Lecture Notes in Computer Science 3473

Commenced Publication in 1973
Founding and Former Series Editors:
Gerhard Goos, Juris Hartmanis, and Jan van Leeuwen

Preface

IICS 2004, the fourth workshop on Innovative Internet Community Systems, successfully dealt with several timely topics of distributed systems, the Internet and virtual communities. The workshop series commenced with IICS 2001 held at the Technical University of Ilmenau. After two more workshops, in Kühlungsborn and Leipzig, this year was the first time that the workshop was held abroad (Guadalajara, Mexico). Due to a broader international environment, the workshop this year was organized by the IEEE in cooperation with the Universidad de Guadalajara.

The papers from the conference were mainly focused on three aspects: system-oriented problems, text processing, and theoretical foundation of distributed and Internet systems. The organizers tried to cover the main issues appearing today with the steady growth of the Internet and the Internet communities. Consequently, the speed and quality-of-service problems of today's Internet protocols, aspects of cooperation and collaboration in Internet systems, as well as agent- and textprocessing-based methods used to compute the large amounts of information in the Internet more or less automatically were all emphasized in most papers and discussions during the conference.

There were two mini-workshops in the workshop because some topics may influence communities and the Internet, and the other way around. Armin Mikler from the University of North Texas at Denton organized the workshop on Computational Epidemiology, considering several aspects of this brand new research area which requires fast exchanges of information from large areas. Helena Unger organized a mini-workshop on the Optimization of Urban Traffic Systems (OUTS), showing the strong connection between social communities and technical systems, and many requirements to use distributed systems and the Net to collect and process current information in the right manner.

We would like to thank all those who contributed to the success of the workshop: all the authors who submitted their papers which demonstrated their excellent research work, and the Program Committee for its selection of the invited talks and the regular papers. In addition, Tomas Herrera and his Department of Information Systems from the CUCEA campus of the Universidad de Guadalajara deserve special gratitude for their great efforts and perfect work concerning all administrative and organizational matters of the workshop.

Finally, we hope all participants enjoyed this workshop, made a lot of contacts, had fruitful discussions which helped to solve their research problems, and had a pleasant stay with our friendly Mexican hosts.

Last but not least, we look forward to meeting you and many new participants at the 5th IICS conference to be held in the attractive city of Paris in France.

April 2005   Thomas Böhme
                                        Victor Larios-Rosillo (Local Chair)
                                                             Herwig Unger
                                                             Helena Unger

Organization

IICS was organized by IEEE

Steering Committee

T. Böhme
G. Heyer
V.M. Larios-Rosillo (Local Chair)
A. Mikler
H. Unger

Program Committee

A. Anbulagan	N. Kalyaniwalla	M.A.R. Dantas
A. Brandstädt	P. Kropf	F. Ramos
J. Brooke	M. Kunde	J. Roth
M. Bui	R. Liskowsky	A. Ryjov
N. Deo	S. Lukosch	D. Tavangarian
D. Dergint	Y. Paker	D. Tutsch
K.-P. Fähnrich	A. Pears	T. Ungerer
T. Haupt	U. Quasthoff	P. Young-Hwan

Co-sponsors

Universidad de Guadalajara
University of Rostock
Technische Universität Ilmenau
Gesellschaft für Informatik e.V. (GI)
Paperdyne

Table of Contents

Workshop Innovative Internet Community Systems 2004

Invited Papers

Contributed Papers

Workshop Computational Epidemiology

Workshop Optimization of Urban Traffic Systems (OUTS)

Random Walks in Distributed Computing: A Survey

Marc Bui[2,*], Thibault Bernard[1], Devan Sohier[1,2], and Alain Bui[1]

[1] Département de Mathématiques et Informatique
Université de Reims Champagne Ardennes,
BP1039 F-51687 Reims cedex, France
{alain.bui,thibault.bernard,devan.sohier}@univ-reims.fr
[2] LRIA – EPHE rue G. Lussac,
F-75005 Paris, France
marc.bui@univ-paris8.fr

Abstract. In this survey, we give an overview of the use of random walks as a traversal scheme to derive distributed control algorithms over a network of computers. It is shown that this paradigm for information exchange can be an attractive technique by using electric network theory as a mathematical tool for performance evaluation.

Keywords: Distributed System, Random Walks, Electrical Network, Distributed Algorithms

1 Introduction

We propose to use random walks in distributed computing to provide uniform and efficient solutions to distributed control of dynamic networks. Random walks have already been successfully exploited to design basic network control algorithms: self-stabilizing mutual exclusion by single token circulation [IJ90], gathering and dissemination of information over a network [AKL+79], random structure over a network [BIZ89].

Indeed, we show that using accidental meetings of *circulating tokens*[1] that merges partial information of the network at each node independently gives an efficient traversal scheme for distributed control. Accidental meetings of several tokens have been ingeniously used in [IJ90] (by merging all tokens to one), in order to insure a single token circulation. It has been shown in [TW91] that all tokens should merge to one in polynomial time.

Random walks are interesting by providing a scalable mechanism to insert information into the distributed computation, for example when node insertion occurs in the distributed system or to update topology modification (edge or node deletion). Ad-hoc networks or pervasive distributed systems, because of their very limited communication bandwidth for network control, can also benefit of this approach.

Because of their inherent complexity, deterministic solutions to control large distributed systems are often unsatisfactory. One solution is to design randomized algorithms which can be simpler, especially for their correctness proof. Precise statement about their performance are, on the other hand, an interesting challenge: by introducing electrical networks, we present an original and elegant manner to compare solutions.

---

[*] Corresponding author
[1] A data structure moving following a random walk scheme in the network

T. Böhme et al. (Eds.): IICS 2004, LNCS 3473, pp. 1–14, 2006.
© Springer-Verlag Berlin Heidelberg 2006

2   Preliminaries

In this section we present the motivation for using random walk in distributed computing, and a formal description of a random walk.

2.1   Distributed Systems

We define a distributed system to be a set of autonomous computing resources, exchanging messages via communication links. The system is modeled as a graph, the nodes of which represent the computers and the edges the communication channels.

We adopt the classical asynchronous message passing model, *i.e.* computers communicate by sending messages to their neighbors, and there is no bound on the time it takes to a message to reach its goal.

2.2   Random Walks Characteristics

A *random walk* is a sequence of vertices visited by a token that starts at i and visits other vertices according to the following transition rules: if the token is at i at time t then at time $t + 1$ it will be at one of the neighbors of i, this neighbor having been chosen according to some time-constant law. Various papers deal with random walks e.g. [Lov93,AKL+79]. More formally, a random walk is a finite homogeneous Markov Chain with state set V and with transition probability matrix $P = (p_{ij})_{(i,j) \in V^2}$ given by

$$p_{ij} = \begin{cases} \frac{1}{\deg(i)} & \text{if } (i,j) \in E \\ 0 & \text{if } (i,j) \notin E \end{cases}$$

where $\deg(i)$ is the degree of node i (*i.e.* the number of its neighbors).

Let P^t the tth power of P, whose entries are $p_t(i,j)$, $(i,j) \in V^2$.

Since G is connected, if it is not bipartite, the Markov Chain has only one acyclic ergodic class of states, then $\lim_{t \to \infty} P^t$ exists and is a matrix Q with identical rows $\pi = (\pi_i, \ i \in V)$, *i.e.* $\forall (i,j) \in V \times V, \lim_{t \to \infty} p_t(i,j) = \pi_i$. π is the stationary distribution and can be computed such that $\pi = \pi.P$. Note that, in the particular case of random walks, the stationary distribution satisfies

$$\pi_i = \frac{\deg(i)}{2|E|} \tag{1}$$

Some characteristic values are useful in the context of distributed computing. The mean time to reach vertex j (state j), starting from the vertex i (state i) which may be regarded as the conditional expectation of the random number of transitions before entering j for the first time when starting at i, is called *hitting time* and denoted h_{ij}. In particular, we have $h_{ii} = 1/\pi_i$. We often use the quantity $\max\{h_{ij}/j \in V\}$, which is an upper bound for a random walk starting at i to hit a fixed, but unknown vertex, for example, when the average time to look for an information owned by a unknown vertex is required. $h_{ij} + h_{ji}$ called the commute time, is the expected number of steps for a random walks starting at vertex i to reach vertex j for the first time and reach i again. It can be viewed as the average time to fetch back to i an information owned by the vertex j. The expected time for a random walk starting at i to visit all the vertices of the graph is called the *cover time* C_i. Let $C = \max\{C_i/i \in V\}$. C_i will be the average time needed by i to build a spanning tree thanks to the algorithm described above. C will be an upper bound of the average time for an unknown vertex to build a spanning tree thanks to the algorithm described above. Results on bounds on cover time can be found in [Lov93].

3   Random Walks and Network Structuration

In [Bro89], the author computes a random spanning tree by using a random walk in a graph. [BIZ89], applies this method to compute a spanning tree over a network. As they mention, a random spanning tree is more resilient to link failures: *"the probability that a bad channel will disconnect some nodes from the random tree is relatively small"*.

In [IJ90], random walks have been used as the design of a self-stabilizing algorithm for the mutual exclusion problem. In their system, a token typifies the privilege to execute critical section code. This token moves with a random walk policy. If several tokens are present in the network, they eventually meet on a site and the protocol will make them merge. [TW91] shows that the protocol developed in [IJ90] stabilizes in polynomial time (this is an average complexity).

In our works, we use random walks to structure a network. Many applications can use this structuration: data transfer in peer-to-peer network, job dispatching in GRID computing... We give here the main idea of the algorithms except in Section 3.3 where we give full specifications of the algorithm.

3.1   Routing with Mobile Agents

In [BDDN01], mobile agents are used to update the shortest path routing table in each site. Two protocols are presented. In the first protocol, there is no interaction between agent. Each site dispatches a mobile agent for a random walk. Each agent carries (and possibly updates) link state of its creator and updates routing tables of visited sites through the network. In the second protocol (the cooperative one), agent caries not only the links states of its creator but the routing table (updated each time the agent returns at home). This protocol increases the convergence of routing table, but increases the size of all agents. The aim of using random walk is to easily manage topological changes. If a channel becomes unavailable, the agent when returning home, is updated. If a new site get connected, it launches an agent with its links state (routing table) and thus updates other routing tables.

3.2   Random Spanning Tree Construction
for Shortest Path Routing Computation

In [Fla01], the author presents how to collect topological informations by the use of a random walk, and more precisely a random circulating word, and a method to deduce a spanning tree of the network from the collected topological informations. That deduced spanning tree is not applied to the entire network, but locally stored in each node of the network. Then he gives original algorithms to reduce the size of the collected information without loss of the needed information for the spanning tree construction. At last, he gives a possible application of that "local" tree construction : the creation of shortest paths routing tables.

3.3   Network Design with Distributed Random Walks

In [BFG$^+$03], we address the problem of constructing such a structure with a protocol that tolerates faults and adapts itself to dynamic topology changes that often occur in mobile ad hoc networks. Tolerating faults is crucial in such networks where mobile devices get frequently out of range or powered off by users. Therefore, we introduce distributed random walk (DRW) as a collection of random walks (RWs) that cooperate in order to establish a computation. The technique uses a collection of RWs that are coalescing into a final one that maintains the control structure. We apply this technique to compute a spanning tree (ST), which is selected uniformly at random among all possible ones for a network. To gather informations, we use a wave scheme. We can informally describe the whole procedure as follows: several mobile devices initiate a RW, with an explorer agent. Every mobile device, upon receiving an explorer token, marks itself visited with the identity of the token, except if it has already been visited by another token. It then forwards at random to one of its neighbors the received explorer token. The network is thus, explored in parallel and decomposed into sub-regions, one per token. Each token constructs a sub-tree of the network. When a token meets another one, or an already visited mobile device, a wave is initiated. This wave is a backward propagation wave that merges the two sub-trees. This process is conducted in parallel and, eventually, the waves will cover the network, resulting in the ST definition. The protocol is ready for termination when a single explorer token remains and all mobile devices of the network have been visited.

Description of the self-stabilizing algorithm for spanning tree construction. We briefly present here the specifications of the algorithm.

Each node maintains:

- *color*, the identity of an agent
- *master*, the (sub)tree root to which the node belongs
- *parent*, the node parent within the (sub)tree
- *sons*, the set of sons of the node

An agent is composed of two fields: a color and a root. When two agents are merging on a site, the site have to decide values affected to the fields. So we need a rule to compare agents:

- $T_1 > T_2$ if $(T_1.color > T_2.color) \lor (T_1.color = T_2.color \land T_1.root > T_2.root)$
- $T_1 = T_2$ if $(T_1.color = T_2.color) \land (T_1.root > T_2.root)$

On timeout, a site flips a coin, generate an agent by a color and the node identity, sends, *local_state* to all neighbors. Once all neighbors' *local_state* received, if *test_validity_state* is not correct *reset(node)*.

We specify the algorithm behavior by means of overall actions driven by agents and waves. Some sites randomly generate an agent identified by a color that is characterized by the initiators of the agent.

Agent Annexing Mode. Whenever an agent $a_i(color_i, rac_i)$ issued from a node q is annexing (or generated at) node p, which belongs to a (sub)tree (i.e. an agent $a_j(color_j, rac_j)$).

AA1 if $color_i < color_j$, the annexing is stopped and the agent is destroyed.
AA2 else (if $color_i > color_j$), one of the 2 conditions holds:

   i One (or more) agent(s) are present on node p

      – if agent is the unique biggest, it continues its traversal and all others are destroyed. Node p marked himself with $color \longleftarrow color_i, master \longleftarrow rac_i, parent \longleftarrow q$

      – if agent a_i is the biggest but not unique (others agents $a_{j1}, \ldots, a_{jd}$ that have respectly $color_{j1}, \ldots, color_{jd}$ equal to $color_i$, agents $a_i, a_{j1}, \ldots, a_{jd}$ are merged to form the unique agent of identity $i+1$ rooted in p (i.e. agent $a(i+1, p)$ is generated).

      – if agent a_i is not the biggest, it is destroyed.

   ii No other agent on node p. Agent continues its traversal scheme. p marks himself with $color \longleftarrow color_i, master \longleftarrow rac_i, parent \longleftarrow q$

Wave Update Mode. Whenever an agent $a_i(color_i, rac_i)$ reaches a node p with its variable color such that $color < color_i$ a wave is generated.

   WU1 The wave is propagated applying a path reversal scheme over the domain identified by color (the domain which p belongs to)

   WU2 The wave stops itself when it reaches the p limit.

Termination of the algorithm is realized with a derivation from the Dijkstra-Scholten scheme known as diffusing computation. This termination detection is periodically initiated by nodes that have initiated an annexing agent.

For proof of correctness and stabilization, refer to [BFG+03]

3.4 Random Self-stabilizing Structures

In [BBF04], we use a random walk for the self-stabilizing construction of a collection of spanning tree rooted in each site. As in [Fla01] this computation is achieved using a circulating word which collects the identity of visited site. Each time a site gets the token, it updates its local spanning tree with the one contained in the word. To stabilize the computation, we need to insure the stabilization of the content of the word (for stabilizing tree construction) and the presence of only one circulating word. We correct the word step by step in each site by processing to an internal test that detects local inconsistencies thanks to the neighborhood of the current visited site. A site at the reception of the token, checks the neighborhood relation declared in the word correspond to the neighborhood of the site. The presence of a token is insured by a timeout process on each site that eventually creates new tokens. The merger of the tokens insures the decrease of the number of tokens to one (by the same process as described in [IJ90]). If several tokens hold on a site at the moment, the site would merge them into one, merging topological information. This algorithm is well adapted for unsafe dynamic networks.

3.5 Conclusion on Structuration

We have a way to construct routing tables ([BDDN01,Fla01]) and adaptative structures ([BBF04] for small scale networks. In [BFG+03], we propose another approach for network structuration : distributed random walks. Our future intend to join the two approaches in order to construct control structures for large scale networks.

4   Random Walks and Electrical Networks for the Complexity of Distributed Algorithms

Random walks offer a pleasant framework to design distributed algorithms in a dynamic context or with self-stabilization. However, evaluating the complexity of those algorithms requires the use of many probabilistic tools. It is important to note that, except in very particular case, there is no hope to give hard bound to the complexity of a random walk based distributed algorithm. Indeed, due to their probabilistic nature, there is no way to guarantee that a walk reaches a given site in a given number of steps.

Some quantities are very useful in the evaluation of the complexity of random walk based distributed algorithms. The hitting time h_{ij} is the average number of steps it takes to a random walk starting at i to first reach j. The commute time is the average time for a round-trip from i to j: $\kappa_{ij} = h_{ij} + h_{ji}$. The cover time C_i is the average number of steps for a random walk starting at i to visit all the sites in the network. The cover time $C = \max\{C_i / i \in V\}$.

Random walks and electrical current have in common two properties: the amount of them that enters a node must leave it; it leaves a node through a channel, proportionally to a time-constant quantity attached to this channel (weight or probability for random walks; conductance for the current). This similarity entails a tight link between random walks and resistive networks, detailed in [DS00,CRR+97], for example. In the sequel, we focus on resistive networks.

The conductance is the inverse of the resistance. The effective conductance C_{ij} of a network, between two of its nodes i and j is the conductance of the resistor to be placed between i and j to ensure the same electrical properties. In other words, it is the current that flows from i to j when a potential difference of $1V$ is imposed between i and j.

In [BBS03,BBBS03], we propose a method based on resistances to automatically compute hitting times, which provides with an evaluation of the complexity of some random walks based distributed algorithms. Our method use the relationship between electrical resistance and random walks established in [DS00,CRR+97]. We provide an automatic way to compute resistances on graphs modeling distributed networks.

A network topology may be viewed as an electrical network (both may be viewed as an undirected graph). Each link (edge) (i, j) is assigned a real value: the resistance $r(i, j)$. Interesting results can be deduced by application of the two Kirchhoff's law and Ohm's law. In particular, through the notion of effective resistance (explained below), we present an innovative method to automatically compute bounds on cover time, exact values of commute time and hitting times, exact values of cyclic cover time and total hitting time for any arbitrary graph.

4.1   Review of Basic Ideas on Electricity

Relation between the potential difference between two nodes, the electrical resistance and the electrical current are given by Ohm's law: $U = R \times I$. Kirchhoff's law states that the sum of currents entering and exiting a node must equal zero. For two resistors (or resistive networks) R_1 and R_2 connected *in series*, we have: $R_{global} = R_1 + R_2$. For two resistors (or resistive networks) R_1 and R_2 connected *in parallel*, we have: $\frac{1}{R_{global}} = \frac{1}{R_1} + \frac{1}{R_2}$.

4.2 Effective Resistance

$R(i, j)$ is the effective resistance (resistance of the electrical network) between i and j, if we replace each edge in the graph by a 1Ω resistor. R denotes the maximal effective resistance between two nodes of the network *i.e.* $R = \max_{(i,j) \in V^2} R(i, j)$.

4.3 Previous Results

A tight relationship between resistances in electric networks and random walks character-istic values such as commute times and cover time, has been established in [CRR$^+$97]. In particular, it has been shown that:

$$\kappa_{ij} = h_{ij} + h_{ji} = 2mR(i,j) \tag{2}$$

where i and j denote two distinct vertices and m, the number of vertices.
From this equation, we have:

$$mR < C < O(mR \log n) \tag{3}$$

In [Tet91], hitting time are expressed only in terms of resistances:

$$h(i,j) = mR(i,j) + \frac{1}{2} \sum_{k \in V} deg(k)[R(j,k) - R(i,k)] \tag{4}$$

4.4 Millman's Theorem

Our method uses the Millman's theorem to compute automatically effective resistance. As shown above, we can compute, thanks to resistances, bounds on cover time, exact values of cyclic cover time, exact values of commute time and total hitting time for any arbitrary graphs.

Theorem 1 (Millman's theorem). *Consider an electrical network, on any node i, we have the following relation:*

$$V_i = \frac{\sum_{j=0,}^{k} \frac{V_j}{r(i,j)}}{\sum_{j=1}^{k} \frac{1}{r(i,j)}}$$

that is

$$\frac{V_i - V_0}{r(i,0)} + \frac{V_i - V_1}{r(i,1)} + \frac{V_i - V_2}{r(i,2)} + \cdots + \frac{V_i - V_k}{r(i,k)} = 0$$

where $1, \cdots, k$ are the neighbors of i, $V_1, \cdots, V_k$ are the voltages on each of these nodes.

By giving the potentials on the two nodes i and j connected to the generator, say $V_i = 0$ and $V_j = 1$, we obtain a single solution. The matrix of the system is obtained from the matrix of the walk by replacing the line i and j by the null line and $M_{ii} = M_{jj} = 1$. Then, we can compute the potential on all the nodes, and the intensity I going out of i. The effective resistance R_{ij} is then $1/I$.

This method is not efficient, since we have to inverse n^2 matrices to obtain all the resistances and hitting times.

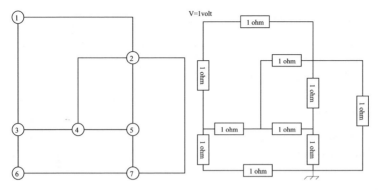

Fig. 1. Example

Example. Let apply Millman theorem to the graph on fig. 1, to compute R_{17}.
Then $V_1 = 1$, $V_7 = 0$.

$$V_1 - V_2 + V_4 - V_2 + V_5 - V_2 + V_7 - V_2 = 0$$
$$V_1 - V_3 + V_4 - V_3 + V_6 - V_3 = 0$$
$$V_2 - V_4 + V_3 - V_4 + V_5 - V_4 = 0 \qquad (5)$$
$$V_2 - V_5 + V_4 - V_5 + V_7 - V_5 = 0$$
$$V_3 - V_6 + V_7 - V_6 = 0$$

From (5), we obtain $V_6 = \frac{2}{7}$, $V_4 = \frac{3}{7}$, $V_5 = \frac{2}{7}$, $V_3 = \frac{4}{7}$ and $V_2 = \frac{3}{7}$. The intensity going out of 1 is $\frac{V_2}{1\Omega} + \frac{V_3}{1\Omega} = 1$, and $R_{17} = 1$. Thus, $h_{17} + h_{71} = 10 \times 1 = 10$.

We can design a more efficient method by noting that we inverse very similar matrices.

Let V_k be the potential on the node k in the graph G. According to the Kirchoff's current law, when a 1A current flows from i to j:

$$\begin{cases} \forall k \in V \backslash \{i,j\}, \sum_{l \in N(k)} c_{kl}(V_k - V_l) = 0 \\ \sum_{l \in N(i)} c_{il}(V_i - V_l) = 1 \\ \sum_{l \in N(j)} c_{jl}(V_j - V_l) = -1 \end{cases}$$

This can be written:

$$\Delta V = v$$

with Δ the matrix built from the conductance matrix by letting the entry $(k;k)$ be $-\sum_{l \in N(k)} c_{kl}$, and v the vector with all entry 0 except the i-th one 1 and the j-th one -1.

However, Δ is not invertible, since the vector $(1, \ldots, 1)$ is in its kernel: the potential is defined up to a constant. The kernel is $(1, \ldots, 1) \times \mathbb{R}$, for if there were other vectors, there would be several steady states in this circuit with one given generator connected to two given nodes, which is false according to electricity laws. Thus, the matrix Δ_2 built by replacing the first line in Δ by $(1, 0, \ldots, 0)$ is invertible, for its electrical interpretation is that the potential on node 1 is given and the Millman's theorem applies on each other node (and the network is connected). Thus, $\Delta_2^{-1} v$ is a solution to $\Delta V = v$.

Knowing the potential on each node, we can compute the effective resistance of the network between i and j: $V_j - V_i$. The effective resistance between i and j is $\Delta_2^{-1}(i,j) - \Delta_2^{-1}(j,j) - \Delta_2^{-1}(i,i) + \Delta_2^{-1}(j,i)$. The hitting times can then be computed thanks to the above formula (4).

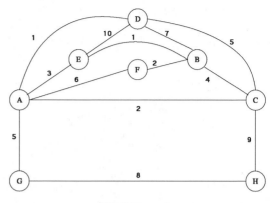

Fig. 2. Example

Thus, this method works with only one matrix inversion, and with no matrices multiplication, which is much better than the previous results we published ([BBS03]). We improved the speed of those computations with a factor of about one hundred, making it possible to apply this on large graphs.

For the graph on figure 2, the matrix Δ_2 is:

$$\begin{pmatrix}
1 & 0 & 0 & 0 & 0 & 0 & 0 & 0 \\
0 & -14 & 4 & 7 & 1 & 2 & 0 & 0 \\
2 & 4 & -20 & 5 & 0 & 0 & 0 & 9 \\
1 & 7 & 5 & -23 & 10 & 0 & 0 & 0 \\
3 & 1 & 0 & 10 & -14 & 0 & 0 & 0 \\
6 & 2 & 0 & 0 & 0 & -8 & 0 & 0 \\
5 & 0 & 0 & 0 & 0 & 0 & -13 & 8 \\
0 & 0 & 9 & 0 & 0 & 0 & 8 & -17
\end{pmatrix}$$

Δ_2^{-1} is:

$$\begin{pmatrix}
1 & 0 & 0 & 0 & 0 & 0 & 0 & 0 \\
1 & -\frac{102091}{627268} & \frac{56049}{627268} & \frac{67339}{627268} & \frac{110783}{1254536} & \frac{102091}{2509072} & \frac{6426}{156817} & \frac{41769}{627268} \\
1 & \frac{56049}{627268} & \frac{84309}{627268} & \frac{53851}{627268} & \frac{84937}{1254536} & \frac{56049}{2509072} & \frac{9666}{156817} & \frac{62829}{627268} \\
1 & \frac{67339}{627268} & \frac{53851}{627268} & \frac{89297}{627268} & \frac{137187}{1254536} & \frac{67339}{2509072} & \frac{6174}{156817} & \frac{40131}{627268} \\
1 & \frac{110783}{1254536} & \frac{84937}{1254536} & \frac{137187}{1254536} & \frac{391027}{2509072} & \frac{110783}{5018144} & \frac{4869}{156817} & \frac{63297}{1254536} \\
1 & \frac{102091}{2509072} & \frac{56049}{2509072} & \frac{67339}{2509072} & \frac{110783}{5018144} & \frac{1356627}{10036288} & \frac{3213}{313634} & \frac{41769}{2509072} \\
1 & \frac{6426}{156817} & \frac{9666}{156817} & \frac{6174}{156817} & \frac{4869}{156817} & \frac{3213}{313634} & \frac{21413}{156817} & \frac{15194}{156817} \\
1 & \frac{41769}{627268} & \frac{62829}{627268} & \frac{40131}{627268} & \frac{63297}{1254536} & \frac{41769}{2509072} & \frac{15194}{156817} & \frac{98761}{627268}
\end{pmatrix}$$

The resistance matrix is:

$$\begin{pmatrix}
0 & \frac{102091}{627268} & \frac{84309}{627268} & \frac{89297}{627268} & \frac{391027}{2509072} & \frac{1356627}{10036288} & \frac{21413}{156817} & \frac{98761}{627268} \\
\frac{102091}{627268} & 0 & \frac{37151}{313634} & \frac{28355}{313634} & \frac{356259}{2509072} & \frac{2173355}{10036288} & \frac{136335}{627268} & \frac{58657}{313634} \\
\frac{84309}{627268} & \frac{37151}{313634} & 0 & \frac{16476}{156817} & \frac{388515}{2509072} & \frac{2257179}{10036288} & \frac{92633}{627268} & \frac{14353}{156817} \\
\frac{89297}{627268} & \frac{28355}{313634} & \frac{16476}{156817} & 0 & \frac{199467}{2509072} & \frac{2246667}{10036288} & \frac{125557}{627268} & \frac{26949}{156817} \\
\frac{391027}{2509072} & \frac{356259}{2509072} & \frac{388515}{2509072} & \frac{199467}{2509072} & 0 & \frac{2477603}{10036288} & \frac{577827}{2509072} & \frac{532883}{2509072} \\
\frac{1356627}{10036288} & \frac{2173355}{10036288} & \frac{2257179}{10036288} & \frac{2246667}{10036288} & \frac{2477603}{10036288} & 0 & \frac{2521427}{10036288} & \frac{2602651}{10036288} \\
\frac{21413}{156817} & \frac{136335}{627268} & \frac{92633}{627268} & \frac{125557}{627268} & \frac{577827}{2509072} & \frac{2521427}{10036288} & 0 & \frac{62861}{627268} \\
\frac{98761}{627268} & \frac{58657}{313634} & \frac{14353}{156817} & \frac{26949}{156817} & \frac{532883}{2509072} & \frac{2602651}{10036288} & \frac{62861}{627268} & 0
\end{pmatrix}$$

and the hitting times matrix is:

$$
\begin{pmatrix}
0 & \frac{6740527}{627268} & \frac{4636113}{627268} & \frac{5079563}{627268} & \frac{6844259}{627268} & \frac{68203479}{5018144} & \frac{1655067}{156817} & \frac{6683885}{627268} \\
\frac{6122939}{627268} & 0 & \frac{1848439}{313634} & \frac{679447}{156817} & \frac{5987869}{627268} & \frac{91460059}{5018144} & \frac{9504503}{627268} & \frac{3771965}{313634} \\
\frac{5986821}{627268} & \frac{2832587}{313634} & 0 & \frac{2140579}{313634} & \frac{7480049}{627268} & \frac{101973699}{5018144} & \frac{7735425}{627268} & \frac{1188563}{156817} \\
\frac{6171859}{627268} & \frac{1106918}{156817} & \frac{2011373}{313634} & 0 & \frac{4373337}{627268} & \frac{100608923}{5018144} & \frac{9680431}{627268} & \frac{3899619}{313634} \\
\frac{10946183}{1254536} & \frac{10468579}{1254536} & \frac{9516347}{1254536} & \frac{3819747}{1254536} & 0 & \frac{98029553}{5018144} & \frac{19278767}{1254536} & \frac{16338531}{1254536} \\
\frac{8632011}{2509072} & \frac{22730653}{2509072} & \frac{20114289}{2509072} & \frac{20465549}{2509072} & \frac{14514859}{1254536} & 0 & \frac{31874379}{2509072} & \frac{30104657}{2509072} \\
\frac{1042971}{156817} & \frac{7673707}{627268} & \frac{3936333}{627268} & \frac{6139751}{627268} & \frac{8562167}{627268} & \frac{95101143}{5018144} & 0 & \frac{3197993}{627268} \\
\frac{5760001}{627268} & \frac{3618817}{313634} & \frac{619915}{156817} & \frac{2891529}{313634} & \frac{8616549}{627268} & \frac{103757699}{5018144} & \frac{4722493}{627268} & 0
\end{pmatrix}
$$

The cover time can be expressed in terms of hitting times. To compute the cover time, we need a criterion to determine whether every vertex has been visited by the token. So, a state of the system will be the site the token is currently visiting, but also the set of sites it has visited.

Consider $G = (V, E, \omega)$ the undirected connected weighted graph modeling a distributed system. To formalize the idea above, we build from G an associated graph $\mathcal{G}$ such that the cover time of G may be expressed in terms of hitting times in $\mathcal{G}$.

First let define $\mathcal{G} = (\mathcal{V}, \mathcal{E}, \omega_2)$ where $\mathcal{V}$ is a set of nodes and $\mathcal{E}$ a set of directed edges.

- $x \in \mathcal{V}$ is defined by $x = (P, i)$ with $P \in \mathcal{P}(V)$ (*i.e.* P is a subset of nodes of G, representing the nodes in G already visited), and $i \in V$ is a node.
- any edge $(x, y) \in \mathcal{E}$ is of the form $(x, y) = ((P, i), (Q, j))$ with $(x, y) \in \mathcal{V} \times \mathcal{V}$ and $(i, j) \in E$ (is an edge).

Suppose that, initially, the token is at node i in G, and next the token moves to j neighbor of i, and next moves back to i. For the associated graph $\mathcal{G}$, we have the following path $((\{i\}, i); (\{i, j\}, j); (\{i, j\}, i))$.

Note that $\mathcal{E}$ is a set of *directed* edges $((P, i), (Q, j))$. Edges in $\mathcal{E}$ are defined by:

- $((P, i), (P, j))$, where i and j are neighbors ; this case corresponds to a token transmission to the node j that has already been visited by the token.
- $((P, i), (P \bigcup \{j\}, j))$ where i and j are neighbors ; this case corresponds to a token transmission to the node j that is holding the token for the first time.

If $x = (P, i)$ and $y = (Q, j)$ in $\mathcal{G}$ are neighbours, $\omega_2(x, y) = \omega(i, j)$.

The probability to obtain a given path in G is equal to the probability to obtain the associated path in $\mathcal{G}$. Indeed, for $i \in P \subset V$ and $j \in V$, there exists some $Q \subset V$ such that the transition probability from (P, i) to (Q, j) and the transition probability from i to j are the same: $Q = P$ if $j \in P$, else, $Q = P \bigcup \{j\}$.

A token in G has visited every node *iff* the associated token in $\mathcal{G}$ has reached a node (P, i) such that $P = V$. Then, we deduce that the cover time in G is the average time it takes to a random walk token in $\mathcal{G}$ starting from a node i to reach any arbitrary node k while having visited all vertices that is

$$
C_i(G) = h_{(\{i\}, i), \{(V, k)/k \in V\}}(\mathcal{G})
$$

The token has covered G when the associated token in $\mathcal{G}$ has hit any vertex in $F = \{(V, k)/k \in V\}$. We do not care at which node (V, k) the token reaches in $\mathcal{G}$, then we lump all nodes F into a single one called f (in fact we obtain an absorbing Markov Chain). Now, the cover time in G is obtained by the average number of steps needed before entering f starting in node $(\{i\}, i)$.

Indeed, let $\mathcal{N}_o(x)$ be the set of vertices that have an incoming edge from x: $\{y \in \mathcal{V}/(x, y) \in \mathcal{E}\}$.

Now, in any graph (even directed), since f can be reached from any vertex (if not, some of the h_{xf} would be undefined), with $p_{xy} = \frac{\omega(x,y)}{\sum_{n \in \mathcal{N}(x)} \omega(x,n)}$:

$$\begin{cases} \forall x \in V, h_{xf} = 1 + \sum_{y \in \mathcal{N}_o(x)} p_{xy} h_{yf} \\ h_{ff} = 0 \end{cases} \tag{6}$$

6 is a square linear system that has a single solution (since it is square and has at least one solution: the vector $h_{.f}$, which we know to exist!): one can compute the hitting time between all vertices and a given vertex by inverting one matrix.

Thus, we can compute the cover time of any graph G by building $\mathcal{G}$ and computing $h_{(i,\{i\}),f}(\mathcal{G})$, which requires the inversion of an approximatively $2^n \times 2^n$ matrix.

Let G be the graph on figure 3. Then $\mathcal{G}$ is the graph on figure 4.

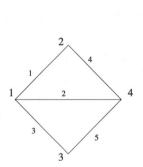

Fig. 3. G

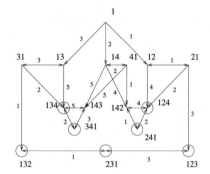

Fig. 4. $\mathcal{G}$

In figure 4 we named sites by giving the set of known vertices, the last mentionned being the current one. We only built the part of $\mathcal{G}$ that corresponds to situations where the token started on vertex 1. We did no write the states in which all vertices are visited: for the sake of legibility, we circled the sites that lead to such a state. Thus, in state 134, the token will reach 2 and finish to cover the graph with probability $\frac{1}{3}$, reach 3 (the state being 143) or 1 (341) also with probability $\frac{1}{3}$.

Since we merge all the states in which the token has covered the graph, every circled state leads to the new site f with an unweighted directed vertex.

The matrix of $\mathcal{G}$ is then:

	1	12	14	13	21	124	41	142	143	31	134	123	132	241	341	231	f
1	0	1	2	3	0	0	0	0	0	0	0	0	0	0	0	0	0
12	0	0	0	0	0	1	4	0	0	0	0	0	0	0	0	0	0
14	0	0	0	0	0	0	2	4	5	0	0	0	0	0	0	0	0
13	0	0	0	0	0	0	0	0	0	3	5	0	0	0	0	0	0
21	0	1	0	0	0	2	0	0	0	0	0	3	0	0	0	0	0
124	0	0	0	0	0	0	0	4	0	0	0	0	0	2	0	0	5
41	0	0	2	0	0	0	0	1	3	0	0	0	0	0	0	0	0
142	0	0	0	0	0	4	0	0	0	0	0	0	0	1	0	0	0
143	0	0	0	0	0	0	0	0	0	0	5	0	0	0	3	0	0
31	0	0	0	3	0	0	0	0	0	0	0	2	0	1	0	0	0
134	0	0	0	0	0	0	0	0	5	0	0	0	0	0	2	0	4
123	0	0	0	0	0	0	0	0	0	0	0	0	0	0	0	3	5
132	0	0	0	0	0	0	0	0	0	0	0	0	0	0	0	1	4
241	0	0	0	0	0	2	0	1	0	0	0	0	0	0	0	0	3
341	0	0	0	0	0	0	0	0	3	0	2	0	0	0	0	0	1
231	0	0	0	0	0	0	0	0	0	0	0	3	1	0	0	0	2
f	0	0	0	0	0	0	0	0	0	0	0	0	0	0	0	0	0

To obtain the cover time, we have to multiply the inverse of the below matrix by $(1,1,1,1,1,1,1,1,1,1,1,1,1,1,1,1,0)$:

$$
\begin{pmatrix}
1 & -\frac{1}{6} & -\frac{1}{3} & -\frac{1}{2} & 0 & 0 & 0 & 0 & 0 & 0 & 0 & 0 & 0 & 0 & 0 & 0 & 0 \\
0 & 1 & 0 & 0 & -\frac{1}{5} & -\frac{4}{5} & 0 & 0 & 0 & 0 & 0 & 0 & 0 & 0 & 0 & 0 & 0 \\
0 & 0 & 1 & 0 & 0 & 0 & -\frac{2}{11} & -\frac{4}{11} & -\frac{5}{11} & 0 & 0 & 0 & 0 & 0 & 0 & 0 & 0 \\
0 & 0 & 0 & 1 & 0 & 0 & 0 & 0 & 0 & -\frac{3}{8} & -\frac{5}{8} & 0 & 0 & 0 & 0 & 0 & 0 \\
0 & -\frac{1}{6} & 0 & 0 & 1 & -\frac{1}{3} & 0 & 0 & 0 & 0 & 0 & -\frac{1}{2} & 0 & 0 & 0 & 0 & 0 \\
0 & 0 & 0 & 0 & 0 & 1 & 0 & -\frac{4}{11} & 0 & 0 & 0 & 0 & 0 & -\frac{2}{11} & 0 & 0 & -\frac{5}{11} \\
0 & 0 & -\frac{1}{3} & 0 & 0 & 0 & 1 & -\frac{1}{6} & -\frac{1}{2} & 0 & 0 & 0 & 0 & 0 & 0 & 0 & 0 \\
0 & 0 & 0 & 0 & 0 & -\frac{4}{5} & 0 & 1 & 0 & 0 & 0 & 0 & 0 & -\frac{1}{5} & 0 & 0 & 0 \\
0 & 0 & 0 & 0 & 0 & 0 & 0 & 0 & 1 & 0 & -\frac{5}{8} & 0 & 0 & 0 & -\frac{3}{8} & 0 & 0 \\
0 & 0 & 0 & -\frac{1}{2} & 0 & 0 & 0 & 0 & 0 & 1 & -\frac{1}{3} & 0 & -\frac{1}{6} & 0 & 0 & 0 & 0 \\
0 & 0 & 0 & 0 & 0 & 0 & 0 & 0 & -\frac{5}{11} & 0 & 1 & 0 & 0 & 0 & -\frac{2}{11} & 0 & -\frac{4}{11} \\
0 & 0 & 0 & 0 & 0 & 0 & 0 & 0 & 0 & 0 & 0 & 1 & 0 & 0 & 0 & -\frac{3}{8} & -\frac{5}{8} \\
0 & 0 & 0 & 0 & 0 & 0 & 0 & 0 & 0 & 0 & 0 & 0 & 1 & 0 & 0 & -\frac{1}{5} & -\frac{4}{5} \\
0 & 0 & 0 & 0 & 0 & -\frac{1}{3} & 0 & -\frac{1}{6} & 0 & 0 & 0 & 0 & 0 & 1 & 0 & 0 & -\frac{1}{2} \\
0 & 0 & 0 & 0 & 0 & 0 & 0 & 0 & -\frac{1}{2} & 0 & -\frac{1}{3} & 0 & 0 & 0 & 1 & 0 & -\frac{1}{6} \\
0 & 0 & 0 & 0 & 0 & 0 & 0 & 0 & 0 & 0 & 0 & -\frac{1}{2} & -\frac{1}{6} & 0 & 0 & 1 & -\frac{1}{3} \\
0 & 0 & 0 & 0 & 0 & 0 & 0 & 0 & 0 & 0 & 0 & 0 & 0 & 0 & 0 & 0 & 1
\end{pmatrix}
$$

By solving this system, we obtain that:

$$h_{.f}(\mathcal{G}) = \left(\frac{15154068}{2185469}, \frac{21601}{5423}, \frac{37223}{5797}, \frac{15217}{2431}, \frac{19062}{5423}, \frac{533}{187}, \frac{39698}{5797}, \right.$$
$$\left. \frac{710}{187}, \frac{1150}{187}, \frac{1321}{221}, \frac{903}{187}, \frac{337}{187}, \frac{267}{187}, \frac{483}{187}, \frac{1063}{187}, \frac{400}{187}, 0 \right)$$

Since the first entry is the average time it takes to the token to first reach any state in which all vertices are known, starting from the state in which no site is known and the token is on vertex 1, the cover time is

$$C_1 = h_{1f}(\mathcal{G}) = \frac{15154068}{2185469}$$

that is to say about 7.

5 Conclusion

Peer-to-peer protocols and wireless connections are two important and widespread examples of dynamic distributed systems. In such systems, the lack of knowledge of the topology of the system is the main problem. Current solutions are based on a control layer, that oversees the connections and disconnections, and updates the the routing tables and all the required topological information accordingly. Such a control layer consumes an important amount of bandwidth, which is problem in systems the bandwidth of which is limited.

Random walks offer an interesting alternative to deterministic control layers. Random walks based deterministic algorithms can provide a completely distributed framework to handle the dynamicity of networks, with a lesser consumption of bandwidth. However, the complexity of those solutions, being based on randomized procedures, is difficult to estimate. The main quantities can now be computed, which allows to compare random walk based algorithms to deterministic ones.

References

AKL⁺79. R. Aleliunas, R. Karp, R. Lipton, L. Lovasz, and C. Rackoff. Random walks, universal traversal sequences and the complexity of maze problems. In *20th IEEE Annual Symposium on Foundations of Computer Science*, pages 218–223, October 1979.

BBBS03. T Bernard, A Bui, M Bui, and D Sohier. A new method to automatically compute processing times for random walks based distributed algorithm. In Marcin Paprzycki, editor, *ISPDC 03, Second IEEE International Symposium on Parallel and Distributed Computing Proceeding*, volume 2069, pages 31–36. IEEE Computer society Press, 2003.

BBF04. T Bernard, A Bui, and O Flauzac. Random distributed self-stabilizing structures maintenance. In Victor Larios Félix F. Ramos, Herwig Unger, editor, *ISADS'04, IEEE Internationnal Symposium on Advanced Distributed Systems Proccedings*, volume 3061, pages 231 – 240. Springer Verlag (LNCS), January 2004.

BBS03.   A Bui, M Bui, and D Sohier. Randomly distributed tasks in bounded time. In *Innovative Internet Community System*, volume 2877, pages 36–47. Springer Verlag (LNCS), 2003.

BDDN01.   Marc Bui, Sajal K. Das, Ajoy Kumar Datta, and Dai Tho Nguyen. Randomized mobile agent based routing in wireless networks. *International Journal of Foundations of Computer Science*, 12(3):365–384, 2001.

BFG⁺03.   H Baala, O Flauzac, J Gaber, M Bui, and T El-Ghazawi. A self-stabilizing distributed algorithm for spanning tree construction in wireless ad-hoc network. *Journal of Parallel and Distributed Computing*, 63(1):97–104, 2003.

BIZ89.   J Bar-Ilan and D Zernik. Random leaders and random spanning trees. In *WDAG89*, pages 1,12, 1989.

Bro89.   AZ Broder. Generating random spanning trees. pages 442–447. FOCS89 Proceedings of the 29st annual IEEE Symposium on foundation of computer sciences, 1989.

CRR⁺97.   Ashok K. Chandra, Prabhakar Raghavan, Walter L. Ruzzo, Roman Smolensky, and Prasoon Tiwari. The electrical resistance of a graph captures its commute and cover times. *Computational Complexity*, 6(4), 1997.

DS00.   Peter G. Doyle and J. Laurie Snell. *Random Walks and Electric Networks*. 2000.

Fla01.   O Flauzac. Random circulating word information management for tree construction and shortest path routing tables computation. In *On Principle Of DIstributed Systems*, pages 17–32. Studia Informatica Universalis, 2001.

IJ90.   A Israeli and M Jalfon. Token management schemes and random walks yield self-stabilizing mutual exclusion. In *PODC90, Proceeding of the ninth ACM Annual Symposium on Principles of distributed Computing*, pages 119–131, 1990.

Lov93.   Laszlo Lovasz. Random walks on graphs: A survey. In T. Szonyi ed. D. Miklos, V. T. Sos, editor, *Combinatorics: Paul Erdos is Eighty (vol. 2)*, pages 353–398. Janos Bolyai Mathematical Society, 1993.

Tet91.   P Tetali. Random walks and effective resistance of networks. *J. Theoretical Probability*, 1:101,109, 1991.

TW91.   P Tetali and P Winkler. On a random walk arising in self-stabilizing token management. In *PODC91, Proceeding of the tenth ACM Annual Symposium on Principles of distributed Computing*, pages 273–280, 1991.

A Simulation Analysis of Multiagent-Based Dynamic Request Placement Techniques

Félix F. Ramos and Fernando Velasco

CINVESTAV del IPN, Unidad Guadalajara, Av. López Mateos Sur 590
Apartado Postal 31-438, Zapopan, Guadalajara, C.P. 45090, JAL., Mexico
{framos,fvelasco}@gdl.cinvestav.mx
http://www.gdl.cinvestav.mx/

Abstract. As many Web services have become very popular over the past few years, users are facing the problem of the perceived QoS. Practical approaches to address this issue are based on service replication at multiple locations and on allocation mechanisms to dispatch requests in such a way that the QoS perceived by the user is improved. In this paper we compare user perceived QoS performance of three Dynamic Request Placement techniques. One technique randomly allocates Web requests while the other two techniques implements a market-based mechanism for QoS negotiation and request allocation. The analysis is conducted via simulation with *SIDE* using a Behavioral Model of Web traffic to simulate accurate traffic conditions and determine the limitations or validity of these techniques.

1 Introduction

The fast growth of the World Wide Web has led to a wider appreciation of the potential of Internet-based global services and applications. Nowadays services are provided in an ad hoc fashion at fixed locations, which users locate and access manually. The first service selection approaches proposed to allocate clients request to the nearest replica are based on some static metric such as the geographical distance in miles [1] and the topological distance in number of hops [2]. However, as several experimental results [3] show, the static metrics are not good predictors for the expected response time of client requests. The main drawback of both geographical and topological network metrics is that they ignore the network's path dynamic conditions. Dynamic replica selection strategies [3, 4, 5] have emerged in order to improve the estimation of the expected user response time, based on active or passive measurements of network parameters, such as: Run Trip Time, bottleneck bandwidth, available bandwidth, and server request latency. As mentioned in [5], the accuracy of response time estimation is still limited in these works, as they don't consider service load.

M. Rabinovich et all. propose a selection strategy [6] that combines both the network proximity and the server load metric in order to select the suitable service for the client. The AQuA framework [7, 8] implements a service selection strategy which uses replica performance measurements in order to determine the subset of services that can satisfy the client timing requirements with the required probability. As their work targets LAN environments, the quality of network connections is neglected. Finally, the anycasting service described in [3] proposes a flexible replica selection

T. Böhme et al. (Eds.): IICS 2004, LNCS 3473, pp. 15–27, 2006.

strategy. The objectives of this system are closed to ours. Similar to our Agent's knowledge model, this service proposes the concept of filters. Filters specify the relevant metrics to be used by the anycast resolver when searching for a suitable service. However, they place at the same level both the basic and the derived metrics contained in the filters. That is, the metrics mentioned in filters (in particular, the response time) are uniformly estimated for all clients and applications. The main contributions of our Multi-agent Dynamic Request Placement approach, compared to previous related work are:

- The ability of agents to adapt to the dynamic behavior of Internet and user preferences; this allows agents to adapt the response time estimation to the QoS requirement of user's requests
- The experimentation in a realistic scenario where actual Internet conditions are considered as high variability, self similarity, hourly effects and servers load.

1.1 Quality of Service

The International Organization for Standards (ISO) [23] defines QoS as a concept for specifying how good the offered networking services are [9]. Generally, QoS parameters are performance measures and the set of parameters for a chosen service determines what will be measured as QoS. We concentrate on the QoS perceived by users specified in terms of:

- *Network Performance*, describing the requirements that the network services must guarantee, it might be expressed as end-to-end delay,
- *Service Performance:* Characterized for the requirements that the Web service must guarantee expressed as the Web service response time.

2 Multiagent-Based Dynamic Request Placement Techniques

In this section we briefly illustrate the system architecture, the agent structure, its knowledge model and the request placement techniques under examination.

2.1 System Architecture

We assume a Web Service as a set of servers, each with his own identity and whose service is replicated through common redundancy mechanisms as mirroring or caching. Figure 1 depicts the basic architecture proposed [10] showing how a set of Service Agents provides a number of services with a defined QoS. The following are tasks performed by Service Agents:

- Monitor services load,
- Control access to services,
- Implement QoS negotiation techniques with clients,
- Collect Client information,
- Poll Service offers to Clients.

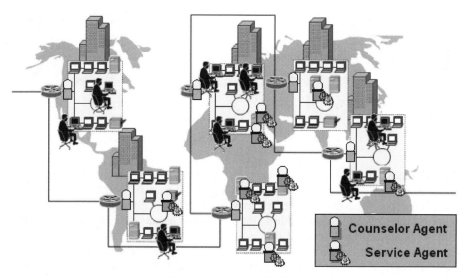

Fig. 1. System Architecture

In the proposed architecture, Counselor Agents are associated with every border node in networks and they are responsible for the assignment of individual request to servers comprising a Web service. The following are tasks performed by Counselor Agents:

- Seek and classify services with a Discovery mechanism,
- Implement a Knowledge mechanism to learn about Service Agents,
- Intercept requests generated by the user,
- Make Dynamic Server Selection decisions based on a negotiation mechanism,
- Collect dynamic QoS service proposals from Service Agents.

2.2 Agents Structure

Each agent in the system is an independent self-contained, concurrently executing thread of control encapsulating a perceived system state. Agents communicate with its environment and with other agents via a common communication protocol. The Internet is the environment where agents inter-operate to improve QoS by reducing response times perceived by users and load balancing at Web services.

Counselor Agent. A Counselor Agent is considered to be a service requestor and a service resolver. Figure 2 depicts the Counselor Agent Structure, each counselor Agent implements a Service Discovery mechanism and a communication manager to be able to communicate with every other agent using common models and communication protocols. The most basic implementation of a counselor Agent uses a MPI (Message Passing Interface), a user interface to intercept requests from users and deliver received responses, a Service Directory to resolve service requests, a Knowledge Model to update the QoS service repository. Finally at the core of the counselor agent it's the Request Placement Strategy to make dynamic placement decisions to a selected server depending on the selected technique.

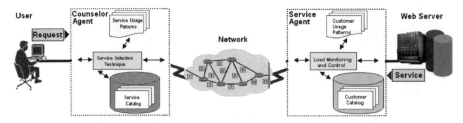

Fig. 2. Counselor Agent and Service Agent Structures

Service Agent. A Service Agent is located on each Web Server and is responsible for controlling access client requests and service load levels by means of monitoring QoS. It's also responsible for appropriately market QoS negotiation protocols avoiding a suboptimal load balance due to the Counselor Agents behavior trying to optimize its individual QoS obtained from popular Web services. Figure 2 also illustrates the Service Agent component structure where we appreciate the QoS information Scheduler who is responsible for the dissemination of QoS information to Counselor Agents in order to enforce load balancing. As part of the Service Agent component structure there's also a QoS passive monitor. Finally, the main component of the service Agent is the Service Manager who incorporates all the necessary components to control access to services, load balancing and forwarding of responses to Counselor Agents.

2.3 Service Discovery Mechanism

When users request a service, the Counselor Agent checks its knowledge base (i.e. service directory) to determine whether or not it is aware of the existence of the requested service. If, based on the information of its knowledge base, the Counselor Agent knows about the requested service then it will contact the corresponding Service Agent directly. But if the Counselor agent can't determine the existence of the requested service, it will start a Service Discovery mechanism to obtain the currently available services and update its knowledge base. The Service Discovery mechanism was originally implemented based on two popular [11] spanning tree techniques:

MST. Multiple Spanning Tree method, this allows Counselor Agents to directly contact each Service Agent available on the system thus identifying the services it offers by constructing a spanning tree rooted at each Counselor Agent., although this techniques has proven to be rather than effective it needs a complex consistency mechanism to keep up to date the service directory.

NPR. Non Predetermined Root, this method builds in parallel a service directory organized in a hierarchical fashion. Each time a Counselor Agent looks for a service, it contacts its Authority Agent to resolve the service request and direct the request to the Service Agent meeting the requirements. This method provides an efficient way to keep the service directory updated, it reduces the complexity of information at each Agent and provides a flexible way to maintain service directory consistency.

2.4   Knowledge Model

The principal responsibility of the Knowledge Model is to maintain and accurate estimate of services QoS in the Service Directory. The Knowledge Model is based on statistical information of the use of Web services. For each service it stores, as a time series, the identity of the Service Agent, the QoS, and time validity for the perceived QoS. This last parameter enables Counselor Agents to consider old information when it becomes obsolete. An example of the knowledge of a Counselor is displayed in figure 4.

Table 1. Parameters considered in the process of knowledge acquisition and evolution

Parameter	Description
x	Service identification
D,H	Time-stamp for collected QoS
$q_x = q(D,H)$	QoS of service provided by service x
V	Validity duration of knowledge

The background to store QoS as a time series is bounded to the well known daily effect on Web services [11], bandwidth and latencies depends on time of day and day of week, therefore, each Counselor Agent stores its QoS parameters as a time series, which is sampled at different hours, and deduces a function representing the QoS by interpolation dealing with large skew, long tails and high variability. Figure 3 shows such QoS as a function of day and time of the day. Whenever a new response is received for an allocated request, the QoS is stored at specific time H of day D, this new value is used to update the Counselor Agent knowledge as follows:

$$q_{x(D,H)} = \mu * q_{x-1(D,H)} + (1-\mu)q \qquad (1)$$

Where μ is comprised between 0 and 1, and represents the Agent capability to keep a reference of past measured QoS. Additionally when service information has not been updated before some delay V, it is considered obsolete. In that case, a Counselor Agent must start a new learning phase based on relevant knowledge.

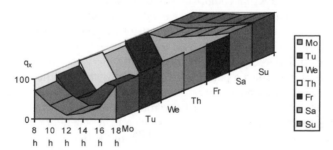

Fig. 3. Web Services QoS as a time series function

2.5   Dynamic Server Selection Algorithms

The problem of finding a request placement technique that improves system QoS perceived by the system users has been extensively investigated analytically, empirical, and via simulation [5, 13, 14] leading to a classification of the request placement techniques into static, statistical and dynamic. Static techniques select a service on the basis of QoS capacity, such as hop count, connection bandwidth, server architecture, etc. Statistical algorithms, instead, reflect typical levels of QoS availability as they consider past QoS data, such as latencies and bandwidths, to choose a service. Finally dynamic or runtime algorithms use small probes in the service negotiation process to detect the current network and service conditions in order to make a decision based on the current QoS perceived.

We have focused our efforts on statistical and dynamic techniques because besides of adapting automatically to changes in the network and service conditions, previous studies [13] show that this technique is easy to implement and adds little traffic or delay overhead. The contribution of this study is the comparison in performance of three algorithms concurrently getting different services from different servers hosting a Web page instead of getting all the required services from a Web Page in the same server. The three algorithms use different knowledge levels and negotiation mechanisms ranging from random passing trough market negotiations concluding with a novel dynamic algorithm.

Random Technique. The first algorithm, hereafter referred as RND, lies under the basic idea that Counselor Agents take advantage of the Service Discovery mechanism and the resulting Service Directory uniformly dispatching the requests without proceeding to any local computation. Though, in some cases this technique may lead to reliability problems because a selection of the same Service Agent leads to an overwhelmed service.

Market-Based Technique. The second algorithm, hereafter referred to as MKT (stands for free market), for every Web service request Counselor Agents starts a QoS negotiation process [15]. Three steps distinguish such process: first a request-for-bidding is launched to all Service Agents proposing the service. Second, Service Agent replies are evaluated; these replies are also used by the Counselor Agent to refresh its knowledge on the QoS of the service requested. Finally, the contract is awarded to the Service Agent comprising the best QoS.

While this negotiation mechanism is general and simple, it still suffers from a high communication cost derived from the request-for-bidding when the set of Service Agents is large and thus the market-based technique can be prohibitive. Therefore this technique is modified to consider only a subset of N Service Agents whose historical information does not reflect a poor QoS. Consequently the modified version of MTK reduces the communication cost for large number of candidate Service Agents.

Although MKT technique uses accurate information about network conditions, it does not offer accurate information about service load. Therefore a novel technique namely Bilateral was proposed, to make use either of the historical knowledge learned by Counselor Agents and a low-cost mechanism implemented by Service Agents to post current service load information to Counselor Agents.

Bilateral Technique. The third technique, hereafter referred to as BIL, technique (stands for Bilateral) is an adaptive one in which Counselor Agents as well as Service Agents make use of their knowledge and learning skills to allocate requests. On the reception of a service request from users, if the Counselor Agent has no actual information about the QoS of Service Agents, it sends a request-for-bidding to select the Service Agent that has the best QoS. At the same time, the Counselor agent takes advantage of such bidding to learn about the QoS of responsive Service Agents. Otherwise, the Counselor Agent uses its knowledge and allocates the request on the Service agent with the best QoS.

On the service side, the reactive agents behave as follows, when a Counselor Agent receives a request-for-bidding; it makes its offer and stores the sender identity. From that moment on it will send QoS offers to register Counselor Agents according to three criteria: the date of the last request for bid, the date of its last request allocation and the number of requests that the Counselor Agent has awarded to it. With this policy, a Service Agent will offer its service to frequent clients, while the others will be less often addressed. This adaptive strategy issued by Service Agents should provide Counselor Agents with accurate knowledge of the QoS of services it frequently request, and this, without perturbing the whole system with useless offers.

3   System and Workload Model

In order to carry out our analysis we have implemented a detailed simulation and a workload model designed to compare the Request Placement Techniques under a realistic Internet scenario. The simulation model for the three Dynamic Request Placement techniques introduced in section 2 has been implemented through an extension we have made to the SIDE [16] package, designed for describe network configurations and specifying distributed programs organized into event-driven threads.

3.1   Web Traffic Model

Web traffic continues to increase and is now estimated to be more than 70 percent of the total traffic on the Internet [17]. Consequently, it is important to have an accurate model to produce a simulated network that closely resembles the pattern of traffic on a real network to be able to determine accurate QoS measures. Web traffic has more structures than most types of Internet traffic. Further the characteristics of traffic change as browsers and services evolve, as the behavior of users change, as the speed of network increases and as protocols change.

Our simulation analysis has devoted special attention to the workload model and we have implemented a Behavioral Model of Web traffic [18] to incorporate the most recent results on Web workload characterization. The high variability and selfsimilarity nature of Web service load is modeled through ON/FF processes with heavy-tailed distributions such as Pareto and Log-normal. Figure 4 describes the traffic generation process where the ON state represents the activity of a Web-request and OFF state represents a silent period after all objects in a Web-request has been retrieved.

This model has adopted as basic unit a Web-request instead of a Web page which has been the basic unit of most past models [19]. A Web-request is a page or a set of pages that result from an action of a user, resulting in a model that closely imitates user behavior. The implementation of this new traffic pattern is one of the most important extensions we have made to the SIDE framework in order to support the simulation of actual network conditions.

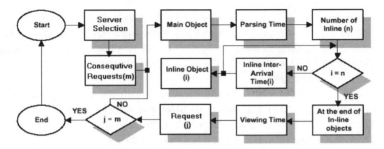

Fig. 4. State transition diagram for Web traffic generation

3.2 System Model

Typically, a program in SIDE consists of a number of source files. The basic unit of execution is called a process and it looks like a specification of a finite state machine. A process always runs in the context of some station, which conceptually represents a logical component of the controlled/modeled system. In our simulation each Client is modeled as a process at some station owing a copy of the presented Web Traffic Model to generate Web requests, such requests are forwarded by an interface to the Counselor Agent process and waits for the Web-request to be retrieved. Counselor Agents process implements one of the three techniques to decide where to send the received requests, allocated requests are sent to Service Agents through the network interface. The network connections have different structures to represent available network bandwidths present in the Internet links and also have different distribution of transmission delays, finally the network topology is defined by a connectivity function. Service Agent process run in the context of Web server stations and receive requests that accept or reject them depending on service load and in the case of Bilateral implementation it sends its QoS offers to clients accordingly to the mechanism presented in section 2. Likewise the process model of Web servers is an abstraction of actions that occur at the session level layer of the HTTP protocol. We model a Web server as a set of resource queues. Service times are based upon two types of requested objects: static and dynamic objects. Service time for static objects is proportional to its size, and dynamic objects require extra time drawn from a Hyper Geometric Distribution representing objects that requires to be processed at Web server before the response is sent to the client.

4 Experimental Setup

The specification of the three dynamic Request Placement Strategies illustrated in the previous section has been analyzed through simulation in the SIDE framework. In this section we describe the scenario within which these experiments have been carried out. Every simulation experiment for a given configuration has consisted of 20 runs, each considering at least 5,000 Web-requests issued from 1,900 users per Autonomous System in the network. The values for the Web traffic model that drives client Web-request generation are shown in Table 2.

Table 2. Web traffic model parameter statistics

Parameter		Mean	Median	S.D.	Distribution
Request Size		360.4	344	106.5	Lognormal
Object Size	Main	10710	6094	25032	Lognormal
	In-line	7758	1931	126168	Lognormal
Parsing time		0.13	0.06	0.187	Gamma
In-line objects		5.55	2	1.14	Gamma
Viewing time		39.5	11.7	92.6	Gamma
Temporal locality		1.5	-	0.80	Lognormal
Service popularity					Zipf

There are two kinds of objects. The file containing an HTML document is referred to as main object and the objects linked from the Hypertext Document are referred to as In-line objects. Parsing time is the time spent parsing the HTML code in order to determine the layout of a page after fetching the main object. Viewing time is the inactive interval between Web-requests. Temporal locality is the number of sequential Web-requests addressed to the same server. Finally to address the issue of popular Web services and client preferences a Zipf distribution is implemented as an extension to the original Work load model.

In the scenario of Fig 5, five Web services has been considered with a replication level of 3 giving 15 available services distributed randomly, Table 3 shows the values for the hyper-exponential distribution parameters defining service time at Web servers for dynamic objects requested by clients. Five services were chosen because it is a large enough number to make the task of correct service selection hard enough for the Agents to learn service values within the time frame of the experiment.

Table 3. List of parameters considered in the work load model

Parameter	Type	Mean	Frequency
	High intensive	0.7	0.01
Service time	Medium intensive	0.1	0.14
	Low Intensive	0.001	0.85

Because the structure on the Internet is not fully understood we use the Inet[20] tool to generate simulated Internet topologies. We have conducted experiments with 10, 30, 50, 70 and 100 Autonomous Systems to evaluate effects of light and heavy traffic load on Dynamic Request Placement Strategies. Network delays at interdomain links model OC-48 speeds with a mean of 2488 Mbps and delays at transit domains with a mean of 10 sec.

5   Results

In order to evaluate the effectiveness of the proposed techniques to Dynamic Request Allocation, the performance of the market-based techniques: BIL and MKT were benchmarked against a Random service selection technique. We consider four metics to evaluate the effectiveness for each technique we measure:

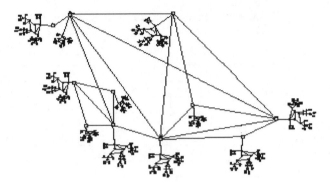

Fig. 5. Case study network topology

- The median of user response times experienced by users to complete a Web-request with 5, 10, 50, 100 (samall Web-request), 250, 500 and 1000K sizes (large Web-requests).
- The median of user response time in presence of the hourly effects, when service load increases at peek hours.
- The numer of sucessfully allocated request.
- Te overhead of each technique given by its communication costs derived from QoS information collection and disemination.

We found positive learning effects and statistical and cognitive benefits for the Multiagent market-based proposed techniques. In Fig. 6, we report the reponsiveness of the three tecniques, for 5..1000K Web-requests, we see that BIL outperform MKT and RND for bigger Web-request, due to the feedback mechanism of BIL technique and the ammortizacion request-bidding over biggers requested Web pages.

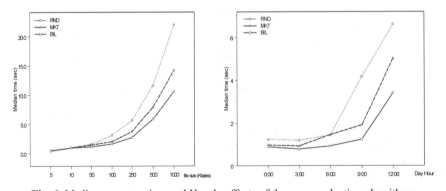

Fig. 6. Median response time and Hourly effects of the server selection algorithms

Differences between request placement techniques are far pronounced during busy daytime hours than for quieter periods (see Fig. 6), reflecting the network load on the techniques, and the periodicity of hourly effects. MKT technique always perform worse than BIL and better than RND, with minor exceptions curves do not cross, implying that as QoS perceived changes clients need not to use a different technique to achieve optimal performance.

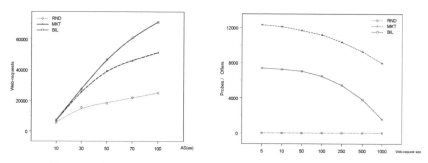

Fig. 7. Performance and Overhead for BIL, MKT and RND techniques

We compare in Fig. 7, the performance of the three techniques using the total number of request allocated and the overhead induced by negotiation techniques implemented by such techniques; we can see that selecting with RND technique has the lowest performance although it does not produce any overhead as compared with MKT whose performance is higher because its QoS actualization mechanism, but it incurs in high overhead too, then the most cost-effective strategy is BIL whose performance is high and overhead remains relative low in comparison with RND and MKT.

We conclude by mentioning the fact that the obtained results have been compared with corresponding figures in [21], which describe the results obtained by conducting some experiments wtih a different configuration of workload model and network topology. The result of the comparission in a total qualitative agrement goes in the sense that the relationship among the improvement of QoS perceived by users of the contrasted curves are preserved. In the quantitative side, the figures presented in this paper show slower response times that those conducted before, the reason being the workload model described in [21] on which experiments where conducted are based on a Non-Homogenous-Poisson Process, showing low variability and uniform response times.

6 Conclusions and Future Work

In this paper we have analyzed three Dynamic request Placement techniques. These techniques are implemented in a Multi-agent based architecture where Autonomous Agents learn about user preferences, network performance and QoS of services to improve QoS perceived by users, assuming a geographical distribution of Web services in the Internet, and taking into account actual conditions as high variability and self-similarity. Such techniques rely on a market-based mechanism to negotiate required QoS by user and applications, and a Service Directory to classify and locate available services on the network. We also have discussed the behavior of our strategies over several configurations as illustrated by our simulation analysis.

This architecture will be adapted to the GEDA-3D[22] project in order to accommodate diverse application requirements by implementing them as techniques tailored to different application-specific requirements. The framework will allow GEDA-3D middleware to assign replicated servers to clients adaptively based on the QoS requirements of the clients and the current responsiveness and state of the services. The experimental results that we have obtained demonstrate the role of feedback from service load and for adaptively sharing the available services among the users in a range of different scenarios. While a random selection technique would be sufficient when the primary goal is load balancing and when the clients do not have QoS constraints, we believe that a dynamic technique, like the Bilateral Technique we have developed, would be useful in an environment in which QoS-aware clients that have different requirements accessing servers that display significant variability in their response times. Although our Bilateral technique was mainly developed to improve QoS perceived by Web service's users, given the diversity of the QoS requirements of client requests when accessing distributed services, such adaptive technique that rely on feedback based control are likely to play an increasing role in solving a range of problems related to building distributed systems.

References

1. J. Guyton and M. Schwartz. Locating nearby copies of replicated internet servers. In Proceeding of ACM SIGCOMM' 95, 1995.
2. Cisco Distributed Director, http://www.cisco.com/warp/public/cc/pd/cxsr/dd/index.shtml
3. E. Zegura, M. Ammar, Z. Fei, and S. Bhattacharjee, Application-layer anycasting: a server selection architecture and use in a replicated web service, IEEE/ACM Transactions on Networking, vol. 8, no. 4, pp. 455–466, Aug. 2000.
4. M. Crovella and R. Carter. Dynamic server selection in the internet. In Proceeding of IEEE Workshop on the Architecture and Implementation of High Performance Communication Subsyste, 1995.
5. M. Crovella and R. Carter, Dynamic Server Selection Using Bandwidth Probing inWide-Area Networks, In Proceedings of IEEE INFOCOM, 1997.
6. M. Rabinovich, I. Rabinovich, R. Rajaraman, and A. Aggarwal. A Dynamic Object Replication and Migration Protocol for an Internet Hosting Service. In Proc. 19th Int'l Conf. on Distributed Computing Systems, pp. 101–113, Austin, TX, June 1999. 18 IEEE.
7. S. Krishnamurthy, W.H. Sanders, M. Cukier, Performance Evaluation of a QoS-Aware Framework for Providing Tunable Consistency and Timeliness, Proc. of The 10th IEEE International Workshop on Quality of Service (IWQoS 2002), May 2002.
8. S. Krishnamurthy, W.H. Sanders, M. Cukier, Performance Evaluation of a Probabilistic Replica Selection Algorithm, Proc. of The Seventh IEEE International Workshop on Object-Oriented Real-Time Dependable Systems (WORDS 2002), Jan. 2002.
9. R. Steinmetz and K. Nahrstedt, Multimedia: Computing Communications & Applications, Prentice Hall., 1995, pp. 420–45.
10. F.Ramos, "Placement dynamique de requêtes multi-agents dans les systèmes d'information globaux", PhD thesis, Université de Technologie de Compiègne, juin 1997.
11. Bui M., Butelle F., Lavault C. (2003). A Distributed Algorithm for Constructing a Minimum Diameter Spanning Tree. Journal of Parallel and Distributed Computing. In Press.
12. Binzhang Liu, "Characterizing Web Response Time" MSc. Thesis, Virginia Polytechnic Institute and State University, Apr. 1998.
13. S.G. Dykes, K.A. Robbins, C.L. Jeffery, "An Empirical Evaluation of Client-Side Server Selection Algorithms", in IEEE INFOCOM 3:1361-1370, 2000.
14. M. Harchol-Balter, M.E. Crovella, C.D. Murta, "On Choosing a Task Assignment Policy for a Distributed Server System", in Parallel and Distributed Computing 59:204-228, 1999.
15. G. R. Smith, "The contract net protocol: high-level communication and control in a distributed problem solver", IEEE Trans. on Computer, 12(29), Dec. 1981, pp.1104-1113
16. Pawel G. Burzynsky, Protocol Design for Local and Metropolitan Area Networks, Prentice Hall, 1996

17. K. Thompson, G. J. Miller, and R. Wilder. Wide-Area Internet Traffic Patterns and Characteristics (Extended Version). IEEE Network Magazine, Nov 1997.
18. Hyoung-Kee Choi, John O. Limb, "A Behavioral Model of Web Traffic", Proceedings of the Seventh Annual International Conference on Network Protocols, 1999.
19. B. Mah. "An empirical model of HTTP network traffic". In Proceeding of INFOCOM '97
20. K. Calvert, M. Doar, and E. W. Zegura, "Modeling internet topology, " IEEE Communications Magazine, June 1997. [10] C. Jin, Q.Chen, S.Jamin, "Inet: Internet Topology Generator," University of Michigan Technical Report, CSE-TR-433-00, September 2000.
21. Ramos F., Chen L., Bui M. (1999). A comparison of two dynamic request placement strategies in large distributed information systems, in Proceedings of the 12th International Conference on Parallel and Distributed Computing Systems (ISCA PDCS), Radisson Bahia Mar Beach Resort, USA, August 1999.
22. Fabiel Zúñiga, H. Iván Piza, Félix F. Ramos. "A 3D-Space Platform for Distributed Applications Management". International Symposium on Advanced Distributed Systems 2002 (ISADS). Guadalajara, Jal., México. 2002.
23. ISO, "Quality of Service Framework", ISO/IEC JTC1/SC21/WG1 N9680, International Standards Organization, UK, 1995.

IP Networks Quality of Service:
Overview and Open Issues

Marlenne Angulo[1,2], Deni Torres-Roman[1],
David Muñoz-Rodriguez[3], and Marco Turrubiartes[1,2]

[1] CINVESTAV Research Center, Guadalajara México
{mangulo,dtorres,mturrubi}@gdl.cinvestav.mx
[2] Universidad Autónoma de Baja California, Mexicali México
[3] ITESM, Monterrey México
dmunoz@cet.mty.itesm.mx

Abstract. Mechanisms to provide Quality of Service (QoS) into Internet have a collection of aspects to consider improving network performance. However, this work focuses only on four of these aspects, as follows: Traffic Models, Queue scheduling, Congestion control and QoS routing. Considering any of the three above mentioned approaches, it is necessary the use of traffic models which capture the real network traffic behavior. This paper introduces some QoS concepts, as well as open-issues in the mentioned areas.

1 Introduction

Most of Internet user applications require superior network performance; some applications even require guaranteed service. This makes Quality of Service (QoS) an area that fulfills users' requirements. The QoS areas research, develop and implement mechanisms to meet users' needs. However, QoS is not a new concept in some telecommunications fields such as telephony.

The QoS development involves mechanisms of network performance evaluation. This allows the provider (e.g. the Internet Service Provider) to verify the QoS degree at the end-user level.

There is a group of suggested mechanisms to provide QoS into Internet, and a collection of aspects to consider. However, this work focuses only on four of these aspects, as follows:

- *Traffic Models* (current models). Besides well implemented algorithms, it is necessary the use of real traffic models in order to obtain valid simulation results.
- *Queue scheduling*. Queue and traffic behavior affect the packet delay variation. It leads to network performance variability in terms of delay, affecting real time applications.
- *Congestion control*. It presents an introduction to TCP-friendly congestion control protocol. The use of this class of transport protocol should be increased in order to avoid the unfair bandwidth competition of UDP versus TCP data.
- *QoS routing*. This subject is important in order to achieve a real guaranteed Quality of Service, instead of attempting a differentiation in service or <Class of Service>.

T. Böhme et al. (Eds.): IICS 2004, LNCS 3473, pp. 28–37, 2006.

This paper introduces some QoS concepts, as well as open-issues in the sub-areas: *Traffic models, Queue scheduling, Congestion control and QoS routing.* The remaining of this article is organized as follows: section two introduces concepts and current models in the above mentioned sub-areas. Section three discusses open issues, followed by section four in which the conclusions of this paper are presented. Finally, references are presented.

2 Literature Review

2.1 Traffic Models

Historically, distributions such as Poisson and Exponential have been used to model telecommunication traffic. However, those models do not suit with some kinds of traffic, specifically data networks. In articles [1][2], the failure of Poisson model to capture variability in time scales of Ethernet traffic is presented. Using traffic models close to reality discards the possibility of overestimating performance in analysis or simulation results due to ideal traffic conditions.

Self-similar Processes
Mathematical analysis shows that the Internet traffic has self-similar properties at the packet level [1]. Moreover, an article published by Feldman shows empirical evidence of fractal characteristics on traffic at the application level [3]. The self-similar term was defined by Mandelbrot to characterize those processes that are scaled in time and do not lose their statistical properties.

Definition: A process X(t) is self-similar if it satisfies the following equation:

$$\{\ X(at),\ t \in \Re\ \} \overset{d}{=} \{a^H X(t),\ t \in \Re\}\quad \forall a,\ H > 0\ \in \Re \tag{1}$$

Where $X(at)$ and $a^H X(t)$ have identical distributions($\overset{d}{=}$), H is the *Hurst parameter* denoting the self-similarity index [4]. For Internet traffic H takes values into the interval (0.5, 1).

Long Range Dependence Phenomenon (LRD)
The self similar property of Internet traffic manifests itself in the autocorrelation function $\rho(k)$. The sum of all autocorrelations from any given time instant is always significant, even if individual correlations are small.

The Internet traffic holds an LRD phenomenon. It means that Internet traffic characteristics, at time *t,* will influence itself in the long term [5].

LRD is defined as the property of some processes in which the sum of the autocorrelation values approaches infinity (see Eq. 2).

$$\sum_{k=0}^{\infty} \rho(k) = \infty \tag{2}$$

Where its autocorrelation function is

$$\rho(k) \sim L_1(k)k^{-\beta} \qquad k \to 0 \qquad 0 < \beta < 1 \tag{3}$$

k is the lag and L_1 is a slow-varying function.

Or equivalently as the power-law divergence at the origin of its power spectrum:

$$f(\lambda) \sim L_2(\lambda)\lambda^{-D} \qquad\qquad \lambda \to 0 \qquad 0 < D < 1 \qquad\qquad (4)$$

λ is the frequency and L_2 is a slow-varying function

The Hurst parameter describes self-similarity of cumulative traffic, while β, from Eq. 3, describes the LRD rate process. β is the most important parameter since it characterizes the LRD phenomenon. Research about L_1, and its relationship with LRD is presented in [6]. The LRD processes expression of the variance of the sample mean with sample size n is defined in [6], denoted by equation 5.

$$\text{Var}\{ X(t) \}=[2L_1{}^{1-\beta}/(2-\beta)(1-\beta)](1/n) \qquad\qquad (5)$$

Heavy Tailed Distributions

It is accepted that current Internet traffic exhibits heavy tail characteristics [2], leading to the development of some designs and analysis tools that consider the tailed nature of traffic [8]

Definition: A random variable X has a heavy-tailed distribution if [7]

$$P[X > x] \sim x^{-\alpha} \qquad \text{as } x \to \infty \qquad 0 < \alpha < 2 \qquad\qquad (6)$$

That is, regardless of the behavior of the distribution for small values of the random variable, if the asymptotic shape of the distribution is hyperbolic, it is heavy-tailed. The simplest heavy-tailed distribution is the Pareto distribution. The Pareto distribution is hyperbolic over its entire range. Heavy-tailed distributions have the following properties:

1) If $\alpha \le 2$, then the distribution has infinite variance.
2) If $\alpha \le 1$, then the distribution has infinite mean.

Thus, as alpha decreases, an arbitrarily large portion of probability mass may be present in the tail of the distribution.

Alpha Stable Distributions

Definition: A random variable X is said to have a stable distribution if for X_1, X_2 independent copies of X and any positive numbers A and B, there is a positive number C and a real number D such that [4]

$$AX_1 + BX_2 \overset{d}{=} CX + D \qquad\qquad (7)$$

Theorem 1: For any stable random variable X, there is a number $\alpha \in (0,2]$ such that the number C (in Eq. 7) satisfies:

$$C^\alpha = A^\alpha + B^\alpha \qquad\qquad (8)$$

A stable random variable X with index α is called *Alfa stable*.

The generalized theorem of Central Limit proposes the alpha-stable distributions to model the aggregated contribution of many random variables, without restricting them to have a finite variance (as central limit theorem does).

Alpha-stable distributions are defined by their characteristic function [4]:

$$\Phi_X(\theta) = \begin{cases} \exp\left[\ j\mu\theta - |\sigma\theta|^\alpha .(\ 1 + j\beta.sign(\theta).\tan(\pi\alpha/2)\ )\ \right]; & \alpha \neq 1 \\ \exp\left[\ j\mu\theta - |\sigma\theta|. (\ 1 + j\beta.\dfrac{2}{\pi}.sign(\theta).\ln|\theta|\ )\ \right]; & \alpha = 1 \end{cases} \quad (9)$$

Where α is a stability index ($0 \leq \alpha \leq 2$), σ is the scaling parameter ($\sigma \geq 0$), μ is the shift parameter, and β is the skewness parameter ($-1 \leq \beta \leq 1$).

2.2   QoS Queue Scheduling

There are different mechanisms to provide QoS, mechanisms such as scheduling and policing. The technique where packets in a waiting queue are selected to be transmitted is known as scheduling discipline. Queue scheduling permits to manage the queues as a network resource, becoming a bandwidth allocation scheme. Moreover, lately different scheduling disciplines have been developed in order to manage multiple queues, which permit the categorization of packets.

The impact of traffic in queuing buffers is a dominant problem in traffic engineering, giving remarkable importance to traffic models. In [9] the demand, capacity and performance of priority access and non-priority access flows (in term of QoS requirements) are reviewed.

Priority Queuing
Under priority queuing discipline packets are classified in two or more priority classes depicted in figure 1 [10]. The classification of packets will be according to the priority mark in the IP packet header (Type of Service field might be used to assign priority). In order to transmit the packet, the scheduling discipline will service the highest priority packets until their queue is empty, after that it will continue offering the service to the lower priority packet.

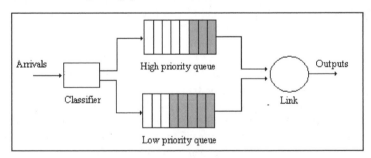

Fig. 1. Priority Queuing Scheduling

Round-Robin Scheduling / Weighted Scheduling
Under Round-Robin scheduling discipline packets are classified and sent to one of the queues according to their class. However, it does not have a strict priority service, transmitting one packet of queue 1, another from queue 2, until the last queue, repeating this pattern forever.

Weighted scheduling uses the same classification method as Round-Robin; however, it differs from that method in the way of servicing the queues, differentiating the time intervals to which the packets of class *i* will be sent. A fraction of bandwidth of

w_i/S_{wi} will be assured to Class i, where w_i is the weight of the class and S_{wi} is the sum of all classes weights. In the worst case, when all queues have packets to transmit, class i will continue having a fraction of bandwidth w_i/S_{wi} [10].

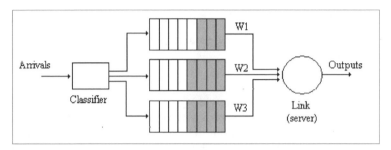

Fig. 2. Weighted Fair Queuing

It is easy to notice that the service method is independent from the classification scheme, where this scheme has many options to be implemented, such as modified Leaky Bucket, where the packets are differentiated according to the traffic contract agreement (if there is one). The differentiation could be implemented in two or three levels, in the case of two levels (commonly called colors) the packets violating the accorded bandwidth to their connection or flow are marked as red, and the complaining packets are marked as green.

Traditional drop tail queue management can not effectively prevent the occurrence of serious congestion and often suffers from large queuing delays. Furthermore, the global synchronization may occur during the period of congestion resulting in underutilization and large oscillation for queuing delay. RED (Random Early Detection) has been proposed to address these problems. In [11] is presented an algorithm that adjust dynamically the RED parameters to improve the network performance, even if exist some little variations on the network.

2.3 Congestion Control Protocols

In order to satisfy QoS requirements have being proposed different congestion methods, such as filters with Leaky Bucket and the jumping window [12].

The jumping window mechanism limits the maximum number of packets (N) accepted from a source in a time interval (window). A new interval begins immediately as the preceding ends. Thus, the associated counter is restarted.

The implementation of this mechanism requires counters to measure the interval T and to count the number of arrivals; and variables are needed for the counter limit and the interval length T.

Exponentially Weighted Moving Average
This mechanism utilizes consecutive windows of fixed time, such as jumping window does. The difference between these two mechanisms is the maximum number of packets accepted in the i-th window N_i. Where N_i is function of the average of the packets allowed by interval N, and S_{i-1} is the exponentially weighted sum of the preceding intervals (X_{i-1}) according to the following equation [13]:

$$N_i = \frac{N - \gamma \, S_{i-1}}{1 - \gamma} \qquad\qquad 0 \le \gamma < 1 \tag{10}$$

Where: $S_{i-1} = (1-\gamma)X_{i-1} + \gamma \, S_{i-2}$

The γ factor controls the algorithm flexibility, regarding the burstiness of traffic. If $\gamma = 0$ and N_i is constant, the algorithm is the same as the sliding window.

Congestion Control Based on Delay
In [14] the performance of DCA algorithms (Delay Based Congestion) in high speed networks is analyzed. Those algorithms are based on round trip time (RTT) as a congestion indicator. That paper refuses the premise of high level of correlation between RTT increment and packet loss.

TCP-Friendly Congestion Control
TCP-Friendly is a transport protocol which implements congestion control mechanisms that interact well with TCP. To provide such fairness, one solution is to satisfy TCP-friendliness, which means the (T_C, p) relationship $T_C \sim 1/(R\sqrt{p})$ should hold, where T_C is the throughput of a flow, p is the packet loss rate, and R is RTT.

TCP-Friendly algorithms are developed because of the increase of UDP applications where congestion control algorithms are not applied. That leads to an unfair bandwidth competition with TCP data [15]
TCP-friendly protocols are classified in:
Rate-based:

- Rate adaptation protocol (RAP) besides short-term RTT average, it utilizes the long-term RTT average to modify the inter-packet gap between consecutive data packets.
- Loss-delay based adaptation (LDA+) uses RTCP feedback messages.
- TCP-friendly rate control (TFRC) adjust rate based on losses by RTT parameter.
- TCP emulation at receivers (TEAR) hybrid protocol utilizes RTT average.

Windows Based:

- Random listening algorithm (RLA) identifies the packet loss by discontinuous acknowledge messages (ACK).
- Multicast TCP (MTCP), in which the participants are grouped in a tree structure.
- Nominee-based congestion avoidance (NCA) The worst receptor uses TCP.

In [16] is presented the study of congestion control mechanism of the TCP-friendly type, compatible with TCP under queuing manage of RED scheme. These authors proposed an SIMD (square-increase/multiplicative-decrease) scheme, where the window size increases proportionally to the square of the elapsed time since the last detection of a loss event. Compared with memory-less schemes based on windows, the SIMD scheme improves the transient behavior using memory. On the other hand, compared with equation-based schemes, the controller presents simple modifications of the TCP scheme.

2.4 QoS Routing Techniques

Routing consists of two basic functions: *distribution of the network state*, and *look for information* to find out a route.

Routing with QoS implies the necessity of including optimization techniques. It could be done by a primary cost function (administrative load, hope counting), in order to select optimal paths. In general, the selection of a multi-constrained path with or without optimization is a not yet solved problem in real time.

To get a multi-constrained routing and a viable solution (complexity and time), some researchers [17] proposed a non-linear cost-function, where minimization provides a wide spectrum of solutions from a linear approximation to an exact asymptotic solution.

There are diverse routing algorithms to find a route that satisfies QoS requirements. In [18] an algorithm to find a route is proposed and it shows less computational complexity compared with Tunable Accuracy Multiple Constrain Routing Algorithm (TAMCRA) and Jaffe algorithms, finding less computational complexity in the proposed algorithm.

In [19] a routing algorithm which adapts to any traffic's stochastic model is proposed. This algorithm does not require knowledge of future demands; authors give a direct application of this algorithm in Multi-protocol Label switching (MPLS) path setup.

3 Open Issues

The parameters of most impact in Quality of Service of IP networks are:

- Bandwidth
- Packet loss rate
- Packet delay
- Packet delay variation

Diverse approaches improve the network performance. In this work the following subjects are considered, and open problems of each subject are presented. The analysis and development of solutions for some of them are left for future work.

a. Traffic Models
b. Queuing scheduling algorithms
c. Congestion Control Protocols
d. QoS routing techniques

a) Traffic Models
Self-Similarity is an important characteristic of current Internet Traffic. Equation 1 shows the definition of a self-similar process X(t), where H is the self-similarity index and its estimation is necessary in order to characterize the self-similarity property.

In the case of self-similar traffic with self-similarity index ½ <H< 1 the LRD phenomenon is captured. The power spectrum of an LRD processes is characterized by: L_2 and β (Eq. 4).

From Eq. 5 the variance of the LRD processes is proportional to L_1. Crovella in [7] describes that the variance of the mean of n samples decreases proportionally to L_1.

In that way the authors of [6] conclude that the value of the function L_1 is therefore critical even for the simplest practical estimation issues for LRD processes.

It is also important to notice that the Internet traffic distributions show heavy tailed characteristics. For so, it is necessary to estimate the α parameter from equation 6 in order to characterize the heavy-tailed traffic distributions.

Moreover, there is still the necessity of increasing the speed of the estimation algorithms (some of them based on wavelets and maximum likelihood techniques).

It is also important to develop a deep analysis on the empirical proposal of Feldmann [3], where the self-similar model could be applied in the application layer. Additionally, it is significant to mention that the traffic is changing constantly and no matter how perfect it fits a model today, it does not have to capture tomorrow's networks traffic behavior.

b) Queuing Scheduling Algorithms
It is important to retake the work done by information theory researchers. In that way queuing scheduling is improved by managing different strategies such as: packets preventive discard, the use of more than one queue, and the manipulation of the service rate (in weighted queuing). However, the utilization of techniques developed in the Information Theory area might improve the scheduling algorithms performance, in terms of: bandwidth utilization, jitter, and packet loss among others.

c) Congestion Control Protocol
TCP-friendly protocols have successful applications in a controlled environment (Intranet rather than Internet). However, under that limitation, there is a huge field of research in order to achieve a congestion control protocol friendly in bandwidth competition with TCP protocols, and at the same time it is able to *tune* a *"friendly parameter"* considering the application priority.

d) QoS Routing Techniques
A trade-off problem between scalability and granularity is present in QoS routing. The problem is that each application has requirements to be fulfilled, and at the same time architectures that treat traffic as per-flow have scalability problem. From the network point of view, it is also important the methodology of metrics measurement, (metrics such as bandwidth, packet delay, etc.), that leads the QoS routing to estimate some metrics from other metric with less complexity and higher speed in the measurement method in order to provide a real-time QoS routing.

Currently, some tendencies are decreasing the complexity of the QoS routing algorithms, improving this characteristic compared with algorithms such as TAMCRA. There is also an important proposal to adapt any stochastic model traffic's without requirement of future demands. Besides, the mathematical model and simulation of these algorithms, it is necessary to prove their convergence and stability.

4 Conclusions

It is not recommendable the use of traditional traffic models such as Gaussian or Poisson to model Internet traffic behavior, because overestimated simulation results might be a consequence of ideal traffic simulated.

As long as Internet Traffic shows self-similar characteristics, it is important to develop estimation techniques of the Hurst parameter in order to characterize the real traffic behavior.

There are different approaches mentioned in section three, where Quality of Service in Internet could be improved, depending on which QoS architecture is implemented. Currently there are three network architectures (defined by IETF) pursuing QoS: Differentiated Services, Integrated Services and Multi-protocol Label Switching. The characterization of QoS mechanisms performance over some network architectures is left for future work.

From a global point of view, working with QoS routing, and/or congestion control consider a significant advance in IP networks. However, it is still not enough to fulfill bandwidth applications requirements. In that way scheduling schemes could be used inside a router, combining different policing mechanisms as the resource management mechanism.

Acknowledgment

First and fourth author want to thank to the Autonomous University of Baja California for their support and to PROMEP funding.

References

1. Leland, H. E., Taqqu, M. S., Willinger, W., Wilson, D.: On the Self-Similar Nature of Ethernet Traffic -Extended Version-. IEEE/ACM transactions on networking, Vol. 2, No 1, February (1994).
2. Paxon, V., Floyd, S.: Wide-area traffic: The failure of Poisson modeling. IEEE/ACM Trans. Networking, vol. 3. June (1995) 226-244
3. Feldmann, G., Willinger, W., Kurtz M.: The changing nature of Network Traffic Scaling phenomena. ACM Computer Communication Review, vol. 28, Apr. (1998) 5-29
4. Taqqu, M., Samorodnisky, G.: Stable non-gaussian Random process. Ed. Chapman & Hall, (1994).
5. Rougham, M., Veitch, D., Abry, P.: Real-Time estimation of the parameters of Long Range Dependence. IEEE/ACM Transactions on Networking, Vol. 8 August (2000) 467-478.
6. Veitch, C., Patrice, A.: A wavelet-based Joint estimator of the parameters of LRD. IEEE Transactions on Information Theory, April (1999).
7. Crovella, M., Bestavros, A.: Self-Similarity in World Wide Web Traffic: Evidence and possible causes. IEEE/ACM transactions on networking Vol 5, No. 6, December (1997).
8. Muñoz-Rodriguez, D.: submitted to IEEE Communication Networks.
9. Roberts, J. W.: Traffic theory and the Internet. IEEE Communications Magazine, January (2001).
10. Demers, A., Keshav, S., Shenker, S.: Analysis and Simulation of a Fair Queuing Algorithm. Internetworking: Research and Experience, Vol 1. No. 1, (1990) 3-26.
11. Tao, Y., et.al.: Adaptive tuning of RED using on-line simulation. Proceedings of GLOBECOM (2002).
12. Parekh, A., Gallager, R.: A generalized processor sharing approach to flow control in integrated services networks: the single-node case. IEEE/ACM Transactions on Networking, Vol. 1, No. 3, June (1993) 344-357.
13. Rathgeb, E. P.: Modeling and performance comparison of policing mechanisms for ATM networks. IEEE Journal on Selected Areas in Communications, vol. 9 issue 3, (1991) 325-334

14. Martin, J., Nilsson, A., Injong R.: Delay-based congestion avoidance for TCP. IEEE/ACM Transactions on Networking June (2003) 356-369.
15. Widmer, J., Denda, R., Mauve, M.: A survey of TCP-friendly congestion control. IEEE Network, May-June (2001) 28-37
16. Jin, S., Guo, L., Matta, I., Bestavros, A.: A Spectrum of TCP-friendly window-based Congestion control Algorithms. IEEE/ACM Transactions on Networking June (2003)   341-355.
17. Ray H.: IP QoS Architectures. Proceedings of International conference on Networking (2001).
18. Korkmaz T., Krunz M.: Routing multimedia traffic with QoS guarantees. IEEE transactions on multimedia, vol.5 no.3, September (2003) 429-443.
19. Oliveira et al.: 'SPeCRA: A stochastic performance comparison routing algorithm for LSP setup in MPLS networks. Proceedings of GLOBECOM (2002)

Efficiency of Wireless Local Area Networks in Clients Moving at High Speed

Andreas Bengsch, Heiko Kopp, André Petry, Robil Daher, and Djamshid Tavangarian

University of Rostock
Department of Computer Science
Chair of Computer Architecture
Albert-Einstein-Str. 21, 18059 Rostock, Germany
{andreas.bensch,heiko.kopp,andre.petry,robil.daher,
djamshid.tavangarian}@uni-rostock.de

Abstract. Wireless communication structures based on the IEEE 802.11 Standard became an important research area within science and economy during the last years. It forms a basis for an area-wide use of mobile services and personalized information within so called hotspots. However, the common usage is a public available stationary installation like at an airport, office building or university. Besides other wireless technologies like DECT or HiperLAN this paper shows, that Wireless LAN is capable for use in clients moving at high speed. To prove the theory a couple of measurements have been made using components of the IEEE 802.11b standard and clients moving at speeds up to 200 km/h. Beside measuring characteristic parameters like signal- and noise level as well as data throughput for different speeds, measurements on the quality of voice transmission have been made for the first time. In addition to a detailed analysis this article covers perspectives for applications using wireless hotspots.

1 Introduction

Wireless LAN relies on the IEEE 802.11 standard [3] which became one of the biggest economy areas for communication technologies in the last few years. In addition to a usage within desktop computers and notebooks as connection to wireless networks nowadays a majority of devices like PDAs and Tablet PCs supports such networks directly.

Most installed wireless networks use the IEEE 802.11b standard as supplement of the original IEEE 802.11 which was standardised in 1999 with a maximum transfer rate of 11 MBit/s and transmitting in the license-free 2.4 GHz ISM Band (Industrial, Science and Medical Band). The up-and-coming supplements IEEE 802.11g inside the 2.4 GHz Band as well as the IEEE 802.11a in the 5 GHz Band support higher transfer rates up to 54 MBit/s and will replace the IEEE 802.11b more or less fast in the future.

Within this paper some terms concerning wireless communication are used of which a definition is mandatory. Therefore, a short explanation of the most important will be given:

Client, Server and User. The term *Client* or *User* in relation to wireless communication is often a synonym for the service-consuming end-device. The server provides this services used by a client. Both, the client as well as the server are using the wire-

T. Böhme et al. (Eds.): IICS 2004, LNCS 3473, pp. 38–48, 2006.

less communication network, but no statement about mobility is associated with one of them.

Ad-Hoc-Mode, Infrastructure-Mode, Hotspot and Access Point. Within the standard IEEE 802.11 two network topologies can be distinguished. In an ad-hoc mode network clients build point-to-point connections between each other. Disadvantages of this kind of topology are the small amount of clients that can communicate and the low scalability. Furthermore a communication between two clients is impossible in case their distance to each other is to small even in the case a third station resides in between and could work as router.

The noted disadvantages do not arise in the infrastructure network. It uses a special device, the Access Point, placed in the centre of a starlike topology to manage all the communication. This means there is no direct connection present between the clients as mentioned for the ad-hoc-network. Each Access Point controls a Wireless LAN cell defined by the physical range of its emitted radiation. Different cells can be combined to cover greater areas. An advantage of this combination is the possibility to hand-over connections between proximate cells. All communication data is send from the actual Access Point to the next using a hand-over protocol (e.g. the Inter Access Point Protocol – IAPP).

Additionally, to achieve a connection between two fixed networks in greater distance, the IEEE 802.11 standard contains bridge-mode functionality.

The availability of wireless networks in public areas lead to the definition of such an accumulation of wireless cells as *hotspot*. A hotspot is a not necessarily contiguous area providing the same wireless network using the IEEE 802.11 infrastructure mode topology. The amount of Access Points within a hotspot is insignificant.

Mobility. As already noted, the definition of a client or server does not associate the mobility as property. In case it is included into the functionality, this leads to some categorization shown in figure 1:

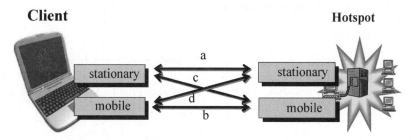

Fig. 1. Mobility as new Characteristic for Client and Hotspot

While in category a) both hotspot and client are stationary, e.g. when providing wireless access to workstations without the need of wires, the categories b) and c) can be found in the area of ad-hoc networks mostly.

This paper covers the evaluation of application fields for mobile clients in stationary hotspots (referred to as category d). Many public hotspots belong to this category, however their mobility is widely restricted. Our evaluation will cover clients moving at high speeds starting at 100 km/h. For this, a comparison with other technologies like GSM, DECT or HiperLAN is useful. Table 1 shows this technologies together with WLAN. Particularly interesting is the maximum speed by user which is high with 250 km/h and GSM but rather low for HiperLAN at 10 m/s.

Table 1. Comparison between wireless communication technologies [10]

Standard	GSM	DECT	WLAN 802.11b,g	HiperLAN
Band	900/1800/1900 MHz	1900 MHz	2,4 GHz	5,15-5,25 GHz
Bit Rate	270,8 KBit/s	1152 KBit/s	1-54 MBit/s	> 20 Mbit/s
Amount Carrier	125	10	14 maximum (differs regional)	
Channels per Carrier	8	24 (12 duplex)	variable	
Cell Size	< 35 km	< 400 m	Indoor < 50 m Outdoor < 500 m	Indoor < 50 m Outdoor < 500 m
Speed by User	< 250 km/h	< 50 km/h	Evaluated up to 90 km/h	< 10 m/s <36 km/h

This paper sets up on measurements with speeds up to 90 km/h in [7]. An important result of that paper is, that no significant interference for speeds up to 90 km/h could be evidenced. Therefore, section 2 covers the description of the testing range and specifies the used equipment for the measurements starting at 100 km/h in detail. Afterwards the test scenarios as well as the measurements will be described in section 3. Finally, section 4 summarizes all measured data and shows perspectives for applications.

2 Test Area and Test Scenarios

2.1 The Test Area

In the planned measurements, speeds up to 200 km/h should be achievable. Therefore, a part of a public highway as graphically shown in figure 2 is used. For the measurements, seven access points have been distributed along the highway part. The access points AP1 to AP3 are responsible for building the local hotspot for the moving client. AP4 and AP5 as well as AP6 and AP7 build a directed radio link to integrate the access points AP1 and AP3 into the communication network. The access point AP2 is connected to the network using a 100 meter wired connection. The stationary server is connected by wire too. Topologically a hotspot with three WLAN cells has been build, where the inner distance between the access points is 700 meters.

Technical Characteristics. For the measurements components from Enterasys Networks are used. The outer access points AP1 and AP2 as well as AP6 and AP7 are R2- Access Points using two wireless interfaces. While the first interface (AP1 and AP6) builds the wireless cell for the local hotspot using a 7dBi omnidirectional antenna, the second wireless interface (AP2 and AP7) is used to create the radio link to the centre station using a 14 dBi Yagi-Antenna.

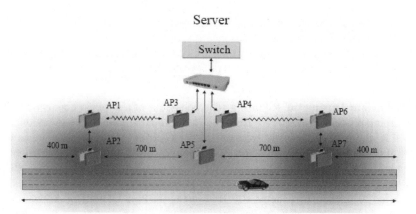

Fig. 2. Testing range at the highway

Because of the high antenna gain and thus too high emitted radiation above 100 mW E.I.R.P (Effective Isotropic Radiated Power) an adapted interface card with reduced power is used for the directed radio links. Besides the Access Points AP3 and AP4 as end points of the radio links at the centre station, AP5 builds the third infrastructure mode WLAN cell for the hotspot.

The wiring of the network itself has been done using a 100 MBit/s switch that connects the end points of the bridges as well as the centre Access Point and the server. For the server a notebook with 100 MBit/s LAN and Windows 2000 is used. The Client inside the car uses Windows 2000 as well as a wireless device with a 5 dBi omnidirectional antenna for in-car-use.

2.2 Measurements at Different Speeds

To evaluate network characteristics during a test run, measurements of parameters of the wireless connection as well as the possible data throughput are made starting at speeds from 100 km/h. Therefore, the mobile client moves along the testing range with constant speed.

The Connection-Quality. To get exact measurements of the connection quality, the software *Network Stumbler* (Version v0.3.30) [9] is used. An advantage compared to the Roamabout Client Utility used in [7] is a more exact logging of important parameters like signal and noise level as well as the resulting signal-to-noise ratio (SNR).

The Data-Throughput. The measurement of characteristic parameters of a wireless connection is no indication for the characteristic of the build data connection. Therefore [7] uses a software based on a round-trip-algorithm that collects characteristic information using a TCP-connection. This information is logged and evaluated.

As this tool does not allow an evaluation on site, our measurements uses the software *NetIQ Chariot* (Version v4.3) [9]. It allows to control the measurements by scripts and allows to measure TCP and UDP data. The used version of *NetIQ Chariot* contains standard scripts, whereas for measurements of the maximum available data-throughput the script `Throughput.scr` can be used. It creates random data with an exact size of 100,000 Byte and transmits them to the client while it moves along the testing range. The data packet size is limited to 32,767 Byte for TCP and 8,183 Bytes for UDP (induced by the used standard script).

All measurements for different speeds are repeated several times to discard measuring errors. In parallel to the evaluated data-throughput, the quality of the connection is logged.

The Behaviour During the Roaming. The behaviour of a wireless connection during the roaming process is measured using the *RoamAbout Client Utility* (Version v2.69) as well as the network analyse software *NetIQ Chariot*. Major disadvantages of the client utility is the low precision for the measured values and the measurement time with approximately four values per second. More detailed measurements are possible with *NetIQ Chariot*. Therefore a new script is created that measures the needed time to transfer 20 packets of exactly 100 Byte using TCP or UDP. This allows conclusions about the latency during the roaming process. A reduction of the amount of packets during the transmission is not possible due to the used software.

2.3   Measurements of Voice-over-IP

Positive results in [7] up to 90 km/h for TCP-connections suggest a possible use of Wireless LAN as media for Voice-over-IP connections. Therefore, two different scenarios are implemented.

In the first scenario, the analyse software NetIQ Chariot is used with a special Voice-over-IP packet that simulates typical voice transmissions to analyse influences of higher speeds on the transmitted voice. Therefore, the client inside the car is defined as performance end-point to measure a single voice communication channel. To account for high traffic, three different speed ranges GB1 to GB3 are used, whereas the ranges are defined as follows:

- GB1 – 70 km/h to 100 km/h,
- GB2 – 100 km/h to 140 km/h, as well as
- GB3 – 140 km/h to 170 km/h.

To analyse the quality of a Voice-over-IP-Transmission mainly network- and speechchannel parameters are responsible. The used transmission rate is adapted by the Access Points. This allows rates from 1 MBit/s to 11 MBit/s. The Voice-over-IP Add On of NetIQ Chariot is initialized with the following parameter:

- Used Codec: ITU G.711 A-Law (G.711a)
- Framesize per packet: 30 ms
- Multimedia Transmission Protocol: RTP over UDP
- No Support for Quality of Service (QoS)
- Di-Jitter Buffer (ITU-Recommendation): 60 ms
- Initial Delay-Value: 0 ms
- No Transcoding
- Total Codec-based Delay by ITU G.114: 91 ms (includes Di-Jitter Buffer, Frame Size and Execution-Delay)

To analyse the quality three different methods are used, and can be classified into three phases:

- Phase 1 – without Silence Suppression and Packet Loss Concealment (PLC)
- Phase 2 – with Silence Suppression and PLC, as well as Voice Activity Detection (VAD) Rate of 50% (default value)
- Phase 3 – with Silence Suppression and PLC as well as additional UDP-traffic, the VAD rate is 50% again. To simulate additional UDP-traffic exactly 100.000 Byte of Data has been transmitted between Server and Client, while moving along the testing range.

In the second scenario a subjective reflection of the voice quality is achieved by using Microsoft Netmeeting. Therefore a real voice-channel is created between the server and the client inside the car. In opposite to the first scenario, the speed varies between 90 km/h and 150 km/h. The Netmeeting tool uses the CCITT A-Low Codec with 8000 Hz and an 8-bit mono-recording connection. This relies to the Codec G.711a. Further configurations are not tested here, but measurements show, that Netmeeting uses a framesize of 32 ms per packet.

3 Evaluation of the Measurements

The described scenarios in section 2 are used in practical measurements to evaluate the characteristics of WLAN in high speed vehicles. To evaluate the results, corelations between the measured values and outer influences must be considered. This influences can be high traffic which prevents a constant speed in some cases, as well as numerous vehicles that become obstacles and lead to significant signal reduction (named as Shadow fading in [10]).

3.1 Evaluation of the Connection Quality

During the measurements between 100 km/h and 170 km/h no direct dependence is recognized between the speed as well as the signal- and noise level. The noise level is measured with minimal deviations at -100 dBi. The signal-to-noise ration (SNR) equals to about 45 dBi in direct line of sight to the access point. An overlap of the three WLAN cells is noted at about 20 dBi. Figure 3 shows the connection quality at a speed of 100 km/h. Figures of other speeds do not show significant differences and are omitted.

3.2 Evaluation of the Data Transfer-Rate

All measurements of the data transfer-rate are done using the network analyse software *NetIQ Chariot* and start at 100 km/h. Consecutively, measurements of 130 km/h, 150 km/h and 170 km/h are done. Because of high traffic measurements with higher speeds up to 200 km/h can be evaluated temporarily only. Therefore, they are not covered by this paper. Corresponding to section 3.1 no significant influences of the speed are recognized. Table 2 shows the average data transfer-rate for the mentioned speeds.

During all measurements no complete loss of connection happens even at a speed of 170 km/h. Therefore, a wireless connection is even possible that this speed. As mentioned in table 2, the deviation of the average data transfer rate is subject to minimal variations only. This leads to no conclusion regarding influences of the speed at the data transfer-rate. In fact it is interesting that the data transfer rate measured while moving is about 25% lower than for fixed measurements. Variations can by means be described with environmental influences.

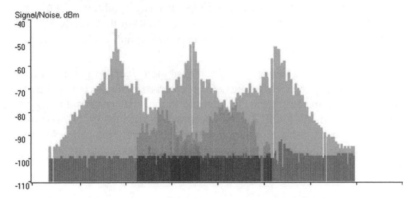

Fig. 3. Connection Quality at 100 km/h, Network Stumbler

Table 2. Average Data throughput for UDP and TCP at different speeds

Velocity	UDP (Mbit/s)	TCP (Mbit/s)
100 km/h	2,8	3,3
130 km/h	2,6	3,1
150 km/h	2,5	2,7
170 km/h	2,6	3,0

3.3 Evaluation of the Roaming Process

The measurements to determine the time of a roaming process are done by sending and receiving 20 packets á 100 byte size. By means of the differences between the measured times while moving along the testing range and during the roaming process an average roaming time can be derived. A transmission of data is impossible during the cell change. Table 3 shows the measured average roaming time for TCP and UDP-connections at different speeds.

The fluctuation of this values leads to a very common conclusion only. While for TCP the roaming time in average is significant lower for higher than for lower speeds, it increased at 190 km/h to its triple value. The measurements of UDP are not subject of this kind of fluctuations. Measurements of other speeds show analogical results. This leads to a necessity of a higher granularity within the measurements to gain more exact conclusions. A direct influence of the speed on the roaming cannot be proven by this measurements.

In consequence of the small size of the packets and its frequency of occurrences, table 4 shows a significantly lower data transfer-rate than measured previously. Nevertheless, the deviation of the average is lower. Clearly visible is the approximately 25% lower data rate of the outer Access Points due to their connection via wireless bridge.

Table 3. Differences of times during the roaming

Velocity	UDP (ms)	TCP (ms)
130 km/h	386	476
150 km/h	423	240
170 km/h	399	265
190 km/h	426	814

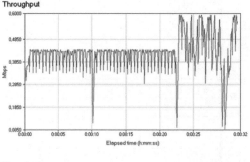

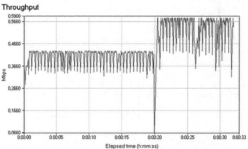

Fig. 4. Roaming at 170 km/h for TCP (top) and UDP (bottom)

3.4   Evaluation of Voice-over-IP

The measurements for Voice-over-IP are divided into two separate scenarios. The results of these scenarios are presented here.

3.4.1   Voice-over-IP Simulation Using NetIQ Chariot

All tests results are shown in table 4. Because of the asymmetric character of the speech channel, the average of the parameters are computed separately from the corresponding single values for both directions. It must be pointed out, that there are excellent results in test case B. All in all the measured values are similar as those gained from static network connections. Although the packet loss exceeds the limit of 1% as specified by the ITU. Therefore an use of PLC at the receiver must be taken into account[12][13]. The resulting speech quality is very good with a MOS-Score above 4.0 with and without additional data transfer (test case D). Our measurements show, that additional data transfer influences the delay significantly but does not have a bearing on the quality of speech and packet loss.

Table 4. Evaluation of Voice-over-IP Measurements

test cases		A	B	C	D
		Speech Channel: G.711a-Full Duplex			
		GB1 + Phase 1	GB2 + Phase 2	GB3 + Phase 2	GB2 + Phase 3
		without VAD/PLC	with VAD/PLC		VAD/PLC and UDP-data
Speed in km/h (min. - max.)		70 - 100	100 - 140	140 - 170	100 - 140
Average data-throughput		117,208 KByte/s	36,512 KByte/s	35,336 KByte/s	2244,464 KByte/s
One-Way-Delay		5 ms	2 ms	4 ms	15 ms
End-to-End-Delay		96 ms	93 ms	95 ms	106 ms
Jitter (Delay Variation)	min. - max	0 ms - 60 ms	1 ms - 20 ms	2 ms - 42 ms	9 ms - 135 ms
	< 11 ms [%]	94	96	96	68
Packet-Loss [%]		1,67	1,045	1,8	1,62
Speech-Quality	Average MOS	3,7	4,2	4,1	4,1
	Consumer satisfaction	some consumer unsatisfied	satisfied	satisfied	satisfied
	Category of quality	average	high	high	high

A direct influence of the speed on any Voice-over-IP communication cannot be proven, even with the worse results in test case C comparing to test case B. Reasons for this worse case can be put down to the dynamically change in the traffic on the highway. In difference the roaming process significantly influences the speech quality in case of additional data communication (test case D).

Below the different measured values shown in table 4 are described in more detail.

Delays. All measurements do not show any influences between speed and measured delay values. In test case D the delay is higher in consequence of the additional UDP data transfer, because of a higher delay in queues and during the serialisation [15]. However, the end-to-end-delay continuously stays between 150 ms as recommended by the ITU [17]. Any influences of the roaming could not be proven, but the measured delays below one millisecond in the test cases A and B are rather interesting.

Jitter. The jitter of incoming packets as shown in table 4 in the case without any VAD is higher, because of the higher amount of speech data to transmit. [13][14]. Nevertheless, 94% of all jitter is lower than 11 ms (in test cases B and C actually 96%). Influences of the speed cannot be proven. Any data transmission raises the runtime deviation because of higher delays within queues. Therefore test case D shows a jitter between 9 ms and 135 ms, which is twice the Jitter-Buffer and corresponds to an End-to-End- Delay up to 181 ms. Consequently this leads to frequent interrupts during a conversation as well as losses of connection [13][17]. Influences of the roaming is noticeable too, but very low. In test case D the runtime jitter lies between 9 and 30 ms, but subsides instantly after the roaming. Other test cases do not show any influences at all.

Data Throughput of Speech Data. For analysing speech data, row data without any protocol overhead is taken into account. The measurements show, that a consequent use of Silence Suppression leads to a significant reduction of used bandwidth. Therefore, test case C shows an about 70% lower amount of data as test case A. No influences of speed and roaming are visible. A variation of the data throughput over all test cases cannot be recognized in the graphical representation.

Packet Loss. By recommendation of the ITU packet los shall not exceed a limit of one percent [13]. All measurements results in higher values. This is mirrored directly in the MOS-Value for the speech quality in test case A which is about 3.7. The use of PLC within the G.711a Codec leads to significant better results in face of a packet loss of 1.8% in test case C. The result was a quality of speech of about 4.1 (MOS). Influences of the roaming are very light. Test case D shows interesting results with no packet loss during the roaming when moving from the eastern access point to the central but a significant higher value of 3% when moving between the central access point and the western access point. This leads to a reduction of the speech quality of 4.37 to 4.1. The packet loss is recognized in bursts, where half of all sent packets are single packets.

Speech Quality. An important factor while evaluating Voice-over-IP is the speech quality. Recommendations of the ITU for G.114 and G.131 demand a minimal quality of 3,6 in the MOS-Score for speech communication systems [17][18]. All test cases achieve this value in average, however high variations can be recognized. For the test case A the MOS-Score varies between 2,2 and 4,37, while test case B has excellent results between 4,1 and 4,37.

3.4.2 Subjective Evaluation of the Speech Quality Using Microsoft Netmeeting

A subjective evaluation using Microsoft Netmeeting leads to a very positive result. Even at a speed of 200 km/h a communication is possible without any complications. Not until high distances (partly over 500 m) to an Access Point and with a SNR-Value clearly below 10 dBi a communication interrupt appears.

Any short timed interrupts during the roaming cannot be recognized subjectively. Refer to the simulated communication how far the influence on the transmission is.

4 Summary and Perspectives

The provided measurements for evaluating the efficiency of mobile clients in wireless networks based on IEEE 802.11b clearly show, that even at speeds up to 200 km/h a data transmission and therefore a use of different services is possible. This is essential for connections using UDP as well as TCP. All measurements take place in an environment with real-time conditions at a public highway and thus high traffic. To gain meaningful results and to eliminate errors multiple measurements are done. A direct influence of speed on the wireless network, physically founded by the arising Doppler-Effect cannot be proven. A consequence leads to the assumption of a very good adjustment of the used wireless hardware to this kind of frequency variations.

However, the results show, that outer influences, like obstacles in direct line of sight between the Access Point and Client (e.g. trucks) have significant impact on the signal level and commonly lead to a loss of the communication stream. Further measurements for more detailed results in this so called shadow fading, are planed.

In case of measurements to evaluate the quality of speech transmissions (Voiceover- IP) within WLAN systems again no direct influence of the speed can be found up to 200 km/h. However, the used codec should support PLC and VAD to improve the quality.

Comprising, the results can be categorised as encouraging for the realization of new architectures based on mobile clients for data as well as for speech transmission.

References

1. Wi-Fi (Wireless Fidelity): http://www.wi-fi.org, 27. Juni 2003
2. IEEE 802.11 Working Group: http://grouper.ieee.org/groups/802/11/index.html, 27. Juni 2003
3. IEEE: IEEE Standard 802.11, Initial Edition 1999, 1999
4. IEEE: IEEE 802.11b Supplement to IEEE 802.11, Edition 1999, 1999
5. J. Knuutila, J. Hämäläinen, T. Sipilä: Data Possibilities of DECT/GSM Dualmode Terminals; The Seventh IEEE International Symposium on PIMRC '96, October 15-18, 1996, Taipeh, ROC
6. ETSI Radio Equipment and Systems: ETS 300 653 – High Performance Radio Local Area Network (HIPERLAN) Type 1, Functional Specification, 1996
7. A. Bengsch, H. Kopp, A. Petry, D. Tavangarian: Test Environment for Mobile Wireless LAN Clients, I2CS Leipzig, Juni 2003
8. Network Stumbler: Network Stumbler V0.30.3, http://www.netstumbler.com, 27. Juni 2003
9. NetIQ: NetIQ Chariot Netzwerkanalyse-System V4.3, http://www.netiq.com, 27. Juni 2003
10. C. Hassania: Packet Scheduling Over Wireless LAN, ECPE 6504: Wireless Networks & Mobile Computing, Spring 2000
11. A. Santamaria, F. J. López-Hernándes: Wireless LAN – Standards and Applications, Artech House Inc., 2001
12. J. Geier: 802.11 Beacons Revealed, http://www.80211-planet.com/tutorials/article.php/1492071, 27. Juni 2003
13. PN-4689 (veröffentlicht als TIA/EIA/TSB116): Telecommunications, IP telephony equipment, voice quality recommendations for ip telephony, 2001
14. J. Janssen, D. De Vleeschauwer, G. H. Petit: Delay and Distortion Bounds for Packelized Voice Calls of Traditional PSTN quality, GMD 2000
15. Cisco White Paper – Understanding Delay in Packet Voice Networks: http://www.cisco.com/warp/public/788/voip/delay-details.html
16. ITU-T Recommendation G.109, Definition of categories of speech transmission quality, 1999
17. ITU-T Recommendation G.114, One-way transmission time, May 2003
18. ITU-T Recommendation G.131, Control of talker echo, August 1996
19. CCITT Recommendation G.711, Pulse Code Modulation (PCM) of voice frequencies, November 1988

Ant-Based Data Traffic Splitting
for Application-Based Routing

Jörg Schulz

D-14467 Potsdam, Germany
j.schulz@imail.de

Abstract. This conceptual paper presents the Ant-based Data Traffic Splitting (ADTS) that uses self-organizing nodes with peer-to-peer properties. ADTS is an addition to the conventional ant-based routing, which belongs to the new defined application-based routing class, whose prime importance is showed by this paper, too. The publication transforms latest biological test results by DIRK HELBING et al. [1] into the field of computer science: If a main path of walking ants is narrowed, natural ants will chose a second path on a given fork. Therefore, if no transmission capacity is available, ADTS nodes will split the data traffic autonomously. Local algorithms realize an interaction of a node only with its direct neighbors inside an ADTS system; this new approach facilitates the organization of large distributed networks. ADTS offers an opportunity to increase the data throughput in nets by automatic path splitting, too. ADTS is divided into two variants, which this paper shortly describes: the Preventive ADTS (PADTS) and the Stream-oriented ADTS (SADTS).

Keywords: application-based routing, ants, data traffic splitting

1 Introduction

Increasingly, large distributed networks like the Internet influence our life. The growing net complexity and new applications often overextend traditional search and routing mechanisms, but users ask for an efficient and comfortable way to find and transmit information. Consequently, special search and routing systems which work in the application network layer are more and more applied inside of peer-to-peer solutions, for instance. Hence, the volume of data traffic of peer-to-peer services in a ratio of the over-all capacity reached a rate of approximately 50 % and 75 % in peak times [2]; another publication reported up to 85 % in case of a typical Internet service provider in Sweden [3]. The ant-based routing [4,5] which is shortly explained in subsection 2.2 belongs to the new defined abstract class of *the application-based routing*.

So the here introduced *Ant-based Data Traffic Splitting (ADTS)* represents a novel contribution to the application-based routing. ADTS applies peer-to-peer and self-organizing principles. This innovative paper transmutes recent results of insect experiments by DIRK HELBING et al. [1] into the computer science:

T. Böhme et al. (Eds.): IICS 2004, LNCS 3473, pp. 49–58, 2006.
© Springer-Verlag Berlin Heidelberg 2006

When you narrow the main path of walking ants, real ants will chose an alternative path on a given parting of the ways. Hence, if there is no available bandwidth, autonomic *Preventive ADTS* nodes will divide the data traffic without a knowledge of the bandwidth values. Biological ants obviate traffic congestions by pushing oncoming conspecific insects into an alternative path. Therefore, when a data packet collision happens, a Preventive ADTS node redirects the packet over another route. Inside an ADTS system nodes interact only with their direct neighbors by local algorithms. Such an approach makes the organization of large distributed networks easier. The automatic path splitting of ADTS could allow higher data throughput values for future technological net products which will work in large distributed environments. The concept of the *Stream-oriented Ant-based Data Traffic Splitting (SADTS)* offers a full new quality to divide data streams in large distributed networks. In opposite to PADTS, SADTS nodes measure bandwidth values and establish splitted connections for any length of time, why a less traffic jam prevention is available in comparison to PADTS.

This paper is structured as follow. Section 2 briefly describes the related work and the background of this paper. Section 3 presents new approaches – the class of the application-based routing and a concept for an ant-based data traffic splitting. This paper concludes with a short summary and thoughts about future tasks in section 4.

2   Related Work and Background

This section discusses shortly related systems and background facts.

2.1   Peer-to-Peer Routing

Only some information about peer-to-peer routing stands in the foreground in this paper – detailed descriptions of peer-to-peer (P2P) networks are to be found in other publications which also serve as sources for these lines: [2,6,7].

The equal peers of a decentralized P2P-network have often a variable connectivity [2]. Thus peers are only reachable under changing addresses or with a limited uptime. Solutions for this problem represent own P2P address spaces whose identifiers are generated with hash functions by taking into account the contents. Consequently, data are identifiable not by the location but by the contents. This fact fulfills an essential condition for a *Content-based Routing* therewith. If there are equal contents on different nodes, then these nodes represent multiple potential routing destinations.

Distributed Hash Tables – DHT. A Distributed Hash Table improves the scalability of P2P networks [8]. DHT uses a distributed indexing of the stored data inside a P2P network. Such a strategy intends to reach a better reliability, fault tolerance and performance, too. If you locate data via DHT, a complexity of $O(\log N)$ will be attained in general. This well value outperforms the mostly linear complexity of representatives of the first P2P network generation. If you insert new contents or new peers, DHT offers complexities of $O(\log N)$ and $O(\log^2 N)$ respectively. Distributed Hash Tables differ in the search methods and the administration: so *rings* which resemble binary or B^* trees are applied; examples represent *Pastry* [9,10], *Tapestry* [11] as well as *Chord* [12] (known predecessor publication: [13]) – the *Content Addressable Network (CAN)* pursues a geometrical approach [14]. Every DHT node gets a part of the search space – replications to neighbor nodes purpose to create redundancy. Distributed Hash Tables are similar to data bases regarding the indexing, but moreover, a DHT owns a distributed administration of the data structure, mechanisms for redundancy, and the ability to locate better reachable data instances which are searched for.

2.2 Ant-Based Routing

Former papers described the utilization of the behavior of ants for solving scientific tasks and for the information management in peer-to-peer-networks [4,5,15,16]: The information transmission between wandering ants is realized by pheromone paths. A wandering ant loses a special amount of pheromone per trail, whereby each of such a pheromone marking dissolves with time. Ants follow the path with the highest concentration of pheromones, unless no pheromone trail is found, then ants go randomly. That makes finding of new paths possible, but existing ways will be also strengthened.

The movement of an ant along a path has an analogy in the message chains of peer-to-peer-networks. Such chains are comparable with ways built by links to the neighborhood of every node. When the setting of the hop-counter of a message has a value of ∞ (symbolized by a negative number), this message can wander forever through the peer-to-peer-network, wherefore optionally a stochastic or cyclic comeback to the origin of the chain may be chosen.

Each entry stored in the neighboring peer-to-peer-warehouse (in relation to a certain node) gets additive parameters as counterparts of ant pheromone paths. A variable symbolizing pheromones will be changed, when a message chain arrives and is forwarded or the pheromone concentration decreases with time. These changes of variables of single nodes do not disturb the whole peer-to-peer-community significantly.

An unsolved problem of ant-based routing is an optimal consideration of communicative performance aspects as an additional criterion for a more effective data routing. Hence, the new ant-based data traffic splitting makes a contribution to a solution for this task.

2.3 Data Traffic Splitting

A splitting of a data traffic stream[1] into partial streams generally allows a higher data throughput for routing purposes. As an example, the *WOSForward Service* stands for an application-based solution for such a splitting strategy.

---

[1] In spite of the known discretization effects of a packet oriented data transfer, this subsection uses the allegory of *streams* because of a better concise verbal presentability.

A characteristic of the WOSForward Service represents the usage of the communication along disjunct paths [17]. The splitting process takes place inside a region **A** where the bandwidth B_{near_1} is obtained and the source node **S** of the stream stands. A target node **T** with an available bandwidth B_{near_2} is located in the region **B**. The Internet with a wide area network bandwidth B_{far} connects both regions **A** and **B**. A fulfillment of the formulas $B_{near_1} >> B_{far}$ and $B_{near_2} >> B_{far}$ forwards an effective application of a communication along disjunct paths. So, in normal cases, local area networks have more bandwidth than wide area networks in practice. With the exception of the standard path, all streams are directed to so-called *WOS-Repeaters* which redirect the partial streams to the target node **T**. The node **T** joins the standard path and the partial streams; **T** reconstructs the origin data stream which is sent by the source node **S**, too. Experimental tests with the WOSForward Service nearly resulted a bisection of the transmission time by using of two disjunct paths in comparison with only one path of a conventional point-to-point data transfer – the bandwidth proportion thereby was $B_{near} \approx 15\ B_{far}$ [17].

3 New Approaches

The first aim of this section is the motivation for the initiation of the new defined abstract class of *the application-based routing*. Secondly, this section explains some facts about the ant-based data traffic splitting: its background, causes, features, and variants PADTS as well as SADTS.

3.1 Application-Based Routing

Definition: The *Application-based Routing Class* unifies all routing methods which work in the application network layer.

Why You Need an Application-Based Routing? As mentioned in section 1, the increasing net complexity and new requirements of users for finding and transmitting information often overstrain conventional search and routing systems. Hence, an intelligent searching and routing are more and more implemented inside the application layer. Thus users can evade the limitations of the underlying network levels. The prevalence of peer-to-peer systems is an example for this general development in the last years – as alluded in section 1, the quantity of data traffic of peer-to-peer services in proportion to the over-all capacity amounted to 85 % in the case of a typic Internet service provider in Sweden [3].

Details of network layers and standards often differ from protocol to protocol. These particulars of the underlying network levels are not of interest for the application-based routing. This high level of abstraction represents an advantage in the development and usage of an application-based routing.

The following paragraph shows new routing possibilities using an application-based concept by means of a thought experiment.

A Constellation when the Application-Based Routing Transmit Data, Although the Underlying Network Levels Refuse It. A thought experiment: two nodes n_1 and n_3 are situated in a network N_1; the nodes n_3 and n_2 belong to the net N_2. If you want to transmit data from n_1 to n_2 without any routes between N_1 and N_2 on node n_3, n_3 will not forward this data to n_2. If an *application-based routing* software runs on n_3, a data transfer from n_1 to n_2 can happen.

The next subsection describes the biological background for a new ant-based data traffic splitting.

3.2   Optimal Traffic Organization in Ants

DIRK HELBING et al. provided an experimental evidence, how ants behave on overcrowded paths [1]. These new facts even met with a wide response from the public in the form of popular scientific publications [18,19].

Two alternative ways for the black garden ants *Lasius niger* (Hymenoptera, Formicidae) were created inside the test environment. The test series utilized five queenless ant colonies each with a population of 500 workers to record the traffic behavior of these ants – the figure 1 sketched the experimental setup. If low traffic occurs, these insects will prefer paths which smelt strongly. Existing modelings and simulations also used before this preference of strong-smelling paths as a common rule for the ant-based routing in computer networks as described in subsection 2.2.

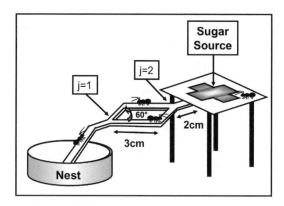

Fig. 1. Experiment setup illustration by Dirk Helbing

A significant discovery by DIRK HELBING et al. is that the ants entered the second path during times of heavy traffic, which was generated via an artificial reduction of the width of the first path [1]. Insects which tried to take the well-known route were pushed and redirected by oncoming ants into another branch – figure 2 shows this fact. There is a remarkable feature of ants' behavior as a paradigm for other fields of research: *before* a too heavy ant traffic and a congestion could occur, the ants chose the alternative path. Thus these insects used

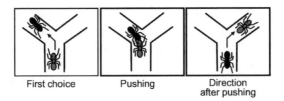

First choice   Pushing   Direction
                                        after pushing

Fig. 2. An ant is pushing and redirecting an oncoming member of the same species into another branch. Illustration by Dirk Helbing

the alternative route *preemptively.* Consequently, the ants are able to transport enough fodder into the nest.

In a press release, DIRK HELBING suggested to use ant-algorithms for data routing purposes on the Internet [20]. The next text makes an innovative contribution to a transformation of the recent results of ants experiments by DIRK HELBING et al. into the field of computer science. Consequently, the new approach of this paper distinguishes from former works by other researchers who could not yet use such novel test results by DIRK HELBING et al.

3.3   Transformation of Test Results into Computer Science

As mentioned before, the *Ant-based Data Traffic Splitting (ADTS)* is an innovative contribution to the new defined abstract class of the *application-based routing.* ADTS applies a *peer-to-peer* paradigm because of a *decentralized* concept using equal peer nodes. Each peer *organizes it-self* and *adapts* the routing behavior in dependence on the local node conditions which are influenced by neighbor nodes, too. ADTS enhances former data traffic splitting approaches as mentioned in subsection 2.3 with ant-based features.

Figure 3 as well as the below-mentioned remarks explain the ADTS method. A set of $k+1$ routes, which direct from a source node n_1 to a destination node n_{l+1}, are given. The sets

$$\begin{aligned}
\mathcal{E}_0 &= \{e_1, e_2, ..., e_l\} \\
\mathcal{E}_1 &= \{e_1^*, e_2^*, ..., e_m^*\} \\
&\vdots \\
\mathcal{E}_k &= \{e_1^{k*}, e_2^{k*}, ..., e_n^{k*}\}
\end{aligned} \tag{1}$$

form a *set system* for the set of all edges $\mathcal{E}$. Another set system

$$\begin{aligned}
\mathcal{N}_0 &= \{n_1, n_2, ..., n_{l+1}\} \\
\mathcal{N}_1 &= \{n_1^*, n_2^*, ..., n_{m+1}^*\} \\
&\vdots \\
\mathcal{N}_k &= \{n_1^{k*}, n_2^{k*}, ..., n_{n+1}^{k*}\}
\end{aligned} \tag{2}$$

is used for the set of all nodes $\mathcal{N}$. The identical nodes n_{l+1}, n_{m+1}^*, ..., n_{n+1}^{k*} represent the destination node. Therefore, the sets $\mathcal{N}_0, \mathcal{N}_1, ..., \mathcal{N}_k$ are not disjointed because of a common element in the form of this destination node.

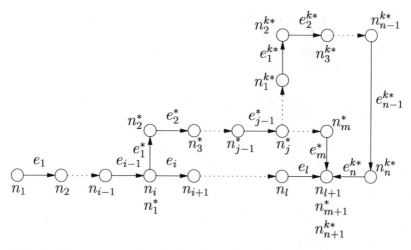

Fig. 3. Data transport by the Ant-based Data Traffic Splitting – ADTS

The bandwidth of computer networks is alike the width of real ant paths – yet another analogy to the ants world.

If there is no necessity for the usage of an alternative path, real ants will prefer a main path [1,20]. As mentioned before in section 2.2, pheromone markings dissolve with time. These two facts promote ant-based algorithms in computer science: The complexity of a distributed path system will be autonomously controlled and reduced. So, ADTS uses only alternative paths as much as needful. Thus, if there is no redundancy for the data transmission, less parallel paths will increase the reliability of ADTS.

There are some differences between previous experiments with biological ants and the ADTS analogy: DIRK HELBING et al. limited to two routes for test purposes with living ants; the ADTS concept tends to split into several new paths per node. Thus, the ADTS model has set systems for edges and nodes – this makes an abstract explanation of the routing and splitting of data traffic possible. A further difference: A natural ant represents a physical existing and moving information processing unit using paths and nodes. The intelligence is located inside a real mobile ant but not in a fixed fork. However, only localized ADTS nodes make decisions for laying new routes because computer nets use other places for the information processing: nodes but not data packets.

The Ant-based Data Traffic Splitting is categorized into two areas: PADTS and SADTS; the following paragraphs shortly present both.

The *Preventive Ant-Based Data Traffic Splitting (PADTS)* applies data packets instead of data streams. The size of the PADTS data packets should be larger than in other network layers because of the PADTS administration overhead. If it is not possible for a PADTS node to send a data packet over a connection with the strongest pheromone concentration, this PADTS node will take the path with the nearest best pheromone concentration.

PADTS reacts very fast to connection quality changes. The reason for this behavior: A routing decision of a PADTS node depends on the last single data packet which has passed the node. Without a knowledge of concrete bandwidth values, PADTS nodes act. Real ants prevent a traffic jam by pushing oncoming members of the same species into an alternative path (cf. section 3.2). Hence, if a packet collision occurs, a PADTS node sends the data packet over another route; consequently, PADTS deserves the adjective *preventive*. There are two types of packet collision situations: Firstly, a system is not able to send and receive at the same time (a practical example: wireless data networks which use the same frequency for sending and receiving); if a data receiving process takes place and a sending is planned, this situation will be interpreted as a collision with the oncoming data traffic. Such a rule fits more to the mentioned analogy of an encounter of natural ants than the other case: A lot of computer networks realize a sending and receiving at the same time. So, if a data sending process runs and another sending is planned, it will be taken as a data collision.

PADTS has a less reliability of the data transmission in comparison to SADTS because PADTS comes with no connection-orientation.

The *Stream-Oriented Ant-Based Data Traffic Splitting (SADTS)* concept allows the splitting of data streams in large distributed networks. The main goal of SADTS should be a better data transmission reliability in comparison to PADTS by an establishing of SADTS connections; thus SADTS is connection-oriented. If no reliable connection is desired, SADTS will not be necessary. SADTS differs from PADTS and hence from the pure ant-based principle: A single real ant must not absolutely reach its target; this ant does not compromise the over-all goal of an ant group to get fodder for the whole ant state.

If SADTS reacts to changes of the connection quality, SADTS will have a higher inertia than PADTS because of three reasons: Firstly, the establishing of a spreaded SADTS connection occurs for any length of time. Secondly, SADTS considers no single data packets but streams. Thirdly, a SADTS node measures the bandwidth of connections to neighbor nodes for routing decision purposes; a measurement analysis will always take a couple of time. Consequently, in comparison to PADTS, the SADTS concept has a less traffic jam prevention.

The publication [16] mentioned in table 1 that the ant-based routing has no link failure notification; hence, a task represents the creation of a SADTS-enhancement for solving this problem.

If a branch of a spreaded SADTS connection was interrupted or a change of the bandwidth appeared significantly, the whole connection would be newly established. Thus, SADTS tries to arrange all the sub paths and their interdependencies for a guaranteed connection between a source and a destination node again; such a behavior differs from the paradigm of local algorithms. This management activity happens parallel to the ongoing impaired data transmission.

4   Conclusion and Outlook

This publication presented and motivated the new class of the application-based routing. The paper also transfered recent biology test results by DIRK HELBING

et al. [1] into the field of computer science: natural ants prevent a traffic congestion by a special behavior which was shortly described. Such real ants react to
narrowing of a path by the parallel usage of another route. Thus, these investigations have provided a basis for the conception of a novel data traffic splitting,
which uses ant-based principles, self-organizing nodes, and peer-to-peer properties. The paper pointed two new ways for such a method out: the Preventive
Ant-based Data Traffic Splitting and a stream-oriented variant; both represent
additions to the conventional ant-based routing that belongs to the mentioned
application-based routing class.

Local algorithms permit to interact only with direct neighbor nodes; this
decentralized approach simplifies the organization of large distributed networks.
The Ant-based Data Traffic Splitting could be applied for a data throughput
increasing of connected nodes, in particular in large distributed nets. ADTS offers
a chance for balanced connection capacities inside complex network topologies,
too.

Simulations with at least 10^2 nodes are planned for validation and optimization purposes – a following paper will contain the results. As noted before, ADTS
routes by pheromones; if you use other local forms of memory or intelligence for
nodes, you can combine the introduced data traffic splitting principles with other
kinds of routing than the ant-based routing.

References

1. Dussutoura, A., Fourcassié, V., Helbing, D., Deneubourg, J.L.: Optimal traffic
   organisation in ants under crowded conditions. Nature **428** (2004) 70–73
2. Steinmetz, R., Wehrle, K.: Peer-to-Peer Networking & Computing. Informatik
   Spektrum, Organ der Gesellschaft für Informatik und mit ihr assoziierter Organi-
   sationen, Springer-Verlag Heidelberg **27** (2004) 51–54
3. Hadenius, P.: Relieving peer-to-peer pressure. In: Technology Review. Technology
   Review, Inc., One Main Street, 7th Floor, Cambridge, MA, 02142, USA (2004)
   MIT's Magazine of Innovation.
4. Caro, G.D., Dorigo, M.: Antnet: A mobile agents approach to adaptive routing.
   Technical Report 12, IRIDIA, Université Libre de Bruxelles, 50, av. F. Roosevelt,
   CP 194/6, 1050 Brussels, Belgium (1997)
5. Dorigo, M., Maniezzo, V., Colorni, A.: The ant system: Optimization by a colony
   of cooperating agents. IEEE Transactions on Systems, Man, and Cybernetics Part
   B: Cybernetics **26** (1996) 29–41
6. Schoder, D., Fischbach, K.: Peer-to-Peer, Anwendungsbereiche und Heraus-
   forderungen. In Schoder, D., Fischbach, K., Teichmann, R., eds.: Peer-to-Peer.
   Springer-Verlag, Berlin, Germany (2002) 3–19
7. Minar, N., Hedlund, M. In Oram, A., ed.: Peer-to-Peer: Harnessing the Power
   of Disruptive Technologies. First edition edn. O'Reilly & Associates, Inc., 1005
   Gravenstein Highway North, Sebastopol, CA 95472, USA (2001)
8. Balakrishnan, H., Kaashoek, M.F., Karger, D., Morris, R., Stoica, I.: Looking up
   data in P2P systems. Communications oft the ACM, ACM Press, New York, NY,
   USA **46** (2003) 43–48

9. Rowstron, A.I.T., Druschel, P.: Pastry: Scalable, decentralized object location and routing for large-scale peer-to-peer systems. In: Proceedings of the IFIP/ACM International Conference on Distributed Systems Platforms (Middleware), Heidelberg, Germany, Springer-Verlag (2001) 329–350

10. Castro, M., Costa, M., Kermarrec, A.M., Rowstron, A., Druschel, P., Iyer, S., Mislove, A., Nandi, A., Post, A., Singh, A., Wallach, D., Hu, Y.C., Jones, M., Theimer, M., Wolman, A., Mahajan, R.: Pastry - A scalable, decentralized, self-organizing and fault-tolerant substrate for peer-to-peer applications. Microsoft Research, Cambridge, UK; Rice University, USA; Purdue University, USA; Microsoft Research, Redmond, USA; University of Washington, USA (2004)

11. Hildrum, K., Kubiatowicz, J.D., Rao, S., Zhao, B.Y.: Distributed object location in a dynamic network. In: Proceedings of the Fourteenth Annual ACM Symposium on Parallel Algorithms and Architectures (SPAA), Session 2, Winnipeg, Manitoba, Canada, ACM Press, New York, NY, USA (2002) 41–52

12. Stoica, I., Morris, R., Liben-Nowell, D., Karger, D.R., Kaashoek, M.F., Dabek, F., Balakrishnan, H.: Chord: A scalable peer-to-peer lookup protocol for Internet applications. IEEE/ACM Transactions on Networking 11 (2003) 17–32

13. Stoica, I., Morris, R., Karger, D., Kaashoek, M.F., Balakrishnan, H.: Chord: A scalable peer-to-peer lookup service for Internet applications. In: Proceedings of the 2001 conference on applications, technologies, architectures, and protocols for computer communications, SIGCOMM (ACM Special Interest Group on Data Communication), San Diego , California, USA, ACM Press, New York, NY, USA (2001) 149–160

14. Ratnasamy, S., Francis, P., Handley, M., Karp, R., Shenker, S.: A scalable content-addressable network. In: Proceedings of the 2001 conference on Applications, technologies, architectures, and protocols for computer communications, SIGCOMM (ACM Special Interest Group on Data Communication), San Diego , California, USA, ACM Press, New York, NY, USA (2001) 161–172

15. Bonabeau, E., Henaux, F., Guérin, S., Snyers, D., Kuntz, P., Thraulaz, G.: Routing in telecommunication networks with smart ant-like agents. In Albayrac, S., Garijo, F., eds.: Proceedings of the Second International Workshop on Agents in Telecommunications Applications (IATA '98). Volume 1437 of Lectures Notes in AI., Berlin, Springer Verlag (1998) 60–71

16. Marwaha, S., Tham, C.K., Srinivasan, D.: A novel routing protocol using mobile agents and reactive route discovery for ad-hoc wireless networks. In: Towards Network Superiority, Proceedings of 10th IEEE International Conference on Networks 2002 (ICON 2002), Singapore, IEEE (2002) 311–316

17. Kropf, P., Unger, H., Babin, G.: WOS: an Internet computing environment. In: Workshop on Ubiquitous Computing, IEEE International Conference on Parallel Architectures and Compilation Techniques. Philadelphia, PA, USA. (2000) 14–22

18. Stieler, W.: Stau-Vermeidung im Schwarm. c't – Magazin für Computertechnik (2004) 58

19. SPIEGEL ONLINE: Stau-Stress. Wenn Ameisen zu Verkehrsrowdys werden. (2004)

20. Helbing, D.: Traffic Regulation in Ants: How to Maintain Efficient Infrastructures by the Right Balance Between Conflict and Cooperation. Press Release. Institute for Economics and Traffic, Traffic Science Faculty 'Friedrich List', Dresden University of Technology, Andreas-Schubert-Str. 23, A-Building, Room No. 420, D-01062 Dresden, Germany (2004)

Search Methods in P2P Networks: A Survey

German Sakaryan, Markus Wulff, and Herwig Unger

Computer Science Dept., University of Rostock,
18059 Rostock, Germany
{gs137,mwulff,hunger}@informatik.uni-rostock.de

Abstract. The peer-to-peer (P2P) file sharing applications have gained a tremendous popularity and now they have millions of users worldwide, since they were introduced in 1999. Due to chaotic structure, achieved scale and network dynamics, they mostly employ a flooding-based search to locate required files and therefore they are the main source of Internet traffic. Thus, the study and development of P2P systems is an important research challenge.
This article presents a survey of existing approaches to organize operations of P2P file sharing systems. It gives a classification of existing protocols and discusses the advantages and disadvantages of each technique. It shows that both network structure and search algorithm influence the operations of P2P applications.

1 Introduction

The peer-to-peer (P2P) file sharing systems are the large scale distributed applications devoted to file exchange among a large number of Internet users.

In contrast to popular client-server applications, end user machines in P2P systems are involved in network operations by providing their resources (e. g., storage space, bandwidth and computer power) and acting as both clients and servers. At the same time, they are not required to have permanent IP addresses as it is necessary for servers in client-server Internet applications. Therefore, they have significant autonomy, i. e., they can join and leave a network [1]. Utilizing user machines in P2P systems helps to distribute the costs of file sharing among the huge number of individual participants [2]. Any centralized server that provides both content and directory service is extremely expensive to run.

Built at the application level, P2P systems consist of the peers connected by a number of point-to-point connections (typically TCP). Due to the chaotic unstructured nature and transient peer population, P2P systems mostly employ flooding-based search mechanisms when many peers are probed whether they have a requested file or not. Such a flooding is the main source of the Internet traffic [3,4], which limits further system growth.

In this paper, it is intended to analyze existing approaches used to search files in P2P systems. More particularly, it is intended to discuss the influence of the methods on the search and network structure as well as methods applicability to real P2P applications. The presented methods are categorized depending on how search is realized and how the network structure is managed.

T. Böhme et al. (Eds.): IICS 2004, LNCS 3473, pp. 59–68, 2006.
© Springer-Verlag Berlin Heidelberg 2006

Accordingly, the article is organized as following. Section 2 presents a classification of the existing search methods in P2P systems. It discusses the advantages and limitation of these techniques. Section 3 presents a detailed description of P2P protocols. The paper ends with a conclusion.

2   A Classification

The P2P protocols can be classified depending on how the search is realized and how the network structure is organized and maintained (Fig. 1).

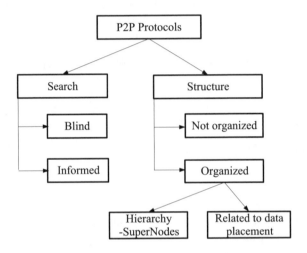

Fig. 1. A classification of P2P protocols

Existing search methods can be split into two main categories depending on how search query forwarding decisions are made:

– **Blind Search.**
  In a blind search, peers has no information related to file location. Therefore, other peers are randomly probed whether they have a requested file or not. Blind search protocols are simple and require peers to maintain a minimum amount of knowledge about network organization.
– **Informed Search.**
  In these systems, peers maintain additional information about file locations which can be useful for the search. For example, a peer may have an index of files offered by other peers connected to it. Based on this additional information, a peer decides which peers should be contacted.

A structure of P2P network is organized by point-to-point connections each peer has. Depending on the criteria used to form these connections between peers, the existing protocol are categorized as follows:

- **Structure is not organized.**
  Connections between peers are made mainly chaotically. They do not represent any dedicated network structure.
- **Structure is organized.**
  Protocols build a dedicated network structure which is an important part of the network operations. Therefore, the connections between peers are set in a special manner to achieve required network organization. Currently, there are two main kinds of protocols which build network structure. In the first one, all the peers are divided into powerful peers which are mainly responsible for network operations and weak peers connected to them. Accordingly, the resulting structure is a two-level hierarchy.
  The second one builds a network structure in accordance to data placement. In this way, connections between peers are related to the data shared by those peers (e. g., to connect peers which offer the similar content).

3   The Main P2P Protocols

The main P2P protocols can be divided into three main groups based on the classification presented above. The protocols of the first group employ blind search with/without network structure building. The majority of existing P2P file sharing applications use protocols of the first group. The second group of P2P protocols uses informed search without structure organization. The last group of protocols employs informed search techniques in addition to network structure organization.

The P2P applications and their protocols are presented in the following sections in groups.

3.1   Blind Search With/Without Structure Building

Gnutella [5] is decentralized both in the terms of file storage and file search. Therefore, it belongs to pure P2P systems. As far as the connections between peers are formed mainly chaotically, Gnutella belongs to unstructured systems in short of complete knowledge. Searching in such networks is mainly done by random search, in which various peers are randomly asked and probed if they have a target file. In Gnutella, a peer initiates a controlled flood of the network by sending a query message to all of the peers connected to it. When receiving a query, a peer checks if it has a requested file. If so, it forwards a special message back toward the search initiator [6]. No matter whether a file is found or not, the peer continues to flood the query. To limit generated traffic, each message can be forwarded only *time to live (TTL)* times. The advantage of such unstructured system is that they easily react to the high dynamics of P2P networks, peers can join and leave network without any notification. The obvious disadvantage is that it is difficult to find desired files without flooding queries which influence the scalability of such systems and significantly increase traffic.

FastTrack [7] protocol is a second generation of P2P protocols. It utilizes the heterogeneity between peers (computer power, bandwidth and availability) to form the two-level organization of a P2P network. FastTrack is based on the Gnutella protocol and extends it with the addition of *supernodes* to improve scalability.

It is used in KaZaa P2P application [8] where a small number of powerful peers (supernodes) handle traffic and routing on behalf of weak peers connected to them. KaZaa peers dynamically elect supernodes which form an unstructured network and use query flooding to locate content. Regular peers connect to one or more supernodes to initiate query and actually act as clients to supernodes [9].

Even though FastTrack utilizes heterogeneity between peers, it still relies on random search which is characterized by big volume of generated traffic. In addition, a limited number of peers responsible for traffic handling and message routing makes P2P networks more vulnerable to planned attacks.

Random Walks [10,11] is a range of blind search methods which benefit from using the properties of overlay topologies. To search for an object using a random walk, a peer chooses a neighbor randomly and sends the query to it. Each neighbor peer repeats this process until the data are found. In addition to random walks, the proactive replication algorithms [10] can be used. It was proposed to replicate files in proportion to the square-root of their query rate; this replication scheme can be implemented in a distributed fashion by replicating objects for a number of times proportional to the length of the search. The proactive replication may take place on the peer even though the peer has not requested the replicated data.

In the case of power-law random graphs [12], it was observed that high degree nodes experienced correspondingly high query loads. Even though the proposed approach helps to decrease generated traffic, it realizes the idea that, due to massive replication, data can be found in the nearness (limited number of hops) from the search initiator and if message will be broadcasted only to part of all the neighbors, the data still can be found almost of the same probability. The disadvantage of this approach is a random choice of a neighbor. The peers available for a long time could be chosen more often.

The **Logical Clustering** [13] approach tries to improve the information management in P2P networks by building dynamic cluster structures. The actual network topology is not changed. The logical clusters are built by circulating messages (wanderers). This provides the basis for a QoS (quality of service) for this high dynamic distributed system, i.e., each peer can be visited by a wanderer within a given time frame.

As mentioned above, the P2P networks can become very huge. The clustering supports a division of the network in such small groups (clusters) that a QoS regarding information management which fulfills certain time requirements can be provided. The time in which a peer wants to be supplied with information is the basis for the creation of the clusters Furthermore, the basic infrastructure for a cooperation between the peers is provided by applying the clustering techniques. Therefore, the clusters described here are defined as a subset of peers in a P2P network which can be covered by a wanderer. This wanderer must be able to visit all peers in that sub-network within a given time-frame.

The algorithm running locally on every peer is able to build the clusters by using just the knowledge about the network which is kept in the local warehouse. The communication between the disjoint clusters is organized by wanderers as well. For this purpose, every cluster has a dedicated peer. These peers are used to build higher-level clusters based on the same mechanisms. The clusters of these peers are connected by wanderers of the next higher level and so on. This results in a tree like structure, which can be used to spread messages (e. g., search requests) in the network.

The advantage is that the number of messages in the system is limited by using wanderers as tokens. The logical tree of clusters is used for search purposes.

3.2   Informed Search Without Network Structure Organization

Query Routing Protocol (QRP) [16] proposes to make informed search instead of network flooding. Peers are responsible for creating their own routing tables which include hashed keywords and regularly exchange them with their neighbors. These keywords are used to describe locally offered files. A Bloom filter [17] is usually used to code a set of keywords in a binary array which is suitable for transmission.

The computed routing tables are propagated up to several hops away from the peer it belongs to. If a peer receives routing tables from its neighbors, it can merge the tables and propagate the merged table further. In this scheme, the peer may decide to which of the neighbors it is worth routing a search query because merged routing tables of its neighbors are available. To decrease a number of hops required to find required data, routing table should be propagated as far as possible. At the same time, the limitations of bandwidth and increasing (with bigger number of propagating steps) ratio of false positives (mistakes with membership checking [17]) limit this idea. In addition, far propagations decrease actuality of information due to network dynamics.

Routing Indices (RI) [18] is an approach which employs ideas similar to QRP. In contrast to QRP, RI does not use Bloom filters to summarize content of neighbors. Instead, they use categorization of documents, which is a complicated task for real applications. Each peer maintains routing indices for each of the neighbors, indicating how many documents of which groups could be found through that neighbor. If a new connection is installed, a peer aggregates all routing indices of its neighbors, adds information about documents shared locally and sends an aggregated RI to a new neighbor. To keep data actuality, peers should inform neighbors of the changes in RI caused by addition or removal of documents or arrival/leaving of other neighbors. For practical purpose, this might cause frequent retransmission of data since network is constantly changing. Routing is done by the evaluation of "goodness" of neighbors against a query. If more documents could be found through particular neighbor, that neighbor is chosen.

Adaptive Probabilistic Search (APS) [19,20] uses the additional information about neighbors to make routing decisions. APS utilizes the feedback from previous searches to make future search more focused. More particularly, each peer keeps a local index describing which objects (files) were requested by each neighbor. The probability of choosing a neighbor to find a particular document depends on previous search results. The update takes a reverse path back to the peer search initiator and can take place after success or failure, adjusting probability accordingly. In this way, a network demonstrates a self-learning property which is supported by the discovered fact that many of the requested files are close to the requesters [4]. In contrast to RI or QRP, no additional overhead is required to obtain additional information about neighbors. Therefore, it could be better adapted to the changing topologies. The used approach leads to the situations when popular files could be located very fast, while other files could be hardly located. Other limitations are caused by the fact that first discovered peer (which has a requested object) might be more used for future routing and might experience more load. At the same time, other peers which are closer (from time or path length) could be ignored.

3.3   Informed Search with Network Structure Organization

Systems with Distributed Hash Tables (DHT). All the systems described above were unstructured so that the connections between peers are made chaotically, and data placement is completely unrelated to the structure formed by connections between peers.

To overcome the scalability limitations of flooding-based unstructured systems, the recently introduced systems like CAN [21], Chord [22], Pastry [23] and Tapestry [24] use another approach to the routing and topology organization of P2P networks. This approach employs the idea of *distributed hash tables (DHT)* functionality—mapping "keys" onto "values"—on Internet-like scale.

In DHT systems, files are associated with a key which is produced by hashing, for example, the file name or the file content. The range of the output values of the hash function forms an ID space. Every peer in the system is responsible for storing a certain range of keys (or partition of ID space). The structure is formed by routing tables locally stored on individual peers. A table includes a list of other peers with addresses and range of keys they are responsible for. Such systems are highly structured. The topology is tightly controlled and files (or information about files) are placed at the precisely specified locations defined by their keys. Depending on the application, the network structure and routing may be different (for details see [25]). Due to careful data placement and tightly controlled topology, DHTs have a scalable routing ($O(\log n)$ steps), where n is the size of a network (number of peers).

The important disadvantages of DHTs concern to the resilience of the system [26]. Since tightly maintained structure is important for correctness of operations, the structured design is likely to be less reliable in the face of a very transient user population.

Another important key problem of DHTs is load balancing. Due to significant file popularity skewness [9,27], peers responsible for storing pointers to the most popular files (or keywords) may become *overloaded*, since the majority of requests for the most popular content come to those peers.

In addition, retrieving content requires the knowledge of the exact file identifier, which is problematic in real P2P file sharing applications. All these require additional functionality which is missing in the original design of DHT systems.

A Content-oriented Approach to Network Structure Building and Search [28] does not require tightly controlled network structure and therefore copes with network dynamics better than DHTs. It includes two main concepts: content-oriented search and content-oriented structure building.

Content-Oriented Search

To avoid flooding, each peer stores content summaries of its neighbors. The summaries of peers can be represented as Bloom filters to code the set of keywords used in file names offered by those peers. If a network is devoted to sharing analyzable documents (e. g., text), the text processing techniques can be applied to create peers summaries. In this case, offered files and accordingly peers content can be represented in vector form (e. g., [29]).

Every time a query is forwarded, a forwarding algorithm will consult these summaries to select the neighbor to be contacted. If Bloom filter is used, the query keywords are hashed by using the same hash functions which were used to calculate Bloom filter. The obtained values are used to check keywords membership in a Bloom filter. In case analyzable documents are used, a query is matched with vector representation of peers content as it was suggested in [29].

In both cases, a neighbor which is supposed to store required content is contacted.

Content-Oriented Structure Building

In contrast to chaotically formed network structure, it is proposed to build connections between peers based on relations between respective users. Those relations in P2P file sharing applications are described and determined by shared (offered) and requested files. For example, if users offer similar content then there is a relation between them. The locally offered content as well as requested content is analyzed to create respective summaries.

Each peer analyzes summaries of its neighbors and restructures its neighborhood.

The experiments have demonstrated [28] that the best system performance was achieved when neighborhood includes two types of neighbors: those which offer the most similar content to the one shared locally (so-called *social neighbors*) and those which offer the most similar content to the one a user is interested in (so-called *egoistic neighbors*). In this case, the resulting global structure is content-oriented which represents grouping of peers based on not only similar offered content, but also users' interests.

Each peer has a possibility to collect information about other peers in a network which are not direct neighbors. To avoid additional messages for network structuring purposes, it was proposed to combine network discovery with a search process. In this way, a search message includes additional data-Log which contains a list of visited peers and summaries of their content. When a search message comes back to the peer-search initiator, it brings a list of visited peers[1]. A peer analyzes a message Log and current neighbors and selects the most appropriate peers for the new neighborhood.

The content-oriented structure building requires neither global control nor complete knowledge for its operations. All algorithms are locally executed. The global structure emerges as a result of individual activities of peers even under the highly dynamic conditions.

The resulting structure improves search operations, since at the beginning, egoistic neighbors are used to forward a query to the peers which might offer required content and then social neighbors are used to forward a message within a group offering similar content.

One can build an analogy with WWW. To search a page, a user can use its bookmarks to go as close as possible to the required content and then it can use the links provided on that page to other pages offering content about the similar topic.

4   Conclusion

The article presented a survey of existing P2P protocols. It was proposed to categorize the protocols depending on how they search data and organize the network structure.

The presented survey has demonstrated that the network structure and the respective forwarding algorithms significantly influence the properties of P2P applications. The existing systems are mainly unstructured so that P2P protocols mostly employ flooding which results to the traffic problem. On the other hand, the application of highly structured systems is limited due to high dynamics of network population.

References

1. Shirky, C.: What is P2P ...and what isn't? The O'Reilly Network. http://www.openp2p.com/pub/a/p2p/2000/11/24/shirky1-whatisp2p.html (2000)
2. Daswani, N., Garcia-Molina, H., Yang, B.: Open problems in data-sharing peer-to-peer systems. In: Database Theory-ICDT 2003, 9th International Conference. Volume 2572 of Lecture Notes in Computer Science., Siena, Italy, Springer (2003) 232–241
3. Internet2: Weekly reports. http://netflow.internet2.edu/weekly/ (2003)
4. Ripeanu, M., Foster, I.: Mapping the Gnutella network: Macroscopic properties of large-scale peer-to-peer systems. In: Peer-to-Peer Systems, First International Workshop, IPTPS 2002, Revised Papers. Volume 2429 of Lecture Notes in Computer Science., Cambridge, MA, USA, Springer-Verlag, Berlin (2002) 85–93
5. Gnutella: http://www.gnutellanews.com (2002)
6. from http://www.LimeWire.com, A.: The Gnutella protocol specification v0.4. (2003)

---

[1] In the current version of algorithms. For practical realization, a peer can analyze passing messages, each carrying the content summary of its starting peer

7. Wikipedia: FastTrack. http://en.wikipedia.org/wiki/FastTrack (2004)
8. Kazaa: http://www.kazaa.com (2003)
9. Leibowitz, N., Ripeanu, M., Wierzbicki, A.: Deconstructing the Kazaa network. In: 3rd IEEE Workshop on Internet Applications (WIAPP'03), San Jose, CA (2003) 112–119
10. Lv, C., Cao, P., Cohen, E., Li, K., Shenker, S.: Search and replication in unstructured peer-to-peer networks. In: ACM, SIGMETRICS 2002. (2002)
11. Adamic, L., Huberman, B., Lukose, R., Puniyani, A.: Search in power law networks. Physical Review **E 64 (2001)** (2001) 46135–46143
12. Deo, N., Gupta, P.: World Wide Web: A graph-theoretic perspective. Technical Report CS-TR-01-001, School of Computer Science, University of Central Florida, Orlando, FL 32816, USA (2001)
13. Unger, H., Wulff, M.: Cluster-building in p2p-community networks. In Akl, S., Gonzalez, T., eds.: Parallel and Distributed Computing and Systems, Cambridge, USA, ACTA Press (2002) 685–690
14. Jain, A.K., Dube, R.C.: Algorithms for Clustering Data. Prentice Hall (1988)
15. Krishnamurthy, B., Wang, J., Xie, Y.: Early measurements of a cluster-based architecture for P2P systems. In: ACM SIGCOMM Internet Measurement Workshop, San Francisco, USA (2001)
16. Rohrs, C.: Query routing for the Gnutella network. http://rfc-gnutella.sourceforge.net (2001)
17. Bloom, B.: Space/time trade-offs in hash coding with allowable errors. Communication of ACM **13(7)** (1970) 422–426
18. Crespo, A., Garcia-Molina, H.: Routing indices for peer-to-peer systems. In: 22 nd International Conference on Distributed Computing Systems (ICDCS'02), Vienna, Austria (2002) 23–33
19. Tsoumakos, D., Roussopoulos, N.: Adaptive probabilistic search for peer-to-peer networks. In: Third International Conference on Peer-to-Peer Computing (P2P'03), Linköping, Sweden (2003) 102–110
20. Tsoumakos, D., Roussopoulos, N.: A comparison of peer-to-peer search methods. In: Sixth International Workshop on the Web and Databases., San Diego, USA (2003)
21. Ratnasamy, S., Francis, P., Handley, M., Karp, R., Shenker, S.: A scalable content addressable network. In: Proceedings of ACM SIGCOMM 2001. (2001)
22. Stoica, I., Morris, R., Karger, D., Kaashoek, F., Balakrishnan, H.: Chord: A scalable Peer-To-Peer lookup service for internet applications. In: Proceedings of ACM SIGCOMM 2001. (2001) 149–160
23. Rowstron, A., Druschel, P.: Pastry: Scalable, decentralized object location, and routing for large-scale peer-to-peer systems. In: IFIP/ACM International Conference on Distributed Systems Platforms (Middleware). (2001) 329–350
24. Zhao, B.Y., Kubiatowicz, J.D., Joseph, A.D.: Tapestry: An infrastructure for fault-tolerant wide-area location and routing. Technical Report UCB/CSD-01-1141, UC Berkeley (2001)
25. Balakrishnan, H., Kaashoek, M.F., Karger, D., Morris, R., Stoica, I.: Looking up data in p2p systems. Communications of the ACM **46** (2003) 43–48
26. Ratnasamy, S., Shenker, S., Stoica, I.: Routing algorithms for DHTs: Some open questions. In: Peer-to-Peer Systems, First International Workshop, IPTPS 2002, Revised Papers. Volume 2429 of Lecture Notes in Computer Science., Cambridge, MA, USA, Springer-Verlag, Berlin (2002) 45–51

27. Chu, J., Labonte, K., Levine, B.: Availability and locality measurements of peer-to-peer file systems. In: SPIE ITCom: Scalability and Traffic Control in IP Networks. Volume 4868. (2002)
28. Sakaryan, G., Unger, H., Lechner, U.: About the value of virtual communities in P2P networks. In: 4th IEEE International Symposium and School on Advanced Distributed Systems (ISSADS 2004), Guadalajara,Mexico (2004)
29. Sakaryan, G., Unger, H.: Self-organization in peer to peer communitites. Technical Report UR-TR-0403, University of Rostock, Computer Science Dept. (2003)

A Formal Framework to Reduce Communications in Communication Systems*

Manuel Núñez, Ismael Rodríguez, and Fernando Rubio

Facultad Informática, Universidad Complutense de Madrid
C/. Juan del Rosal, 8, E-28040 Madrid, Spain
{mn,isrodrig,fernando}@sip.ucm.es

Abstract. In this paper we present a method that, given a communicating system, allows us to reduce on average the number of messages sent. The basic idea is to *shortcut* the most frequent *dialogs* appearing in the communications. By doing so, some large dialogs can be reduced to only two messages. In addition, not only the number of messages, but also the size of them, can be minimized, on average, by considering the probabilities of sending each message in each state.

1 Introduction

Compression algorithms are useful to reduce the size of huge amounts of data. In this paper we are only interested in those compression algorithms that are *reversible*, that is, it is possible to recover the original data from the compressed version. This is the case of algorithms as Huffman codes, LZ, and LZW (see e.g. [4,7,6]) which are used in most data compression tools. Even though compression/decompression is usually a computationally costly process, it is often worth to sacrifice this computing capacity because of the limited storing capacity of computing systems. Let us remark that compression algorithms are not only useful to *enlarge* storing capacity. In fact, and this is the use of compression that we consider in this paper, compressed data is getting nowadays very popular to overcome transmission limitations through the Internet.

In this paper we consider communications between distant partners where computational power is *cheaper* than transmission power. Examples of these systems are partners communicating through the Internet or located in a network. A first approach consists in compressing isolated messages, that is, compression at the *message level* (to the best of our knowledge, this is the only method studied in the literature). In this situation, each separate message is independently compressed. We propose a more elaborated reversible method where compression is applied in such a way that not only isolated messages are taken into account but *whole dialogs*. Obviously, in order to compress a dialog we should know it before the transmission starts. This requires that each partner knows in advance what the corresponding communicating partner is going to answer to a given message, and again for the answer to the answer of the first message,

---

* Work supported in part by the projects TIC2003-07848-C02-01 and PAC-03-001

T. Böhme et al. (Eds.): IICS 2004, LNCS 3473, pp. 69–80, 2006.

and so on. Unfortunately, all this information can be known with certainty only when the whole dialog has finished. But it is completely useless to worry about compressing information that has been already transmitted!

Even though we cannot know beforehand a future dialog, we may try to *guess*, with a certain probability, that dialog. For example, let us suppose that P_1 is going to send the message a to P_2. In addition, P_1 could decide that if P_2 replies b then the message c will be sent to P_2. Moreover, it could have already decided (even before the first message is sent) that if P_2 replies with d then e will be sent. Thus, P_1 knows that the complete dialog will be *abcde assuming* that P_2 will reply b to a and d to c. Let us also suppose that we can deduce that the dialog *abcde*, between P_1 and P_2, has a high probability[1]. In this case, it is obvious that it will be profitable to code the whole dialog in such a way that it is not necessary to deliver five messages. In this case, the number of transmitted messages is reduced in a high number of situations (because of the high probability of the corresponding dialog).

Thus, assuming the previous conditions, how does one *anticipate* dialogs? Let us consider again the previous simple example. Let us suppose that P_1 observes that the previous conditions hold, that is, that P_1 decides to send a to P_2, that if afterwards b is received then c will be sent, etcetera. So, P_1 will ask P_2 whether it is willing to perform the whole dialog σ, where both partners know in advance that $\sigma = abcde$. If the dialog σ is compatible with its situation then P_2 will reply *yes*. Otherwise, it will reply with a different message (e.g. b') and the dialog will be continued from that moment on. Let us remark that in the first case we have sensibly reduced the number of messages while in the second case we have not incurred in any lost. Moreover, our approach does not only reduce the size of dialogs by reducing the number of transmitted messages. In fact, it also reduces the size in bits of the most common messages. Thus, the average size of dialogs is reduced, although some low-probability dialogs can be increased.

Following these intuitions, we propose a formal method that, given a communicating system, allows us to compress the most frequent dialogs. In order to know which are the most frequent dialogs, log files recording the past communications can be used. However, they can also be computed by using specifications including the probabilities of sending each message in each state of the machines. We will use this probabilistic information to find out which dialogs should be compressed to decrease the average length of communications in a system. Besides, we will provide a method to compress them by introducing *shortcuts*. Let us remark that our notion of minimizing protocols communication is completely different to the idea of minimizing the number of states of a given protocol, issue that has been extensively studied in the literature (see e.g. [3]).

The rest of the paper is structured as follows. In Section 2 we introduce the basic definitions related to our notion of *dialog finite state machines*. Then, in Section 3 we define how to reduce their communications by introducing *shortcuts*. Finally, in Section 4 we present our conclusions and some lines of future work.

---

[1] This high probability can be deduced either from the historic record of dialogs or from the specification of the possible communications between the partners

2   Dialog Finite State Machines

In order to apply our method, we need to use a formalism to specify the corresponding systems. Finite state machines have already been considered in the literature for specifying protocols and communicating systems (see e.g. [2,1,5]). Following this idea, in this paper we suppose that the partners of the studied system are formally defined as finite state machines[2]. Thus, by composing them we can get a whole view of the system. This composite view of the system will be formally defined by means of *dialog finite state machines*.

Intuitively, a dialog finite state machine, in short DFSM, represents all the possible communications among the components. In every DFSM, states can be classified into two classes, depending on the partner that has to send a message. In this sense, we assume a strict alternation between the partners while sending messages. Thus, in any DFSM there are only transitions from states associated with a partner to states associated with another partner. Let us remark that a transition represents that a given message has been sent. For example, if the origin of the transition is a state associated to partner P_1 then the destination must be a state associated to P_2. In addition, each transition of the DFSM has attached a probability p. Its meaning is that the probability of sending the message attached to that transition is p.

In our notion of DFSM we will consider some special messages representing *compound* messages. A message $(m_1 \cdots m_n?)$ represents that one of the partners is proposing to perform a predefined dialog containing n *atomic* messages. A message $(m_1 \cdots m_n!)$ represents that the other partner accepts to perform such a dialog. When this is the case, the whole n-steps dialog is communicated by using only two messages (the proposal and the acceptance). In case the dialog is not to be completely accepted, a message $(m_1 \cdots m_i!b)$ is sent, where $m_1 \cdots m_i$ is the accepted prefix of the dialog, and b is the first message sent after rejecting the rest of the dialog. Finally, if the first partner desires to send m_1 but not to perform the whole dialog $m_1 \cdots m_n$, it can send the message $(m_1 \cdots m_n\#)$. This message allows a partner to distinguish between communicating $m_1 \cdots m_n$ and communicating any other message beginning by m_1 when the compound message $(m_1 \cdots m_n?)$ is available. Let us remark that if $(m_1 \cdots m_n\#)$ is communicated then we do not send only m_1. In fact, we also know that the partner cannot perform the whole dialog. Thus, we can recompute the probabilities of each transition. In order to ease the presentation, we consider systems composed of two partners. From the technical point of view, the extension of our formalism to deal with n-partner systems is trivial (but cumbersome).

In the next definition we introduce the notion of dialog finite state machine. In this definition, and during the rest of the paper, we use the trick of indexing some related sets by i and $3-i$. Let us note that if $i = 1$ then $3-i = 2$, and $i = 2$ implies $3 - i = 1$. Since our communicating partners will be denoted by indexes 1 and 2, this trick will be used to relate each partner with its counterpart.

---

[2] Actually, we only require that formalizations concern the portion of the behavior of each partner where we want to apply our methodology

Definition 1. A *Dialog Finite State Machine*, in short DFSM, is a tuple $D = (S_1, S_2, M_1, M_2, T_1, T_2)$ where S_i, M_i, and T_i are the sets of *states*, *messages*, and *transitions* of the partner i.

Each message set M_i is defined as a disjoint union $M_i = \alpha_i \cup \beta_i$, where α_i is the set of *atomic messages* and β_i is a set of *compound messages*. Each compound message $m \in \beta_i$ is a sequence of atomic messages of either the form $(m_1 \cdots m_{n-1}!m_n)$ or $(m_1 \cdots m_n\$)$, where for any $1 \leq j \leq n$, if $odd(j)$ then $m_j \in \alpha_i$, while if $even(j)$ then $m_j \in \alpha_{3-i}$. The symbol $\$ \in \{?, !, \#\}$ indicates that the sequence is a *proposal*, a (partial or full) *acceptance*, or a *not-proposal*.

Each transition $t \in T_i$ is a tuple (s, m, p, s') where $s \in S_i$, $s' \in S_{3-i}$ are the initial and final states, $m \in M_i$ is the message communicated in the transition, and $0 < p \leq 1$ is the probability of taking the transition t at state s. Each transition $t = (s, m, p, s')$ will also be denoted by $s \xrightarrow{m}_p s'$.

Let $\mathtt{Tran}(s)$ denote the set of transitions (s, m, p, s') departing from state s. Then, for any state $s \in S_i$ we have $\sum\{p \mid (s, m, p, s') \in \mathtt{Tran}(s)\} \in \{0, 1\}$, where this value is 0 only when the set is empty. Besides, for any state $s \in S_i$ and message $m \in M_i$ there exists at most one transition $t \in T_i$ such that $t = (s, m, p, s')$. □

Let us comment on the previous definition. First, let us remark that any state belonging to S_i represents that the next partner communicating in the system is partner i. In that state, the communications that i can perform are given by the transitions in T_i departing from that state. Transitions are labelled by both the message transmitted in the communication and the probability of performing such a transition. Let us note that probabilities of all transitions departing from the same state must add 1 (unless there is no transition leaving that state). Simple and compound messages are dealt equally, and they are both transmitted by single transitions. Let us note that any transition performed by partner i leads a DFSM to a state in S_{3-i}, that is, a state where the next communication will be performed by partner $3 - i$. It is worth to point out that this restriction does not decrease the expressivity of the system. For instance, if we want a partner to be able to transmit the sequence of messages ab, then we can consider a single message c representing ab.

Example 1. Let us consider a communication protocol that describes the communications that take place in a peer to peer environment. Specifically, the protocol denotes the negotiation process that takes place when a peer asks another peer to share and transfer some file. The DFSM associated to this protocol is depicted in Figure 1. We suppose that the sharing negotiation process is performed by autonomous agents, where each of them behaves on behalf of its respective user and its preferences. Sharing is a voluntary act, but agents remember previous negotiations, so their behavior with other agents can change depending on their previous decisions (e.g., if an agent A refuses to share files with other agent B, then agent B will punish agent A by refusing to share files with A in the future). Moreover, after a refusal an agent can complain to communicate the other agent that if the request is not accepted then the future sharing with this agent will suffer. Our peer to peer environment includes also some non-standard features.

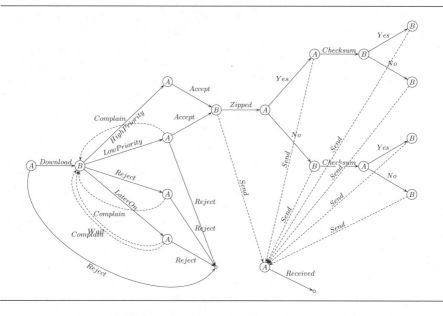

Fig. 1. Example of peer to peer system

For instance, after agents agree to transmit a file, the sender can ask the other agent whether it wants the file to be compressed with a *zip* compressor before sending it. Moreover, it can ask the receiver whether it wants the sender to check the integrity of the file before sending it (i.e., whether it can be correctly open with its respective reader application). In both cases, the sender will ask the receiver only if it has the suitable applications to perform them.

Let us comment the details of the protocol. As no dialog has been compressed yet, all represented messages are atomic. States of the requester and of the provider are marked by letters A and B, respectively. Firstly, the requester asks the provider for sharing and sending the file. Then, the provider can accept to send it with high priority, accept to send it with low priority, refuse the sharing, or ask the requester for waiting for a while and ask again. In the first two cases, the requester can accept. In the last case, the requester can wait for a while and ask again. In the last three cases, the requester can complain and ask for a better deal. Finally, in all cases the requester can abort the operation. Let us suppose that both partners accept to share and send the file. Then, if the provider has a zip compression application, it asks the requester whether it wants the file to be compressed. After, if the provider has the corresponding application to check the integrity of the file, it asks the requester whether it wants that application to be used before the sending. After this operation (or in a previous point if the needed application was not available) the provider begins the sending of the file, and finally the requester acknowledges the reception of it. Later on we will recall this example to present how dialogs are compressed.   □

Let us note that any communication a partner i can perform from a state $s \in S_i$ must be distinguishable from any other communication it can perform from s; otherwise, the receiver of the message would be unable to properly interpret it. Without loss of generality, let us assume that we use the simplest signature to code our messages, that is, the binary signature. The binary code used to denote a message in each state should be different to any other binary code representing a different message in that state. Moreover, we must require that the binary code associated to a transition is not a *prefix* of another binary code associated to another transition of the same state. Let us suppose that c and c' are codifications of the messages m and m' respectively, and let us also suppose that c is a prefix of c'. Then, when a partner receives the codification c it cannot know whether the message m has been completely sent, or whether the message m' is still being sent. Let us include explicitly the binary codes associated to transitions in our formalization. Given a DFSM we construct a derived *codified* DFSM by assigning binary codes to each message/transition.

Definition 2. We say that a pair $C = (D, \eta)$ is a *Codified Dialog Finite State Machine*, in short CDFSM, if $D = (S_1, S_2, M_1, M_2, T_1, T_2)$ is a DFSM and the function $\eta : T_1 \cup T_2 \longrightarrow \{0,1\}^*$ assigns a binary code to every transition in D such that for any state $s \in S_i$ there do not exist two transitions $t_1, t_2 \in \text{Tran}(s)$ fulfilling that $\eta(t_1)$ is a prefix of $\eta(t_2)$. □

Let us note that any code is a prefix of itself. Hence, equal codes in different transitions of the same state are forbidden according to the previous definition.

In order to reduce the length of communications, it is desirable that codes associated to messages are as shorter as possible, while keeping their distinguishing power. In any codification, binary codes associated to different transitions from the same state might have different lengths. Obviously, it is preferable that most frequent messages are associated to shorter codes. Next we introduce a notion to denote a CDFSM where the codification of transitions in all states is *optimal*. A locally minimal codification is a CDFSM where the weighted average length of the messages is minimal. That is, when the length of each message is multiplied by its probability, the average of these products is minimal.

Definition 3. Let $D = (S_1, S_2, M_1, M_2, T_1, T_2)$ be a DFSM. A *locally minimal codification* of D is a function $\eta : T_1 \cup T_2 \longrightarrow \{0,1\}^*$ such that (D, η) is a CDFSM and there does not exist another function θ such that (D, θ) is also a CDFSM and there is a state $s \in S_1 \cup S_2$ with

$$\sum \{\text{length}(\theta(t)) \cdot p \mid t = (s, m, p, s') \in \text{Tran}(s)\}$$
$$< \sum \{\text{length}(\eta(t)) \cdot p \mid t = (s, m, p, s') \in \text{Tran}(s)\}$$

If η is a locally minimal codification of D then we say that $C = (D, \eta)$ is a *locally minimal* CDFSM. □

A locally minimal CDFSM represents an optimal codification when we deal with compression *at the message level*, that is, when compression is applied only to atomic messages. Let us suppose that we construct a DFSM where all messages are atomic, and we obtain its locally minimal CDFSM. If we constrain ourselves to perform a compression at the message level, then such a CDFSM provides a codification where the average length of any dialog between partners is minimal. However, as we will show later, our compression strategy will go one step further by introducing compound messages and compressing whole dialogs. Let us note that after the suitable compound messages are found and inserted into our DFSM, the best codification for our compression *at the dialog level* is provided by the corresponding locally minimal CDFSM as well.

The codification of the available messages in a state is independent from any other codification in other state. Thus, the problem of finding the locally minimal codification in a DFSM can be decomposed into the simpler problem of finding the optimal codification for each state. Let us define how to codify a set of pairs *(message,probability)* representing the messages of a state. This codification will be applied to each state of a DFSM to create its corresponding CDFSM.

Definition 4. Let $R = \{r_1, \ldots, r_n\}$ be a set of pairs $r_i = (m_i, p_i)$ where m_i is a message and $0 < p_i \leq 1$ is a probability. A *codification function for R* is a function C which returns for every message m_i a binary codification $\alpha \in \{0, 1\}^*$ such that there do not exist $(m_j, p_j), (m_k, p_k) \in R$ such that $C(m_j)$ is a prefix of $C(m_k)$. We say that C is a *minimal codification function* if there does not exist another codification function B for S with $\sum\{\texttt{length}(B(m_i)) \cdot p_i \mid (m_i, p_i) \in S\} < \sum\{\texttt{length}(C(m_i)) \cdot p_i \mid (m_i, p_i) \in S\}$. □

As it is well known, the Huffman algorithm [4] computes the minimal codification function associated to a set of *symbols* (in our context, messages) and *frequencies* (in our context, probabilities). Thus, if we apply it to each state, we trivially obtain the locally minimal codification of a DFSM.

Lemma 1. Let $D = (S_1, S_2, M_1, M_2, T_1, T_2)$ be a DFSM. Let η be a function $\eta : T_1 \cup T_2 \longrightarrow \{0, 1\}^*$ such that for every transition $t = (s, m, p, s') \in T_1 \cup T_2$ we have $\eta(t) = C_s(m)$, where C_s is a minimal codification function of $\{(m, p) \mid (s, m, p, s') \in \texttt{Tran}(s)\}$. Then, η is a *locally minimal codification of dialog D*. □

Let us remind that atomic messages transmit a single message while compound messages can represent proposals, refusals or acceptance of dialogs. Thus, to identify the actual messages communicated in a sequence of transitions, each message must be analyzed. Let us define the *real* meaning of a concatenation of messages (either atomic or compounds). For the sake of clarity, in the next definition we represent the sequences of messages as lists.

Definition 5. We define the *effective messages* belonging to a given list of messages by the following recursive expression:

$$\texttt{effec}([\,]) = \varepsilon$$
$$\texttt{effec}([(m_1 \cdots m_n?) \mid S]) = \texttt{effec}(S)$$
$$\texttt{effec}([(m_1 \cdots m_n!) \mid S]) = [m_1 \cdots m_n \mid \texttt{effec}(S)]$$
$$\texttt{effec}([(m_1 \cdots m_k!m') \mid S]) = [m_1 \cdots m_k m' \mid \texttt{effec}(S)]$$
$$\texttt{effec}([(m_1 \cdots m_n\#) \mid S]) = [m_1 \mid \texttt{effec}(S)]$$
$$\texttt{effec}([m \mid S]) = [m \mid \texttt{effec}(S)]$$
□

Let us remark that a compound message as $m_1 \cdots m_n$? does not represent any effective message, as it is necessary to wait until the other partner decides whether to accept the proposal or not. Hence, such messages do not add any effective message to the list.

Let us now consider how the current state of a DFSM evolves after a given sequence of transitions. Sequences of messages will be denoted by *evolutions*. Evolutions will be labelled by the sequence of messages labelling each transition and the probability of performing the whole sequence. That probability will be computed by multiplying the probabilities of each transition involved in the evolution. Let us remark that loops of states may appear in evolutions. However, it is not possible to have loops of length 1 since this would mean that a partner can send two messages before the other one sends anything.

Definition 6. Let $D = (S_1, S_2, M_1, M_2, T_1, T_2)$ be a DFSM. Besides, let $t_1 = (s_1, m_1, p_1, s_2), \ldots, t_{n-1} = (s_{n-1}, m_{n-1}, p_{n-1}, s_n)$ be transitions such that for any $1 \leq i \leq n - 1$, if $odd(i)$ then $t_i \in T_j$ and otherwise $t_i \in T_{3-j}$ for some $j \in \{1, 2\}$. Then, we write $\sigma = s_1 \xrightarrow{\texttt{effec}([m_1 \cdots m_{n-1}])}_{\pi} s_n$, where $\pi = \prod p_i$, we say that σ is an *evolution* of D. We denote the set of evolutions of D by $\texttt{Evol}(D)$.

Let $C = (D, \eta)$ be a CDFSM. Then, the *code length* of the evolution σ, denoted by $\texttt{clength}(C, \sigma)$, is defined as $\sum_{1 \leq i \leq n} \texttt{length}(\eta(t_i))$. $\qquad\square$

3   Introducing Shortcuts

A *shortcut* is a sequence of states and transitions that are added to the original machine to reduce the codification length of a frequent evolution[3]. The aim of a shortcut is to allow communicating partners to perform a given sequence of messages with only a pair of messages (a proposal and an acceptance). In order to do it, new compound messages are inserted to represent the whole sequence. Obviously, reducing the codification length of a single evolution may produce a penalty in the codification lengths of other evolutions. Actually, the addition of available messages in some state requires, in general, to enlarge the codes of the messages to properly distinguish them. Nevertheless, if shortcuts are carefully introduced, the overall weighted average length of the evolutions will be reduced.

Next we explain the basic ideas underlying the construction of a shortcut, ant then we present them more formally in Algorithm 1. Let us suppose that there is an evolution from a state s_1 to a state s_n labelled by messages $a_1, a_2, \ldots, a_{n-1}$ in a DFSM, and we wish to shortcut it. This evolution will also appear in the modified DFSM. In addition, two new types of evolutions are added:

- First, a new evolution of two-steps is introduced. In s_1, the first partner proposes the whole compound evolution and then the second partner can accept it, reaching the state s_n in only two steps. These two new transitions

---

[3] The length of this evolution must be even. The reason is that the second partner is the one finishing the shortcut. Thus, the next message after the shortcut sequence should be sent by the first partner

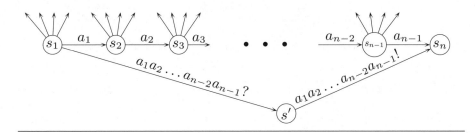

Fig. 2. First approach for shortcutting $a_1 a_2 \ldots a_n$ from state s_1 to state s_n

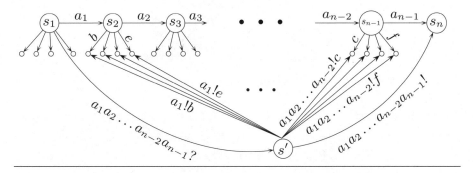

Fig. 3. First approach for including refusals in a shortcut

are labelled by $a_1 a_2 \cdots a_{n-1}$? and $a_1 a_2 \cdots a_{n-1}$!, respectively (see Figure 2). Alternatively, after the initial compound proposal, the second partner can decide not to accept it. In such a case, we must indicate both the accepted part of the proposal and the first message b sent after that part. Let us suppose that the first i messages of the shortcut are accepted, but the $(i+1)$-th is not. The final state after the refusal will not be the $(i+1)$-th state of the original evolution. In fact, the final state must be the state reached after the $(i+1)$-th state when a message b is produced (see Figure 3). However, some information is missing: When the first partner does *not* want to perform the whole dialog, we must recompute the rest of probabilities of the original path, as these probabilities are *conditioned* to that fact.

– The second step of the construction comes from that case, that is, the case when the first partner is interested in sending the first message of the considered compound message but not the whole compound message. For dealing with such a case, we need to *clone* all the intermediate transitions and states of the original evolution (see Figure 4). This new cloned evolution will be as the original regarding actions, but the probabilities will be updated with the new extra information: We know that the first partner does not desire to perform the shortcut dialog. Moreover, the last transition of the evolution, denoting the willingness to perform the whole dialog, is not cloned.

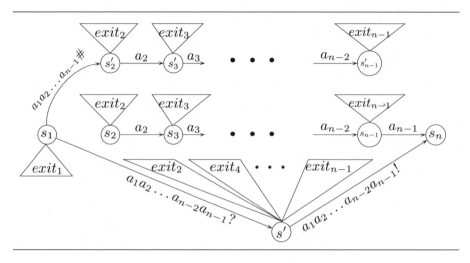

Fig. 4. A shortcut for $a_1 a_2 \ldots a_{n-1}$ from state s_1 to state s_n

Algorithm 1. Let $D = (S_1, S_2, M_1, M_2, T_1, T_2)$ be a DFSM and let us consider a sequence of transitions $s_1 \xrightarrow{m_1}_{p_1} s_2 \xrightarrow{m_2}_{p_2} \cdots \xrightarrow{m_{n-1}}_{p_{n-1}} s_n$. Let $\sigma = s_1 \xRightarrow{\rho}_{\pi} s_n$ with $\pi = \prod_{i=1}^{n-1} p_i$ and $\rho = \texttt{effec}(m_1 \cdots m_{n-1})$. Let $s_1 \in S_k$ and let $l = 3 - k$. A *shortcut* for σ in D is a new DFSM $D' = (S_1', S_2', M_1', M_2', T_1', T_2')$ constructed as follows:

- $S_k' = S_k \cup A_k$, where $A_k = \{s_i' \mid 1 \leq i \leq n-1 \wedge odd(i)\}$ is a set of fresh states. Intuitively, this step represents the inclusion of the odd states of the *cloned* evolution.
- $S_l' = S_l \cup A_l$, where $A_l = \{s_i' \mid 1 \leq i \leq n-1 \wedge even(i)\} \cup \{s'\}$ is a set of fresh states. Intuitively, this step represents the inclusion of the even states of the *cloned* evolution plus the accepting/rejecting state s' of the whole dialog.
- $M_k' = M_k \cup \{(\rho?), (\rho\#)\}$. Intuitively, we add a proposal to perform the shortcut as well as a message to perform the first step of the shortcut but not the whole one (i.e., going to the cloned evolution, see Figure 4).
- $M_l' = M_l\{(\rho!)\} \cup \bigcup_{1 \leq i \leq n-1, even(i)} \{(\texttt{effec}(m_1 \cdots m_{i-1}!m)) \mid \exists p, t : s_i \xrightarrow{m}_p t\}$. Here we add the acceptance and rejections (that is, acceptances up to a certain point) of the proposal.

Besides, transitions sets T_k' and T_l' are constructed as follows, where $\pi_0' = 1$, $\pi_i = \prod\{p_k \mid odd(k) \wedge i \leq k \leq n-1\}$ and $\pi_i' = \prod\{p_k \mid even(k) \wedge 1 \leq k \leq i\}$:

- $T_k' = (T_k \setminus \{s_1 \xrightarrow{m_1}_{p_1} s_2\})$
  $\cup \{s_i' \xrightarrow{m_i}_{p \cdot \pi_i} s_{i+1}' \mid s_i \xrightarrow{m_i}_p s_{i+1} \wedge odd(i) \wedge 3 \leq i \leq n-2\}$
  $\cup \{s_1 \xrightarrow{(\rho?)}_{\pi_1} s'\} \cup \{s_1 \xrightarrow{(\rho\#)}_{p \cdot \pi_1} s_2'\}$
  $\cup \{s_i' \xrightarrow{m}_{p + p \cdot \pi_i} u \mid s_i \xrightarrow{m}_p u \wedge u \neq s_{n+1} \wedge odd(i) \wedge 1 \leq i \leq n-1\}$

After removing the first transition of the original evolution, we have to add the odd steps of the cloned evolution. The probabilities change because we

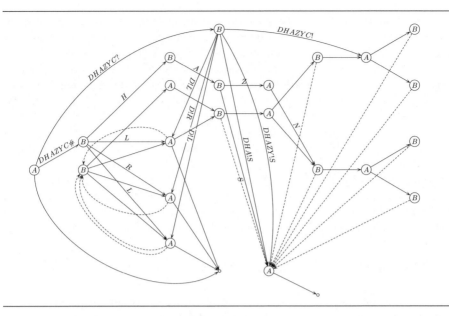

Fig. 5. Example of shortcut in the peer to peer system

know that the whole shortcut was not proposed. Additionally, we add the shortcut proposal, the first step of the cloned evolution, and the transitions to leave the cloned evolution.

$$- \ T'_l = T_l \cup \{s'_i \xrightarrow{m_i}_p s'_{i+1} \mid s_i \xrightarrow{m_i}_p s_{i+1} \wedge \ even(i) \wedge \ 2 \le i \le n-2\}$$
$$\cup \{s'_i \xrightarrow{m}_p u \mid s_i \xrightarrow{m}_p u \wedge \ u \ne s_{n+1} \wedge \ even(i) \wedge \ 1 \le i \le n-1\}$$
$$\cup \{s' \xrightarrow{(\rho!)}_{\pi'_r} s_n \mid r = max\{i \mid 1 \le i \le n-1 \wedge \ even(i)\}\}$$
$$\cup \{s' \xrightarrow{(\mathbf{effec}(m_1 \cdots m_{i-1}!m))}_{p \cdot \pi'_{i-2}} u \mid s_i \xrightarrow{m}_p u \wedge \ u \ne s_{n+1} \wedge \ even(i)$$
$$\wedge \ 1 \le i \le n-1\}$$

First we add the even steps of the cloned evolution. Note that in this case probabilities do not change because the second partner is not the one rejecting the shortcut. Then, we also add the corresponding transitions to leave the cloned evolution. Finally, we add both the acceptance of the shortcut proposal and the set of rejections to it. For the rejections, we specify which part was accepted and the probabilities are changed accordingly.   □

Example 2. Let us consider that a shortcut is introduced in the system described in Example 1. Let us suppose that two agents A and B use to share with each other every file they have, always with high priority. Besides, most of the times they want the file to be compressed, but they do not want the integrity of the file to be checked. Let us suppose that this sequence of acts is performed in 95 per cent of times they negotiate. Then, it is clear that the whole trace of transitions performing all of this acts (from the initial request up to the sending of the file) is a good candidate to perform a shortcut. Let σ denote this whole shortcut from the first state. Let us note that, in spite that the first message (the simple request to download) will have to be denoted with a larger code of bits, the average length of symbols will decrease, because symbol σ will be performed most of the times, while the original first transition will be so rare (actually, the original request transition will be performed *only* if the requester does not want to perform σ). As a result, a lot of communications will be saved. Obviously, after the requester proposes σ, the provider can refuse it (though it will also be rare). In this case, depending on the part of σ the provider accepts, it will be conducted to a different state. Besides, if the requester wants to download a file but it does not want to perform σ, the DFSM is conducted to the sequence of *cloned* states. Each cloned state is related to the corresponding state of the original path. The resulting DFSM after the inclusion of the shortcut is depicted in Figure 5. For the sake of clarity, only those transitions directly related to the new states are included. Besides, messages are referred by their initials.   □

4   Conclusions and Future Work

In this paper we have presented a method to reduce the communications in communicating systems and network protocols. By *shortcutting* frequent dialogs, the number of messages needed for performing them is notably reduced. Moreover, not only the number of messages, but also the *size* of them can be reduced (on average) by applying our strategy.

We think that this methodology can be applied to the design of new protocols. However, further research must be done to make our framework completely practical. Besides, the reciprocal influence of shortcuts must be studied. We have provided a method to decide whether we should introduce a single shortcut in a DFSM, but our framework allows to introduce several shortcuts consecutively in the same DFSM.

References

1. B.S. Bosik and M.U. Uyar. Finite state machine based formal methods in protocol conformance testing. *Computer Networks & ISDN Systems*, 22:7–33, 1991.
2. G.J. Holzmann. *Design and Validation of Protocols*. Prentice Hall, 1990.
3. J.E. Hopcroft and J.D. Ullman. *Introduction to Automata Theory, Languages, and Computation*. Addison Wesley, 1979.
4. D.A. Huffman. A method for the construction of minimum redundancy codes. *Proceedings of the Institute of Radio Engineers*, 40(9):1098–1101, 1952.
5. R.P. Kurshan. *Computer-aided Verification of Coordinating Processes*. Princeton University Press, 1995.
6. T.A. Welch. A technique for high-performance data compression. *IEEE Computer*, 17(6):8–19, 1984.
7. J. Ziv and A. Lempel. A universal algorithm for sequential data compression. *IEEE Transactions on Information Theory*, 23(3):337–343, 1977.

Quality of Service on a Distributed Virtual Reality System for Robots Tele-operation over the Internet

M. Patricia Martínez-Vargas[1], Maria E. Meda-Campaña[1],
Victor M. Larios-Rosillo[1], and Francisco Ruíz-Sánchez[2]

[1] Research Center on Systems and Information Management,
Information Systems Department,
CUCEA University of Guadalajara,
Periferico Nte. 799, Mod. L-308, 45100 Zapopan, Jalisco; Mexico
Phone: +52 (33) 37.70.33.52, Fax: +52 (33) 37.70.33.53,
{mmartinez,emeda,vmlarios}@cucea.udg.mx
[2] Sección Mecatrónica Departamento de Ingeniería Eléctrica
CINVESTAV-IPN
A.P 14-740 07300 México D.F., Mexico
Phone: +52 (55) 51 60 37 89, Fax: +52 (55) 51 60 38 66
fruiz@mail.cinvestav.mx

Abstract. Virtual Reality applications for tele-operation are the base for nowadays development of virtual laboratories where researchers can share work at distance. Such systems must support a distributed framework to scale and a good Quality of Service (QoS) support to be effective. This paper proposes such a system, where the aim is the teleoperation of robots for complex cooperation tasks between peers. The system has multimedia components and virtual reality interfaces to control and monitor the real robots state. To ensure the QoS, good politics must be defined to manage the resources of the system to reduce bandwidth consumption over the internet. To apply the QoS policies, an online algorithm is adapted and compared against a greedy version. The online algorithm is taken from a financial set of algorithms used to invest in stock markets. The analogy between stock markets and the QoS control is shown as promising for further applications with QoS support over the internet.

1 Introduction

Multimedia and Virtual Reality applications [8] running over the Internet requires a high demand of connectivity among users communities. These applications are helping to increase the interaction necessary to share work at distance. Therefore, communities can work on complex team tasks for example, to manipulate and to teleoperate physical devices from remote environments with precision and effectiveness. However, one problem to overcome is when using the internet related in how to avoid the possible perturbations of the network produced by latency, jitters and data loss. Hence, the aim is to implement the adequate

T. Böhme et al. (Eds.): IICS 2004, LNCS 3473, pp. 81–90, 2006.

Quality of Service (QoS) management policies, resulting in good communication helping to users to coordinate complex tasks at distance. Moreover, if the users are seen like peers on the internet network, then some works in optimization can be done from the side of each peer to support the QoS.

This paper presents a strategy to dynamically support the QoS of a distributed peer to peer system with the goal to control robots tele-operation over the internet. Such strategy is related and built in from the software level. The organization of the paper is as follows: on section two we give the context of our specific application and the requirements to keep satisfactory conditions for robots tele-operation, on section three we describe the proposed architecture, the communication strategy and the QoS politics to implement; on section four we advance a distributed solution on QoS based in a financial on line-algorithm; on section five, we introduce the obtained results for this work and finally, on section six conclusions are shown as well as the perspectives where we propose future alternatives for QoS development.

2   The Problem Context

Universities and research centers in Mexico are joining efforts to support technologies helping to share resources from physical devices and computers. These resources can be integrated into the concept of Virtual Laboratories, where students and professors can tele-operate interconnected devices through networked virtual reality user interfaces. The University of Guadalajara (UdeG), the Centro de Investigación y de Estudios Avanzados IPN (CINVESTAV) and the Universidad Nacional Autonoma de Mexico (UNAM) are working together, in a collaborative project to support the development of virtual laboratories over the Internet. A first step, was to set up an environment allowing the tele-operation of real robots by means of virtual reality and multimedia applications over the internet.

To drive solutions to increase the coordination and communication among the peers teleoperating the robots, the system is aimed with a virtual reality interface and a video/audio channel on each peer. This configuration, result in an important bandwidth consumption because each peer on the network receives simultaneously the audio/video signals from all other peers and because the virtual reality interface acts like a shared memory where coherence must be kept. Furthermore, the virtual reality interface have one communication line for the robots control and other to feedback force information from robots sensors to be reflected in haptic interfaces. As a case of study, the system intents to control a pair of robots performing a simple writing task on a blackboard (each robot with tree degrees of freedom). While controlling the robots, the main constraint for the communication system is to prevent latency behaviors between peers. The communication bandwidth is used by separate channels related to the robot control data stream, the video/audio inputs and outputs, and the messages for peers management. The control of the system bandwidth consumption is done by deciding the granularity of information packages to send on each channel by means of the QoS online algorithms.

The QoS can be defined as the capacity to provide better network services for application users requirements, providing satisfaction and understandability of all subjective or objective parameter values [5]. The QoS goal is to provide a resource management strategy by priority including policies considering issues like bandwidth, jitter, loss, and latency [4]. This paper is related with the solutions that optimize the use of resources on each peer to deal with the QoS.

One of the main tasks for the virtual laboratory system, is to monitor and to supervise the communication lines over the internet. Thus, the aim is to get a stable communication among peers depending on available information such as bandwidth, latency, jitter, and data loss. To get the best control over these parameters and to ensure the safe tele-operation of robots, is necessary to establish the adequate QoS policies.

Our contribution is to offer an scalable architecture that preserves the QoS and to provide security (by means of stable signals) for the interconnected devices that must be controlled in real time. The system implements the QoS resource control based in policies. Policies are divided in tasks, actions and rules to provide the security and QoS issues.

3   The Architecture of the System

The architecture of the system is shown in figure 1 illustrating collaborative peers tele-operating the robots. Each peer is supported in different communication ports and protocols like the RTP (Real Time Protocol) for video, audio and Virtual Reality updates and like the TCP/IP protocol for the system administration messages. There are different kinds of peers states that can be settled as: *device tele-operation state, device master control state* and *observer state*. Tele-operation state is only possible when a haptic device is present to control at distance one robot through the Virtual Reality interface. Video and audio are available to look other peers participating in the tele-operation session. The device master state is the peer where the real robots are interconnected and controlled. This master peer, get control instructions from the tele-operation peers and has a virtual reality interface also with audio-video channels. The video channels are implemented for security to check that the real state of robots is coherent against the virtual reality interface. The robots sensors send force feedback information to the haptic devices. Finally, the observer state belongs to each additional peer that is not going to tele-operate any device and just only wants to observe via the virtual reality interface the cooperation tasks.

The system is OS independent via the Java Virtual Machine with a dependency only from the C++ programs to support the data acquisition cards for sensors and the interconnected haptic devices. Such program interfaces are supported by the Java Native Interface. However, for these devices the most frequent OS systems are linux and windows for the available drivers and libraries in C++ or C, on the external hardware devices used.

Video confering is supported by the java media framework library and an implementaton of the RTP protocol that is used both for video and virtual reality updates. The virtual reality interface is built in the top of the Java 3D library

with support for sterographic devices. An administration module is implemented
to manage the security on the system, validate the users and have a general
overview of the other peers via the TCP/IP protocol. Finally, there is a QoS
module that implements the QoS policies and that is able to connect/disconnect
or reduce the bandwith consumption of all the networked peers in order to
preserve the QoS. This module can load different kinds of algorithms to improve
the performance of the QoS policies decisions to take. In this paper, we are
presenting two algorithms, one online and another determinist called greedy.

Next section will shown the policies to apply on the system before start
explaining the QoS algorihms implementation.

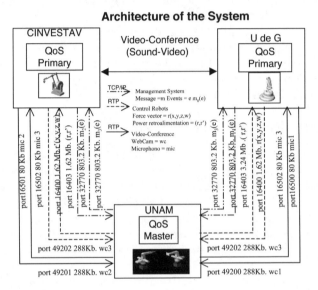

Fig. 1. The VE is partitioned in regions managed by a cluster

3.1   QoS Adaptation Policy

To manipulate efficiently the system resources for the QoS application support;
in general terms we have defined the following policies on each pear:

- A robots control stream always has a higher priority to use network bandwidth, CPU and other related resources than a video stream.
- An Audio stream always has higher priority to use network bandwidth, compared with the video stream.
- To avoid the QoS oscillation, the QoS system self-adaptation only performs
  quality-degrading activity.
- The system may perform quality-upgrading adaptation under receivers requests. The receiver request will be made using the administration channel.

The correct selection of the required QoS policy will depend on the latency
of the system and also on the current system state. A system state involves the

state variables of each one of the peer to peer connections of the application. In our case these state variables are Video (V) and Audio (A), the associated values of these states variables are the following:

Normal Video	NV
Degraded Video	DV
Without Video	WV
Normal Audio	NA
Degraded Video	DA
Without Audio	WA

Notice that these states variables describe the performance of each one of the peer to peer connections of the application, for instance we are considering three peer to peer connections: 1) UNAM-CINVESTAV, 2) UNAM-UdeG and 3) UdeG-CINVESTAV, if we are monitoring the UNAM-UdeG connection then it is possible that the latency reaches high values, in this case the state variable V takes the DV value. However, the situation in another peer to peer connection could be different and the state variable V in this connection could take another value.

Given the architecture of the application, the QoS policies will be implemented by peer to peer connection considering its latency in the video-conference channel and its state variables. This is illustrated on figure 2.

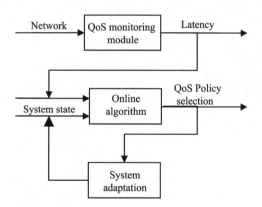

Fig. 2. QoS policies process

Following are described each one of the QoS policies.

a) QoS policies when the latency value is less than 15 ms.

1. NV Continuing in same state;
2. DV Upgrade video under receiver request;
3. WV Open video session under receiver request;
4. NA Continuing in the same state;
5. WA Open audio session under receiver request;

b) QoS policies when the latency value is in the interval $15 \leq L \prec 17ms$.
6. NV Degrading video;
7. DV Continuing in same state;
8. WV Open video session under receiver request in a degrading mode;
9. NA Continuing in the same state;
10. WA Open audio session under receiver request;

c) QoS policies when the latency value is in the interval $17 \leq L \prec 19ms$.
11. NV Close video session;
12. DV Close video session;
13. WV Continuing in the same state;
14. NA Close audio session;
15. WA Continuing in the same state;

d) QoS Policies when the latency value is in the interval $19 \leq L \prec 20ms$
Send warning messages over the administration channel

e) QoS policies when the latency value is greater or equal than 20 ms.
16. NV Close video session;
17. DV Close video session;
18. WV Continuing in the same state;
19. NA Close audio session;
20. WA Continuing in the same state;

The automatas representing the change of values of the states variables video
and audio given a latency value are depicted on figures 3 and 4 respectively.

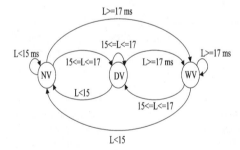

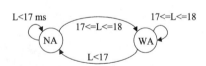

Fig. 3. Automata representing the values taken by state variable video (V) given any latency value

Fig. 4. Automata representing the values taken by state variable audio (A) given any latency value

4   The Distributed Solution in QoS

An important component to control the QoS is the network monitor which provides as a return value the latency between peers. Latency is estimated as the
time for one package to travel from one peer to another. To avoid transients
on the latency lectures, the monitor also implements statistical functions to get

some form of average latency providing a final value to be used by an online algorithm which is the responsible of taking the optimal decisions to apply the QoS policies.

An online algorithm is defined as one that must produce a sequence of decisions on incoming inputs based only in past with out knowledge about the future [6]. Controlling the QoS of an application is an intrinsically online problem. The study of online algorithms include concepts of scheduling, optimization, data structures, game theory, combinatorial problems and other computational topics. The framework of online algorithms includes the approach of competitive analysis where the quality of an online algorithm is measured against an optimal offline algorithm which is an unrealizable algorithm that has the knowledge of all the future. Competitive analysis falls in the framework of worst case complexity.

One way to analyze the algorithm is to view the online problem as a game between an online player and a malicious adversary. The online player runs the online algorithm over an input created by the adversary. The adversary, based on the knowledge of the algorithm used by the online player tries to put the worst input to make the decision task costly for the online algorithm and to minimize its competitive ratio.

Our original idea is to relate the problem of QoS to an online financial problem where the online player seek to invest its wealth among a number of investment opportunities in the most profitable way [3]. In our problem, the online player look for the network state and must decide which QoS policy to apply based on the online network latency measure. The network can be seen as a market of s securities that can be stocks, bonds, currencies or commodities. Each security has a price that fluctuates with the time and depending on the price (related for us as the online latency measure), the online player must decide to buy or sell a QoS policy in order to get a trading strategy that keeps a wealth in our system or in other words, that keeps the QoS. If the latency start to increase its value, the system must sell its services applying a policy that means to decrease the use of bandwidth in communications. Moreover, if the latency goes down on its value means that the price is good to buy and is related to apply again a QoS policy to connect or increase the use of communication components to increase the QoS to the optimal level. If the algorithm have not an optimal performance on decisions, the system may operate with a negative profit called loss but in the contrary keep a good QoS means a profit.

The adapted algorithm for the QoS control is based on a Money Making online trading strategy from [2]. On such strategy, we must define market sequences by relative prices as $X = x_1, x_2, ..., x_{n-1}$. This market sequence is related in the system to a set of lectures from the network monitor. Fixing $n \geq 2$, assume that each feasible sequence is of length n and impose the restriction that the optimal offline return associated with an online sequence is at least ϕ where $\phi \geq 1$. Is not difficult to see that ϕ can be obtained as $\phi = \prod_{1 \leq i \leq n-1} \max\{1, x_i\}$ Consider the following algorithm wich is defined recursively in terms of (n, ϕ). Use $R_n(\phi)$ to denote the return of the algorithm for a n period sequence. The algorithm is decribed as follows:

Algorithm: if n = 2, invest the entire wealth and otherwise invest b units in QoS policies where

$$R_2(\phi) = \phi$$

$$R_n = \max_{0 \leq b \leq 1} \inf_{x \leq \phi} \{(b_x + 1 - b)R_{n-1}(\phi_{n-1})\}$$

The b units is a probability number meaning the trustability on a market and in the case of our QoS application, is related to the network stability. If b is higher, it means that the network is in bad state and that is necessary to invest in more QoS policies to optimize the use of communication lines. Depending on the value of R_n we have a set of ranges meaning the policy by priority to invest. So, to lower values of R_n the policy is less aggressive in terms of resources to reduce in use.

On next section we will compare this algorithm with a Greedy one, which structure is very simple taking also its input online. Then, Greedy gets an average from a set of lectures (equivalent to the market sequence for the Money Making algorithm) and directly maps to a QoS policy.

5   Experimental Results

To test the proposed algorithm a set of 50000 inputs taken from the internet and representing time of data traveling in milliseconds between two peers. The market sequences were organized in packages of 10 inputs where both Greedy and Money Making algorithms started. The Greedy makes an average of the 10 lectures and then maps the value to a table pointing to the QoS policy to apply. In the case of the Money Making algorithm the result from R_n is scaled and adapted to map it to the QoS policy table. Also, for Money Making the value $b = 0.4$ was set to have a conservative output. All the algorithms and programs where implemented in Java using the UDP protocol to manage the data packages. The obtained result in cost (added and accumulated value when a policy must be applied) is shown in figure 5.

It can be seen that the cost of the Money Making algorithm is over 2000 compared against Greedy that grows faster with the time.

6   Concluding Remarks and Perspectives

This paper presented a strategy to control the QoS of a peer to peer application with the aim to tele-operate robots. One of the main problems is related to preserve the stability of the communication lines by priority where the proposed solution deals with resource management and optimization by reducing bandwidth consumption of the peers in the system. This issue drives to identify and build the QoS policies for the system and then to find an algorithm to have an optimal use of policies to get the QoS. The optimal algorithm is taken from a financial online algorithm where the paper shows how it was related and applied

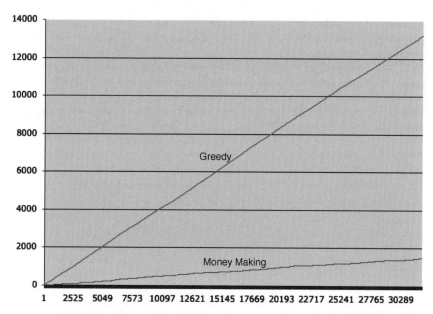

Fig. 5. Accumulated cost between a Greedy and a Money Making for the QoS system where horizontal axis represents the inputs of network latency and vertical axis the accumulated cost per choosing a policy

to the QoS system. The use of the financial recursive algorithm Money Making in QoS open a framework for future works to improve the QoS under different conditions of the network where some parameters can be better adapted as the b factor for the reliability of the network that was fixed as a constant. Other algorithm can detect the network state and adapt a better value for b. Another work to continue is to compare not only greedy but different families of online algorithms (deterministic and random) to improve the system and study how can help the optimization of resources among communities of hundred of users.

References

1. Borodin, A., El-Yaniv, R.: Online Computation and Competitive Analysis. Cambridge University Press (1998)
2. A. Chou, J. R. Cooperstock, R. El-Yaniv, M. Klugerman, and T. Leighton The statistical adversary allows optimal money-making trading strategies In proceedings of the 6th annual ACM/SIAM Symposium on discrete algorithms, 1995.
3. Competitive solutions for online financial problems ACM Computing surveys, Vol30 No.1 March 1998
4. Quality of Service Networking www.cisco.com/univercd/cc/td/doc/cisintwk/ito-doc/qos.html Cisco, December 2003.
5. Kalkbrenner, Gerrit., Pirkmayer, Teodor., Dornik, Arnd, Van., Hofmann, Peter.: Quality of Service (QoS) in Distributed Hypermedia-System Technical University of Berlin, IEEE, (1995)

6. Manasse, M. S., McGeoch, L.A., Sleator, D.D.: Competitive Algorithms for On-Line Problems. Proceedings of the 20th Annual ACM Symposium On Theory of Computing (1988) 322–333
7. Park, K.S., Kenyon, R.V.: Effects of Network Characteristics on Human Performance in a Collaborative Virtual Environment. Proceedings of the IEEE VRAIS 99 Houston Texas, USA, March (1999) 104–110
8. Singhal, S., Zyda, M.: Networked Virtual Environments: Design and Implementation. ACM Press SIGGRAPH Series - Addison Wesley, New York (1999)

A First Approach to Build Product Lines of Multi-organizational Web Based Systems (MOWS)⋆

David Benavides[1], Antonio Ruiz-Cortés[1],
Miguel A. Serrano[2], and Carlos Montes de Oca Vázquez[2]

[1] Departamento de Lenguajes y Sistemas Informáticos,
E.T.S.Ingenieros Informáticos,
Universidad de Sevilla,
Avda. ReinaMercedes s/n, 41012 Sevilla, España
benavides@us.es, aruiz@lsi.us.es
[2] Centro de Investigación en Matemáticas
AP 402, Guanajuato, Gto., CP 36000, México
{masv,moca}@cimat.mx

Abstract. From the recent past and current state of the Internet, it is possible to
forecast a wide growing of Multi Organizational Web–based Systems (MOWS).
Therefore, the reduction of both costs and time–to–market is desirable. On the
other hand, the success of building software in Product Lines (PL) is being demonstrated in different contexts reducing both time–to–market and costs. However,
research on PL topics has not been oriented to include web–based assets. In this
article, we propose a first approach to use PL methodologies to build MOWS. We
identify quality aspects as a key point when building Product Lines of MOWS and
we give a way to specify quality aspects in PL.

1 Introduction

The term "Product Line" (PL) was first introduced in 1976 by David Parnas [13] and it
has been widely studied in Universities and in the industry since then [12,16]. The PL
concept means that similar products share a common set of components and functionality
(called core assets) and still, each individual product have some functionality specific to
it (variable part). For the software industry, it is a good approach since similar parts (e.g.
those belonging to the core assets) are developed only once and reused since then. The
goal for organizations that follow a PL development approach is to be able to develop
their products, by developing the variable parts only, and not developing the whole
product.

MOWS have been described in [14] as a particular case of federated systems [1]
or work–flows with multiple organizations [7]. The main difference between federated
systems and MOWS is that in federated systems providers are often reduced in number,
known beforehand and do not change along the system life–cycle. In MOWS, providers
are numerous, they are not necessarily known a priori and they can change along the
system life–cycle.

⋆ This work was partially funded by the Spanish Ministry of Science and Technology under grant
TIC2003-02737-C02-01 (WEBMADE)

T. Böhme et al. (Eds.): IICS 2004, LNCS 3473, pp. 91–98, 2006.
© Springer-Verlag Berlin Heidelberg 2006

Until now, PL engineering has not taken into account web–based assets. At the same time, a process to build MOWS reducing both time–to–market and costs is not well defined. In this paper, we propose a first approach that uses PL engineering when building MOWS. The products in the PL are composed by web–based assets offered by providers on the Internet. In this article, we focus on giving a step ahead to use PL methodologies to build MOWS pointing out the importance of quality aspects. In addition, we propose an approach to specify quality aspects in product lines.

The paper is organized as follows. In section 2, we give an introduction to MOWS. In Section 3, we briefly explain the PL concept and we mention some of the benefits of this approach. In Section 4, we present our approach to build PL of MOWS. Finally, in section 5, we present conclusions and related work.

2   MOWS in a Nutshell

The incredible success of the Internet has paved the way for an industry devoted to developing and running web services, which some authors tend to describe as the core of the next–generation Internet. Web services bring programmers a new way to develop advanced applications that are able to integrate a group of services available on the Internet into a single solution. These systems have been defined as Multi–Organizational Web–based System (MOWS) [5,14].

The reason why many experts forecast such a change from site-centric applications to web-service-based applications is the recent bankrupt of dotcoms. They have failed, not because of a lack of customers, but because of a lack of plans to make profit on them. In the near future, profit will be as important as ever, but the model will change from one based on competition to one based on collaboration. The success of the overall collaboration will lead the way to the success of each of the individual units.

We provide an example to illustrate MOWS. Consider that someone is interested in setting up a web portal specialized in providing movies. The portal offers a potentially infinite catalog of films and the same functionality as a domestic video player. The portal has three kinds of web services: a service for streaming videos over the Internet, a service for managing catalogs and keeping them up-to-date, and a service for managing virtual shops. Consequently, the portal becomes a service that integrates other more basic services that are provided by other organizations.

3   Product Lines in a NutShell

PL engineering has been widely used in several industries such as hardware or telecom-munications. For instance, there are PL of processors that share some commonalities but still each processor has some specific characteristics. However, the PL approach has not been widely adopted in the software industry [4].

The PL concept means that in an industry there are a set of products sharing a common part, called core assets, and each of those products adds a set of specific characteristics, called variable parts. PL is a promising approach to achieve one of the main goals of software engineering which is software reuse.

It has been said that PL engineering is a good approach for product–oriented organizations [2], which have a well known market domain. PL engineering might not be suitable for organizations that are project-oriented because each project might have a different domain.

A PL includes an application domain, where PL engineering is applied, and assets that cover the derivation of products of such domain. An asset is a partial solution such as a component, a design document, or knowledge that engineers use to build or modify software products in PL [18]. The term 'domain' may have different meanings for the customers and the software engineers. We refer to domain in the same way that Bosch does [2]. He makes difference between *application domain* and *software domain*.

- *Application domain* is the definition from the customer's point of view where they refer to the product as a whole as being part of a particular domain. For instance, a word processor can be considered as part of the domain of building office suits software.
- *Software domain* is the definition from the software engineers' point of view where they refer to the product that may belong to different domains. For instance, the word processor may contain functions from different domains such as graphical user interfaces, text parsing, spell checking, etc.

3.1 Activities

There are three main activities in product line engineering: core assets development (also found in the literature as domain engineering), product development from core assets (also found in the literature as application engineering), and management tasks (the interaction between the first two activities). Core asset development is the part of the process where the analysis, design, and management of the assets of the application domain is done. Product development deals with the derivation or construction of new products from the different assets in the application domain. If there is a part of a product that is needed and it does not exist in the application domain, it may be developed, bought, rented or even shared from other domain. An optimal state for organizations would be to put most of the effort on core asset development activities and to put minimal effort on product development. Unfortunately, this situation does not happen often.

3.2 Example: A PL of Web Videos

We use the example of a web video provider mentioned in section 2 to illustrate a PL. The set of core assets are those that give the functionality of streaming videos on the Internet, manage catalogs and keep them up-to-date, and manage virtual shops. There could be a product line in this application domain. One product could offer access trough mobile phones, another could offer access trough digital TVs or other similar devices with different format. Both products share the same core and each of them has a variable part. The organization offering this service would be clearly product-oriented since it is specialized in a specific application domain. Once the set of core assets are developed, the main activities will be addressed to integrate a short amount of assets covering the variable part of each different product.

3.3 Benefits

PL approach has several benefits:

- Cost reduction because of assets reuse.
- A reduction of time–to–market because once the core assets are developed it takes less time to produce a new product.
- Many activities of the product life-cycle are shared among the products in the PL.
- There are common requirements, architecture, models, planning and so on.
- It is predictable that a quality improvement will appear due to the reduction of rework.

The main weakness we have identified in this approach is that if an organization wants to follow a PL approach, a large amount of work has to be carried out beforehand (e.g., defining the set of core assets, processes, architecture, common requirements).

4   Our Approach

Up to now, there have not been efforts to create a methodology to develop PL of MOWS. We propose a first approach to build MOWS in PL that follows three steps:

1. Include web–based assets in PL.
2. Study the impact of including web-based assets in the PL methodology.
3. Identify and specify quality aspects in the PL.

Our approach brings together two separates worlds of software engineering: MOWS and PL. We use PL to improve the techniques to produce MOWS and to profit from benefits of the PL approach such as cost and time-to-market reduction and quality improvement.

Our approach offers two important benefits:

- Reuse of components when developing MOWS.
- Reduction of work in core asset development because some of the core assets could be rented or outsourced.

Following with the example of a web video provider, it is possible to identify an application domain in this context and some parts that appear in all the products of this PL. Three kinds of web services, at least, will shape the set of core assets: a
service for streaming video on the Internet, a service for managing catalogs and keeping them up–to–date and a service for selling videos. From this base, it is possible to define different products in the PL. Movies could be visualized through mobile phones or through digital TVs. They are two different products addressed to different customers. Moreover, they share a set of common core assets and they have variable parts (e.g., a web video server or a mobile video server).

Features diagrams are used in the literature and industry to specify PL [6,8,11,9,17]. This type of diagram specifies a PL differentiating the common and variable parts.

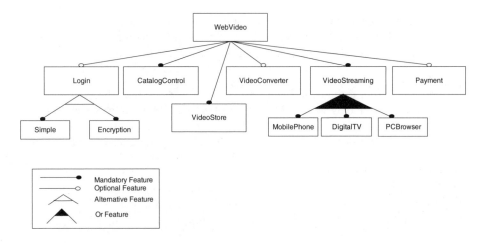

Fig. 1. Feature Model of a PL of Web Videos

In figure 1, we use the notation proposed in [6, pag. 86] to clarify our example. In this notation, there are four types of relations between features:

– Or-features: an or-feature of a set of or-features may be present in a feature model instance if its parent feature is included. Then, one or more features of the set may be present. It has the same meaning of an OR logical relation.

– **Mandatory features:** a mandatory feature is present in a feature model instance when its parent feature is present.
– **Optional Feature:** an optional feature may or may not be present in a feature model instance when its parent feature appears.
– **Alternative Features:** an alternative feature of a set of alternative features may be present in a feature model instance if its parent feature is included. Then, exactly one feature of the set is present. It has the same meaning of a XOR logical relation.
– **Or-features:** an or–feature of a set of or–features may be present in a feature model instance if its parent feature is included. Then, one or more features of the set may be present. (It has the same meaning of an OR logical relation).

In this example of a Product Line of Multi–Organizational Web–Based System (MOWS-PL), it is possible to define different products. In figure 1, there are five parts where different decisions define the set of possible products:

– First decision refers to whether to include a login service (optional feature) or not.
– Second decision implies to have a product in the video server with an image converter service or without it (optional feature).
– Third decision: if the login service has been including in the product, it will be a simple login service or an encrypted login service. In this case it is possible to decide only one option (alternative features).
– Forth decision represents the possibility of having visualization through a mobile phone, or a web browser or a PC Internet browser. However, it is possible to decide on having one or more services at the same time (or-features).

- Last decision represents the possibility of including a payment functionality (notice the possible dependency between this feature and the login feature. If a virtual payment is needed, an encrypted login service might be needed. This complex problem about dependencies is out of the scope of this paper).

With the present technologies and web services provided over the Internet, every feature of the feature diagram can be implemented by a web service. Several services interacting at the same time conform a MOWS, therefore it is possible to define a MOWS Product Line (MOWS–PL). As discussed in section 2, a particularity of MOWS is that providers are not necessary known beforehand and may change along the system life cycle. Thus, the key point that differentiate product lines using MOWS from those using local components, is that quality aspects of the features become more important. The functionality represented by a feature may be provided by more than one service, the decision of which service will provide the specific functionality is going to be based on quality aspects.

Up to now, we have not found any proposal in which quality aspects have been taken into account when specifying PL. With the inclusion of web–assets, the quality aspects become fundamental. Therefore, quality aspects need a specific way to describe them.

We propose to augment the feature diagram of figure 1 with quality features. In figure 2 only a fragment (Video Streaming) of the diagram is presented because of space constraints.

To be understandable, a feature diagram that includes quality information, must be accompanied with a catalogue of attributes describing the quality features. In figure 2, the catalogue is defined using the QRL (*Quality Requirement Language* notation [14]. Furthermore, we use discontinuous lines in quality features to distinguish between functional and quality features.

A quality feature is directly related to a quality attribute. Nevertheless, the values of these attributes should not appear in the feature model because different instances of the PL can have different values for each quality feature.

5   Conclusions and Related Work

There is a significant amount of research done about PL issues. The European research project, called CAFE [16] [16] whose main research area is on PL, has the collaboration of some of the most important organizations with representation in Europe. However, they have not addressed the introduction of web-based assets in PL.

There are some works in the literature suggesting the need of dealing with quality features. Kang *et. al* [9, pag. 38] suggested the need of taking into account quality features since 1990, when they described a classification of features. Later in 1998 Kang *et. al* [10] made an explicit reference to what they called 'non-functional' features (i.e., quality features or extra–functional features). However the authors proposed to include in the same model both functional and non-functional features without making any distinction in the model between them. Later in 2001 Kang *et. al* [3], proposed some guidelines for feature modeling. The authors made a distinction between functional and quality features and pointed out the need of an specific method to include quality features. However, they did not provide an specific way to do it.

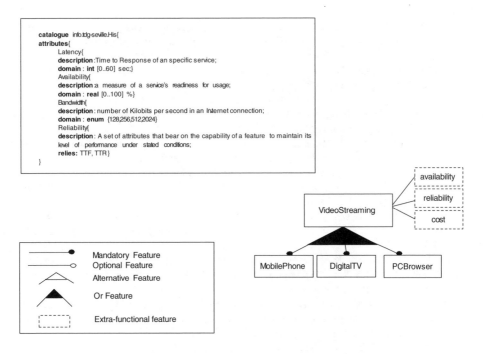

Fig. 2. Fragment of a feature model including quality features

In [15], the authors made a distinction between functional and what they called "parameters". The authors marginally introduced a way to deal with this kind of features. There is a drawback in this proposal: the authors proposed to include the values of the parameters in the feature model. With this proposal, the possible instances of the PL are limited to the values specified in the feature model. In this paper we introduced a way to specify quality features separating the definition of this kind of features at feature level and the range of values at instance level.

Any of the previous works was not focused on the inclusion of web-based assets. They only marginally describe the need of coping with quality features without giving an specific way to do so. In this paper, we identified that quality might become a major research topic when building Product Lines of MOWS (MOWS–PL). We have given a brief description of our approach to deal with quality features in MOWS-PL. We are currently working on implementing automated support tools for the derivations of products in MOWS–PL. This automates support will take into account quality issues.

References

1. P. Bhoj, S. Shingal, and S. Chutani. SLA management in federated environments. *Computer Networks*, 35:5–24, 2001.
2. J. Bosch. *Design and Use of Software Architectures*. Addison-Wesley, 1th edition, 2000.

3. G. Chastek, P. Donohoe, K.C. Kang, and S. Thiel. Product Line Analysis: A Practical Intro-duction. Technical Report CMU/SEI-2001-TR-001, Software Engineering Institute, Carnegie Mellon University, June 2001.
4. P.C. Clements and L. Northrop. *Software Product Lines: Practices and Patterns*. SEI Series in Software Engineering. Addison–Wesley, August 2001.
5. R. Corchuelo, A. Ruiz-Cortés, J. Mühlbacher, and J.D. García-Consuegra. Object–Oriented Business Solutions. In *Chapter 18 of ECOOP'2001 Workshop Reader, LNCS nº 2323*, pages 184–200. Springer–Verlag, 2002.
6. K. Czarnecki and U.W. Eisenecker. *Generative Programming: Methods, Techniques, and Applications*. Addison–Wesley, may 2000. ISBN 0–201–30977–7.
7. P. Grefen, K. Aberer, Y. Hoffner, and H. Ludwig. CrossFlow: Cross–organizational workflow management in dynamic virtual enterprises. *International Journal of Computer Systems Science & Engineering*, 15(5):277–290, 2000.
8. M. Griss, J. Favaro, and M. d'Alessandro. Integrating feature modeling with the RSEB. In *Proceedings of theFifthInternational Conference on Software Reuse*, pages 76–85, Canada, 1998.
9. K. Kang, S. Cohen, J. Hess, W. Novak, and S. Peterson. Feature–Oriented Domain Analysis (FODA) Feasibility Study. Technical Report CMU/SEI-90-TR-21, Software Engineering Institute, Carnegie Mellon University, November 1990.
10. K.C. Kang, S. Kim, J. Lee, K. Kim, E. Shin, and M. Huh. FORM: A feature–oriented reuse method with domain–specific reference architectures. *Annals of Software Engineering*, 5:143–168, 1998.
11. K.C. Kang, J. Lee, and P. Donohoe. Feature–Oriented Product Line Engineering. *IEEE Software*, 19(4):58–65, July/August 2002.
12. L. Northrop. SEI's Software Product Line Tenets. *IEEE Software*, 19(4):32–40, July/August 2002.
13. D.L. Parnas. On the design and development of program families. *IEEE Transactions on Software Engineering*, SE-2(1):1–9, March 1976.
14. A. Ruiz-Cortés, R. Rorchuelo, A. Duran, and M. Toro. Automated Support for Quality Requirements in Web-Services-Based Systems. In *Proc. of the 8th IEEE Workshop on Future Trends of Distributed Computing Systems (FTDCS'2001)*, pages 184–200. IEEE-CS Press, 2001.
15. D. Streitferdt, M. Riebisch, and I. Philippow. Details of formalized relations in feature models using ocl. In *Proceedings of 10th IEEE International Conference on Engineering of Computer–Based Systems (ECBS 2003), Huntsville, USA. IEEE Computer Society*, pages 45–54, 2003.
16. F. van der Linden. Software product families in Europe: The Esaps & Café Projects. *IEEE Software*, 19(4):41–49, 2002.
17. J. van Gurp, J. Bosch, and M. Svahnberg. On the notion of variability in software product lines. In *Proceedings of the Working IEEE/IFIP Conference on Software Architecture (WICSA'01), IEEE Computer Society*, pages 45–54, 2001.
18. J. Withey. Investment Analysis of Software Assets for Product Lines. Technical Report CMU/SEI-96-TR-010, Software Engineering Institute, Carnegie Mellon University, November 1996.

New Technical Services Using the Component Model for Applications in Heterogeneous Environment

Colombe Herault, Sylvain Lecomte, and Thierry Delot

LAMIH/ROI/SID, UMR CNRS 8530 University of Valenciennes
Le Mont Houy, 59313 Valenciennes Cedex 9 France
{colombe.herault,sylvain.lecomte,thierry.delot}
@univ-valenciennes.fr

Abstract. Nowadays, execution environments of applications are more and more heterogeneous: from powerful servers to smart cards. In order to assume the heterogeneity and the portability of applications, the component–based model has emerged as a model to develop new distributed applications. Thus, these applications are built as an assembly of interchangeable software blocks. Nevertheless, the gain of adaptability that comes from the use of component does not stretch to non-functional services (such as transaction management, security, etc). So, we suggest complementing the existing solution by facilitating the adaptability of non-functional services to their environment. Therefore, we propose to design a non-functional service as composition of small components. Besides, it is possible to supply the most appropriate version of a non-functional service to an application. So, in our approach, the application is composed by assembling both business components and non-functional components.

1 Introduction

Today, computers in distributed systems are more and more heterogeneous. These computers may be very powerful servers, but also personal computers, personal digital assistants, mobile phones, smart cards and so on. In such environments, the programmers of new distributed applications have to manage the heterogeneity, and to assume the portability of their applications. A good solution to achieve this is to use the programming component model. An application is then realised by assembling business components. In addition, a component may be replaced by another, to fit with the terminal requirement.

However, current component based platforms do not take into account the adaptability to the environment for non-functional services. These services (for example: transaction management, security, services localisation, etc...) facilitate to users the management of some specifics tasks and the application development. These services are essential to assume an easy application deployment on distributed terminals.

The aim of this paper is to propose a solution to adapt non-functional services to their environment. In section 2, we present the new needs for distributed applications deployed on heterogeneous environments. Then, section 3 presents the component model, which allows to develop an application, by assembling existing components. This model provides more flexibility in the conception of distributed application. In section 4, we present non-functional services, and explain how these services facili-

T. Böhme et al. (Eds.): IICS 2004, LNCS 3473, pp. 99–110, 2006.

tate the task of the programmer in distributed application. At the end of this section, we highlight the major drawbacks of classical non-functional services in applications based on the component model. In this section, we illustrate our purpose with the example of lookup services, which can be very different depending to the protocol used and the terminals capacities. Finally, in section 5, we propose to use the component model itself, to realise new non-functional services, based on the assembly of small components, to facilitate the adaptation of a non-functional services for a specific environment. Then, a complete distributed application will be an assembly of business components and non-functional components.

2   New Needs for Applications

The emergence of both handheld devices and wireless networks has implied an exponential increase of terminals users [1]. Today, users can be connected to distributed applications by using:

- Personal computers at home or/and at their office. These users may also share data between their computer at home and the computer at their office which are usually more powerful (storage capacity, CPU power, etc) and are connected to the Internet using a permanent connection (LAN or ADSL).
- Handled devices: thanks to such devices, users can retrieve their information anywhere and anytime. Basically, handheld devices characterise small terminals such as Personal Digital Assistants (PDA), pocket PC or cellular phones. These devices offer communication functionalities, storage capacity, I/O unit and display facilities.
- Many other computers at home, such as a SetTopBox used for the digital and interactive television, digital cameras, game consoles, MP3 readers, etc, which share a lot of characteristics with handled devices.

The use of many computers by a same user is known as the *ubiquitous computing* [2,3]. However, to develop scalable applications in ubiquitous environments, it is necessary to consider several drawbacks, notably due to the heterogeneity of this environment. Moreover, Thanks to the evolutions of mobile and wireless networks, new proximity services can be proposed to handheld devices users [4], which are deployed in highly distributed environments, to offer new devices use perspectives to users. In this case, application development has to become more generic and flexible.

An example of application is proposed in figure 1. This application is based on a classical auction service. However, the user executes this application by using several kinds of terminals. Each one of these terminals has specific characteristics (the mobile phone uses a Wireless LAN and has a confined execution environment, the SetTop-Box uses specific connection to the network, with a high rate download link, and a low rate upload link, and so on).

The ubiquitous computing is also used in the health context since it can help health professionals to consult important data when they are at home, at the hospital or anywhere else. Mobile devices can be used either by health professionals or by patients. Homecare represents a very interesting field of application and evaluation of wireless technologies [5]. First, let us consider that the patient's health information is stored on the patient HAN (the remarks of patient close relatives) and doctor, fitted with a

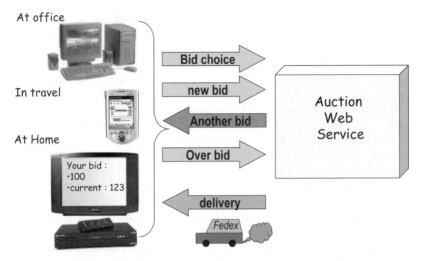

Fig. 1. Auction services in heterogeneous environment

handheld device such as a PDA, making his/her house calls. When he/she goes to a patient, he/she recovers the health information about this patient. Then, based on all the information, the doctor can make a diagnostic more easily. Finally, he/she updates the patient electronic health record stored on a patient's smart card.

In this kind of applications, due to the heterogeneous context, the programmer has to adapt its application to each terminal. Moreover, these clients do not use the same non-functional services. For example, you can not use the same security protocol on a personal computer and on a mobile phone or a PDA. So, today, a lot of non-functional services have to be adapted to the application participants.

3 An Overview of the Component Model

Today, platforms based on the component model facilitate the development of distributed applications in heterogeneous environments. These platforms allow to better distribute the different tasks necessary to develop an application. The business logic of the application (that will run on the application server) and presentation layers are notably separated in three tier architectures. In this part, we begin with a general description of the component-based programming model. Then, we describe existing component-based platforms.

3.1 Component-Based Models

A component is an autonomous and intelligent software module. It can be run on different networks, using different operating systems [6]. A component is described by one or more interface(s), by configurable properties (to personalize the component) and technical constraints (for example, security or transactional needs). To be used, a component provides interfaces, which describe its features, and uses the interfaces of one or more components. This process is called assembly of components.

In component-based applications, each business activities defines its own set of components. For instance, the developer of the bank application will create specific components for the payment. This solution assures a better tasks distribution. Indeed, developers of each "community" propose the piece of software that they know perfectly. Then, operational applications are simply obtained by assembling existing components.

To be used, a component must be deployed on an application server, which may contain several containers and proposes non-functional services, as the transactional service, the persistency service or the security service. These services are configured and parameterised during the deployment of the component. The code of a component only contains the business logic. The deployment of the application consists in configuring data sources, the distribution of tasks on a given execution platform, the policy of security, and so on, for a given assembly of components. Once deployed, the component is managed by a container. This container provides to the component all the services necessary for a correct execution.

A customer accesses a component using its interface. A component can also use one or more other components through their interfaces. These components can be managed either by the same container or by distinct ones.

3.2 Existing Platforms

Today, there are four main component-based platforms:

- Microsoft .NET: The .NET platform [7] is the last evolution of component-based platforms proposed by Microsoft© and started with COM (Component Object Model [8]) in Windows environment. This platform is very influenced by Web Services [7] and uses Web technologies to assure interoperability (SOAP [9] for the transport of requests, UDDI/WSDL [10, 11] for service location and XML for data management).
- CORBA Component Model (CCM [12]) is a very recent specification promoted by OMG. This specification provides the richest component model. However, there is no complete implementation of the CCM specification available on the market for the moment. The CCM platform relies on CORBA technology, both for transport protocols (IIOP/GIOP) and "non-functional" services (Naming, Transaction, Security, etc.).
- Enterprise Java Beans (EJB[13]): Numerous implementations of Sun's EJB specification have been proposed such as IBM WebSphere [14] or JONAS [15] promoted by the ObjectWeb consortium. The EJB model essentially relies on Sun's technologies (RMI/GIOP for the transport of requests). Nevertheless, some of the services proposed are inspired from the CORBA world.
- Frameworks for the assembly of components: FRACTAL [16, 17] and AVALON [18] are frameworks of composition of components: a Fractal component allows a dynamic composability i.e. a composition of components is seen as a component itself. Moreover, thanks to different controllers, it is possible to monitor the constitution and the bindings of composite components, which are explicit and exposed. Thus, the system has a representation of itself. It also allows one component to be shared by two compositions of components. An implementation of the

FRACTAL model, called Julia, is proposed by the Objectweb consortium. AVALON is a service-oriented component model. The provided implementation of AVALON is Excalibur proposed by Apache.

With all these platforms, the programming of business services is largely facilitated.

Moreover, these applications can use non-functional services to facilitate the application management (localisation services, such as Naming or Trading, Transaction services to assume data coherence and fault tolerance, security services, and so on). However, currently, existing non-functional services are not adapted to new heterogeneous environments such as those described in section 2. In the following section, we present the non-functional services used in component platforms, as well as their major drawbacks.

4 Non-functional Services and the Component Model

Non-functional services (also called technical services) are used to assume specific tasks in distributed applications. A non-functional service is a service that does not add new functionality to the infrastructure but a better quality of service (QoS). They can be used by all the components of the service implementation. Non-functional services are provided by the middleware and the component container. Each one of the quoted component models provides its own implementation of non-functional services. In this section, we present the different classes of non-functional services in the component-based platforms presented in the previous section. Then, we study the major drawbacks of current implementations of these technical services.

4.1 Non-functional Services in Component-Based Model

We can classify non-functional services defined in the component model in four distinct categories:

- Interactions between components: In this category, we find the services which allow components to interact and/or to collaborate (distribution management, synchronous transport requests, asynchronous transport requests, ...)
- Life cycle management: These services allow to manage the component life cycle (deployment, activation, execution, destruction). In this category, we also find localisation services, such as Naming or Trading Services.
- Information system management: These high level non-functional services allow data persistence, transaction management, security, ...
- Quality of service: These services include load balancing, synchronisation, and so on. They guarantee a minimal level of quality for services execution.

To use these non-functional services, the application assembler indicates in the deployment file the technical services he/she wants to use. For example, in the Enterprise Java Bean platform, the application assembler uses a transactional attribute to select if he/she wants to use (or not) the transaction management. This transactional attribute (for example: NEW_TRANSACTION_REQUIRED to create a new transaction) is specified in an XML deployment file.

Technical services also facilitate the programmers' task, by managing distributed constraints (such as naming or trading services, load balancing, …). However, when the programmer wants to use one of the technical services, this service is used on his terminal (cf. figure 2).

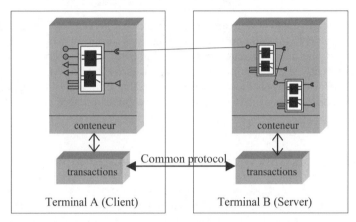

Fig. 2. Transactional mechanism in component oriented application

For example, in figure 2, the distributed application is running on two terminals (terminal A, which can be a PDA, and Terminal B, which can be an application server). On terminal A, there is an application formed by one or several components. This application also uses localisation services to retrieve remote services and transaction services to secure actions performed by the user. On terminal B, there is the merchant application.

Technical services on both terminals must be compliant with each others (for example, in figure 2, Transaction services on Terminal A must be compliant with transaction services on terminal B, to perform a correct transaction management). Currently, the only solution in existing component based platforms is to use the **same service** on each terminal.

4.2 Major Drawbacks

Currently, non-functional services do not allow to adapt their functionalities to the environment. In the following, we will illustrate our purpose with the example of lookup services. Many lookup services have been proposed these last years. In distributed environments, these services are required for users to retrieve data or services in a transparent way. Several kinds of lookup services may be distinguished. First, naming services (like the Internet DNS Protocol[1] or the CORBA Naming Service[2]) are used to retrieve an object according to its name. Naming services provide location transparency of objects to users. Using a naming service, a user can bind a name to an

---

[1] Domain Name Service Protocol: http://www.ietf.org
[2] CORBA Naming Service:
    http://www.omg.org/technology/documents/formal/naming_service.htm

object and then, later on, he/she can query the naming service to localize his/her objects. Then, trading services (such as the CORBA Trader[3]) are used to retrieve information according to its properties. These services propose a yellow pages service and so facilitate the offering and the discovery of services instances of particular types. A trader can be viewed as an object through which other objects can advertise (or export) their capabilities and match their needs against advertised capabilities (called import). Export and import facilitate dynamic discovery of (and late binding to) services. To export, an object gives the trader a description of a service and the location of an interface where that service is available. Directory services (like LDAP [19] or UDDI[4]) provide both white pages and yellow pages services. They propose to retrieve an information using either its name or/and its properties. A network directory service is a highly distributed information system in which directory entries are organized into a hierarchical namespace and can be accessed by names or by using declarative queries.

These systems provide means for managing security, scale and heterogeneity, as well as allowing conceptual unity and autonomy across multiple directory servers in the network. Compared to directory services, naming services are of course very limited since only services administered in remote servers can be named in such services. No property (i.e. attribute) can be added or stored in naming services to characterize the association realized between a name and a service. These properties are usually exported in a trader.

According to the environment where the applications are deployed, very different lookup solutions are required. So today, we have to face to an important need of adaptability for lookup services. For instance, a traditional CORBA application where objects are created dynamically will only require a naming service so that created objects may be named and then easily retrieved by client applications. On the other hand, other applications have much more complex requirements as it is the case for M-Commerce applications for example. In such an application, a potential client, fitted with a handheld device such as a cell phone, enters in a virtual Commerce Zone. Thus, the potential client can receive several merchants offer broadcasted on the LAN's commerce zone and then select the most interesting offers in function of his/her preferences. If the client is interested in specific offers, he/she goes to the merchant who is close to him/her and finally buys the products. Lookup services deployed in such environments for clients to easily retrieve an offer, a vendor and so on have to face numerous constraints compared to our first example. In particular, they generally have to support a very important number of clients. These lookup services also have to manage many updates since the vendors have to maintain up-to-date the information about the products available in their stores. Besides, these services have to provide advanced querying capabilities. Indeed, in our example, clients will not retrieve information using a logical name but will execute complex queries to get for example the list of vendors who sell red shoes at the first stage of the shopping mall.

Today, the solution adopted to answer the needs of such applications consists in using several lookup services, a naming and a trading service for example. Nevertheless,

---

[3] CORBA Trading Service:
   http://www.omg.org/technology/documents/formal/trading_object_service.htm
[4] Universal Description, Discovery and Integration: http://www.uddi.org

the coherence of information stored in these different services is not maintained what can cause severe inconstancy problems. In the following, we discuss the interests of the component model in this context.

5   Non-functional Services Using the Component Model

In this section, we describe how to use the component model to implement new non-functional services. These services will be designed as a composition of components, to allow the modularity and the adaptation to all applications specificities. In the first part of this section we propose a definition of non-functional services as a composition of components. Then, we will focus on the assembly of an application using such non-functional services. Finally, we will illustrate our purpose with the example of a lookup service based on the component model.

5.1   Definition of Non-functional Services as Components

The best way to easily create adapted non-functional services is to use the component model. With this model, non-functional services can be decomposed in many sub-tasks. Each one of these tasks is programmed as a component. To propose a specific version of a given non-functional service, the programmer has to assembly all the components he/she needs (cf. figure 3).

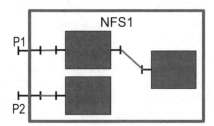

Fig. 3. An example of non-functional service seen as a composition of components

When the programmer wants to use another implementation of a non-functional service, he/she has to define a new assembly to generate a well-adapted non-functional service. Therefore, it is naturally important to use a component model that allows to create a component as a composition of existing components. So, a non-functional service will be itself a component, that is an assembly of elementary components. With the FRACTAL model, you can easily assemble several components to generate a new bigger one. Moreover, you can easily take over a component, by using a component, which presents the same interface. So, with the FRACTAL model, we can easily change the non-functional services version for a specified environment. Moreover, thanks to different controllers, it is possible to monitor the constitution and the bindings of composite components, which are explicit and exposed. Thus the system has a representation of itself. It also allows one component to be shared by two compositions of components.

Since a non-functional service is considered as a component, it has the same characteristics: separation of meta-data, expression of required and supplied API (facets and receptacles), automatization of sending and receiving messages (event sources and sinks), reusability. Moreover, with the Fractal model, a composition of components is a component itself. Then, a non-functional service can be seen as a composition of all the components which implement its models.

5.2 An Application as a Assembling of Functional and Non-functional Components

The composition of a business component plus its non-functional services is also a component. In this part, we describe in depth the composition and the binding that should be constituted of such a composite component. Then we focus on the advantages of this concept by shortly explaining how two components can use the same non-functional service.

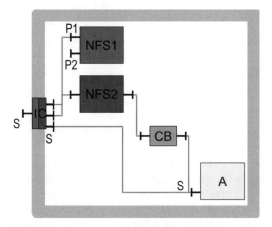

Fig. 4. An application gifted of non-functional services

An application (A), gifted of non-functional service (NFS1, NFS2) is an assembly of its functional components (seen as one big composition A) and its non-functional services (see figure 4). As long as non-functional services are components, they are invoked through one of their interfaces (ex: P1 or P2 for NFS1) thanks to bindings. The application is thus reachable through an "interceptor component" (IC) that exposes the same client interface as the application (S). When a method call is invoked on the application, it is intercepted by the "interceptor component", which executes this method call but also the non-functional services. As this "interceptor" is based on AOP (Aspect Oriented Programming), it is possible to define for each NFS a policy of execution, e.g. if it has to be executed before or after the method call.

Note that we define a "call-back component" (CB) that represents the functionality that a component must provide to some non-functional services (for example NFS2).

For example, methods defined in the *javax.ejb.SessionBean* interface or in the *javax.ejb.EJBContext* are call-back methods. They are used by the container to manage the non-functional services of life cycle, transaction and security.

In order to write those call-back methods, the developer has to know both about the non-functional service and the application. Then, the application has to provide the

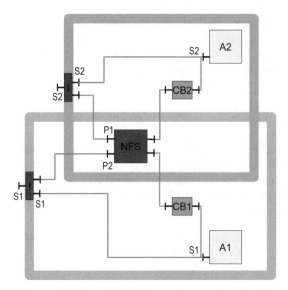

Fig. 5. Two applications gifted with a unique non-functional service

"call-back component", which was written separately. If the application does not use the non functional service which needs the callback component, there is no need to add it to the composition.

When two components use the same non-functional service (NFS in figure 6), it is possible for them to use the same instance of it through different facets. Thus they can access the appropriate version of the non-functional service. Each service of the application is accessed through its "interceptor component" and if the non-functional service needs "call-back methods" then for each component it uses the corresponding "call-back component" (e.g. CB1 for A1 and CB2 for A2) thanks to appropriate bindings.

5.3 Application to Lookup Services

To propose an adaptable lookup service solving the problems mentioned in section 4, our purpose is to design an adaptable lookup service based on the component model. This service may provide either naming or trading features to users according to users needs. For instance, querying capabilities proposed by the adaptable lookup service vary from the simple resolve operation proposed by naming services to retrieve an object using its name to evolved query languages for users to better specify their requirements.

The main interest of the component model in this context is the possibility to design a service as the association of several different components (storage manager, query manager schema manager and security manager). Using the component model, these components can be dynamically assembled according to the requirements of the user at the deployment time. Different components will be implemented for each feature proposed by the service. For instance, a component will implement the resolve operation traditionally proposed by naming services and another one will propose an operation to evaluate queries in a particular language. This dynamic composition approach makes the service completely extensible since components can be added according to the users needs. Then, when the lookup service is deployed, the components the most adapted for the application are selected to propose users a convenient solution and to avoid them the delicate management of several interdependent services.

6   Conclusion

The increasing development of heterogeneous terminals in distributed environments requires a high level of adaptation for distributed applications. Today, these applications are built by assembling business components (with EJB, CCM, or FRACTAL models) and non-functional services. The component model allows to easily substitute a component by another one to adapt the application to a given context. However, currently, the developer of a distributed application cannot adapt the non-functional services.

In this paper, we have proposed to consider non-functional services as an assembly of components. This allows to reconfigure, at the application deployment time, the non-functional services to take into account all the terminals need. At the end of the application building, business and non-functional components are assembled to generate the complete application.

We have presented the example of a lookup service, which needs a high level of adaptability. Indeed, according to the environment where the applications are deployed, lookup protocols are very different (based on a broadcast protocol, or in the opposite with Peer to Peer (P2P) protocols). We have shown how different lookup services could be designed, by assembling several different components (storage manager, query manager schema manager, security manager and distributed protocol manager).

Currently, a prototype of a transactional manager in a component way is under implementation, based on the FRACTAL model. Our goal is to allow to manage many transactions model (flat transaction, nested transaction) dependent from the application needs.

References

1. Strategis Group, Global Wireless Devices: Market Trends & Forecasts, 2002. http://www.strategisgroup.com.
2. M. Weiser, *The Computer for the 21st Century*, Scientific American, Vol. 265, N° 3, 1999.
3. M. Golm, and J. Kleinöder, *Ubiquitous Computing and the Need for a New Operating System Architecture*, International Conference on Ubiquitous Computing (UbiComp'2001), 2001.
4. M. Thilliez, T. Delot, S. Lecomte, N. Bennani, *Hybrid Peer-To-Peer Model in Proximity Applications*, IEEE AINA 2003, Xi Ang, Chine, 2003
5. N. Bennani, S. Lecomte, T. Delot, N. Souf, L. Watbled, *A new generation for HomeCare Systems based on the use of PDA and WAP/WEB technologies*, Proceedings of the international workshop on Main Issues in Designing Interactive Mobile Services, 2002.
6. R. Orfalie, D. Harkey, J. Edwards, Client/Serveur Survival Guide, 3ème édition, Vuibert, 1999.

7. T. Thai, H.Q. Lam, .NET Framework Essentials, O'Reilly & Associates, 2001.
8. R.J. Oberg, Understanding & Programming COM+. A practical guide to Windows 2000 DNA, Prentice-Hall PTR, 2000.
9. D. Box, D. Ehnebuske, G. Kakivaya, A. Layman, N. Mendelson, H.F. Nielson, S. Thatte, D. Winer, Simple Object Access Protocol (SOAP) 1.1, W3C note, 2000.
10. B. McKee, D. Ehnebuske, D. Rogers, UDDI Version 2.0 API Specification, UDDI.org, 2001.
11. E. Christensen, F. Curbera, G. Meredith, S. Weerawarana, Web Services Description Language (WSDL) 1.1, W3C note, 2001.
12. Object Management Group, CORBA Components. Specification, OMG TC Document or-bos/99-02-05, 1999.
13. Sun MicroSystems, Enterprise JavaBeans Specification, Version 2.1, 2001.
14. O. Takagiwa, A. Spender, A. Stevens, J. Bouyssou, Redbook: Programming J2EE APIs with WebSphere Advanced, IBM Corp., 2001
15. Java Open Application Server (JOnAS) for EJB, Objectweb, 2001. Disponible à l'adresse http://www.objectweb.org.
16. http://www.objectweb.org/fractal/index.html.
17. E. Bruneton, T. Coupaye, J.-B. Stefani, « Recursive and Dynamic Software Composition with Sharing », Proceedings of the 7th ECOOP International Workshop on Component-Oriented Programming (WCOP'02), Malaga, Spain, 2002.
18. http://avalon.apache.org/
19. M. Wahl, T. Howes, S. Kille, Lightweight Directory Access Protocol (v3), Internet RFC-2251, 1997.
20. G.T. Heineman, W.T. Council., Component-Based Software Engineering, Putting the Pieces Together, Addison Weysley, 2001.
21. OMG, CORBAservices: Common Object Services Specification, 1995

Toward an Agent-Based Platform
for Learning Objects Management

Nicandro Farias Mendoza, Gabriel Cruz, Orvil Ceja, Miguel Díaz, and José Macías

Facultad de Ingeniería Mecánica y Eléctrica, Universidad de Colima,
Kilómetro 9, Carretera Colima-Coquimatlán, Coquimatlán, Colima, México
{nmendoza,gcruz,orvil_zaiz,Miguel_Arturo,jmacias}@ucol.mx

Abstract. The current paper proposes a platform for learning objects management, based on the paradigm of intelligent agents. Such platform offers a personalization of the information based on user's behavior, an intelligent search capability for seeking some information between the objects and their ramifications, as well as the current state of the resources that compose to a certain object. This will allow the identification of the right objects to create suitable educative courses. The main contributions of the paper are: in first place, the proposal of integrating the technology of intelligent agents to a platform of learning objects, which makes more easy and precise the search of objects in several repositories located, mainly, in geographically distributed places; Second of all, the improvement of a technological tool which supports the process of education, through a scheme of distance education, utilized by the University of Colima; Finally, we intend to promote the adaptation of these educative schemes to the new technological advances, brought by Computer Science and Telecommunications in last years.

1 Introduction

In last years, Internet has changed the form in which people communicate trade and learn. In the educative context this change is reflected on the form that materials are designed, developed and distributed. Nowadays, the demand of education has increased by diverse social and demographic factors. Before this situation, new educative schemes have arisen in the academic world. One of them is distance education, which intends to satisfy such demand and to apply new technological paradigms to the daily task of teacher and student. Within this scheme, a new technology called learning objects is being increasingly outlined as a technological innovation in instructional design due, primarily, to his generative, adaptive and scalable potential.

A learning object, according to [1], is defined as a digital entity with instructional design features that can be used, reusable or referenced during the computer-enabled learning process.

The characteristics of an object are:

- *Interoperability:* The Capability of integration.
- *Reusability:* The capability of being combined within new courses.
- *Scalability:* Allows integrating to more complex structures.
- *Self-generation:* The capability of new objects generation based on it.
- *Management:* Concrete and correct information about offered content ad possibilities.
- *Interactive:* The capacity to activity and communication generation between involved users.

T. Böhme et al. (Eds.): IICS 2004, LNCS 3473, pp. 111–119, 2006.

- *Accessibility:* Access facility to appropriate content in appropriate time.
- *Durability:* An Expiration Time of object's information in order to avoid to become obsolete.
- *Adaptability:* Characteristic to fulfill the needs of learning of each individual.
- *Conceptual Self Contention:* The capability of being self explained and to allow integral learning experiences

The most important characteristics in this case of study are: scalability and self-generation, which allow the creation of knowledge networks that can become too complex for searching objects in order to fulfill a specific criteria.

The University of Colima, aware of the relevance of this sort of educational resources, has developed a platform to manage learning objects which gives to the academic community the opportunity of knowing and using the objects that have been implemented on the different centers which generate educational resources within the University itself (CEUPROMED, CIAMs Network, CEUVIDITE, CENEDIC, etc).

Along with the creation of this platform, new problems have emerged. For instance, every time a new resource is attached to an existing object, it is mandatory that this resource could be considered by the search engine, because it could happen that neither the original object fulfill the specified criteria nor the resource match the profile of the user that request it. In addition, there is the case that these criteria could be either fulfilled within an attached resource, by combining two related objects or, yet, by combining an internal object with an external one.

Our proposal is strongly based on the framework of a technological platform previously developed by the University of Colima which allows managing the set of learning objects that have been implemented on the different centers of this house of studies. Some related works to this field of study have been accomplished. It is the case of M.Chan that in [3] is proposing a Mexican Repository of Learning Objects. L.Iriarte and others in [4] propose a mechanism to create repositories of learning objects automatically. A.Saad in [5] introduces a model to interconnect Learning Objects in specific learning paths via a spreading activation mechanism. On the other hand F.A.DorÇa and others in [6] propose a multiagents architecture to distance education where they contribute with the idea of a pedagogic agent able to conforming courses according to the user's capacities.

In this paper we deal with an improvement for such platform which uses a multi-tier architecture, based on intelligent agents, that is divided as follows:

- **Presentation Layer:** It allows to the user to interact with the platform.
- **Agent Layer:** It gives the required functionality for creating, transferring and using one or several intelligent agents that will easier the search of learning objects. It will also allow content personalization according to the preferences showed by the user and based on his behavior.
- **Management Layer:** It gives the required business logic to retrieve information both, from this platform and from external ones
- **Communication Layer:** It offers a set of physical protocols and standards that allow interacting to different devices and agents over a communication network.

We consider that, by using a schema like the above to manage learning objects, will bring the next advantages to the current platform:

- User Notification of any object which has been recently created in the platform and that matches user's behavior.
- Intelligent object search for composed or core objects that fulfill thoroughly user's criteria and his objectives.
- State notification of each resource that compounds the object.

The rest of the paper is divided as follows: section 2 broadly explains the proposed platform and its details. Section 3 explains the presentation layer of the platform. Section 4 shows the parts in which the agent layer is divided into as well as introducing the basic concepts for agent-s usage. Section 5 gives an outline of the proposed management and communication layers. Finally, in section 6, it is mentioned the obtained conclusions and future work.

2 The Architecture

As it was previously mentioned, the University of Colima, pursuing to improve its distance education solution (EDUC), has implemented a learning objects set from the different research and study centers of the same institution [1]. These learning objects comprise a diversity of fields of study and they range from medicine to engineering, etc. However, the raising number of objects implemented by this institution has brought the necessity of having a technological solution that may their manipulation easily and suitably. To satisfy such necessity, the University of Colima implemented an XML-based ASP-built technological tool that allows managing the objects previously indicated.

Such tool is supported on a platform of two layers, constituted, mainly, by a presentation layer and a data management layer which, in turn, are in charge of providing the required functionality to the user. In spite of having a tool like the previous one, the University of Colima platform has met some problems. Firstly, the problem, due to the constant increment of the object's resources of finding the appropriate object that can satisfy the designed of a desired course. Another problem founded is represented by instructor's exhaustive work to control and managing his distance course groups. The architecture for this platform is shown in the following figure:

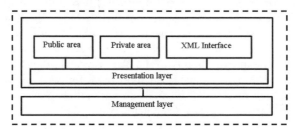

Fig. 1. Current platform's architecture for learning objects management

Based on the exposed necessities, we propose an improvement to the platform previously developed through an integration of intelligent agents that can make easier the search of objects or resources that match a certain profile. This integration is focused on the insertion of two additional layers to the previous model, achieving, in this way, a high level modularity and interoperability.

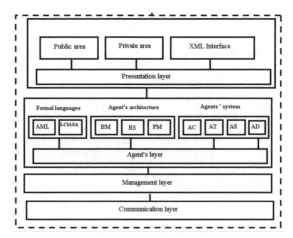

Fig. 2. Proposed platform's architecture

The architecture of the new platform is shown in figure 2. As it can be appreciated, the proposed architecture is a multi-tier one where each one communicates through a physical interface based on the communication protocols that are defined on its last layer. It is worthy to point out that, even though the model suggests a communication in a top-down way, it is possible to access to any layer in an independent way.

Once the user has decided to access to the platform, the presentation layer is in charge of authenticating the user's identity and of presenting the information to the user. This layer carries out a double work. On one hand it authenticates the user and on the other hand it formats the retrieved information in each interaction with the tool. Next, the agent's layer organizes the information according to the preferences and necessities of the user. This situation causes that the management layer carries out the work of recovering the information from the different repositories that are managed by the platform. Once the information has been retrieved, the communication layer is in charge of transferring it, based on the protocols that are defined inside this layer, to the end user.

As for the security part, the proposed model has two main security mechanisms that assure a reliable access to the resources of the platform. The first one is the authentication method given by the presentation layer that allows the user to use the complete features of the solution through a customized username and password. However, to assure the interoperability of the platform, it is proposed that this access could be based on XML by using the standard of IEEE for XML digital signatures on the future. The second mechanism is based on an intelligent agent that assures the invocation of other agents or objects in a reliable way.

While respecting the modular design of the solution, not only is it achieved to re-use the technology already developed, but also a solution that could be used in similar platforms for learning objects management.

3 Presentation Layer

The presentation layer of the platform is divided into three main areas: a public area, a private area and a XML Interface. Each one offers different types of access to the users of the platform, allowing them to use different features or, in the case of the XML Interface through a standard interface to other users and even to connect external platforms. The presentation layer also has the peculiarity of formatting the recovered information through XSL to offer the user a more appropriate approach of the information. Figure 3 sample in detail the areas that compose to the presentation layer.

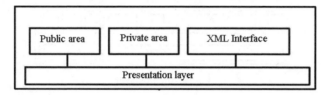

Fig. 3. Presentation layer

The first area, allows the user to be authenticated, it shows the objects recently attached to a repository to the user, the most visited objects and the disciplines in which are classified. Also, it allows carrying out searching and provides a summary of the content of the objects that are returned as a result; besides, the user can create an account that allows him to enter and to obtain more information or the complete content of the objects. The purpose that the user could be identified is to create a profile that allows observing his behavior and that will be useful to offer suggestions.

In the second area, the user's authentication is required through a customized username and password. Once authenticated, the platform offers the possibility to carry out queries that show the complete profile and location of the object, as well as adding to each one: comments, resources and calendars. In this section it is possible to define the preferences and profile of the user, what allows an easy access on the future. Although all users can also add objects to the platform in this section, those will be revised by a committee observer of the same institution before doing it. This revision will only be carried out regarding the structure and form; this is done with the purpose of assuring that the given information corresponds to the topic of the object.

The third area allows that any application could carry out queries to the platform by using XML. Only if the query is requested in a private area, it will be necessary the user identification since, otherwise, an error message will be returned. This feature allows the integration of the platform to external platforms, either compatibles or incompatibles. As XML is a broadly utilized standard, we believe that by offering this characteristic will cause an extensive collaboration, among private and academic institutions, to share the different repositories of learning objects from all over the world.

4 Agent's Layer

Once the user has access to the platform through some of the three areas of the presentation layer, the logic of the platform uses the layer of intelligent agents. This layer is in charge of providing the necessary functionality for the manipulation of the intelligent agents that will guide the searching process of learning objects on the different repositories. The main purpose of these agents resides in offering the contents of the objects according to the preferences shown by the user, based on his behavior. It is important to mention that intelligent agents try to solve the problem of finding the appropriate object for the desired course. These agents help us to identify learning objects that have been recently modified and that, by ignorance of the user or insufficient descriptions of the object, are not in the right classification.

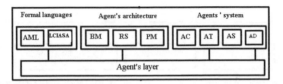

Fig. 4. Agent's layer

The agent's layer is conformed by an agent's system that, in turn, is based on agent's architecture and a formal model. In figure 4 these elements are shown.

An agent's system is a platform that can create, to interpret, to execute, to transfer and to eliminate agents. An agent's system can only be identified by its name and by its address; a host can have one or more systems of agents.

It is defined three common types of relative interactions to the interoperability of agents:

1. Agents' remote creation (AC)
2. Agents' transfer (AT)
3. Agents' invocation method (AS and AD)

Agents' remote creation: In the remote creation of agents, a program of the client has an interaction with the agent's target system to request an agent, of a particular class, to be created. The client authenticates the agent's target system, establishing the authority that the new agent possesses. The client provides the initialization arguments and, when necessary, the class to create an instance and to execute the agent.

Agents' transfer: When an agent is transferred to another agent's system, the agent's system creates a request providing a name and location that identifies the target place. If the agent's source system links the agent's target system, the agent's target system must fulfill the request or to return a failure indication to the agent. If the agent's target system is unreachable, a failure indication must be returned to the agent's source system.

Agents' invocation: An agent's invocation takes place when methods from another agent references to the source agent objects, if it is authorized. The communication infrastructure should invoke the suitable method and return the result of the invocation or return failure identification. When an agent invokes to a method, the security of the information that is given to the communications infrastructure that performs the invocation of the method, must correspond to the agent's authority.

To this end, the agent's system is based on an agent's architecture BI (Belief-Intentions), which can be considered as a subset of the BDI architecture [7] that, in turn, is included as a special case in the ICE architecture (abbreviation of $I^2C^2E^2$: Information, Intention, Communication, Cooperation, Evaluation, Empowerment). The proposed Architecture is used to specify the functionality of the agents within the system. This architecture contains the needed data and storage structures to define the agent's capabilities.

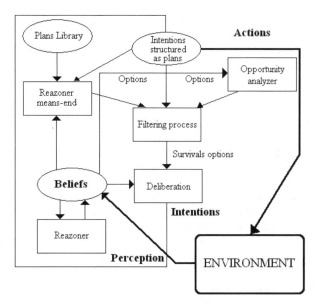

Fig. 5. Agent's architecture

In Fig. 5 the key data structures and their organization to describe the functionality of the agents are shown. Below it is given an outline of the concepts that are associated to the agent's architecture.

This architecture has its foundation on the philosophical tradition of the practical reasoning understanding witch is the process of deciding time after time which action must be execute in the attainment of the proposed goals. The practical reasoning involves two important processes: first, to decide which goals are pursued, which is called deliberation process and second, to decide how to achieve such goals, this process is called "means-end" reasoning.

Plans' library: Set of plans stored as procedures, this plans' library can be seen as a subset of the beliefs that an agent has about the plans and under which circumstances they are required to perform a task. *The Intentions structured as plans, are the plans that the agent is performing in the current time.* Additionally, the agent's architecture contains a reasoner that allows him to decide about the world. The "means-end" reasoner is invoked once that an intention has been created, for each of the existing partial plans, with the purpose of proposing sub-plans to determine which plans could be used to reach the agent's intentions, an opportunity analyzer that senses the environment with the purpose of determining subsequent options for the agent.

A filtering process and deliberative process, the filtering process is the responsible one of summing up the subset of the courses of the potential agent's actions, that have property of being consistent with the current agent's intentions, the selection among the options that compete is made by the deliberative process which receives the remaining options after being filtered and it ponders the options some against other and it updates the structured intentions as plans.

The beliefs repository contains a representation of what the agent knows from itself and from its environment, as shown in Fig. 5.

The Agent's system is also based on a formal model that contains two main parts: an Agents Meta language (AML) and an object language (LCIASA). These two languages are proposed by N. Farias in [2] as verification and specification languages for agent-based system. The Agent's system uses this model to describe functions and operations of the system in a precise way.

5 Management and Communication Layers

The management layer has as purpose to retrieve all the information from one or several repositories. On other hand the communication layer, includes all the standards and protocols that are required for the information transfer, as well as its corresponding retrieval. Because of this reason, the management and communication layers work as closed to achieve these goals that, sometimes, they get overlapped offering, one to another, the requested or required features.

Following the process of information retrieval, which is performed by the management layer, is explained. Every time that any user sends a query to the platform, this carries out a request to the database servers, which generates a XHTML document that is returned as the answer. If the query is sent through the XML interface, then the returned document is XML.

To conclude, a brief mention of the protocols and standards that conform to the communication layer and the parts in that they are used is made. The platform is designed to work on the WEB; also by having XML interface, it allows the integration of mobile devices through WAP (Wireless Application Protocol) or any other application that wishes to obtain information from the platform itself. As the communication protocol, the platform uses TCP/IP.

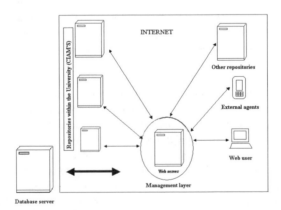

Fig. 6. A schematic view of management and communication layers

The database is designed in MS-SQL Server, which allows a large storage, security and stability capacity. It is based on the recommendation AMS v3.2, which provides a technological infrastructure that supports the indexation, management and storage of educational objects that work under LOM and KPS standards (Knowledge Pool System). LOM (Learning Object Metadata) it is a standard that specifies syntax and semantics of educational objects metadata. LOM is defined by the IEEE P1484.12

(Learning Objects and Metadata Working Group that is part of the IEEE Learning Technology Standards Committee), at the moment this initiative is denominated LTSC.

The proposed programming language is ASP (Server Activates Pages) that allows an express development besides other benefits that are beyond the context of this article.

6 Conclusion

The platform for learning objects management proposed in this article intent to provide a better option to the user so he could find the right learning objects, within one or more geographically distributed repositories.

It is important to point out that in the case of the selected platform; the objects implemented by the University of Colima are attached to the IEEE LOM standard. This could give the idea that the platform can only be used with platforms that use the same standard. This is a mistake. Since the platform offers an XML interface, it enables to the external user to integrate it to his daily use. In future work we propose to build web services that allow to the platform to use learning objects repositories that are based on different standards.

We suggest continuing this work in future, incorporating coordination, and cooperation and negotiation protocols in order to generate a tool useful for distance teaching instructor.

References

1. Galeana, L.: La Plataforma de Gestión de objetos de aprendizaje. Presentado en el XII Encuentro Internacional de Educación a Distancia, Jalisco, MX, (2003).
2. Farías M.N., Ramos C.F.F., LCIASA: Lenguaje de Capacidad de Interacción de Agentes en Sistemas Abiertos: LCIASA, ELECTRO 2000 technologic Institute of Chihuahua. Published in proceedings, MX. (2000) 337-343.
3. Chan, M.E., Martínez, J., Morales, R., Sánchez, V.: Prototipo de patrimonio público de recursos educativos basados en una red institucional y un repositorio distribuido de objetos de aprendizaje., presentado en CUDI Reunión Otoño 2003. Puebla, MX, (2003).
4. Iriarte, L., Such, M., Pernías, P., Morón, D.: Creación automatizada de una biblioteca de objetos de aprendizaje (LO). Presentado en ENC'03, Tlaxcala, MX, (2003).
5. Saad, A.: A Multi-Agent Spreading Activation Network Model for Online Learning Objects, Multi Agent-Based Learning Environments (MABLE) Workshop, 10th International Conference on Artificial Intelligence in Education (AIED), San Antonio, TX, May 19, (2001), pp. 55-59 (workshop proceedings).
6. Fabiano A. Dorça, Carlos R. Lopes, Márcia A. Fernandes: A Multiagent Architecture for Distance Education Systems. en Proc. 3rd International Conference on Advanced Learning Technologies, ICALT 2003, Atenas, Grecia, (2003), 368-369.
7. Haddadi A., Sundermeyer K. " Chapter 5 – Belif-Desire-Intentions Agent Architectures, "Foundations Of Distributed Artificial Intelligence., G.M.P. O`Hare and N.R. Jennigs (eds) Jhon Wiley & SonsInc., (1996) 169-186.

Notes on Agent-Oriented DBMS Toward a Robust KDBS

Juan Salvador Gómez Álvarez, Gerardo Chavarín Rodríguez,
and Victor Hugo Zaldivar Carrillo

Instituto Tecnológico de Estudios Superiores de Occidente A.C.,
Periférico Sur Manuel Gómez Morín 8585, Tlaquepaque, Jalisco, México
{vithar,gchavarin,victorhugo}@iteso.mx

Abstract. The work on Agent Based Systems lead us to gather different components in order to provide our agents the necessary tools to deal with their environment and tasks. But there is a gap when we want to provide agents individual database capabilities, developers do not have a reliable KDBMS (Knowledge Database Management System)that could be attached to a single agent and design agents with their own Agent-Oriented KDBMS designed specifically for agent based technology needs. This paper exposes the needs of an Agent Oriented Knowledge DBMS, and how this would be useful on Knowledge DB Systems, crucial for agent learning, evolution capabilities and Agent Community Knowledge.

Background

Our research team has been working on a MAS (Multi-Agent Systems) test bed that is designed to be a useful tool for developing MAS and testing them without wasting valuable time making everything from scratch. This way we have achieve good results on different areas of MAS design [ISSADS] (Agent Communication, graphic representation of agents, script processing and Agent Interaction).

While working on this test bed we realize that there is not a set of tools to provide agents knowledge-base capabilities as they are for Communication and Interaction. When we look for communication tools, we can find several libraries and technologies that help developer to add easily communication capabilities to an agent (TCP/IP, sockets, etc.) and even if you want to provide agents an upper level of communications using ACL (Agent communication languages) such as FIPA's ACL, or transport protocols as KQML you can find lexical analyzers and parsers (flex, bison, etc.) that could be attached to the agent without spending a lot of time implementing it.

But the problem opens up when we want to provide a KB to a single agent. When we design an agent, we design it to be autonomous and proactive, we do not want it to depend on a central KDBMS to make its own decisions, we conceive it as an autonomous piece of software capable to work individually.

When we read "Enabling technology for knowledge sharing" [KNWSHARE] years ago from now, and we analyze the four impediments mentioned there, we realize that we are now capable to provide agents Knowledge capabilities as described on their paper, and enabling our agents to have more robust reasoning tools.

There are certainly new approaches on this area but we would like to start from a particular quote on that paper that inspired us to develop new technologies on this area: "One mode of reuse is through the exchange of techniques". We trim it to be: "One mode of reuse is through the exchange".

T. Böhme et al. (Eds.): IICS 2004, LNCS 3473, pp. 120–128, 2006.

Against a centralized DB, a community of agents could share knowledge between them and have Agent Community Knowledge. Each agent would be expert on specific areas, but will be able to share and learn from other agents. Agents would be even capable to work with their own knowledge and create new knowledge to share to the community.

Project Overview

Jennings talks us about how Complex Software Systems could be easily designed using Agent-Oriented paradigm [JENN01], and before he also talked to us about the possibilities of this technology [JENN98]. Therefore, there is a need to fulfill all technology gaps. Providing developers and researchers robust and easy to use tools will let us create smarter Agents that could perform more complex and important tasks. In other words, take advantage of this technology.

This paper it is an initiative to create KB(Knowledge-Base) systems designed to be part of Software Agents. This KB would have characteristics that could help agents to improve their performance and perform complex tasks autonomously.

We want to provide an easy-to-use tool for developers on their different applications. That would enable them to create agents capable to understand their knowledge, use it when they perform their tasks, use it when they are doing planning. Even knowledge could be a weighted argument for decision on Plan-Merging algorithms.

The initial focus of this research is for investigation on AI area and information technologies. But the focus is not limited to research.

Design Considerations

We start from the earlier design of an agent a scratch without having the model even on a standard format such as UML or AUML. We get a simple diagram which shows the different components that our agent would need. This is an initial scratch:

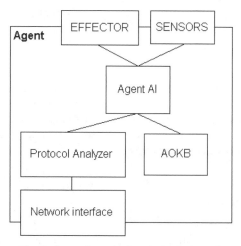

Fig. 1. Agent Scratch, first design approach

After we have this model we could start gathering the tools required for each module, for instance the network libraries, flex and bison for the protocol analyzers, and so for. But when we want to provide the agent Knowledge Base capabilities we found a gap were specific tools are not available. At this point we need to take a decision: Make a KB from scratch for this agent, or adapt some existing technology.

We believe that the better answer is to create a new tool that could be useful for different kinds of agent implementations, that could be attached to our agents without wasting developer's time on this specific module and move on to higher level programming.

For this AOKB (Agent-Oriented Knowledge Base) we start from a basic scratch, defining some of the suggested modules that it should have to provide the agent KB capabilities. This is a first approach on this technology:

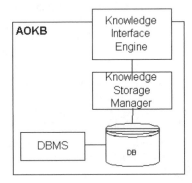

Fig. 2. AOKB: First approach scratch

Now we explain each module:

DBMS

This module will work almost the same way that conventional DBMS works, it will perform maintenance tasks such as indexing, backup, archiving, etc.

Knowledge Storage Manager

The responsibility of this module is to know how and where is stored the different Knowledge. All new data structures added to the knowledge base will have to update this module in order to use correctly the new knowledge added. The scripts or algorithms to use specific kind of data will be stored on this module. This will allow to process different kind of knowledge, handle different information that could be stored or retrieved from the DB.

Knowledge Interface Engine

The agent must handle knowledge in a format that he could compute and make use of it. There could be different formats to share knowledge (XML [XML], KIF, etc) and the agent must be able to understand them.

This Module gives the agent the information in a format he can use and makes the link to the Knowledge Storage Manager which stores and retrieves the information from the Database.

This interface engine should be able to support different kind of formats allowing the agent to understand many different agent knowledge architectures.

Advantages and Possibilities

Flexible MAS Design and Implementation

When designing software agents, developer could be able to consider a KB to help the agent in decision process, agent could be able to find a better solution based on the knowledge he owns.

What we want to provide is a easy-to-use API that could be added and configured to the agent in a short time. This KB would run embedded to the agent, linked exclusively to it.

The main difference between this kind of KB and normal DBMS linked to a KB or Expert System it is that many Agent-Bases KBs could be running on a single system. As many AOKBs (Agent-Oriented Knowledge Base) as agents are in the system. In this way we give agents full independence that can only be simulated on centralized, conventional DBMS and KBs.

This AOKB could be added to different kind of agent, is an independent component that has its own inputs and outputs, therefore different application or specific characteristics of the agent should not be an obstacle to add this AOKB.

Agent Dynamically Add New Data Structures to Their Knowledge

Agents are not sharing only Data and Communication Messages, they are interchanging Knowledge, therefore it is needed to share as well different ways to store knowledge. For instance, if an agent it is training another agent about some business hierarchy, it might be easier to represent this on a tree graph. And this knowledge will be complemented with a script that could let agent know how to read and use this kind of new data structure. The data structure and the procedure to use are both the knowledge that enables this agent to learn new ways to store, use and share knowledge.

In other words, agents can learn to learn. They could start sharing KIF format knowledge but they could learn to use more knowledge interchange formats according to the task needs.

If some agent is learning business information an agent could add it to his own DB the information and at the same time the KB will be updated to add the necessary procedures (scripts) to allow agent to use correctly this new data.

For instance an agent that uses KIF could learn how to parse XML objects in order to share information to another systems or agents.

Complex Hierarchical System Requirements

Jennings [JENN01] talks us about the benefits of agent-based paradigm and how this could be a good approach on many complex systems. But in order to provide agents the strength needed to work by their self and cooperate with each other, tools are needed to cover all gaps on this technology.

This initiative on AOKB wants to help agent developers to have more tools when they are implementing software agents.

Share Workload of DBMS and Agent Autonomy

If we are considering the use of a single DBMS to share knowledge to an Agent community we are having a single server providing information to many agents. Even more, if we want smarter agents we would like them to take decisions based on their available knowledge. Were is all that knowledge? Shared on a single DBMS, were all agents are trying to find the desired information and they could reach a certain answer. Meanwhile they may not be able do any other activity than waiting a response to continue with their other activities. This is not a desired behavior for an agent which should be far more autonomous, at least ideally.

If each agent has his own knowledge, each agent could make his own decisions without depending on the environment or busy servers. The next obvious answer to this problem is to attach a DBMS to each agent. But this is not necessary right, since an agent has different needs than a ordinary application with Database capabilities.

AOKB must be lighter enough to be attached to the agent and been robust enough to provide the agent quick and reliable response. Agents may run on different platforms, could be distributed and this would make the workload to be shared along the agent community. If an agent is requesting too much information from the KB he and just he will be slowed down. If some query to the KB will take much time the agent could decide if he request help to another agent that has equivalent knowledge. This can spread the workload between more than one agent and the resources could be used in a more efficient way.

Even more, while an agent is doing an specific task there is the possibility to perform "meditation queries" where he could browse the KB or even query other agents about his current task, asking if there is a way to do his task more efficiently.

Data and Knowledge Store

There is a difference between data and knowledge when we talk about data, we talk about tables or data structures without any particular meaning. They could be used to generate statistics, predictions, or reports. But when we talk about knowledge we talk about behaviors, procedures, etc. Information that give agent a complex pattern of behavior, information that is used to achieve decisions based on previous experience, logical rules, and even new algorithms learnt to process the information.

As a matter of fact Knowledge and Data are stored the same way (Bits), but the way data is used makes the big difference. That is important to remark, an AOKB is designed to allow the agent to decide based on previously stored knowledge. Knowledge is not only the information stored, it is also the way to store and use it.

Agent Cross-Training

When agents are able to share knowledge, also they are capable to share behaviors, procedures and information. Agents could teach other agents to handle different situations that they may face.

This opens up the possibility for leader agent that recruit generic agents, and train them in specialized tasks. Agents could cooperate without previous experience once they are fully trained.

The KB therefore adds the agents the possibility to grow in capabilities and been more flexible to the environment. This is also useful on risky task were an agent could share his knowledge to the others and backup this experience to the community. If for any circumstance this agent is lost (Mine detector robot, space rover), there are other agents who learnt from him and can share the knowledge for future agent generations.

Less Resources than Standard DBMS

This KB should not consume more resources than the agent it self. Against conventional DBMS use on industry, the AOKB is designed to share resources with other agents and their KBs, therefore this AOKB must be compact and have just the necessary elements. There are many components on standard DBMS that are simply not adequate to fit agent oriented requirements.

When we talk about resources we have three main focal points: CPU, Memory and Human resources (developer). The use of CPU and Memory per agent and his KB is not an static requirement (or limitation), depends on the application. But agent need a KB that provides them the necessary knowledge capabilities, consuming only the necessary resources.

A standard DBMS, installs several components that are oriented to Human-user interactions, and the lack of features that could make easier the access for the information to the agent. That is why we suggest adding XML (or KIF or other format, also new ones that could be learnt from other agents) processing engine, which makes knowledge easier to understand for the agent and easier to store in the KB.

The developer should concentrate on agent's intelligence programming, giving it reasoning, interaction, communication and behavior capabilities. Developer will be able to design agents that query their own KB and make decisions with this knowledge. It is much easier to design software this way than trying to predict all possible situations. Agents will take their own decisions. Providing this kind of tools the developer resource will be better used, he will use his time for more advanced activities than starting over and design from scratch a KB or trying to adapt some existing DBMS.

Disadvantages

We are aware that this technology it is not a silver bullet, but might be very useful for many applications, here there are some disadvantages we see at this time.

Robust Existing DBMS

There are in the market and development several Database Technologies, for instance it is possible to find something as simpler as MS Access [MS] and as complex as Oracle [ORCLE] or ESS Base[ESS]. The problem with this technologies is that they are not designed for agent systems. And even when they could be adequate to agent systems, they are not supposed to run inside the agent, but on a system.

What is really needed is to gather all the experience on Database Technologies that has been maturing for several years and merge this best practices with agent technology. Create a new wave of tools capable to make our agents smarter each time.

Existing technologies, allows developers to simulate agent's knowledge, but the agents needs to be really independent. And this tools need to be fully designed for this purpose.

Knowledge Duplication and Inconsistency

Different agents with individual AOKB will generate duplicated information, and some of the information will not be updated within the community, at least for the moments where the agents are not capable to share and receive knowledge updates.

Data may be inconsistent and duplicated. But there is an interesting workaround here, agents are able to keep working even if they are totally insolated. They do not depend on a centralized base of knowledge to work. They can work on their tasks while the others can work on their own. Of course it would be needed to define priority criteria for the tasks, some tasks will require to confirm specific knowledge with the community in order to avoid working with not updated information. But this is a problem that could be treated and could be a topic of future work.

Existing Working Solutions

This are just a few examples of available technologies:

JESS: This tool allows agents to access Expert Systems. Can be used along JADE, but this is still a centralized Expert System. The next step needed here is to make the Expert system to be attached to the agent, and not depending on other layers. The agent should include the expert system and the necessary capabilities to query it. And of course the capability to understand and use this Knowledge.

Protégé [PROTEG]: This is an interesting approach, from here the distance to reach AOKB needs seems to be quite short. This tool allows developer to create and model KB easily. And also provides the necessary java API to query this KB. From here we only need that this KB could have the dynamic features here described and the possibility to run stand-alone on each agent.

Possible Applications

It is necessary to analyze what are the possible applications for this technology, and some of them could be found here:

In-Communicated Mobile Robots

Real world situations can not guarantee that agents will be communicated between them nor with a centralized Base of Knowledge. We can imagine infinite reasons why agents are not communicated at some moment. But they must be able to continue their task with the own knowledge and been able to share and receive knowledge when communication is available.

Also agents will be able to backup their learnt knowledge to the other agents as soon as they can establish communication again.

For instance a platoon of Agent-Based planet explorer robots with AOKB capabilities could share and distribute the information obtained.

Embedded Systems

Compact devices such as cell phones, PDAs, etc. could have agents with KB capabilities that could improve their performance updating their software, or adding new functionalities and so on.

It is not practical to add a big robust DBMS, it could be more adequate to add just the Agent-oriented needs to make devices smarter and more flexible.

Research Purposes

Researchers could use this tool for testing purposes, they could really simulate distributed environment, where each agent has his own knowledge and it has to interact with the others.

Current Status

This is a first approach on this technology from our team, we are on design phase gathering all the possible needs and ideas. We are also working on the test bed, where we can test different kind of agents. But we would like to add our agents more capabilities and make them more complete and useful.

Future Work

Our first goal, is to gather a team interested on this research line and work together to define all the needs and features that this AOKB should have. Then we could do the necessary planning for it's implementation and follow up.

We believe that this technology will be growing on possibilities and the project could stay for long time creating new tools for MAS developers.

Conclusions

This initiative is open for further discussion, and will be very interesting see what will result of this discussion. This technology pretends to improve the Agent Systems, allowing them to be easier to develop and make agents smarter than they are now.

We would also like to invite research teams from different locations to gather and work together on this project or new projects that might created around this investigation field.

AOKB could be a useful addition to agent technology, that could lead us to create more complex systems in a shorter time.

I2CS 2004 Guadalajara, Mexico Discussion and Observations

After conferences we had some observations regarding our work, it´s use and existing resources.

Some new applications that we did not considered before were epidemic disease simulations, network routers with special capabilities to understand contents and improve Peer-to-Peer services. Smarter routers could be able to understand the requests and route connection to a server he believes (Knowledge Based query) has the requested information.

We also found at ObjectWeb [OWeb] several existing tools that could be used for many Agent based applications. There does not exist a tool with the exact characteristics of a AOKB, but there are many working solutions that could be used as workaround.

References

[KNWSHARE] R. Neches, R. Fikes, T. Finin, T. Gruber, R. Patil, T. Senator, & W. R. Swartout. Enabling technology for knowledge sharing. *AI Magazine*, 12(3):16-36, 1991.

[GFP94] Peter D. Karp and Thomas R. Gruber. A Generic Knowledge-Base Access Protocol. SRI International Technical Report, 1994.

[KIFABS] M. R. Genesereth. Knowledge Interchange Format. *Principles of Knowledge Representation and Reasoning: Proceedings of the Second International Conference*, Cambridge, MA, pages 599-600. Morgan Kaufmann, 1991.

[JENN98] Nicholas R. Jennings and Wooldridge, M, Eds. Agent Technology: Foundations, Applications and Markets. Springer Verlag 1998.

[JENN01] Nicholas R. Jennings, An Agent-Based approach for Building complex software systems, Communications of the ACM april 2001/Vol. 44. No.4

[UML2003] OMG Unified Modeling Language Specification V. 1.5, March 2003, formal/03-03-01.

[FIPAACL] FIPA 97 Specification, Version 2.0, Part 2,Agent Communication Language, Publication date: 23 rd October, 1998.

[KQML01] Finin T., Labrou Y. & Mayfield J., KQML as an agent communication language, 1995.

[MABS] Paul Davidsson, Multi Agent Based Simulation: Beyond Social Simulation, Department of Software Engineering and Computer Science, University of Karlskrona/Ronneby.

[OGL] OpenGL specification version 1.4, released on July 24, 2002.

[KQML02] Tim Finin and Rich Fritszon, "KQML – A Language and Protocol for Knowledge and Information Exchange", Computer Science Department, University of Maryland, UMBC, Baltimore MD 21228.

[AIW2002] Edited Steve Rabin, AI Game Programming Widsom,, Charles River Media, INC., 2002.

[AIW_Script01] Lee Berger-Turbine, Scripting: Overview and Code Generation, Entertainment Software.

[AIW_Script02] Jonty Barnes – Lionhead Studio, Jason Hutchens – AmristarScripting for undefined Circumstances,

[JAFMAS] JAFMAS: http://www.ececs.uc.edu/~abaker/JAFMAS/, Multi-Agent Technology at the University of Cincinnati.

[ORBacus] ORBacus and Corba : http://www.iona.com

[JADE] JADE Framework: http://sharon.cselt.it/projects/jade/

[MS] Microsoft Corporation. All rights reserved.

[ORCLE] Oracle is a registered trademark of Oracle Corporation and/or its affiliates.

[ESS]ESSBase Hyperion Solutions Corporation. All rights reserved.

[PROTEG] Copyright © 2003 Stanford Medical Informatics: http://protege.stanford.edu/

[JESS] Jess is a trademark of Sandia National Laboratories. Java and all Java-based marks are trademarks or registered trademarks of Sun Microsystems, Inc. in the U. S. and other countries. http://herzberg.ca.sandia.gov/jess/

[Oweb] ObjectWeb http://www.objectweb.org

Anticipative Emergence in Environment Virtual

Marco A. Ramos[1,2], Alain Berro[1,2], and Yves Duthen[1]

[1] UT1/IRIT, Allées de Brienne, 31042 Toulouse cedex, France
{mramos,berro,Duthen}@univ-tlse1.fr
[2] Virtual Reality Department, C-S, Toulouse, France
{Marco.Ramos,Alain.Berro}@univ-tlse1.fr

Abstract. This paper describes how a group of agents can anticipate the possible changes within a virtual environment, than this concept the actors explore and adapts to the environment, thanks to mechanisms of evolution and adaptation, that provide the genetic algorithms and the classifier systems, with this capacity to learning and take one action by resolve a problem or change his objectifies. The main idea of the anticipation is based on the acquisition of knowledge of events happened in the environment of the past, later to compare them with the actions that appear in the present, in a time specify. The events of the past to like learning and make the calculus and the interpolating with the actions that happen in the present, this way to be able to make all the calculations necessary to be able to anticipate the possible changes in the environment [Hoffmann, J (1993)].

Keywords: Adaptation, Agents, Anticipation, Classifier System, Intelligence Artificiel.

1 Introduction

The main idea of the anticipation is base on the capacity to predict changes in the environment, that allow developed one new condition many favorable. One approach to designing intelligent agents systems is to look to the different studies in the biological systems for clues and design principles. The result is a system that builds an environmental model that applies reinforcement learning techniques. The main learning mechanism of the agents is a classifieur (CS) that introduce a genetic algorithm (GA). However, recently the concept of anticipations need more techniques in artificial learning systems, because is necessaries implementer the aspects the learning cognitive. Inside the world of artificial and evolutionary learning systems to allow incorporate techniques based to fitness to the eXtended Classifier System (XCS), or Learning Classifier System (LCS) [Wilson, 1995] the accuracy-based approach in XCS over comes the previously encountered problems in LCSs where especially deferred reward lead to over-generalization and unequal distribution of classifiers in the problem space [Wilson, 1989]. Moreover, XCS solves the problem of speciation and what mating restriction schemes should be used implicitly by the accuracy measure combined with genetic algorithm (GA).

2 The Anticipatory Classifier System (ACS)

The ACS [Stolzmann, 1998] has its origins in LCSs and cognitive psychology. The framework of the ACS shows many similarities with LCSs. Differences can be de-

T. Böhme et al. (Eds.): IICS 2004, LNCS 3473, pp. 129–135, 2006.

tected in the enhanced classifier structure as well as the application of the learning process. For explain with work this type of system; we start with the environment interaction. The ACS interacts autonomously with an environment. In the behavioral act at certain time t, it perceives a situation $\sigma(t) \in I = \{t_1, t_2, ..., t_m\}^L$ where m is the number of possible values of each attribute and L is the string length, is not necessarily coded binary but can only take discrete values. The system can act upon the environment with an action $\alpha(t) \in A = \{\alpha_1, \alpha_2, ..., \alpha_n\}$ where n specifies the number of different possible actions in the environment and $\alpha_1,..., \alpha_n$ are the different possible actions. Note, after the execution of an action, the environment provides a scalar reward $\rho(t) \in R$.

2.1 Knowledge Representation

The knowledge in the ACS is represented by a population [P] of classifiers. Each classifier represents a condition action anticipation rule having the following components:

- The condition part (C) specifies the set of input situations in which the classifier can be applied.
- The action part (A) proposes the classifier's action.
- The effect part (E) anticipates the effects that the classifier believes to be caused by the specified action.
- The mark (M) records all values in each attribute of the classifier that do not anticipate correctly sometimes.
- The quality (q) measures the accuracy of the anticipations;
- The reward prediction (r) predicts the reward expected the execution of action A.

The condition and effect part consist of the values perceived from the environment and '#'symbols (i.e. C, E $\in \{t_1, t_2,...,t_m, \#\}^L$). A # symbol in the condition called don't care symbol means that the classifier matches any value in this attribute. However, a # symbol in the effect part called pass through symbol means that the classifier anticipates that the value of this attribute won't change after the execution of specified action A. An action can be any action possible in the environment. The mark has the structure $M = (m_1,...,m_L)$ with $m_i \subseteq \{t_1,...,t_m\}$. The measures q and r are two scalar values where $q \in [0, 1]$ and $r \in R$. A classifier with quality greater than the threshold θ_r is called reliable and becomes part of the internal environmental model. A classifier with a quality g lower that the threshold θ_i is considered as inadequate and is consequently deleted. All these parts are modified according to de reinforcement learning mechanism.

2.2 Reinforcement Learning

In XCS, the reinforcement learning approach adapts the Q-learning idea in reinforcement learning [Watkins, Dayan, 1992]. A first mathematical analysis of Q-learning in generalizing systems such as LCSs can be found in [Lanzi, 2002] In order to learn an optimal policy en the ACS, the reward prediction r of each classifier in an action set is updated. For the reliability of the maximal Q-value in the successive state, we con-

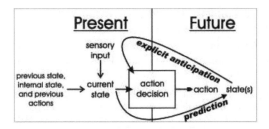

Fig. 1. Decision by predictions about the future

sider the quality of the classifier assuming that the reward converges in common with the accuracy of the anticipation. Once an accurate, reward sufficient model of the environment is evolved, the update method converges to the Q-learning theory and the formation of an optimal policy is assured.

$$r = r + b_r * (\rho(t) + \gamma^*) \max(q_{cl} * r_{cl}) - r)$$
$$cl \in [M](t+1)$$

The parameter $b_r \in [0, 1]$ denotes the reward learning rate and $\gamma \in [0, 1]$ the discount factor similar to Q-learning.

2.3 The Anticipatory Learning Process (ALP)

The ALP is derived from the psychological learning theory of anticipatory behavioral control [Hoffmann, 1993]. While the similarity with the learning theory is discussed elsewhere [Stolzmann, Butz, Hoffmann & Goldberg, 2000]. The ALP compares the anticipation of each classifier in an action set with the real next situation. According to this comparison and the current structure of the classifier, the classifier is modified and new classifier may be generated.

3 Prototype Model

This prototype simulates an environment in which two different agents that both exhibit realistic natural behaviors can be placed. The entire agent will have rules that will apply to them as individuals (i.e. local rules), [Reynolds, 1987], and each of the agent will change their objectives with regard to environment.

The objective of this prototype system is to show emergent and anticipated the actions complex global behavior this complex global behavior will emerge from the interactions of moderately simple local rules.

Emergence is an essential aspect of Artificial Life, as was stated by [Langton, 1989]. "Artificial Life is concerned with tuning the behaviors of such low-level machines that the behavior that emerges at the global level is essentially the same as some behavior exhibited by a natural living system. Artificial Life is concerned with generating lifelike behavior." Emergence can lead to *self-organizing behavior*, which means the spontaneous formation of well-organized structures, patterns, or behaviors, from random initial conditions. The behavior of interest is often found in the area between order and chaos, which could be described as *organized complexity*.

These ideas are based on natural living systems, where dynamical structures are not devised to exhibit this behavior, but they develop it spontaneously from random initial conditions. The theory is that in nature there is a tendency for spontaneous self-organization, which is universal, [Kauffman, 1993]. This process of self-organization can also be interpreted as the evolution of order from chaos.

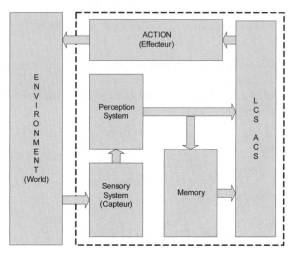

Fig. 2. Virtual behavior Framework

3.1 The Environment

A formal abstraction exists between the agent and the world. The world model's primary function maintains the list of agents and objects and to act as an event blackboard for the posting and distribution of the world events. It also coordinates network synchronization and manages rendering.

World events take the form of data records, perceptual nuggets than can be processed by an agents sensory and perception systems.

3.2 Sensory System

The sensory system is a filter though which all world events must pass. Unlike its physical equivalent, where any data that passes through is fair game, the sensory system plays an active role in keeping the virtual agents. In a simulated world, there is potentially much more accessible information that the agent, limited by its sensory module, should be able to sense. For example inside in world of species carnivores, herbivores, the carnivores can locate the herbivores that are behind him, he shouldn't be given it. While often the role of the sensory system is to filter out data that cannot be sensed [Sanchez, E. 2003], other times its role is to transform it. It converts visual location information in to local space of the sensing an object or identify other agent in the environment. The agent receives all local information from the world.

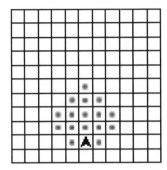

Fig. 3. Map of perception of agent   **Fig. 4.** Agent in environment virtual

3.3 Perception System

Once the stimulus from the world has been sensed it can then perceived. The distinction between sensing and perceiving is important. An agent may sense an event but it is up to the perception system to recognize a process the event as something that has meaning to the agent. Thus, it is within the perception system that meaning is assigned to events in the world. The perception system takes the form of a percept tree. A percept tree is an atomic classification and data extraction unit models some aspect of the sensory it returns both a match probability, the probability represents the experience.

3.4 Memory

Memory is a repository for the events that pass in the environment. The memory is itself a useful structure by caching together the various perceptual impressions made by a world event, to the decision making, the agents status system monitor and stores internal states of the virtual actor in order to simulate its knowledge of its actual situations. The memory provides of the world can be informed by more just direct perception. Much like our own perception where unobserved data is subconsciously by low-level prediction an assumption, agents implemented under the framework can be designed to act upon events that are like to have. We believe that the ability to recognize temporal patterns and act on them is an essential component of common sense intelligence. Sometimes prediction is used not to predict the future but simply to maintain a coherent view of the present. The stream of sensory data coming from object is out of the agent's visual field, or because it is occluded by another object. In theses cases, prediction can allow in agent to maintain a reasonable estimate of where the object is even though it is not being observed. The actual mechanisms of prediction can take many forms. Whit objects contain histories of percept data are vector or scalar, to use function approximation techniques to extrapolate values. These mechanisms of prediction could conceivably extend to common sense knowledge about the world if an object is suspended with no visible support, it light be predicted to fall. The occasional deviation of predictions from the actual state of the world and the magnitude of that deviation also provide a basis for anticipate or surprise, a surprising is an excellent method for focusing perception.

134   Marco A. Ramos, Alain Berro, and Yves Duthen

4 Anticipation

Consider that for each agent, for each state, and at each time, there is a computable values for the probability that active agent could successfully collaborate with passive agent. As the world constantly changing, the values for the probability of collaboration are computed as a function of the dynamic world. Assuming that the transition between states for each agent take time or other type cost, then anticipation consists of the selection of a new state that maximizes the probability of future collaboration. Anticipation therefore allows for a flexible adjustment of team agent towards the increase of the probability of being useful for team.

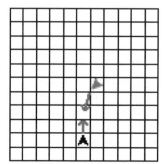 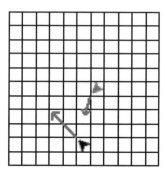

Fig. 5. Anticipation of collision of the agents

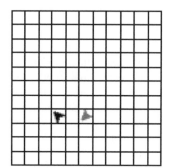 

Fig. 6. Agents in the environment virtual

5 Conclusion

In this paper, we described several LCSs, each of the then casting a new light on the concept of generalization in the LCS framework. In particular, we enlighten how most LCS like XCS consider generalization with respect to an expect payoff, while other LCS like ACS consider it with respect to anticipated effects in terms of situations. We also enlighten some limitation of the formalism of ACS. A lot of future research is needed to understand exactly when and which anticipation is useful or sometimes even mandatory in an environment to yield competent adaptive behavior. Although psychological research proves that anticipations take place in at least higher animals, a clear understanding of the how, the when, and which is not available. Any system of agents system requires some coordination of action. Thus, one essential direction of future research is to identify environmental characteristics in which distinct anticipatory mechanism are helpful or necessary.

References

[Butz, M. 2003] Martin V. Butz, Olivier Sigaud, Pierre Gerard. Internal Models and Anticipations in Adaptive Learning Systems, Department of Cognitive Psychology, University of Würzburg, Germany

[Isla D. 2000] Damian Isla, Robert Burke, Marc Downie, Bruce Blumberg. A Layer Brain Architecture for Synthetic Creatures. The Media Laboratory Massachusetts Institute of Technology, USA.

[Hoffmann, J. 1993] Anticipation and Cognition. Hogrefe, 1993.

[Holland, J.] John H. Holland. Adaptation in Natural and Artificial Systems. (pp. 171-198), MIT press edition.

[Kauffman, 1993] The Origins of Order: Self-Organization and Selection in Evolution, Oxford University

[Langton, 1989] Artificial life, Addison-Wesley.

[Lanzi, 2002] Learning classifier system from reinforcement perspective. Soft Computing, 6(3-4), 162-170

[Reynolds, C. 1987] Craig Reynolds. Flocks, Herds, and Schools: A Distributed Behavioural Model, in Computer Graphics, 21(4) (SIGGRAPH '87 Conference Proceedings) pages 25-34.

[Sanchez, E. 2003] Stéphane Sanchez, Hervé Luga Yves Duthen, Olivier Balet. Virtual Behavior: A framework for real-time animation of animation of autonomous characters. International Symposium and School on Advanced Distributed Systems 2002 (ISSADS). Guadalajara, Jal., México. 2003.

[Stolzmann, 1998] Wolfgang Stolzmann. Anticipatory classifier systems, Genetic programming 1998: Proceedings of the third Annual Conference (pp. 658-664). San Francisco, CA.

[Stolzmann, 2000] Wolfgang Stolzmann. Introducing a genetic generalization pressure to the anticipatory classifier system: Part 1 theoretical approach, Proceeding of the Genetic and evolutionary Computation Conference (GECCO-2000) pp. 34-41. San Francisco, CA.

[Veloso, 1998] Manuela Veloso, Peter Stone, Michel Bowling. Anticipation: A Key For Collaboration in Team of Agents. Computer Science Department. Carnegie-Mellon University.

[Watkins, Dayan, 1992] Learning whit delayed rewards. Doctoral dissertation, Psychology department, University of Cambridge, England.

[Wilson, 1995] Wilson S. W. Classifier Fitness Based on Accuracy Evolutionary Computation, 3(2) 149-175.

Towards Logical Hypertext Structure
A Graph-Theoretic Perspective

Alexander Mehler[1], Matthias Dehmer[2], and Rüdiger Gleim[2]

[1] Universität Bielefeld, D-33501 Bielefeld, Germany
Alexander.Mehler@uni-bielefeld.de
[2] Technische Universität Darmstadt, D-64289 Darmstadt, Germany
{dehmer,gleim}@informatik.tu-darmstadt.de

Abstract. Facing the retrieval problem according to the overwhelming set of documents online the adaptation of text categorization to web units has recently been pushed. The aim is to utilize categories of web sites and pages as an additional retrieval criterion. In this context, the bag-of-words model has been utilized just as HTML tags and link structures. In spite of promising results this adaptation stays in the framework of IR specific models since it neglects the content-based structuring inherent to hypertext units. This paper approaches hypertext modelling from the perspective of graph-theory. It presents an XML-based format for representing websites as *hypergraphs*. These hypergraphs are used to shed light on the relation of hypertext structure types and their web-based instances. We place emphasis on two characteristics of this relation: In terms of *realizational ambiguity* we speak of functional equivalents to the manifestation of the same structure type. In terms of *polymorphism* we speak of a single web unit which manifests different structure types. It is shown that polymorphism is a prevalent characteristic of web-based units. This is done by means of a categorization experiment which analyses a corpus of hypergraphs representing the structure and content of pages of conference websites. On this background we plead for a revision of text representation models by means of hypergraphs which are sensitive to the manifold structuring of web documents.

1 Introduction

Text representation is a preliminary task of any approach to automatic text analysis. Among other things, this relates to the summarization, categorization, and mining of textual units. Analogously, *hypertext representation* is fundamental to *automatic hypertext analysis* [31]. This comprises, for example, the identification of patterns (e.g. compound documents [10], or small worlds in WWW graphs [1]), the categorization of links [3,27] or the retrieval of information from large hypertext bases [2]. In this context, the bag of words model of IR has been utilized as a starting point for hypertext representation just as HTML metadata, tags and link structures. That is, hypertexts are represented as vectors of features reflecting wording or markup as found in the hypertexts to be analyzed.

T. Böhme et al. (Eds.): IICS 2004, LNCS 3473, pp. 136–150, 2006.
© Springer-Verlag Berlin Heidelberg 2006

In spite of promising results this approach stays in the framework of *text representation* as elaborated in IR. Particularly with regard to categorization the predominance of traditional representation models is evident: Categorization is designed as an assignment of predefined category labels to feature vectors without the preceding exploration of hypertext structures (e.g. compound nodes or paths).

In this paper we plead for an integrative view of graph-theoretical analysis and categorization. Our starting point is a system of hypertext structure types and their nondeterministic manifestation by web-based units. We propose a four-layer model of hypertext structure types and focus on the many-to-many relation to its instances as units of Internet-based communication. We place emphasis on two characteristics of this relation: In terms of *realizational ambiguity* we speak of functional equivalents to the manifestation of the same structure type. Conversely, in terms of *polymorphism* the phenomenon is addressed that the same hypertext unit may manifest different structure types. Polymorphism occurs when, for example, the same page provides information about different topics (e.g. a page as part of an academic's homepage lists courses beneath her biographical information) or serves different functions (e.g. a page offers the registration form of a research group beneath its brief description).

Our central hypothesis is that (comparable to natural language texts) realizational ambiguity and polymorphism are prevalent characteristics of web-based units. This has fundamental implications for hypertext categorization which normally presupposes to result in a non-overlapping separation of the object space, i.e. into an assignment of at most one category per object. If polymorphism is prevalent in this area, it does not make sense to view hypertext categorization as a process of disambiguating category assignments. As a consequence, two implications have to be balanced: Either the category system has to be revised, or – and this is our central thesis – the object space has to undergo a structural analysis as the result of which categorization *and* segmentation of the focal objects occurs. Since we view polymorphism to be a characteristic of web-based hypertexts, we expect *multiple, interdependent* categorizations to occur regularly. In other words: Proper hypertext categorization is bound to a preliminary structure analysis in which the regular realizational ambiguity and polymorphism of hypertext units is resolved. In order to support this line of argumentation we present a categorization of web pages of an area which is supposed to follow more stable authoring patterns and thus to be a profitable field of categorization: conference websites. This analysis operates on an XML-based representation format of hypertexts whose presentation is the second central focus of this paper. It is based on the idea to represent web-based units, their content and links as attributed typed directed nested *hypergraphs* [5].

The paper is organized as follows: After an outline of related work, our conceptual framework is presented in section (3): a four-layer model of hypertext structure types. This framework is used as the background of an XML-based format for representing web-based hypertexts as hypergraphs. The basic idea is to combine data-oriented representations of link structure, wording and markup in a uniform model. In other words: The format integrates information relevant to structural analysis *and* categorization. It is proposed as a data-oriented alternative to the document-oriented representation of web pages as DOM trees based on their HTML tags [7]. Section (5) describes the automatic mapping of a corpus of conference websites onto a set of categories. The uniqueness of category assignment is measured in order to shed light on the range of polymorphism in the area under consideration. The practical relevance of our study is outlined in section (6). The paper closes with some conclusions.

2   Related Work

Structural analysis is a much considered topic in hypertext research. Beginning with the seminal article of Botafogo et al. [6], graph theory was utilized as a generic format of hypertext representation. This relates, for example, to the identification of spanning trees in hypertexts [6]. The idea is to markup hypertextual aggregates in order to enhance retrieval and browsing [22]. More recently, candidates of web-based hypertext types (e.g. web hierarchies, directories, corporate and web sites) have been identified by exploring the link structure of their pages [4]. Moreover, plenty of approaches deal with the structuring of single such types [24], their constitutive paths [20] and intentionally defined structural units as, for example, *compound documents* and their leaders [10], *logical domains* and their entry pages [19] or *logical documents* [28]. Whereas these approaches operate on the level of websites and their constituents, another group of approaches focuses on macrostructures. This relates to the distribution of links per node and web-topologies based on these distributions (e.g. the small-world problem [1]) as well as clusters of interrelated web pages and their hubs [9,16,21,22].

This paper also explores aggregates in web-based hypertexts which it conceives as informationally uncertain instances of latent authoring patterns. According to this view, structural analysis is always concerned with two aspects of markup: it includes (i) the exploration and annotation of patterns in concrete hypertexts whose frequent observation allows (ii) their abstraction as hypertext structure types which in turn serve as a precondition of pattern identification. In other words: We view structural analysis always to aim at a model of the underlying authoring patterns, and not only at a segmentation and annotation of their instances. As a preliminary step towards such a *grammar of authoring patterns*, the paper integrates three domains of research: graph theoretic modelling, structural analysis and explorative data analysis.

3   Logical Hypertext Structure

Our starting point is a four-level hypertext model which relies on the distinction of *abstract* structure types and their *concrete* instances as observable parts of the web (see figure 1). According to this view, compound hypertext document types are representations of stable authoring patterns on the level of homepages (e.g. academics' personal homepages). They are defined as systems of more elementary

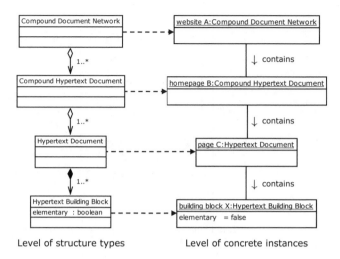

Fig. 1. A class and object diagram of hypertext structure types and their instances

hypertext document types and their regular dependency relations, whereby these document types are defined on their own as regular compositions of types of either complex or elementary building blocks. This multilevel type system is instantiated on four levels (see fig. 1):

1. On the lowest level *types of hypertext building blocks* are manifested by paragraph tags, horizontal rules, lists, tables, etc. Since these building blocks exist only as dependent parts of pages as elementary self-contained units of web-based communication, diagram (1) associates them with document types by *composition* which in UML is symbolized by a filled rhombus.

2. *Hypertext document types* and their dependency relations are instantiated by one or more web pages and their links, respectively. In the literature on web-based documents, these dependency relations have predominantly been classified with the help of rhetorical structure theory [17,26,29]. In terms of the Dexter Hypertext Reference Model [13] this means that the rhetorical relation (e.g. elaboration, exemplification, contrast) served by the target of a link l with respect to its source determines the type of l.

3. *Compound hypertext document types* are instantiated by *compound documents* in the sense of [10], i.e. by networks of pragmatically homogeneous web pages as instances of document types whose coherence is provided by the uniform intention of one or more hypertext authors. Document types are distinguished from *compound* document types by not only being pragmatically, but also functionally homogeneous in the sense of serving the same content function.

4. Finally, *compound document network types* are instantiated by *websites* and thus are characterized by pragmatic *and* content-based heterogeneity.

This multilevel type-instance model is illustrated by *conference websites* whose regular composition supports their expectation-driven processing: They

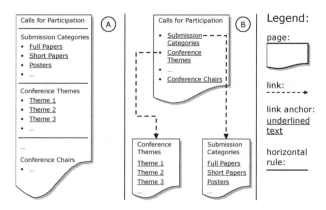

Fig. 2. Schematic drawings of functionally equivalent presentations of the same information as (A) a list and (B) a compound document of three pages

typically consist of pages on calls for participation, the conference program, additional workshops and tutorials etc. as instances of compound hypertext document types. The regular composition of conference websites can be observed on the level of their constitutive compound documents, too: A call for participation typically includes units about submission categories, topics, chairs and the submission procedure, whether they occur on the same page or not. Last but not least, the regular manifestation of building blocks is illustrated by HTML lists as the preferred means of enumerating conference topics.

The distinction of building blocks, document types and their recursive composition to networks of such types follows the linguistic differentiation of elementary text patterns and text (network) types. Evidently, this analogy does not stop with the alignment of both type systems. Rather, it is continued by what is called *realizational ambiguity*: Just as the same text pattern may be realized by different, but functionally equivalent text structures [23], the same kind of realizational ambiguity is observed in web-based communication. In other words: The realization of hypertext document types by websites, web pages, and (X)HTML building blocks is nondeterministic – their exist *functional equivalents* to the realization of the same hypertext structure type. This is once more illustrated by conference websites: In order to inform about a conference's calls for participation, the hypertext author may list all submission categories and conference themes as well as information about the submission procedure on one single page, possibly structured by horizontal rules and section headings (see figure 2.A). Functionally equivalent to this alternative is an instance of a document type leaded by a web page which enumerates the headers 'submission categories', 'conference topics', etc. as anchors of links to pages listing the corresponding subsets of categories (see figure 2.B). Obviously, these two alternatives do not exhaust the range of functional equivalents existing in this area. Moreover, realizational ambiguity is accompanied by what is called *polymorphism*. That is, the same web page may realize *different* hypertext document types. In terms of conference websites polymorphism occurs when for example tutorials are listed on the same page as submission categories. The upper bound of this polymorphism is given by a conference website which manifests all constitutive document types (e.g. calls for participation, program, workshops, etc.) on a *single* page. Polymorphism and realizational ambiguity constitute the $n{:}m$-relation of hypertext structure types and their instances as distinguished in figure 1. Obviously, the range of this relation has not been explored so far.

In order to grasp this type-instance relation, we utilize the document structure model of [23] which has recently been proposed to account for the divergence of rhetorical, logical, and layout structure in written texts. Power et al. systematically report on examples where the same document structure is manifested by different but functionally equivalent texts. The added value of this approach is that it proposes a *document grammar* which supposes hierarchical text structures. This is in accordance with the linguistic tradition to represent structures as hierarchies as reflected by the OHCO-model, which describes texts as Ordered Hierarchies of Content Objects [25]. There is a long debate on the adequacy of the OHCO-model, which for the time being resulted in the proclamation of a poly-hierarchical text structure model [25]. It is well-known that even poly-hierarchies do not adequately model the network structures of hypertexts. This also holds for instances of (compound) hypertext document types: Although they prove to have a kernel hierarchical structure they also contain page internal links as well as *outside links* [4,10] which link pages of different sites and thus transcend the kernel hierarchy.

On this background, we view an extension of the model of Power et al., which also accounts for non-hierarchical links transcending the kernel (poly-)hierarchy, to be the favourite candidate for modelling the relation of hypertext structure types and their instances as shown in figure 1. This model is referred to by the term *LOGical hypertext dOcument Structure* (LOGOS). Its assumptions are:

- Observable web-structures are instances of usage-based and hence probabilistic hypertext structure types on at least four levels (see figure 1).

- The relation of these types to their instances is characterized by realizational ambiguity and polymorphism.

- Compound document types impose a kernel hierarchical structure on their instances on the basis of hierarchy constitutive links.

- An adequate model of hypertext structure types and their dependency relations is a *probabilistic grammar* which represents prototypical web structures on the level of compound document types.

A probabilistic grammar of compound hypertext documents is a formal representation of the yet unknown range of realizational ambiguity and polymorphism in this area. The goal of this paper is to shed light on this range as a preliminary study to such a grammar. It is approached by a quantitative analysis of the structure of conference websites as described in the subsequent sections.

4   Hypertext Representation

In order to approach a grammar of compound hypertext documents, a format is needed which allows to represent web-based hypertexts in a *uniform* and *standardized* as well as *flexible* and *extensible* way. That is, we do not only need a format expressive enough to represent the range and structural variety of functional equivalents of hypertext structure types. We also need a format which proves to be conceptually clear and computationally processable as regards the divergent tasks of automatic hypertext analysis. In order to approach this task of *adequate hypertext representation*, three requirements have to be met:

1. Page-internal and external, outside, inside, up, down and across links have to be mapped as well as the graph structures they induce (e.g. sequences, hierarchies and networks of interlinked pages).

2. User and system perspective (i.e what is seen on the screen vs. its underlying markup) have to be kept apart without ignoring their reciprocal mapping.

3. Link and node classification are two more use cases of machine learning. They demand a hypertext model which includes representations even of the wording of single pages – comparable to the bag-of-words model of IR, but with the difference that now graphs of such representations have to be managed since web pages are embedded into hypertext graphs.

The subsequent section presents an XML-based format for representing hypertexts as graphs. It is based on the Graph eXchange Language (GXL) [30], which has been developed as an XML-based format for data interchange between information systems. We utilize this format for hypertext representation:

4.1   XML-Based Hypertext Representation

Hypertext representation serves to map hypertexts onto instances of a format which supports the different tasks of hypertext analysis. The idea of our approach is that hypertexts are adequately modelled as graphs. This is in accordance with hypertext modelling [6,12]. We continue this tradition by using the GXL DTD against which automatically generated *hypertext graphs* are validated. The graph model of the GXL distinguishes six graph classes which we utilize as follows:

Graphs are ordered pairs (V, E) of a vertex set V and an edge set E. In the GXL, vertices are referred to as XML-elements named `node`. In the LOGOS framework, instances of this element are commonly used to represent single web pages identified by an ID and an GXL-attribute named URI (see table 1). Accordingly, instances of the elements `edge` and `rel`(ation) are commonly used to represent links of these nodes (see below).

Typed graphs are graphs with typed vertices and edges. We use typing to distinguish anchor nodes and page nodes as well as standard links and frame source links. Typing is manifested by the `type` element and its `xlink:href` attribute. Since we need several type systems to independently classify the same set of hypertext constituents, we also construct attributed graphs:

Table 1. A hypertext graph of a conference website (dots indicate omitted content)

```
<gxl xmlns:xlink="http://www.w3.org/1999/xlink">
  <graph hypergraph="true" edgemode="directed" id="HyperGraph0">
    <attr name="Title"><string>Hypertext 2004</string></attr>
    <node id="Page1">
      <attr name="URI"><locator xlink:href="http://www.ht04.org"/></attr>
      <attr name="Title">
        <string>Hypertext 2004 - Fifteenth Annual Conference on
        Hypertext and Hypermedia</string>
      </attr>
      <graph hypergraph="false" edgemode="directed" id="EmbeddedGraph2">
        <node id="Anchor5"> ... </node> ...
      </graph>
    </node> ...
    <node id="Page843">
      <attr name="URI">
        <locator xlink:href="http://www.ht04.org/cfpPapers.php"/>
      </attr>
      <attr name="Title">
        <string>Hypertext 2004 - Papers Call for Participation</string>
      </attr> ...
    </node> ...
    <rel id="HyperLink875">
      <attr name="LinkStructureType"><enum>kernellink</enum></attr>
      <relend direction="in" target="Page1" role="sourcepage"/>
      <relend direction="in" target="Anchor5" role="sourceanchor"/>
      <relend direction="out" target="Page843" role="targetpage"/>
    </rel> ...
  </graph>
</gxl>
```

Attributed graphs are graphs whose nodes and edges are assigned possibly nested bags, sets, tuples or sequences of boolean, integer, real or string valued attributes. In hypertext representation they are inter alia used to model the URL of a web page and its metatags as an attribute-value pair and a bag of such pairs enclosed by an GXL-attribute named `MetaTags`, respectively. Analogously, the content of a page (i.e. the wording and HTML tags enclosed by its `body` element) is modelled by a `TokenVector` element. This vector serves as a representation model in automatic hypertext categorization (see section 5). Furthermore, links are assigned a GXL-attribute named `LinkType` whose values distinguish between up, down, inside, outside and across links (see below). Finally, the GXL attribute model may also be used to represent HTML lists, tables and embedded objects as attributes of nodes.

Directed graphs are graphs whose edges are ordered pairs of nodes, *adjacent from* their source and *adjacent to* their target node. They are the default means of representing HTML links whose source and target anchors belong to the same web page, i.e. page internal links (see link C in figure 3). This is done

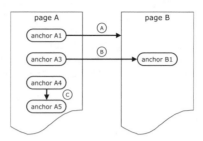

Fig. 3. Internal (C) and external links with (B) and without (A) target anchor

with the help of two attributes assigned to the **edge** element (see table 1): **from** and **to** take as values the **ID** of the corresponding source and target node anchor, respectively. Thus, they behave as **IDREF** attributes in **XML**. In spite of this preferred usage, **edge** elements, their attributes and content model are not restricted to map only **HTML** links. As the **GXL** model of hypergraphs (see below) shows, even sophisticated links following the **XLink** standard can be modelled in **GXL** – it is this expressive power of the **GXL** which underlies our decision to use it as the primary format for representing web-structures.

Ordered graphs are directed graphs whose arcs are assigned ordinal numbers reflecting any order dependent on their respective source node. In linguistics, such assignments can be used to model the syntagmatic order of immediate constituents of superordinate nodes. In hypertext representation they are analogously used to model the order of links (dependent on the textual order of their anchors) which are adjacent *from* the same node. This order is manifested by a **GXL**-attribute named **order** and assigned to the respective **rel**(ation) element.

Stratified graphs are graphs whose nodes (may) embed graphs on their own. In hypertext representation they are used to model page-internal structures composed of links whose source and target anchors belong to the same page (see link C in figure 3). In order to map this membership, the graph spanned by the links internal to a page is included by the content model of the node modelling this page. Following this approach, the **GXL** realizes a kind of document-oriented modelling – *complementing its predominant data-oriented character*. Since page-internal links simply consist of a (possibly attributed) association of two anchors belonging to the same page, the **edge** element suffices as the **GXL** analogon of graph theoretic edges to model this kind of links. In case of all other links, so called hyperedges of hypergraphs are used:

Hypergraphs are graphs whose *hyper*edges are subsets of the vertex set V. Hyperedges may also be ordered and directed. This qualifies them for modelling **HTML** links whose anchors belong to different web pages (see link B in figure 3). Table (1) illustrates an instance of the element **rel**(ation) which models a link of two pages (identified by **Page1** and **Page843**). The content model of the hyperedge in question comprises a **relend** element targeting at **Page1** as its **sourcepage**, a **rel**(ation)**end** targeting at **Page843** as its **targetpage**, and a **relend** element targeting at the link's source page anchor.

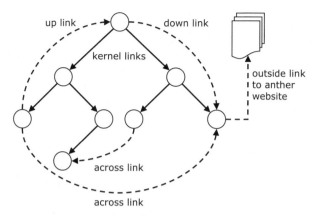

Fig. 4. The kernel hierarchy with additional up, down, across and outside links

Links with a target anchor specification in the URL value of their href attribute (see link B in figure 3) are modelled as rel elements with a relend element of role targetanchor. Since relation ends can be extended by any GXL-attribute and since hyperedges of this kind are not restricted regarding the number of their targets, they allow to model any relation of any valency. In other words, hyperedges are the preferred means to represent complex links of the XLink standard *using the same representation format as in case of* HTML *links.*

With the help of the GXL, web-based hypertexts on the level of compound documents, their constitutive pages and the internal link structure of these pages are mapped onto XML documents – henceforth called *hypertext graphs* – as instances of the GXL DTD. As claimed by the LOGOS model in section (3), these hypertext graphs have a kernel hierarchical structure whose constitutive links are tagged as rel(ation) elements of LinkType kernellink (see for example HyperLink875 in table 1). This kernel hierarchy is illustrated by a conference website leaded by a title page and continued by a page on the corresponding call for papers which in turn is continued by a page on style sheets, etc. The root of the kernel hierarchy of a hypertext graph is identified by the GXL-attribute RootID of the global graph element. The web page corresponding to that root has to be explored in advance as the leader (or home page) in the sense of [10]. The compound document leaded by that page is for the time being identified by a breadth first search starting with the leader and identifying the spanning tree rooted by it.

Kernel links are distinguished from up, down, inside, outside and across links [4,10,26], which in the following are defined on the basis of the kernel hierarchy spanned by the kernel links of the respective hypertext graph (see figure 4):

Kernel links associate dominating nodes with their immediately dominated successor nodes.

Down links associate nodes of the kernel hierarchy with one of their (dominated) successor nodes in terms of that kernel hierarchy.

Up links associate analogously nodes of the kernel hierarchy with one of their (dominating) predecessor nodes.

Across links associate nodes of the kernel hierarchy none of which is an (im-)mediate predecessor of the other in terms of the kernel hierarchy.

Inside links are node (i.e. page) internal links.

Outside links associate nodes of the kernel hierarchy with nodes of other websites.

These types of links are tagged by means of the GXL-attribute named `Link-Type` whose string-value belongs to the set {`uplink, downlink, insidelink, outsidelink, acrosslink`}. Table (3) lists the frequencies of these types as found in our test corpus of 13,481 pages of 1,000 conference/workshop websites from computer science and mathematics.

According to our LOGOS model, web-based hypertexts are represented as typed attributed directed ordered hypergraphs supplemented by graph stratification and markup of a kernel hierarchy. This is done with the help of the GXL as a uniform format for representing hypertexts, their nodes, links and other building blocks. These hypertext representations serve as a *uniform* input/output format of any subsequent qualitative/quantitative hypertext analysis. It is this general requirement hypertext graphs are generated to meet.

5   Hypertext Categorization

Hypertext categorization is the task of automatically assigning category labels to hypertext units [8]. It utilizes HTML markup, metatags and link structure beyond representations of the units' wording as input of feature selection [11,31]. In our categorization experiment pages of conference websites are categorized (see table 2). The aim is to shed light on the range of polymorphism which we expect to be accompanied by a regular multiple-categorization. If polymorphism is a characteristic of web-based units, their pages cannot serve as the elementary unit of hypertext categorization, since polymorphic pages simultaneously instantiate several categories. In order to verify this we use Support Vector Machine (SVM) classification which proves to be successful in text categorization especially in cases of high dimensional, sparse and noisy feature vectors [15]. Handling noisy data is of outmost importance in hypertext categorization since we cannot expect to observe instances of well established authoring practices comparable to well established text types.

To implement this we use the LibSVM implementation of SVMs [14]. We use C-SVM and an RBF-*kernel function* of type $K(u,v) := e^{-\gamma \|u-v\|^2}$. In order to derive optimal parameter vectors (C, γ) for our training sets we perform a search in the parameter space $P := \{(C, \gamma) | C = 2^g, \gamma = 2^s, g \in \{-4, 0, 4, \ldots, 20\}, s \in \{-16, -12, -8, \ldots, 8\}\}$ in combination with a 5-fold cross validation. For each category we choose those parameter vector which minimizes the error of cross validation with respect to the training set. As features all tokens and HTML tags enclosed by the `body` and `head` element of the respective page are used. The training set of category C_i was designed as follows: starting from the overall

Table 2. The set of categories and their uniqueness coefficient U_i

category	label	prec.	recall	acc.	#matchings	U_i
submission and author instructions	C_1	29,1%	99,0%	70,8%	2107	0,10
call for papers	C_2	41,6%	99,0%	82,5%	2661	0,05
important dates	C_3	41,2%	99,0%	90,4%	1992	0,05
committees	C_4	50,0%	99,2%	88,2%	1546	0,24
accepted papers	C_5	66,6%	99,0%	72,1%	3846	0,02
topics and general information	C_6	35,0%	99,1%	90,4%	3616	0,02
program	C_7	25,5%	66,0%	68,4%	2716	0,14
travel and accommodation	C_8	50,0%	99,2%	80,3%	2245	0,03
venue	C_9	32,0%	99,0%	66,3%	3045	0,02
invited speakers	C_{10}	25,0%	99,0%	80,1%	2206	0,01
registration	C_{11}	46,1%	99,0%	71,3%	3339	0,03
sponsors	C_{12}	41,6%	99,0%	82,9%	4627	0,03
workshops	C_{13}	52,1%	99,2%	94,1%	1141	0,02

training set (of about 800 pages) all positive examples of C_i were selected and a random sample of negative examples was chosen whose cardinality equaled the set of positive examples of C_i in the overall set, whereby the negative examples were uniformly distributed over the set of remaining categories. The evaluation of performance on the basis of our corpus (see table 3) is shown in table 2. It demonstrates very high recall, but low precision values; with the exception of category C_7, the categories are in many cases wrongly applied. In other words: the categorization is highly error-prone. This result is confirmed by the uniqueness coefficient $U_i \in [0, 1]$ which relates the number of test cases assigned solely to category C_i to the total number of assignments to this category, where $\|C_i(u)\| = 1$ iff the page u belongs to category C_i; $|C| = 13$ is the cardinality of the set of categories:

$$U_i := \frac{|\{u \in U \mid C_i(u) \wedge \neg(C_1(u) \vee \ldots \vee C_{i-1}(u) \vee C_{i+1}(u) \vee \ldots \vee C_{|C|}(u))\}|}{|\{u \in U \mid C_i(u)\}|}.$$

Table (2) demonstrates the extremely low discriminatory power of our category set. There are at least four possible reasons for this deficiency: Either, the category set is erroneous in the sense of not being fine-grained enough, for example, or the training corpora have to be redesigned, or SVM categorization has to be replaced by another method, or – and this is our preferred reading – the pages in question are systematically polymorphic: they simultaneously manifest – as a sample of the websites has shown – more than one function in conference announcement. That is we do not directly cast doubt on the category set, but rather argue for a preceding exploration of patterns of page internal structures in order to disentangle functional equivalents and polymorphic units as a preliminary step to any categorization. In this sense, hypertext categorization is bound to an integration of vector space and structure oriented models.

Table 3. The corpus of conference web sites used in the categorization experiment

Attribute	Value	Attribute	Value
Number of web sites	1,000	Number of up links	10,535
Number of web pages	13,481	Number of down links	13,012
Number of frame set links	1,236	Number of across links	43,145
Number of kernel links	12,382	Number of internal links	6,323

6   Applications

In hypertext analysis various graph theoretic measures are investigated [6]. These measures generally ignore syntactic, semantic and pragmatic types of nodes and links as well as the sub-structures they induce. We plan to develop measures which focus on that deficit. We especially focus on measures that are based on node sequences and sequence alignments. Measures and *spectral algorithms* to describe maximal subgraphs in the sense of semantic similar regions will be defined on the Matrix $(s_{ij})_{ij}, 1 \leq i \leq n, 1 \leq j \leq n, i, j \in \mathbb{N}$, where s_{ij} is the similarity between the text sequences representing the nodes v_i and v_j computed by the metric explained in [18]. The application area of these measures is the exploration of WWW patterns, i.e. the classification of web-units based on fine-grained representations of their structuring.

A further application area of structural hypertext analysis is the enhancement of browsing and information retrieval from large hypertext bases. The idea is to gain an additional guideline for browsing and retrieval from the markup of hypertext aggregates above the level of elementary nodes and links. We also follow this line of argumentation, but propose a further field of application, namely *large-scale hypertext authoring and maintenance*. This proposal follows Power et al. [23] who describe a text authoring tool which allows a text designer to chose among a set of parameters which control the manifestation of the same logical document structure by different texts. Analogously, we plan an authoring tool which automatically produces and maintains web pages on the basis of their GXL hypertext graphs and the designers choice of functional equivalents to the manifestation of hypertext structure types. The application scenario of this tool is a large scale intranet or website with a tremendous number of heterogeneously designed web pages. The first task is to map these pages onto a set of GXL hypertext graphs. The next step would be a redesign by standardizing, for example, the functional equivalents to the manifestation of the same structure type (e.g. presentation of project descriptions). That is, we plan to use hypertext representation not only for the *analysis* of existing, but also for the *synthesis* of new web documents.

7   Conclusions

Starting from a four-level hypertext structure model we introduced the concepts of realizational ambiguity and polymorphism. That is, we view web-based units to be informationally uncertain manifestations of latent authoring patterns. We argued that in order to derive an adequate hypertext model this informational uncertainty has to be explored first. In order to show this we performed a categorization experiment according to which even higher performing categories do not prove to be stable predictors of hypertext units – due to multiple and fuzzy categorizations. Our conclusions are twofold: First, we argue for structure analysis which tries to identify functional equivalents to the manifestation of hypertext structure types and to resolve the pages' inherent polymorphism as a preliminary step of any hypertext categorization. We are convinced that without such an analysis it does not make sense to compare different websites since there may exist hypertext graphs which manifest the same structure types by means of radically divergent surface structures and at the same time there may exist graphs which manifest divergent structure types by means of similar surface structures. Second, we plead for a reconstruction of (hyper-)text representation models used in content analysis, which depart form the vector space model in the sense that they map both, the structure and content of units to be represented.

References

1. L. A. Adamic. The small world of web. In S. Abiteboul and A.-M. Vercoustre, editors, *Research and Advanced Technology for Digital Libraries*, pages 443–452. Springer, Berlin/Heidelberg/New York, 1999.
2. M. Agosti and A. F. Smeaton. *Information Retrieval and Hypertext*. Kluwer, Boston, 1996.
3. J. Allan. Automatic hypertext link typing. In *Proceedings of the 7th ACM Conference on Hypertext*, pages 42–52. ACM, 1996.
4. E. Amitay, D. Carmel, A. Darlow, R. Lempel, and A. Soffer. The connectivity sonar: detecting site functionality by structural patterns. In *Proc. of the 14th ACM conference on Hypertext and Hypermedia*, pages 38–47, 2003.
5. C. Berge. *Hypergraphs: Combinatorics of Finite Sets*. North Holland, Amsterdam, 1989.
6. R. A. Botafogo, E. Rivlin, and B. Shneiderman. Structural analysis of hypertexts: Identifying hierarchies and useful metrics. *ACM Transactions on Information Systems*, 10(2):142–180, 1992.
7. S. Chakrabarti. Integrating the document object model with hyperlinks for enhanced topic distillation and information extraction. In *Proc. of the 10th International World Wide Web Conference, Hong Kong, May 1-5*, pages 211–220, 2001.
8. S. Chakrabarti, B. Dom, and P. Indyk. Enhanced hypertext categorization using hyperlinks. In L. Haas and A. Tiwary, editors, *Proceedings of ACM SIGMOD International Conference on Management of Data*, pages 307–318. ACM, 1998.
9. S. Chakrabarti, M. Joshi, K. Punera, and D. M. Pennock. The structure of broad topics on the web. In *Proc. of the 11th Internat. World Wide Web Conference*, pages 251–262. ACM Press, 2002.
10. N. Eiron and K. S. McCurley. Untangling compound documents on the web. In *Proceedings of the 14th ACM conference on Hypertext and hypermedia, Nottingham, UK*, pages 85–94, 2003.
11. J. Fürnkranz. Using links for classifying web-pages. Technical report, TR-OEFAI-98-29, 1998.

12. J. Furner, D. Ellis, and P. Willett. The representation and comparison of hypertext structures using graphs. In M. Agosti and A. F. Smeaton, editors, *Information Retrieval and Hypertext*, pages 75–96. Kluwer, Boston, 1996.
13. F. Halasz and M. Schwartz. The Dexter hypertext reference model. *Communications of the ACM*, 37(2):30–39, 1994.
14. C.-W. Hsu, C.-C. Chang, and C.-J. Lin. A practical guide to SVM classification. Technical report, Department of Computer Science and Information Technology, National Taiwan University, 2003.
15. T. Joachims. *Learning to classify text using support vector machines*. Kluwer, Boston, 2002.
16. J. M. Kleinberg. Authoritative sources in a hyperlinked environment. *Journal of the ACM*, 46(5):604–632, 1999.
17. R. Kuhlen. *Hypertext: ein nichtlineares Medium zwischen Buch und Wissensbank*. Springer, Berlin/Heidelberg/New York, 1991.
18. M. Li, X. Chen, L. Xin, B. Ma, and P. M. Vitányi. The similarity metric. In *Proceedings of the 14th Annual ACM-SIAM Symposium on Discrete Algorithms*, pages 863–872. ACM Press, 2003.
19. W.-S. Li, O. Kolak, Q. Vu, and H. Takano. Defining logical domains in a web site. In *Proc. of the 11th ACM on Hypertext and Hypermedia*, pages 123–132, 2000.
20. Y. Mizuuchi and K. Tajima. Finding context paths for web pages. In *Proceedings of the 10th ACM Conference on Hypertext and Hypermedia*, pages 13–22, 1999.
21. S. Mukherjea and Y. Hara. Focus+context views of world-wide web nodes. In *Proceedings of the eighth ACM conference on Hypertext*, pages 187–196, 1997.
22. P. Pirolli, J. Pitkow, and R. Rao. Silk from a sow's ear: Extracting usable structures from the web. In *Proc. of the ACM SIGCHI Conference on Human Factors in Computing*, pages 118–125. ACM Press, 1996.
23. R. Power, D. Scott, and N. Bouayad-Agha. Document structure. *Computational Linguistics*, 29(2):211–260, 2003.
24. G. Rehm. Towards automatic web genre identification – a corpus-based approach in the domain of academia by example of the academic's personal homepage. In *Proc. of the Hawai'i Internat. Conf. on System Sciences*, January 7-10 2002.
25. A. Renear. Out of praxis: Three (meta)theories of textuality. In K. Sutherland, editor, *Electronic Text. Investigations in Method and Theory*, pages 107–126. Clarendon Press, Oxford, 1997.
26. L. Routledge, B. Bailey, J. van Ossenbruggen, L. Hardman, and J. Geurts. Generating presentation constraints from rhetorical structure. In *Proceedings of the 11th ACM Conference on Hypertext and Hypermedia*, pages 19–28. ACM, 2000.
27. E. Spertus. ParaSite: mining structural information on the web. In *Selected papers from the sixth international conference on World Wide Web*, pages 1205–1215. Elsevier, 1997.
28. K. Tajima and K. Tanaka. New techniques for the discovery of logical documents in web. In *Internat. Symposium on Database Applications in Non-Traditional Environments*, pages 125–132. IEEE, 1999.
29. M. Thüring, J. Hannemann, and J. M. Haake. Hypermedia and cognition: Designing for comprehension. *Communications of the ACM*, 38(8):57–66, 1995.
30. A. Winter, B. Kullbach, and V. Riedinger. An overview of the GXL graph exchange language. In S. Diehl, editor, *Software Visualization*, pages 324–336. Springer, Berlin/Heidelberg, 2002.
31. Y. Yang, S. Slattery, and R. Ghani. A study of approaches to hypertext categorization. *Journal of Intelligent Information Systems*, 18(2-3):219–241, 2002.

Calculating Communities by Link Analysis of URLs

Gerhard Heyer and Uwe Quasthoff

Leipzig University Computer Science Institute,
Natural Language Processing Department, Augustusplatz 10 / 11 D-04109 Leipzig
{heyer,quasthoff}@informatik.uni-leipzig.de

Abstract. Collocation analysis finds semantic associations of concepts using large text corpora. If the same procedure is applied to sets of outgoing links of web pages, we can find semantically related web domains to a large extent. The structure of the semantic clusters shows all properties of small worlds. The algorithm is known to work for large parts of the web like the German internet. As a sample application we present a surf guide for the German web.

Introduction

When analyzing the internet, the term „community" generally refers to a collection of web pages that offer content to one and the same topic and contain links of each other. It is well known that within internet communities there exists a characteristic link structure that can be measured and described by graph theoretical means [Gibson 1998], [Barabasi 2000]. Among the key aspects that need to be taken into account by an algorithmic description of communities, we briefly rehearse the following (cf. [Brinkmann 2003]):

- **Structure:** Prototypical structures comprise centralistic structures, generally known as authorities and hubs, and so-called webrings [Deo 2001]. In reality, however, an internet community will contain a *variety* of link structures.
- **Non-exclusiveness:** Participants in a community can be members in another community, too. Membership to a community must not be exclusive.
- **Hierarchy:** Communities can themselves be part of larger communities. In general, a community that is contained by a larger community can be considered a specialisation of the more general one.
- **Communication:** Communities can be related, i.e. there may be communication links between communities.

It is also generally accepeted, that an algorithm for detecting communities must fulfill the following requirements:

- **Stability:** The algorithm should yield nearly the same results when fed with the slightly disturbed data. In particular, the choice of a starting point for calculating the community should have no effect on the result.
- **Performance:** In order to efficiently calculate community structures, the performance of the algorithm should have a complexity between linear and quadratic complexity. Otherwise communities could be computed by means of clustering algorithms known to have cubic complexity.

In what follows, we present an approach to calculating internet communities based on a natural language processing technology for calculating semantic networks of words. The basic idea is that if we are interested in the characteristic concepts of a

T. Böhme et al. (Eds.): IICS 2004, LNCS 3473, pp. 151–156, 2006.
© Springer-Verlag Berlin Heidelberg 2006

certain subject area, we can take some known concepts of this subject area and look for concepts co-occurring significantly often with those starting concepts. This co-occurrence can be measured for texts using a window size of one sentence at a time. Here we want to apply the same procedure to URLs: Assuming that URLs often mentioned on the same web page belong to the same subject area, we want to generate a cluster of semantically related URLs.

It turns out that the algorithms developed for the semantic analysis of natural language yield promising results for the semantic analysis of the internet.

Background: Collocations

Some words co-occur with certain other words with a significantly higher probability and this co-occurrence is semantically indicative. We call the occurrence of two or more words within a well-defined unit of information (sentence, document) a *collocation*. For the selection of meaningful and significant collocations, the following collocation measure has been defined (cf. [Quasthoff 2002]).

Let a, b be the number of sentences containing A and B, k be the number of sentences containing both A and B, and n be the total number of sentences.

Our significance measure calculates the probability of joint occurrence of rare events. The results of this measure are similar to the *log-likelihood*-measure:

Let $x = ab / n$ and define:

$$sig(A,B) = \frac{-\log\left(1 - e^{-x}\sum_{i=0}^{k-1}\frac{1}{i!}\cdot x^i\right)}{\log n}$$

For $2x < k$, we get the following approximation, which is much easier to calculate:

$$sig(A,B) = \frac{(x - k\log x + \log k!)}{\log n}$$

In general, this measure yields semantically acceptable collocation sets for values above an empirically determined positive threshold. Hence, we can use this measure to select the relevant words in a sentence and to determine the context of a word in a collection of texts.

Example: *Detroit*

Fig. 1 shows the collocations of the word *Detroit*. Two words are connected if they are collocations of each other. The graph is drawn useing *simulated annealing* (see [Davidson 1996]). Line thickness represents the significance of the collocation. In Fig. 1 we find three different aspects of *Detroit*: Mainly other cities related to Detroit and Names of Organizations based in *Detroit*.

Link Analysis

The following link analysis was performed for a significant part of the German web, i.e. for ".de"-domains.

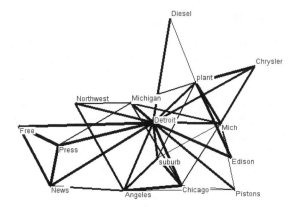

Fig. 1. Collocation Graph for *Detroit*

The analysis of URLs follows the collocation analysis described above as close as possible. Analyzing sentence collocations, we analyse a large corpus of monolingual text and look for words (or concepts) occurring significantly often together within sentences. Both, the number of sentences and the number of different words are usually in the range of 10^6. A typical sentence contains about 10 words.

In the case of link analysis we will get numbers in the same range if we consider the following units for our analysis:

1. URLs found in link targets replace words. Web pages replace sentences. For a given web page, the corresponding 'sentence' just contains sets of link targets found on this page. Their order is irrelevant.
2. Two URLs co-occur in such a sentence if there are links to both of them on the original web page generating the sentence.
3. We only consider top-level-domains. Hence, both www.xyz.de/index.html and www.xyz.de/programm/2004.html are mapped to the same URL www.xyz.de. Dubletts are removed from the sentences.

The number of sentences generated this way again is in the range of 10^6. The number of different words also has the desired size of 10^6. The reason for these numbers, relatively small compared to the actual number of web pages, is as follows. First, only part of the German web was crawled. Second, many web pages do not contain links to other URLs. This reduces the number of sentences about a factor of 10. And for many URLs we did not crawl incoming links which reduces the number of words. Let us consider the individual steps of the analysis in detail.

Step 1: Sets of Links as Sentences

The following box gives two sample sentences as stored in the database. For inspection reasons the fist entry is the URL of the page containing the links given in the second part:

```
http://www.jazzdimensions.de/interviews/portraits/craig_schoedler.html
        www.craigschoedler.com  www.atomz.com  www.phonoclub.de
http://www.google.de/appliance/index.html                www.reuters.com
        www.infoworld.com  www.ecommercetimes.com  services.google.com
```

Step2: Collocations of Links

In the analysis of natural language text, collocations have proved to be useful to discover pairs of words connected by a semantic relation. The software available for calculating collocations between words works for large texts of 10^9 running words (tokens) containing 10^7 different words (types).

Now, the same procedure is applied on sets of URLs instead of sentences of words.

To calculate the similarity of two URLs A and B using the formula given above, now let a, b be the number of incoming links for A and B, k be the number of pages containing both links to A and B, and n be the total number of pages.

Due to the data structure we can apply exactly the same algorithms. Sample results are given in the next section.

Comparison of URLs and Words

Figure 2 shows the most similar URLs for www.heidelberg.de both in a list ordered by similarity and drawn using simulated annealing as described above.

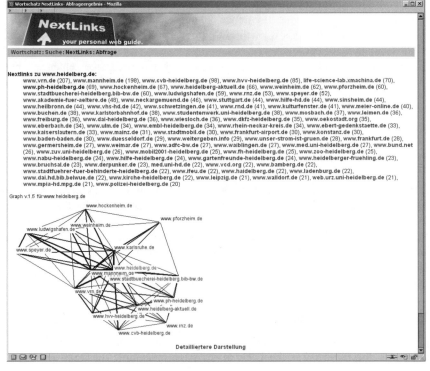

Fig. 2.

The graph of the URL *www.heidelberg.de* shows strong similiarities to the graph of the word *Detroit*: Both the word and the URL of the cities are connected to the same type of objects. On one hand, they are connected to other cities nearby and/or of the same size, on the other hand, they are connected to organisations of the city. Hence, the identical ananalysis of both text and links represent the underlying semantics in the same way. This might lead to the conclusion that human authors use links the same way as they use words: In the typical case, both words and links are choosen carefully according to their semantic content. In the case of proper names, both the word and the URL are used to denote the same object. What the algorithms find out mihgt be the relations between those objects, regardless of their representation

Application: NextLinks

In order to test the results for user acceptence, we implemented a *surf guide* called NextLinks which displays the top-10 similar URLs for the URL found in the browser window, see figure 3 for www.heidelberg.de.

Fig. 3.

At the moment, the following data are used:

Table 1. Amount of data for domain similarity

Number of URLs crawled	980.751
Number of different domains found	886.107
Number of domains with similar domains found	351.033

NextLinks is available from http://wortschatz.informatik.uni-leipzig.de/nextlinks/

Further Steps

To get deeper insights into the link structure of the web we need more data. The data used here were crawled with nedlib [NEDLIB], but this crawler does not scale very well. The next dataset will be crawled by a distributed system having many clients for crawling and link extraction.

The similarity between links and words shown for cities can be carried further if one analyses the strings used to name domains and subdomains. Here we can find even more relations between URLs and words.

References

[Barabasi 2000] A.L. Barabasi et al.. Scale-free characteristics of random networks: the topology of the World-wide web, Physica A (281), 70-77. 2000

[Brinkmeier 2003] M. Brinkmeier. Communities in Graphs, in: Böhme, Th., Heyer, G., Unger, H. (eds.), Innovative Internet Community Systems, Proceedings of the Third International Workshop I2CS 2003, Leipzig, 20-35, Springer: Berlin, Heidelberg, New York 2003

[Davidson 1996] R. Davidson, D. Harel. Drawing graphs nicely using simulated annealing. ACM Transactions on Graphics. vol. 15, num. = 4, pp. 301-331. 1996

[Deo 2001] N. Deo, P. Gupta. World Wide web: a Graph Theoretic Approach. Technical Report CS TR-01-001, University of Central Florida, Orlando Fl. USA, 2001

[Gibson 1998] D.Gibson, J.Kleinberg, P.Raghavan. Inferring Web Communities from Link Topology. in Proceedings of the 9th ACM Conference on Hypertext and Hypermedia, Pittsburgh, Pennsylvania, pp. 225-234, 1998

[NEDLIB] NEDLIB Harvester, http://www.csc.fi/sovellus/nedlib/

[Quasthoff, U. 2002] U.Quasthoff, Chr. Wolff. The Poisson Collocation Measure and its Applications, in: Proc. Second International Workshop on Computational Approaches to Collocations, Wien, Juli 2002.

Automatically Building Concept Structures and Displaying Concept Trails for the Use in Brainstorming Sessions and Content Management Systems

Christian Biemann, Karsten Böhm, Gerhard Heyer, and Ronny Melz

University of Leipzig, Institute of Computer Science
{biem,boehm,heyer,rmelz}@informatik.uni-leipzig.de

Abstract. The automated creation and the visualization of concept structures become more important as the number of relevant information continues to grow dramatically. Especially information and knowledge intensive tasks are relying heavily on accessing the relevant information or knowledge at the right time. Moreover the capturing of relevant facts and good ideas should be focused on as early as possible in the knowledge creation process.

In this paper we introduce a technology to support knowledge structuring processes already at the time of their creation by building up concept structures in real time. Our focus was set on the design of a minimal invasive system, which ideally requires no human interaction and thus gives the maximum freedom to the participants of a knowledge creation or exchange processes. The initial prototype concentrates on the capturing of spoken language to support meetings of human experts, but can be easily adapted for the use in Internet communities that have to rely on knowledge exchange using electronic communication channels.

1 Introduction

With a growing number of communities in the Internet, tools are needed that provide aid in communication within and between them. People with different backgrounds might use the same term for different concepts or call one concept with different names – often without even noticing. The result is an inherent misunderstanding between people who want and need to cooperate, leading to communication problems, frustrations and finally to financial losses.

Our goal is to support the communication and mutual understanding in two ways: On one hand we provide a visualisation tool for spoken language, having its application in informal creative and usually highly innovative meetings like brainstorming sessions or open space workshops (cf. [Owen, 1998]. In these scenarios the tool does not only serve as an automatic documentation method by arranging the keywords in a meaningful way, but also provides corpus-based associations in order to enrich the conversation with concepts that are related but might have been forgotten by the participants.

On the other hand we use the same visualization engine for displaying single documents as trails on a so-called *semantic map*. The idea of a semantic map is heavily relying on the well known concept of geographical maps, in which visual structuring of interesting locations and the emphasizing of relevant paths between them are the key concepts to provide an orientation for the user. Other important properties of geographical maps that deal with an appropriate information filtering are the different

T. Böhme et al. (Eds.): IICS 2004, LNCS 3473, pp. 157–167, 2006.

levels of scale and thematic scopes (e.g. political maps vs. hiking maps). The semantic maps introduces in this paper will reflect this properties too. Since the location of the concepts on the map is fixed, users can grasp the contents of a document rapidly and compare documents in a visual way.

The description of these features and the discussion of possible applications will be the topic of this paper. Both features are part of a prototype implementation called "SemanticTalk" which has been presented to the public in at the worlds largest IT-Exhibition CeBit in Hanover, Germany, in spring 2004.

The remaining paper is organized as follows: In the following section we will introduce the underlying technologies for our approach. Section 3 describes the current implementations in the prototype. Current applications are shown in section 4. The concluding section 5 shows some issues for further research.

2 Base Technologies

After introducing the notion of statistically significant co-occurrences, we describe how the results of this calculation method – the global contexts – give rise to the construction of semantic maps and the automatic associations provided by the system in brainstorming mode.

2.1 Statistically Significant Co-occurrences

The occurrence of two or more words within a well-defined unit of information (sentence, document) is called a co-occurrence. For the selection of meaningful and significant collocations, an adequate co-occurrence measure has to be defined: Our significance measure is based on a function comparable to the well-known statistical *G-Test* for Poisson distributions: Given two words *A*, *B*, each occurring *a*, *b* times in sentences, and *k* times together, we calculate the significance *sig(A, B)* of their occurrence in a sentence as follows:

$$sig(A,B) = x - k \log x + \log k!$$

with n = number of sentences,

$$x = \frac{ab}{n}.$$

Two different types of co-occurrences are generated: based on occurrence *within the same sentence* as well as *immediate left and right neighbors of each word*. For further discussion on co-occurrences, see [Biemann et al. 2004].

In short, the co-occurrence statistics result in connection strengths between words, which tend to appear in the same contexts. In the following, connections below a significance threshold are dropped, leading to the notion of the global context of words: Whereas words occurring with a reference word in a single sentence are called local contexts, the global context of the reference consists of the most significant co-occurrences.

2.2 Visualization with TouchGraph

TouchGraph (see also *www.touchgraph.com*) is a freely available 2D visualization tool for dynamically developing complex graphs. It is written in Java and provided under the conditions of the apache-style software[1]. Within our solution the software is used as a framework for the visualization of semantic maps.

The layout mechanisms of TouchGraph provide methods to add, change/delete both nodes and edges to a graph already being visualized, causing it to jiggle and find a new stable state. The principle can be captured if you consider the nodes to be positive electrical charges, dispersed due to the electrical force but some of them bounded by a constraint force imposed by the edges. This is exactly the effect we want to visualize: unbounded objects (which can be whole clusters or single word forms) are drifting away until they find a stable position, because semantically they do not have anything in common. Different nodes representing semantic objects can be connected with one or more semantic relations while the network grows. As a result the distance between them decreases, nodes related to each other are automatically repositioned. Aside from the automatic layout mechanism, TouchGraph provides generic zoom- and other scrollbars and a context menu for user interface that can be used to parameterize the shape of the displayed network.

The following enhancements were added to the basic functionality, mostly motivated by our application of visualizing word semantics:

- various zoom scrollbars (see section 2.3)
- colored nodes and edges depending on semantic categories (see section 3.1)
- a possibility to disable the convergence towards total equilibrium, thus "freezing" the graph in its current layout

Furthermore, the necessity arose to add new edges without changing the positioning of the graph (see section 3.2), which could be obtained by freezing it.

As the main panel only represents a detail of the whole graph, a function dynamically scrolling and zooming has been implemented to keep track of the red thread.

2.3 From Co-occurrences to Semantic Maps

Based on methods described in [Faulstich et al. 2002], it is possible to extract keywords that reflect important concepts of a document collection describing a domain automatically and language-independently. For this analysis, based on differences in relative corpus frequency, a large reference corpus, such as the Wortschatz Corpora, containing the result of an analysis of a large, representative document collection in German language (see http://www.wortschatz.uni-leipzig.de) is needed.

These keywords serve as a basis for generating a semantic map of the domain: by analyzing the co-occurrence of words within the same sentence statistically (see [Quasthoff et al. 2003]), and techniques of visualization (see [Schmidt 2000]), it is possible to display the keywords on a two-dimensional plane in a way that relatedness between keywords is reflected by short distances on the map.

By use of this method the keywords arrange themselves in clusters. All keywords of one cluster are related to a single event. Keywords can be part of several clusters, but are painted only once during the visualization process. As a consequence they will be located between the clusters they belong to. Figure 1 shows a cluster for "Tastatur" (keyboard), and the two clusters of "Monitor" (monitor), being part of the cluster related to computer hardware and a TV magazine called "Monitor".

[1] The software can be obtained at *http://prdownloads.sourceforge.net/touchgraph*.

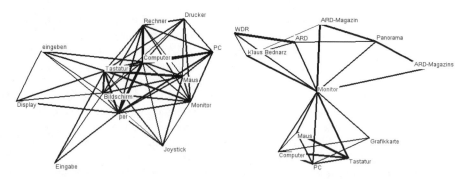

Fig. 1. One cluster for "Tastatur" (keyboard) and two clusters for "Monitor" (monitor)

Note, that the graphs in the figure above are centered on the reference words ("Tastatur", "Monitor"). This causes the effect that the cluster from the left graph in figure 1 is being reproduced in the right graph of the figure in a somewhat distorted way. As opposed to this, when visualizing the semantic map of the whole domain, the relative position between the keywords remains the same.

The automated creation of the semantic map for a specific domain consists of the following processing steps:

1. Extracting keywords using a relative corpus frequency comparison
2. Adding global context sets from the domain
3. Adding connections between words that are members of each other's global context

The size of the resulting map can be parameterized by the number of extracted keywords and the size of the global context sets.

Naturally, the number of important keywords is varying with the size of the text collection that has been used to define a domain. Especially when thinking of large domains, like newspaper archives or document collections of companies, a single screen for displaying the whole map will clearly not suffice for showing all the keywords in lexicalized form. As a practical solution, we introduced two windows for visualizing the same semantic map at two different zoom factors: the "topic survey window" serves as an overview of the whole domain, the "local context window" displays highly granular relations between specific content units. For a screenshot, see figure 2.

To adjust the granularity of the display according to the user's needs, three rulers have been implemented:

- *Conceptional zoom:* display of nodes as dots (see topic survey window) vs. lexicalized display i.e. as words in the local context window, larger words are keywords with higher rankings
- *Granularity:* the total number of nodes displayed
- *Scale:* ratio of the size of the local context compared to the whole semantic map

The visualization of the semantic map is pre-calculated for a specific domain and serves as constant background knowledge to visualize the content-path of each spoken sentence in the semantic net. When extending the domain, the map has to be recalculated. An initialization of the visualization software with positional information of the previous domain map ensures resemblance to the previous map on order to facilitate re-orientation: When e.g. visualizing newspaper content, politics will stay in the lower right corner while sports is always in the upper middle part.

3   SemanticTalk – A Tool for Innovation Acceleration

As mentioned in the introduction, the SemanticTalk tool supports two operation modes: a *brainstorming mode* in which a semantic map will be constructed dynamically from the input and a *red-thread mode* that visualizes a communication trail in a pre-calculated map. Both modes will be described in detail in this section. The input for the system can be obtained from different sources: it may be loaded from text files, directly typed in using a provided input field or spoken text recorded from a headset. For the conversion of spoken text, we use *Linguatec*'s VoicePro 10[2], which is speaker-dependent general-purpose dictation software for German language.

The SemanticTalk user-interface that represents the different views of the semantic map as well as the controls that modify the behaviour of the tool is show in the figure below.

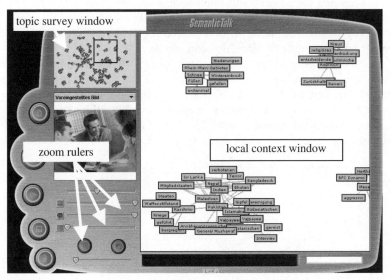

Fig. 2. The *SemanticTalk* user interface. The local context window is a zoomed variant of the topic survey window and can be changed with the three zoom rulers. Other controls: New, Load, Save, Exit, Microphone on/off, Freeze graph, Brainstorming / Red thread Switch, Input text bar and scrolling

3.1 Visualization of Associations in Brainstorming Mode

Project planning and realization usually starts and is further accompanied by brainstorming sessions where several people simply talk about possibilities of what to do. In the beginning, every participant has an isolated view on the issue, whereas the goal

---

[2]   For more information, visit: http://www.linguatec.de

of the brainstorming session is the exchange of the views in order to share the same view afterwards. In brainstorming mode, the software acts as a common brain that contains the views of all participants and proactively gives associations itself.

For preparation, a text collection of the domain has to be processed as described in [Biemann et al. 2004] to provide the terminology and the global contexts to the system. If existent, ontology or some typological system can be loaded in order to assign types to concepts and relations.

The brainstorming session starts with a blank screen. Words of the conversation that are considered to be important (an easy strategy is to use only nouns of a substantial frequency in the domain corpus) are thrown into the visualization. These words are in the following referred to as *core words*. If two words stand in the global context relation they are connected, which leads to an arrangement of concepts that reflects semantic relatedness by smaller distance. Each word is painted in a single frame with white background, indicating the human source.

The global contexts of words serve as candidate sets for *associations*. These global contexts are over-generating, first of all because the sets are usually too large, second because of the lexical ambiguity of words that leads to mixed semantics in the global contexts: i.e. when speaking about bank transactions, one would not want a system to associate river (bank) or park-bench related words. The strategy for associations is as follows: only words that appear in two ore more global contexts of core words are displayed and connected to their related core words.

When choosing associations, preference is given to typed relations, assuming that relations from the ontology are of higher interest to the brainstormers than other, untyped relations. The number of associations as well as the number of necessary core words for displaying an association can be parameterized, making the system tuneable with respect to associative productivity. The frames of associated words are painted in grey background colour, indicating machine source.

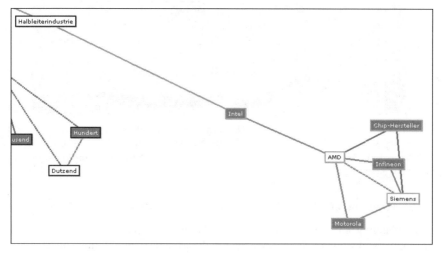

Fig. 3. Brainstorming Mode: core words and associations

Figure 3 shows an example for some semiconductor companies: *AMD, Halbleiter-industrie* (semiconductor industry) and *Siemens* are core words and *Motorola, Infineon, Intel* and Chip-Hersteller (chip manufacturer) have been associated by the system. All company names are coloured in pink, reflecting organisations, the typed connections between the companies reflect co-hyponomy, between *Chip-Hersteller* and two companies the IS-A-relation holds. The connection between *Halbleiterindustrie* and *Intel* is not typed. Typization of words and relations can either be loaded from an existing domain-specific ontology or annotated manually or semi-automatically.

The resulting graph can be exported via a template engine into XML-like description languages for example RDF to be used and further refined in domain specific applications. Depending on the target structures an export into other graph and concept-oriented knowledge structures, such as Topic-Maps or ontologies are possible.

An important aspect of the export functions will be the domain- or role specific filtering, using typed nodes an edges which can be used to build contextualized knowledge structures. Possible applications are the knowledge management applications that rely on a contextual information provision that could be gained from a business process, for example (see [Hoof et al. 2003]).

3.2   Visualization of Concept Trails on Semantic Maps in Red Thread Mode

Semantic maps (see section 2.3) provide a good overview of a domain by visualizing keywords and their relatedness. While they are extracted from a document collection and serve as model for the whole domain, it is possible to display single documents as paths through them.

We visualize the content of the broadcast as trajectory in the pre-calculated semantic map. Words of interest from the document are marked in red and are connected in sequence of their occurrence by directed edges. Here we distinguish between two kinds of connections (see figure 4):

1. A connection between two concepts has already been present in the semantic map: the two keywords are semantically related and therefore connected by a red colored line.
2. The connection has not been present in the semantic map: this indicates a shift of topic, just like the introduction of a new piece of information. These kinds of connections are drawn in orange.

When using spoken input, the colored connections are visualized in real time; the local context window is moving in a way that the most recent keyword always is located in the middle of the plane. For text file input, the resulting train is pre-calculated and visualized after processing the whole text file.

Words that are contained in the semantic map are marked in red in the input. The input document gets connected to the semantic map, which gives rise to bidirectional retrieval: the semantic map's local context window adjusts to (clickable) red words in the input, and document contexts from the single document and from the underlying collection can be retrieved by selecting a word from the semantic map.

By using a fixed semantic map and dynamically representing input as indicated, it is possible to examine

- coverage of domain: the more clusters are visited, the more the document covers the domain

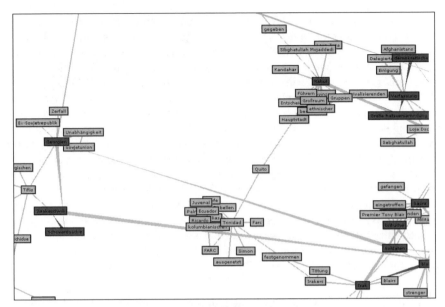

Fig. 4. Red thread visualization: topic shift to and from Georgian politics (left part of the window). Other clusters visited: Afghanistan (right upper corner) and Iraq politics (right lower corner), not visited by red thread: Trinidad and Columbia politics (lower middle). Data basis: *Tagesschau* broadcast news in red on one-day newspaper corpus in grey

- coverage within topics: the more words in a cluster are marked in red, the more extensively the document treats the topic of the cluster
- relatedness of document to domain: few red words in the input indicate non-relatedness
- contiguity of document: many successive long range orange connections indicate semantic incoherence
- comparison of different documents: either in a visual way by displaying several documents in different colors or by using semantic map concepts as features for classification or clustering

The great advantage of this representation lies in displaying what is described in the document, and the same time, what is *not* being dealt with. By using a fixed representation for the domain, the practiced user can grasp the document's content in a few seconds and then decide whether to read it or not.

4 Applications

To some extent this model captures important aspects of our cognitive processing of language. One natural application will therefore be in the area of natural language dialogue systems, in particular in Question-Answering systems: When evaluating a path in a semantic net for certain key concepts alternative continuations to the path actually followed become apparent. This indicates possible questions that the system might ask back to the user. We might also evaluate the actual path with respect to its information value (with reference to the domain specific conceptual expectations), and better structure the dialogue accordingly.

A further application may be found in the area of content and knowledge management. By mapping a document onto the semantic background net (instead of spoken natural language input), we get an indication of the topics that it treats, and of the topics that it does not cover as well. This may be used to evaluate, for example, the coverage of technical descriptions (e.g. instructions for the use of technical devices/user manuals). Also, by evaluating the conceptual path, documents may be compared with respect to the way they verbalize conceptual relations. Thus the SemanticTalk can be seen as a tool supporting the digestion of electronic documents, which in turn will help to find the relevant information within a large document collection faster and more easily.

With respect to Internet Communities we are currently evaluating another promising area: the analysis of high volume discussion forums in its various forms (Mailing lists, newsgroups, Wikis and blogging systems). Many of these community-centric systems propose a significant entry barrier to a newcomer in the community, since the sheer amount of information and its dynamic change makes it difficult to find the relevant information or follow the communications threads within an established community. In order to apply the SemanticTalk we will carry out a background analysis of a complete high volume Mailing list (to be used as a semantic map) and use single positing or communication threads as inputs for the red thread functionality to highlight the mentioned topics and concepts and draw relevant association from the background knowledge.

The full paper will present some result of the experiments currently carried out with some high volume mailing lists and newsgroups.

5 Related Research

The general issues of supporting group meetings with IT-systems are dealt with in [Krcmar et al. 2001] at a general level, whereas the extraction of theme structures from spoken language relates to different research areas and can be seen as the task of information or topic extraction (see [Cowie & Lehnert 1996]) and [Grishman 1997]). Information extraction from spoken language was discussed in [Palmer et al. 1999] but focuses on the template-based extraction of named entities. Another interesting approach in which the computer plays the role as a mediator within a session is illustrated in [Jebara et al. 2000], although the scope of this approach is limited to a restricted set of trained topics using a machine learning approach. The proposed solution is not limited to a set of topics and therefore only dependent on the analysis of an appropriate document collection in the background.

To our knowledge there is no related work of visualizing concepts in semantic maps automatically. While [Bergmann & Dachs 2003] visualize documents on maps due to relatedness of extracted keywords, the content description of the documents is inserted manually and rather high conceptual. Other approaches for visualization of semantics, like [Mertins et al. 2003] or [Paier 2003] who both display organisational structures, assume a well-defined database or ontology, whereas this work finds its data basis by statistical analysis.

6 Future Work

For the future, we plan to extend the tool in different ways. We identified another necessary zoom method: A simple hierarchical clustering algorithm could group the concepts into sensible clusters using their closeness on the map. When using the cluster-zoom, several close concepts are collapsed into a multi-node with a circular label. This multi-node is positioned at the center of gravitation to preserve the topology of the map. Lexical labels for multi-nodes can be chosen by heuristics from the labels of the collapsed nodes; when in red thread mode, the grade of redness indicates the fraction of red nodes in a multi-node. Multi-nodes should be expandable and collapsible by automatic means, but also by the user who defines a personalized view on a fixed, underlying map.

For improving usability, we will implement a variety of import formats, in as well as provide means to export the resulting graphs into machine-readable markup-files (e.g. in RDF Format) and printable graphics formats.

References

1. Bergmann, J. and Dachs, B. (2003): Mapping Innovation in Services. A Bibliometric Analysis. Proceedings of I-KNOW'03 International Conference on Knowledge Management, Graz, Austria
2. Biemann, Chr.; Bordag, S.; Heyer, G.; Quasthoff, U.; Wolff, Chr. (2004): Language-independent Methods for Compiling Monolingual Lexical Data, Proceedings of CicLING 2004, Seoul, Korea and Springer LNCS 2945, pp. 215-228, Springer Verlag Berlin Heidelberg
3. Cowie, J.; Lehnert, W. (1996): Information Extraction. In: Communications of the ACM. Vol. 39, Nr. 1, S. 80-90.
4. Faulstich, L.; Quasthoff, U.; Schmidt, F.; Wolff, Chr. (2002): Concept Extractor - Ein flexibler und domänenspezifischer Web Service zur Beschlagwortung von Texten, ISI 2002
5. Grishman, R. (1997): Information Extraction: Techniques and Challenges. In: Maria Teresa Pazienza (Hrsg.): Information Extraction, Lecture Notes in Artificial Intelligence. Rom: Springer-Verlag.
6. van Hoof, A.; Fillies, C.; Härtwig, J.: Aufgaben- und rollengerechte Informationsversorgung durch vorgebaute Informationsräume, Aus: Fähnrich, Klaus-Peter; Herre, Heinrich (Hrsg.): Content- und Wissensmanagement. Beiträge auf den LIT'03. Leipzig (2003).
7. Jebara, T.; Ivanov, Y; Rahimi, A.; Pentland, A. (2000): Tracking conversational context for machine mediation of human discourse. In: Dautenhahn, K. (Hrsg.): AAAI Fall 2000 Symposium - Socially Intelligent Agents - The Human in the Loop. Massachusetts: AAAI Press.
8. Krcmar, H., Böhmann, T., & Klein, A. (2001). Sitzungsunterstützungssysteme. In G. Schwabe, N.A. Streitz, & R. Unland (Eds.), CSCW Kompendium - Lehr- und Handbuch für das computerunterstützte kooperative Arbeiten. Heidelberg: Springer.
9. Mertins, K., Heisig, P. and Alwert, K. (2003): Process-oriented Knowledge Structuring. Proceedings of I-KNOW'03 International Conference on Knowledge Management, Graz, Austria and Journal of Universal Computer Science (JUCS), Volume 9, Number 6, Pp. 542-551, Juni 2003
10. Owen, H. (1998): Open Space Technology: A User's Guide, 1998, Berrett-Koehler Publishers Inc., San Francisco

11. OpenspaceWorld: Portal on OpenSpace information in the Internet: http://www.openspaceworld.org
12. Paier, D. (2003): Network Analisys: A tool for Analysing and Monitoring Knowledge Processes, Proceedings of I-KNOW'03 International Conference on Knowledge Management, Graz, Austria
13. Quasthoff, U., Richter, M., Wolff, C. (2003): Medienanalyse und Visualisierung: Auswertung von Online-Pressetexten durch Text Mining, in Uta Seewald-Heeg (Hrsg.), Sprachtechnologie für die multilinguale Kommunikation, Beiträge der GLDV-Frühjahrstagung 2003, Gardez!-Verlag, Sankt Augustin
14. Schmidt, F. (2000): Automatische Ermittlung semantischer Zusammenhänge lexikalischer Einheiten und deren graphische Darstellung, Diplomarbeit, Universität Leipzig

GeDA-3D a Middleware Useful to Handle the Evolution in *Behavioral Animation*-Based Virtual Worlds with a Multi-agent Architecture

Félix F. Ramos, H. Iván Piza, and Fabiel Zúñiga

Multi-Agent Systems Development Group at CINVESTAV del IPN, Guadalajara, Jal., México
{framos,hpiza,fzuniga}@ gdl.cinvestav.mx
http://gdl.cinvestav.mx

Abstract. In this article is proposed a distributed middleware useful to handle the evolution of deterministic virtual scenes in a 3D world. The proposed middleware allows interaction necessitated among virtual humans [1] and the environment. This interaction allows virtual humans to get user defined goals. As stated in the behavioral animation [3,4] paradigm, the user only tells characters "what to do" (goals) instead of "how to do it" (actions). Every virtual human computes dynamically by means of an intelligent algorithm, the actions to achieve its goal based on: a) its actual state; b) the stimuli perceived from the environment, and c) the personality of the virtual human. Main components of the proposed middleware is part of a more complex system we call GeDA-3D [5,6], this system includes a Declarative Virtual Editor useful to create the virtual world, an Context Descriptor used to define the physic laws ruling the environment, increment the language declarative language with definitions, concepts etc. A Rendering Tool useful to display the evolution of the scene, an Agent's Control module to control the agents managing the different virtual life creatures and all this is around a Geda-3D's kernel that provides all the stuff necessary to all these modules interact. Briefly the behavior of these middleware is: The scene controller receives the actions, validates them, handles the effect of the actions according to the natural laws of the world, resolves a set of graphic primitives to render and launches an event for every goal achieved. The cycle of sending local states and receiving actions loops until no goal is left to fulfill.

1 Introduction

The development of distributed systems is well adapted to human behavior; however it is necessitated at same time to offer better interfaces to humans. With this aim, we propose a middleware useful to develop distributed application where a 3D interface is useful. More of these distributed applications recreate a virtual environment o virtual world. When we say a virtual world we mean all programs necessitated to represent a world with all things objects creatures interactions etc. For instance it a world can be all the stuff necessitated in a manufacture plant or in a thermoelectric station. The term virtual creature is typically defined as a representation of a real or fiction creature generated and managed by a computer. Virtual creatures have gained great popularity in the recent years, especially on the entertainment industry – to develop animated movies and video games- and on the academic field, to recreate prehistoric

T. Böhme et al. (Eds.): IICS 2004, LNCS 3473, pp. 168–177, 2006.

environments. When dealing with real-time applications, for instance video-games, it is not so simple to handle the behavior of the virtual humans to make them look realistic.

As a consequence, several researchers from around the world have led their works toward the behavioral animation [3,4] of virtual humans in order to create virtual scenes less predictable, where virtual humans take autonomous decisions in real-time. The spirit of behavioral animation techniques lays in the concept of telling characters "what to do" instead of "how to do it". In behavioral animation, a virtual human determines its own actions, at least to a certain degree. This gives the virtual human an ability to improvise, and frees the animator from the need to specify each details of every human's motion. Unfortunately, it is not clear how the current works provide means for users to: a) develop behaviors and assign them to virtual humans, b) specify the natural laws ruling the interactions in a virtual world, and c) take advantage of existing rendering tools in order to avoid low-level implementations.

We propose an agent-oriented middleware useful to handle the evolution of virtual scenes based on behavioral animation. This middleware is the core of a complex system called GeDA-3D, and introduced in [5,6]. The main goal of this first stage of GeDA-3D concerns allowing inexpert users –scenarists, hereafter– to provide a human-like description of any scene and, as a result, a 3D-graphical representation of such scene is rendered. This overall operation is depicted in Figure 1. During the evolution of the scene, virtual humans [1,2], or characters, interact with each other in order to achieve a number of goals specified formerly by the scenarist.

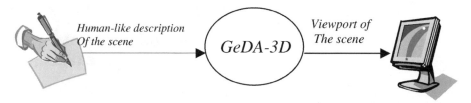

Fig. 1. Context-DFD of GeDA-3D

This article is organized as follows. Section 2 introduces the architecture of the system together with a brief explanation of the components' competencies. Section 3 depicts the internal operation of an agent in GeDA-3D. Section 4 shows the information flow between the components of the middleware. Section 5 summarizes the conclusions and future work.

2 Architecture

The middleware proposed in this paper follows an agent-oriented architecture which allows management of distributed applications and assists the development of virtual environments. It represents the core of GeDA-3D. The behaviors of the characters are actually distributed applications treated as agents attached to the platform. An agent can control the behavior of more than one character. The platform provides templates allowing the programmer to easily develop simple or complex behaviors.

The core of GeDA-3D is primarily in charge of: a) sending the agents the next set of goals their characters have to fulfill and the current local state of the world, b) managing the interaction of the virtual entities according to the natural laws of the world being modeled, and c) sends a set of lower-level commands to a 3D-tool to render the scene. Every agent sends back to the core an action sequence to encourage the fulfillment of the current goal. Figure 2 depicts a data-flow diagram of GeDA-3D considering some components required to accomplish the main goal of the project.

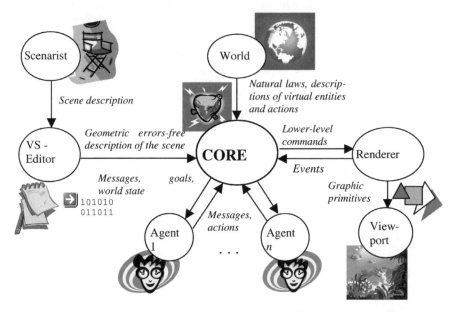

Fig. 2. Level 0-DFD of GeDA-3D

The overall operation of GeDA-3D is as follows. The scenarist provides a declarative [7] description of the scene using geometric constraints [8]. Such description includes: a) creation of virtual entities, b) assignment of behavior for characters, c) arrangement of entities in the world, and d) description of the goals to be fulfilled by the characters. The Virtual Scene (VS) Editor translates the declarative description in a geometric one, only if the description is errors-free and valid according to a number of rules. The world (or context) defines a set of natural laws that rules the interaction between the virtual entities, and includes descriptions of the actions and entities admissible.

The core manages the evolution of the scene: it validates and executes actions, and handles the effect of interactions between entities. Every agent receives the state of the world and sends back actions to achieve the goal-specification. Finally, the renderer receives low-level commands useful to display continuously the scene.

The architecture of the core is constituted primarily by two modules called *scene* and *agents control*. The scene control addresses all the issues related to the evolution of the scene as a result of the interaction of characters, while the agents control manages the distributed issues of the platform. Figure 3 shows a more detailed data-flow diagram depicting the architecture of the middleware proposed.

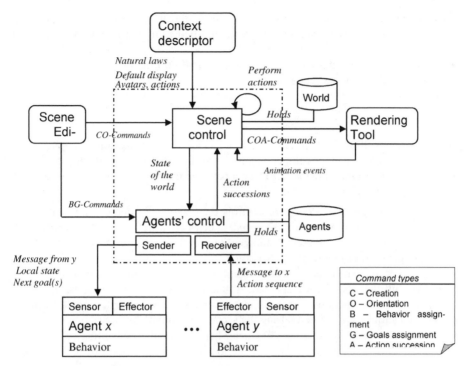

Fig. 3. Middleware architecture

2.1 Scene Control

The scene control is in charge of control the interactions and evolution of the virtual scene. It receives high-level commands to, initially, create and arrange virtual entities in the scene and, iteratively, to request the execution of actions. As a result, the scene control produces low-level commands to be sent to a specific renderer who translates each command in a set of graphical primitives. A low-level command indicates either the creation/placement of a virtual entity, or the animation of one or more entities. A high-level command can produce zero or more low-level ones. The tasks performed by the scene control include the following:

- Receive a sequence of high-level commands for the display of the virtual objects in a certain position
- Receive periodically – coming from the agents – sequences of actions for the characters to perform
- Validate the execution of all the actions received; it has the ability to delay or cancel the execution of a single action or an action succession
- Resolve a sequence of animations to execute as a result of an interaction, and send it to the renderer; the natural laws have much influence in this task
- Whenever an action succession is finished, successfully or prematurely, the scene control determines and sends updated local world-states to the agents through the agents' control. A premature finalization is usually due to unexpected contacts

with other moving entities or by gravity effects: the ground was not enough for all the actions. In either case, the agents are notified right away with the new local world-state.

- It holds a World database containing fundamental information about all the virtual entities involved in the scene

2.2 Agents Control

The agents controlling the behavior of characters are actually distributed applications. The agents' control manages the connection and disconnection of the agents and all the issues related to the transference of data between the community of agents and the middleware. Such data include the following:

- Control assignment. Every agent controls the behavior of one or more characters and enforces them to accomplish a goal-specification defined by the scenarist. A character is said to be linked to an agent during the scene. More details about the agent operation can be found in Section 3.
- Goals required. The operation of an agent is oriented to achieve one or more goals not yet fulfilled and already enabled. A goal is enabled as soon as some preconditions are given, including external events or previously-assigned goals fulfilled. Such conditions are defined during the scene description.
- Local state of the world. Every character has a particular perception of the world around. This perception depends on the location and orientation of the character, and is represented as a set of entities reachable from the character's field of view. The information of an entity seen can be full or partial depending on how far it is from the eyes of the character.
- Action sequences. An agent computes an action sequence as a result of the current goal required, the personality definition and the local perception. The agents control continuously receives action sequences from all the agents and sends them to the scene control for validation and execution.
- Messages between agents. Very often, characters work as a team and hence need cooperation from each other, for instance, to increase the local perception of the environment. In such cases, agents are capable to exchange messages in order to provide information about the scene.

3   Agent Architecture

This section introduces a generic architecture useful to develop the behaviors of the characters. These behaviors are attached to the platform as distributed agents. The scenarist specifies *what* characters must do, instead of *how* they have to do it. The behavior is in charge of solving the second part. Therefore, two similar specifications might produce different simulations. The agent relies on a Beliefs, Desires and Intentions architecture, as described by Georgeff [9], so that each agent makes decisions by itself. In general terms, the agent operation consists on iteratively receiving goals and current states of the environment, and sending back action sequences. The local perceptions received from the environment represent agent's beliefs. Before introducing the agent architecture, some background concepts must be defined.

A **skill** symbolizes a non-trivial action or complex action [10,11], that a character knows how to carry out, and involves the execution of an appropriate sequence of *primitive* (trivial) actions. In order to start working on a skill, some initial conditions about the current status (location, visual state, orientation) of the virtual entities involved have to be fulfilled. Likewise, there are similar final conditions indicating a skill was successfully carried out.

The **goals** symbolize the author's requirements and an agent's desires. All the interactions occurring in a scene lead to the fulfillment of the goals submitted by the scenarist. A simulation is finished as soon as all the goals have been achieved successfully. A goal specification includes a character, a skill and a target. The target is optional and represents either a zone in the environment, or a virtual entity. Sometimes, the scenarist structures the goal-description in such a way that sets of goals enable other sets of goals. That is, goals g_{j1}, g_{j2}, ... g_{jn}, have to be achieved (concurrently, sequentially, or optionally) necessarily before start working with goals g_{k1}, g_{k2}, ... g_{km}. In this context, we call j and k **goal-cycles**. Whenever a goal-cycle is started, an agent is told to fulfill a new set of goals.

Often, the fulfillment of a goal is not a straightforward process of just selecting a series of actions and that's all. Since we are dealing with dynamic environments, the actions selected at a specific time may not lead us to the goal, because of unexpected presence of new obstacles or adversary entities. Therefore, characters frequently divide their current goals in **tasks** or subgoals, where every task lists a sequence of actions required to solve the current trouble. The tasks are also useful to achieve the initial conditions of the skill involved in the current goal. The tasks represent the intentions of an agent.

A **personality** is defined as everything that makes a difference between the behavior of two different characters sharing the same set of goals, skills and actions. The personality resolves the best sequence of actions (within tasks) in order to achieve the current goal of the character, according to the current state of the character inside the environment.

Figure 4 depicts the architecture of an agent. *Msgs* stores all the messages received by an agent; the purpose for the message-passing is to allow cooperation between agents, in the cases where an agent has information useful for any other. *GNF* (Goals Not Fulfilled) stores the goals left to fulfill, while *GF* (Goals Fulfilled) stores the goals successfully achieved. Let $\mathcal{A}$, $\mathcal{N}$ be, respectively, the set of all the actions and entities valid in the current context where the scene carries out, and $\mathcal{G}$ be the set all the goals specified by the scenarist.

The task-tree depends on the current skill selected and it is built up from a Process Algebras [12] expression. The following operators are considered:

- $t_1 >> t_2$: <u>Prefix operator</u>: The agent will have to perform first task t_1, then task t_2
- $t_1 [] t_2$: <u>Choice operator</u>: The agent perform either task t_1 or t_2.
- $t_1 ||| t_2$: <u>Parallel composition operator</u>: The agent must perform goals t_1 and t_2 without concerning the order of execution.

GA is a Genetic Algorithm embedded in every agent, which computes the best sequence of actions to perform. The objective function (*OF*) in *GA* is based on: a) the coordinates of the target place the character is leading to through the execution of the current task, and b) the state of the world, i.e. the presence of moving entities avoid-

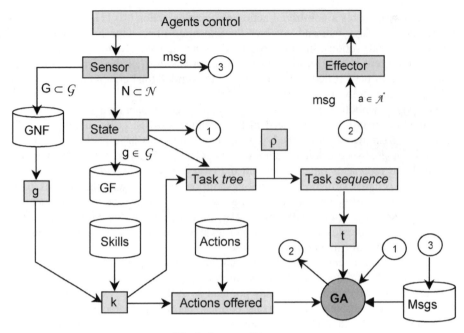

Fig. 4. Agent architecture

ing straight trajectories toward the target. A chromosome represents a sequence of actions to carry out. Two chromosomes may have different length. An allele is a pair <orientation, action> where orientation denotes the amount of degrees to turn about the 3-axes before carrying out the action. Two genetic operators are employed to get the offspring: crossover and mutation. The former combines two chromosomes using random crossover points. The mutation involves slight random changes in the orientation and action values, and the size of the chromosome. *OF* is in terms of: a) the distance between the character and the target, b) the trajectory length, and c) the presence of obstacles during the trajectory computed. The evaluation function computes large fitness values if the *OF* is minimized.

The agent operation is as follows:

1) At goal-cycle n, the sensor receives the next set of goals G to fulfill, and they become GNF; a goal g is selected from GNF. If GNF was not empty at cycle n, then the previous goals in GNF are discarded.
2) The underlying skill k from g is found in *Skills*, and a set of actions available for k is obtained
3) A task-tree structure is created according to the current state of the world and the current skill k.
4) The personality ρ chooses a task sequence from the tree.
5) Having as input data: a) the current local state of the world, b) a set of actions available, c) the current task and d) a list of messages, GA computes a sequence of actions and sends it to the effector; additionally, the GA may send messages to other agents through the effector.

6) Whenever the sensor receives a new local state of the scene, the agent checks if the current goal was successfully achieved; if positive, then a new goal g is obtained from GNF.

4   Information Flow

This section introduces the information flow between the VS-Editor, the core and the community of agents. Figure 5 depicts a zoom-in of the architecture in Figure 3, and shows a more detailed interaction between the agents control, the scene control and the community of agents. Such interaction involves sending and processing the components in a goal-description.

In addition, we introduce two modules, a goals manager and an event launcher, which belong to the agents control and the scene control, respectively. The former is in charge of: a) retaining the goals that are not enabled yet because of the lack of events, and b) sending back to the agents control those goals required to be fulfilled at the current time. Then, the agents control sends every agent the goals assigned to the characters it controls. The event launcher is given the state of the world every time it is changed, as a consequence of actions, and then it determines whether an event can be launched or not. This decision is taken using first-order logics. The behavior of all the components of the middleware is specified using process algebras notation, where they are treated as agents. First of all, let's define some functions and sets useful to resolve the set of goals an agent has to fulfill in a specific time, and hence, tu understand the information flow.

Let C be the set of characters (intelligent virtual entities) existing in the current scene, G be the set of goals assigned to characters, A be a set of agents available within a specific context, Σ is an indexing set of goal-cycles, and E be a set of events occurred in the scene. An event has one of two possible values: true or false. P stands for the power function.

Let $\delta_\sigma : C \rightarrow P\,(2^E \times G)$ be a function that assigns goals to a character, to be fulfilled during goal-cycle σ. Each goal will be enabled as soon as all the events associated are set to true. Let φ_σ be a logical expression that, if true, indicates the fulfillment of the required goals, and so, the finalization of a goal-cycle. This expression is built up with events. The logic operators employed are: $\wedge$, $\vee$, $\Rightarrow$. Δ, Φ denote, respectively, sets of δ and φ. More details about computing $(\Sigma, E, G, \Phi, \Delta)$ from the goal-specification will be included in a further paper.

Let λ: $A \rightarrow 2^C$ *be a* mapping *from agents* to characters, and having the following constraint: two different agents are not allowed to control *the same character*. Formally, $\forall c \in C$, if $c \in \lambda(a_1)$, then $c \notin \lambda(a_2)$, having $a_1, a_2 \in A$ and $a_1 \neq a_2$.

Let FIL: $\mathcal{P}(2^E \times G) \rightarrow 2^G$ be a filtering function that resolves a set of goals enabled and not fulfilled yet, according to the events associated to each goal. Formally:

Let $\mathcal{D}$ stand for the domain of the FIL function, $e_1,\ldots,e_n \in E$, $g_k \in G$

$\forall <\{e_1, \ldots, e_n\}, g_k> \in \mathcal{D}$, if $v(e_1 \wedge \ldots \wedge e_n) = true$ and $v(e_k) = false$
then $g_k \in$ FIL(D).

Finally, let δ': $A \rightarrow \mathcal{P}(C \times 2^{\underline{G}})$ be a goal-assignment relation for agents $\ni \forall a \in A$, if $c = \lambda(a)$, then $<c, \text{FIL}(\delta_\sigma(c))> \in \delta'(a)$, having $c \in C$, $\sigma \in \Sigma$. This relation tells an agent which goals are currently enabled and required to be fulfilled by the different characters the agent controls.

$$AC \overset{\text{def}}{=} in_1(\Sigma, \Phi, \Delta, G, E).out_1(\Sigma, \Phi, \Delta).out_2(G) +$$
$$in_2(\delta').out_i(\delta'(a_i))...out_k(\delta'(a_k))$$
$$+ in_i(actions_i).out_3(actions) + in_3(e).out_4(e)$$

$$GM \overset{\text{def}}{=} (in_4(\Sigma, \Phi, \Delta) + in_5(e)).get\delta'().out_5(\delta')$$
$$get\delta'() \overset{\text{def}}{=} \text{ if } v(\varphi_\sigma) \text{ is } true \text{ then } \sigma = next\_\sigma()$$
$$\text{if } \sigma \text{ is not } null \text{ then compute } \delta' \text{ as follows:}$$
$$\forall a \in A, \forall c \in \lambda(a): \delta'(a) = <c, FIL(\delta_\sigma(c))>$$

$$SC \overset{\text{def}}{=} in_6(actions).perform(actions).out_6(world)$$

$$EL \overset{\text{def}}{=} (in_7(G, E) + in_8(world)).event()$$
$$event() \overset{\text{def}}{=} \text{ if a new event e is launched then } out_7(e)$$

$$AG_i \overset{\text{def}}{=} in_9(\delta'(a_i)).action().out_8(actions_i)$$
$$action() \overset{\text{def}}{=} \text{ run the underlying intelligent algorithm to compute the next set of}$$
$$\text{actions for every character controlled}$$

Notice that the agent control has a pair of ports $<in_1, out_i>$ (input and output) for every different agent$_i$ available in the current context. A further work will introduce the formal description of the actions assigned to characters, the virtual world and the event handling. The last one involves declaring a number of logic-based rules allowing an event to be launched.

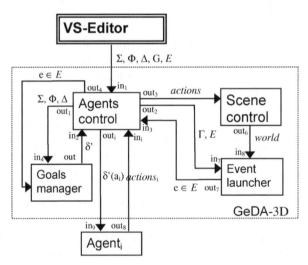

Fig. 5. Information-flow across the middleware

5 Conclusions and Future Work

In this paper we present our work regarding the development of a middleware useful to develop distributed applications where a 3D interface is useful. The design of this middleware is based on agents. Main characteristic of our middleware is that it hides from final user. Till now our middleware allows interactions completely specified. This is useful for applications where user specify all interactions goals to be achieved.

For instance, in entertainment industry this is useful to in the development of a theater scene or a chapter of a film. In industry, the construction of a product must be completely specified. We have work with some very simple examples for instance the simulation of a soccer game, a small piece of theater.

Our future work is addressed in two directions first to provide formal specification of our middleware and second more applicative: to improve our middleware to support interactions not specified; to allow user interact with applications, for instance allowing the control of objects; to evolve our character agent architecture to support in case of virtual human some characteristics like mood, and personality. Also we are developing infrastructure to support several real time engines for rendering the 3D results. In parallel we are developing some applications for final users.

References

1. Badler, N. Real-Time Virtual Humans. Pacific Graphics (1997)
2. Musse, S., Garat, F., Thalmann, D. Guiding and Interacting with Virtual Crowds in Real-Time. In Proceedings of EUROGRAPHICS Workshop on Animation and Simulation. Milan, Italy (1999) 23-34
3. Thalmann, D. Monzani, J.S. Behavioural Animation of Virtual Humans: What Kind of Laws and Rules? In Proc. Computer Animation 2002, IEEE Computer Society Press (2002) 154-163
4. Reynolds, C.W. Flocks, herds, and schools: A distributed behavioral model. Proceedings of SIGGRAPH 87 (1987) 25–34
5. Ramos, F., Zúñiga, F. Piza, I. A 3D-Space Platform for Distributed Applications Management. International Symposium and School on Advanced Distributed Systems 2002. Guadalajara, México. ISBN 970-27-0358-1 (2002)
6. Piza, I., Zúñiga, F., Ramos, F. A Platform to Design and Run Dynamic Virtual Environments. CyberWorlds. Tokyo, Japan. ISBN 0-76952140-1 (2004) 78-85
7. Kwaiter, G., Gaildrat, V., Caubet, R. DEM²ONS: A High Level Declarative Modeler for 3D Graphics Applications. In Proceedings of the International Conference on Imaging Science Systems and Technology, CISST'97. Las Vegas (1997) 149-154
8. Le Roux O., Gaildrat V., Caubet R. Design of a New Constraint Solver for 3D Declarative Modeling: JACADI. 3IA: Infographie Interactive et Intelligence Artificielle, Limoges (2000)
9. Rao, A.S., Georgeff, M.P. Modeling rational agents within a BDI architecture. In J. Allen, R. Fikes, and E. Sandewall, editors, Proceedings of the Third Internacional Conference on Principles of Knowledge Representation and Reasoning. Morgan Kaufmann (1991)
10. Bindiganavale R., Schuler W., Allbeck J., Badler N., Joshi A., Palmer P. Dynamically altering agent behaviors using natural language instructions. In Autonomous Agents Proceedings (2000)
11. Badler N., Bindiganavale R., Allbeck J., Schuler W., Zhao L, Palmer M. Parameterized Action Representation for Virtual Human Agents, in Embodied Conversational Agents, J. Cassell, J. Sullivan, S. Prevost, and E. Churchill, Eds. Cambridge, MA: MIT Press (2000) 256-284
12. Katoen J., Langerak R., Latella D. Modeling Systems by Probabilistic Process Algebra: An Event Structures Approach. Proc. on the IFIP TC6/WG6.1 Sixth International Conference on Formal Description Techniques, VI (1993) 253-268

A Mathematical Model for the Transitional Region Between Cache Hierarchy Levels

Michael Krietemeyer, Daniel Versick, and Djamshid Tavangarian

Chair of Computer Architecture, Department of Computer Science
University of Rostock, Albert-Einstein-Str. 21, D-18059 Rostock, Germany
{michael.krietemeyer,daniel.versick,
djamshid.tavangarian}@informatik.uni-rostock.de

Abstract. The knowledge of internal structures of the cache-memory hierarchy and its performance is very important in modern computer systems. Therefor, this paper introduces a mathematical model that describes the transition between Level 1 and Level 2 cache of current processors. The theoretical predictions are proved by measurements for two Intel CPUs and an UltraSparc II system.

1   Introduction

As the performance gap between CPU and I/O devices increases rapidly in modern computer systems the understanding of I/O systems is of great interest. In the context of the IPACS project that develops benchmarks for distributed systems a mathematical model was introduced that characterizes some performance issues within the memory subsystem.

Modern computer systems have a hierarchical architecture of storage called the memory hierarchy. Each level of the hierarchy is slower and of larger size than higher levels. Typically the memory hierarchy consists of CPU registers, Level 1 cache, Level 2 cache, main memory and disk storage. Often referenced memory can be stored in the fastest possible hierarchy level to increase the performance of memory access, especially in cache and main memory. This technique can strongly improve the application performance. However it complicates the exact understanding of the processes that influence the performance of memory accesses.

This paper describes a mathematical model that helps to understand the performance within the cache hierarchy levels. It focuses on the performance description of the Level 1 and Level 2 cache. Especially, it describes the performance of accesses to the transitional region between that two cache hierarchy levels. While Section 2 presents some former work Section 3 discusses the measuring method and the mathematical model for the memory performance. Section 4 presents some measured results of three chosen example architectures before Section 5 concludes the paper.

T. Böhme et al. (Eds.): IICS 2004, LNCS 3473, pp. 178–188, 2006.
© Springer-Verlag Berlin Heidelberg 2006

2   Related Work

Most of the related works that try to characterise the performance of cache memories, describe methods for implementing memory benchmarks and present measurements for different architectures. Mathematical models that establish a theoretical background for the effects are rare. Saavedra describes in [1] and [2] the characteristics of cache systems. Cache parameters are measured by varying the stride size of memory accesses. As the papers focus on the performance in dependency of the stride size of memory accesses, conclusions about the effective memory bandwidth in different operating ranges are missing. In addition both papers do not give any conclusions about the performance in transition regions between memory hierarchy levels.

Hockney discovers in [3] the phenomenon of a very low bandwidth in the transitional region between cache and main memory. He does not explain it in detail and refers to [4] where the cache memory effect is explained by means of a mathematical model. The model is based on Hockneys linear timing model $(r_\infty, n_{1/2})$ described in [5]. The mathematical model described in [4] uses a very abstract model that does not take cache specifics like associativity into account. As modern computer systems widely use set-associative caches with *least recently used* as replacement strategy, our approach for characterising the cache memory effect will adhere to that. It will introduce a model that can easily be used in most modern computers to predict the performance of consecutive memory accesses for a better optimisation of program behaviour.

Hristea [6] describes some benchmark kernels written in C that measure different performance parameters of the memory hierarchy. The advantage of the suggested benchmarks is that they are completely hardware-independent. To prove the introduced mathematical model a benchmark was written that is based on a benchmark kernel from [6]. Based on that kernel we measured cache memory characteristics on some example architectures to compare it with the expected values acquired by the introduces mathematical model. The comparison between theoretical and measured results gives us the potentials of the suggested theoretical model.

3   Measuring Method and Mathematical Model

This section describes with priority the mathematical model and its theoretical fundamentals.

3.1   Measuring Method

The mathematical model characterizes the performance of reading different block sizes of consecutive memory. Additionally, it allows to calculate the associativity of caches from bandwidths in the several hierarchy levels. A program measures the time for reading memory blocks with an increasing size. The acquired times for the different vector sizes are used to determine the different bandwidths. The main part of the program is a slightly modified *back-to-back memory latency benchmark kernel*, as described in [6].

To minimize disturbing effects, like task switching or memory swapping within the benchmark kernel, and to make sure that all cacheable memory is located inside the caches, the code for traversing the pointer-list is performed 100 times. The program only reports the best time. This guarantees reliable and reproducible values.

In the measured values some straight lines can be identified. Each line represents a memory hierarchy level or a transition between two levels. As described in [3] the asymptotic bandwidth for the sections can be calculated as:

$$B_i = \frac{1}{t_i} \qquad (1)$$

B_i – *Bandwidth in region of line i*

t_i – *slope of straight line i*

For memory vectors that fit into one cache hierarchy level, the time for reading the memory-block increases linear with its length. By increasing the vector size over the size of a cache, the reading time rises faster than in the last level. This is caused by the inevitable cache misses when reading the linear memory area. The change from one hierarchy level to the next is not a simply degradation of the reading time. Because of the cache organization, there is a short transition area between two levels where the reading time per byte rises faster than in both – the faster and in the slower hierarchy level. These effects and their reasons are described in the next section.

3.2   Set Associative Caches

In order to understand the arising effects within the transitions between two memory hierarchy levels, it is important to understand the function and organization of cache memory. There are three forms of cache organization:

- direct mapped (1-way set associative),
- n-way set associative, and
- fully associative caches.

The fact that the cache memory is divided into lines with a specific length of e.g. 16 bytes is applicable to all three forms. These cache lines are organized in sets. For n-way set associative caches a set is containing n lines. In the case of a fully associative cache there is only one set containing all cache lines. Each memory block can only be stored in one cache set. *Least recently used* is a commonly used replacement strategy for loading a further memory block if all cache lines in a set are engaged (see [7] for explanation of LRU).

The functionality of the three cache types is explained in [8].

An example for a 2-way set associative cache will be discussed in order to understand the transition effects between two hierarchy levels. Figure 1 shows such a cache. In order to make this example simpler, the block size is exactly the

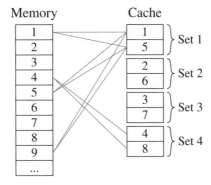

Fig. 1. 2-way set associative cache example

size of a vector element. Additionally Figure 1 shows the contents of the cache memory after reading a vector with a size of eight. As this is the size of the cache, no cache misses occur under the condition that a read is performed more than once. If the size is increased to nine, more cache misses will occur and it will be necessary to replace blocks inside the cache. For this purpose the LRU algorithm is used.

When reading a vector with nine elements, cache misses arise only in the first cache set. For a pointer-list with ten elements, misses appear in the first and second set, and so on. Figure 2 shows the cache content after reading areas with a size of nine to thirteen elements (every range was read twice). The more interesting part in the figure is the number of occurred cache misses. The misses only arose in the gray colored cache sets.

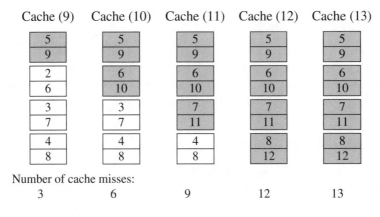

Fig. 2. Occurred number of cache misses for rising vector sizes

The transition effects can be explained with these values. For vector sizes between nine and twelve elements the number of cache misses rises by three with every step, against the rising by one for greater vector sizes. The generic equation for the number of cache misses in the transition area is:

$$m(n) = \frac{n - c}{c_L} \cdot (a + 1) \qquad \text{if} \quad n > c \qquad (2)$$

$m(n)$ — number of cache misses

n — number of read bytes

c — cache size of faster memory[bytes]

c_L — cache line size of faster memory[bytes]

a — associativity of faster memory

The first part is the number of cache lines of the vector that exceeded the size of the cache. This number of lines must be reloaded $a + 1$ times when reading the vector. Increasing the associativity by one is necessary because the first cache line has to be loaded twice. The size of the transition area depends on the associativity of the cache:

$$size_t = \frac{\frac{c}{c_L}}{a} \cdot c_L = \frac{c}{a} \qquad (3)$$

$size_t$ — size of the transition area

Summary: For vectors that fit into the maximum number of cache lines of the faster hierarchy level, the number of cache misses is zero (the vector size is less or equal to the cache size). Vectors that are greater than the cache, need a reload of memory blocks from the slower level into the assigned cache lines. For vector lengths that do not require reloads in all cache sets, the number of misses, and therefore the reading time rises faster than for vectors that need reloads in all sets. In the first case the vector size is between c and $c + size_t$.

3.3   Mathematical Model

The following section explains the mathematical model that describes the memory access performance in the L1 and L2 cache of uniprocessor systems with multiple cache hierarchy levels. Additionally we present a method to calculate the cache associativity from the bandwidths for n-way set associative caches.

The time of every memory access to n consecutive bytes consists of the time that is necessary to read $m(n)$ bytes from the slower memory hierarchy level and the time that is needed to read $n - m(n)$ bytes from the faster level:

$$t(n) = t_s \cdot m(n) + t_f \cdot (n - m(n)) \qquad (4)$$

t_f — access time per byte in faster memory hierarchy level

t_s — access time per byte in slower memory hierarchy level

The Fast Hierarchy Level ($n \leq c$): In case the number of read bytes is smaller than the size of the faster memory no cache misses ($m(n) = 0$) will occur. Applying this in conjunction with Equation (4) results in:

$$t(n) = t_f \cdot n \qquad \text{if} \qquad n \le c$$
$$t_1 = t_f \tag{5}$$

Thus the measurable slope of the straight line in the fast hierarchy level is equal to the access time per byte in that level.

The Slow Hierarchy Level ($n > c + \frac{c}{a}$): Consecutive memory accesses in the slower memory level are more complicated, as the number of cache misses in the slower level depends on the number of read bytes and the cache line size in the faster level. As stated in Section 3 an access to a new memory block with the size of one cache line causes exactly one cache miss in the slower hierarchy level. Other accesses to this memory block can be served by the faster memory. Therefor, the number of cache misses $m(n)$ is the quotient of the number of accesses and the cache line size. Referring to Equation (4) this leads to:

$$m(n) = \frac{n}{c_L} \qquad \text{if} \quad n > c + \frac{c}{a}$$
$$t(n) = t_s \cdot \frac{n}{c_L} + t_f \cdot \left(n - \frac{n}{c_L} \right)$$
$$= \left(\frac{t_s - t_f}{c_L} + t_f \right) \cdot n$$
$$= t_3 \cdot n$$

Thus one can see there also is a linear interrelation between the read time and the number of read bytes in the slower memory hierarchy level. The slope of that function is the measurable slope t_3. It is possible to calculate the real access time to the slower memory t_s using this value:

$$t_3 = \frac{t_s - t_f}{c_L} + t_f$$
$$t_s = \left(t_3 + \frac{t_f}{c_L} - t_f \right) \cdot c_L$$
$$= t_3 \cdot c_L - t_f \cdot (c_L - 1)$$

Hence, the access time t_s can be seen as a complex dependency between the measurable slopes in the memory hierarchy levels and the cache line size in the faster hierarchy level.

The Transitional Region ($c < n \le c + \frac{c}{a}$): The former acquired equations are used to determine the interrelations in the transition area. Therefor, the calculated number of cache misses in the transitional region from Equation (2) can be used in Equation (4):

$$t(n) = \left(t_3 + \frac{t_f}{c_L} - t_f \right) \cdot c_L \cdot \frac{n - c}{c_L} \cdot (a + 1)$$

$$+t_f \cdot \left(n - \frac{n-c}{c_L}(a+1) \right)$$
$$= ((t_3 - t_f) \cdot a + t_3) \cdot n + (t_f - t_3) \cdot (ac + c)$$
$$\text{if} \quad c < n \le c + \frac{c}{a}$$

Thus a linear dependency between n and the time $t(n)$ is shown. The slope t_2 of this straight line is of great interest because it can easily be measured and depends on the associativity of the faster memory hierarchy:

$$t_2 = (t_3 - t_f) \cdot a + t_3$$
$$a = \frac{t_2 - t_3}{t_3 - t_f} = \frac{t_2 - t_3}{t_3 - t_1} \qquad \text{because } t_f = t_1 \text{ from (5)}$$

The associativity of the faster memory hierarchy level can now be calculated from the measurable slopes of the three regions. The following bandwidth equation is equivalent to the last one:

$$a = \frac{(B_3 - B_2) \cdot B_1}{(B_1 - B_3) \cdot B_2} \tag{6}$$

$$\implies B_1 > B_3 > B_2 \quad \text{for} \quad a > 0$$

As one can see in this equation, the bandwidth in the transition area must be smaller than the bandwidths in both memory hierarchy levels to get a positive result for the associativity.

Comprising the following equation describes the reading time for consecutive bytes from the two cache hierarchy levels and their transitional region:

$$t(n) = \begin{cases} t_1 \cdot n & \text{if} \quad n \le c \\ ((t_3 - t_1) \cdot a + t_3) \cdot n + (t_1 - t_3) \cdot (ac + c) & \text{if} \quad c < n \le c + \frac{c}{a} \\ t_3 \cdot n & \text{if} \quad n > c + \frac{c}{a} \end{cases} \tag{7}$$

4   Experimental Results

To verify the model described in Section 3, some measurements were done on three different example architectures.

The first example architecture is an Intel Xeon 2.4 GHz with a L1 cache size of 8 kB. The 1st level cache on this architecture is organized 4-way set associative.

The used Pentium III system has a clock frequency of 1.4 GHz and cache sizes of 16 kB for the 1st level data cache and 512 kB for the 2nd level cache. The 1st level cache of this CPU is organized 4-way set associative and the 2nd level cache 8-way set associative. More detailed information about the architecture can be found in [9].

The third architecture used for these measurements was a Sun UltraSPARC-II with 300 MHz clock frequency. This CPU has a direct mapped 1st level cache of size 16 kB. Some more information can be found in [10].

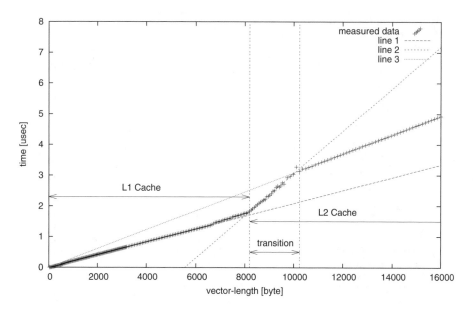

Fig. 3. Reading time for different vector lengths up to 16 kB on Intel Xeon

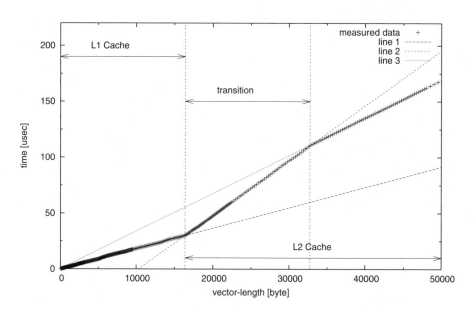

Fig. 4. Reading time for different vector lengths up to 50 kB on SPARC

In all cases the time for reading a number of n consecutive bytes is measured. Figures 3 and 4 show the reproducible results for the Xeon and SPARC CPU. The results for the Pentium III CPU are only given below in Table 1 since the

Table 1. Asymptotic bandwidths on example architectures and associativities calculated by means of mathematical model

region	straight line [μs]	bandwidth [MB/s]
	Intel Xeon	
1st level cache	$t(n) = 5.44 \cdot 10^{-4} \cdot n - 3.18 \cdot 10^{-3}$	4561.28
transition zone	$t(n) = 1.07 \cdot 10^{-3} \cdot n - 3.81$	1387.94
2nd level cache	$t(n) = 6.52 \cdot 10^{-4} \cdot n - 2.89 \cdot 10^{-3}$	3095.04
associativity	calculated: 3.83 expected: 4	
	Pentium III	
1st level cache	$t(n) = 2.09 \cdot 10^{-4} \cdot n + 7.22 \cdot 10^{-3}$	1752.74
transition zone	$t(n) = 6.87 \cdot 10^{-4} \cdot n - 8.62$	888.88
2nd level cache	$t(n) = 3.08 \cdot 10^{-4} \cdot n + 1.00 \cdot 10^{-2}$	1463.15
associativity	calculated: 3.91 expected: 4	
	SPARC	
1st level cache	$t(n) = 1.82 \cdot 10^{-3} \cdot n + 6.39 \cdot 10^{-2}$	521.28
transition zone	$t(n) = 4.92 \cdot 10^{-3} \cdot n - 50.77$	193.73
2nd level cache	$t(n) = 3.38 \cdot 10^{-3} \cdot n + 5.37 \cdot 10^{-2}$	282.22
associativity	calculated: 0.996 expected: 1	

results look much like the ones obtained from the Xeon system. One can see that every curve consists of three straight lines. The first line is equivalent to the region of the 1st level cache. The 2nd line is the transition zone between the first and the 2nd level cache and the 3rd line is equivalent to the 2nd level cache. It can be seen that the slope of the curve in the transition region is greater than in the other regions. Since the reciprocal value of the slope is the asymptotic bandwidth B_i in that region, it is even less than in the 2nd level cache. It should be a design goal to minimize this bandwidth breaking in the transitional region.

Table 1 shows the cache bandwidths on the example architectures. They were calculated from the slopes of the three curves that are determined by means of least-square fits. The shown figures also demonstrate that the transition region on the Xeon architecture is smaller than on the SPARC architecture. Equation (3) points out that this length is reciprocally proportional to the associativity of the first level cache. The smaller the associativity of the cache, the larger the transition region. Since the SPARC architecture has a direct mapped 1st level cache, the transition region is as large as the 1st level cache itself.

Table 1 also shows the associativities of the first level caches calculated by means of Equation (6). It is shown that the calculated values for the associativity are approximately the expected values described in the architectural manuals of the three CPUs. Xeon and Pentium III have a 4-way set associative 1st level cache and SPARC a direct mapped 1st level cache. The bandwidths in the transition regions on the architectures are interesting. On the Pentium III the bandwidth in the transition area between the 1st and 2nd level cache is about 50 percent smaller than in the 1st level cache and about 40 percent smaller as in the 2nd level cache. On SPARC the bandwidth in that area is about 62 percent smaller than in the 1st level cache but only 30 percent smaller as in the 2nd level cache. On

Xeon systems the difference is even larger than on SPARC. There the bandwidth in the transitional region is about 70 percent smaller than the bandwidth in the 1st level cache and about 55 percent smaller than in the 2nd level cache.

The calculation of the axis intercepts of the lines that describe the transitional regions by means of the mathematical model also resulted in the measured values. As shown in Equation (7) the axis intercepts of the lines in the 1st and 2nd level caches are zero. Approximately this applies to the measured lines. Only the straight line of the transitional region has a negative axis intercept as the mathematical model predicts.

5 Conclusion and Further Work

This paper introduced a mathematical model that describes the transition between two cache hierarchy levels in widespread memory architectures that use set-associative caches and LRU or FIFO as replacement algorithms within the sets. The model allows the calculation of the associativity of the L1 cache and the performance prediction of consecutive memory accesses within the transitional region between two cache level hierarchies in case that the bandwidths in the hierarchy levels are known. The model was proved by means of measurements on three hardware architectures with different memory system designs. It was possible to show that the presented model creates reasonable results.

The sample measurements of Section 4 were acquired on UNIX like operating systems (Solaris 5.8 for the SPARC system and Linux 2.4.x on the Intel systems). One problem of these operating systems is that it is impossible to get large blocks of consecutive memory in user space. Hence, at the moment it is only possible to prove that the introduced model describes the performance behaviour of the first and second level cache. Further work will include the extension of the model to other memory hierarchy levels since it should also be applicable to the transitional region between cache and main memory. Besides performance measurements will be done on more than the current three architectures.

Acknowledgement

This research was sponsored by the German Federal Ministry of Education and Research grant 01IRB03E in the context of the IPACS project [11]. We thank the sponsors and the project partners Fraunhofer Institute for Techno- and Business Mathematics, T-Systems, National Energy Research Scientific Computing Center and the University of Mannheim for their support.

References

1. Saavedra, R.H., Gaines, R.S., Carlton, M.J.: Characterizing the performance space of shared memory computers using micro-benchmarks. In: Proceedings of Hot Interconnects. (1993) 3.3.1–3.3.5

2. Saavedra, R.H., Smith, A.J.: Measuring Cache and TLB Performance and Their Effect on Benchmark Runtimes. IEEE Transactions on Computers **44** (1995) 1223–1235
3. Hockney, R.W.: The Science of Computer Benchmarking. Society for Industrial and Applied Mathematics, Philadelphia (1996)
4. Getov, V.S.: Performance characterisation of the cache memory effect. Supercomputer **11** (1995) 31–49
5. Hockney, R.W.: Performance parameters and benchmarking of supercomputers. In Dongarra, J.J., Gentzsch, W., eds.: Computer benchmarks, Amsterdam, Elsevier Science Publishers B.V. (1993) 41–63
6. Hristea, C., Lenoski, D., Keen, J.: Measuring memory hierarchy performance of cache-coherent multiprocessors using micro benchmarks. In: Proceedings of the ACM/IEEE SC97 Conference (SC'97). (1997) 1–12
7. Belady, L.A.: A study of replacement algorithms for a virtual-storage computer. IBM Systems Journal **5** (1966) 78–101
8. Smith, A.J.: Cache memories. ACM Comput. Surv. **14** (1982) 473–530
9. Intel Corporation: Pentium Processor Family, Developer's Manual – Volume 3: Architecture and Programming Manual (1996)
10. SPARC International Inc.: The SPARC Architecture Manual, Version 9 (2000)
11. IPACS: IPACS Benchmark. http://www.ipacs-benchmark.org (2004)

From Medical Geography to Computational Epidemiology – Dynamics of Tuberculosis Transmission in Enclosed Spaces

Joseph R. Oppong, Armin R. Mikler, Patrick Moonan, and Stephen Weis

Introduction

Medical geographers study the geographic distribution of health and health-related phenomena such as diseases, and health care facilities. Seeking to understand *who* is getting *what* diseases or health services *where* and *why*, they examine spatial disparities in access to health care services, and the geographic distribution of health risks. Medical geographers apply tools of geographic enquiry such as disease mapping and geographical correlation studies to health-related issues (Elliot *et al.*, 2000; Pickle, 2002). Some have called this research endeavor spatial epidemiology (Cromley, 2003; Rushton, 2003a).

Disease mapping is an important tool for medical geographers. Such maps help to identify associations between disease and related factors such as environmental pollution. Inevitably, disease maps stimulate the formation of causal hypothesis. By enabling the simultaneous examination of multiple factors associated with disease linked by location, Geographic Information Systems (GIS) facilitate medical geography research. In fact, recent developments in GIS and proliferation of spatially referenced health data sets are spawning new ways to examine health-related issues. Projects such as the *Atlas of United States Mortality* (Pickle *et al.*, 1996) have prompted researchers to explore various measures of morbidity and mortality (Goldman and Brender, 2000; Pickle et al., 1999), their visual representation in geographic contexts (James *et al.*, 2004), and the application of spatial statistics to morbidity and mortality data (James *et al.*, 2004; Pickle, 2002; Rushton 2003).

GIS has revolutionized the way researchers explore the geography of health (Gatrell, 2002; Gatrell and Senior, 1999; Melnick, 2002; Ricketts, 2003), and their utility for the study of health issues is widely documented (de Lepper *et al.*, 1995; de Savigny and Wijeyaratne, 1995; Scholten and de Lepper, 1990). GIS and health research focuses on the quantitative analysis of health-related phenomena in spatial settings (Gatrell and Senior 1999:925) and, thus, isolates locations of health-related phenomena for analysis and interpretation.

While GIS has enabled Medical Geographers to address previously inconceivable complex health-related phenomena, their ability to deal with the dynamic processes of disease transmission among population groups, which usually requires complex interactions among numerous variables, is quite limited. High Performance Computing provides the requisite tools for breaking this barrier and is the focus of a new field of endeavor that we have called computational Epidemiology.

T. Böhme et al. (Eds.): IICS 2004, LNCS 3473, pp. 189–197, 2006.

Epidemiology, Medical Geography and High Performance Computing

Although the role of Epidemiologists and Medical Geographers has become more pronounced in light of public health threats, computational tools that would enhance quality of information, facilitate prediction, and accelerate the generation of answers to specific questions are still lacking. In fact, at a time when global health threats make precise epidemiological information a critical necessity, epidemiologists continue to draw conclusions and make predictions using sparse, widely dispersed, incomplete or compromised data. Meanwhile, the complexity surrounding disease diffusion continues to escalate. Diverse populations traveling extremely long distances in unprecedented short times due to increased globalization mean that disease causing organisms circulate freely in a rapidly shrinking global village. An imperative response is to develop new tools that leverage today's cyber infrastructures for disease tracking, analysis, surveillance, and control.

The ability to predict how a disease might manifest in the general population is essential for disease monitoring and control strategies. Traditionally data collected during previous outbreaks are used. However, for newly emerging or re-emerging infectious diseases, such data is often unavailable or outdated. Changes in population composition and dynamics require the design of models that bring together knowledge of the specific infectious diseases with the demographics and geography of the region under investigation. New scientific methods that enhance understanding of the intricate interplay of disease and population are needed.

In a world of bioterrorism, where new and reemerging local disease outbreaks threaten all mankind, disease monitoring cannot continue to be fragmentary and inadequate focusing on small spatial domains (CDC 1994). As the recent outbreak of Severe Acute Respiratory Syndrome (SARS) showed, effective surveillance is critical to an effective defense against global disease threats, and requires consideration of huge volumes of data from other parts of the world. Developing tools that will accelerate epidemiological research, disease tracking and surveillance is thus, imperative. Computational models for the simulation of global disease dynamics are required to facilitate adequate what-if analyses.

What is needed is a novel interdisciplinary research program that facilitates epidemiology and Medical Geography research through high performance computing (HPC). Specifically, we envision the collaboration of Biologists, Medical Geographers, Epidemiologists, Computer Scientists, Biostatisticians, and Environmental Scientists to develop and implement computational tools in support of epidemiological research. These tools include simulation, visualization, and analysis tools that require HPC infrastructure.

Researchers in computational biology and medical informatics have relied on the availability of HPC infrastructures consisting of parallel computing architectures, cluster computing, and high performance visualization. Computational biologists have concentrated primarily on computational models at the molecular level, addressing specific computational problems in genomics, proteomics (protein folding), drug design etc. Most notable is the use of HPC in the design of drugs to cure or prevent specific diseases such as HIV. The field of medical informatics, particularly in Europe, has utilized HPC to manage the vast volumes of patient data. Further, HPC and high performance visualization tools have been used to design medical devices and test their functions in a simulated environment. To the best of our knowledge, there exists no single comprehensive program that aims at utilizing HPC in the field of Epidemiology or Medical Geography to build and analyze computational models of how a given disease manifests in the general population. This may include models of Tuberculosis (TB) outbreaks in different environments (homeless shelters, factories etc.), a West Nile Virus outbreak in a specific geographic region, or the progression of infectious diseases such as measles in the United States.

For these models to yield adequately precise information, many different factors must be considered. These factors may include socio-economic status of geographic regions, travel behavior of people, or airflow in a factory building. This clearly requires the use of a computing infrastructure that is capable of yielding computational results in a reasonable amount of time. To interpret the data, visual metaphors or data visualization that permits the epidemiologist to interact with the data are needed. For example, we envision an investigator immersed into a simulated model of a factory in which a TB outbreak is being investigated. The scientist is thus able to interact with the model, change functional parameters and thus engage in a what-if-analysis that currently is not available.

One computational challenge is to combine the spatially and temporally disparate datasets. This necessitates a fundamental knowledge of database systems, data management, and data retrieval. Even if a comprehensive dataset, containing individual health data for a large section of the population could be constructed, the extraction of relationships among the data constitutes a second computational challenge. For example, the domain of Artificial Intelligence and Machine Learning has been successfully used in Bio-informatics and is likely to be a valuable tool for discovering relationships among epidemiological data. Geographical Information Systems (GIS) help visualize spatial relationships of epidemiological data.

Whereas the collection of epidemiological data is essential for research, the need for Homeland Security, Disease Tracking and Surveillance requires sharing data among different federal, state, and local agencies. Healthcare providers in hospitals and private practice may be required to provide information to respond quickly and decisively to possible community health threats. A corresponding communication infrastructure can dramatically improve the precision with which health threats are analyzed, predicted, or traced. Such a system requires the combined effort of epidemiologists and computer scientists, each with a detailed understanding of each other's domain. For instance, issues that are central to the analysis of health-related data may dominate the requirements for a network infrastructure to interconnect healthcare providers. Examples of such issues include the type of information to be shared, format of information, and possible privacy and security issues.

Recent breakthroughs in sensor technology and wireless communication have led to the concept of Sensor Networks. Sensors of different types (biological, chemical, physical) have been deployed to monitor conditions in a variety of diverse environments. Ecologists, meteorologists, soil scientists, and others rely on such sensors to collect information about the environment. Connected via wireless networks, sensors can cover extended geographic areas, generating information instantaneously. The National Science Foundation (NSF) has announced special interdisciplinary programs to advance the field of Sensor Networks at a fast pace. This technology facilitates the monitoring for biological and/or chemical agents, and is expected to play a major role in Homeland Security. Environmental surveillance is essential in the field of public health, as it leads to early detection of adverse conditions and hence the ability to alert the population. However, to optimize this technology, scientists need to understand the technical (computational) as well as the epidemiological domains. New algorithms that autonomously extract data from sensors and auto-correlate sensor events must be developed. This leads to the design of intelligent systems, capable of learning from sensor data, and being able to classify events expediently.

Another example of convergence of epidemiology and computer science is the modeling and simulation of infectious disease outbreaks. Such an endeavor requires modeling demographics of the geographic domain within which a simulated outbreak is to take place. It further requires a high-fidelity representation of the disease pathology. Although very small models may be executed on a single computer, the simulation of a geographic region of moderate size will require computational resources beyond those of a single workstation. This leads to the use of a high performance computing infrastructure or computing clusters with tens or even hundreds of processors. Similar to computational biology and bio-informatics, computational epidemiology can utilize modern communication and computation infrastructures to solve computationally complex problems. The next generation of national (and international) cyber-infrastructure to provide access to high-bandwidth networks and high performance computing is about to be developed. The field of Epidemiology must develop tools that will enable scientists to effectively use such an infrastructure. To illustrate the need for computational epidemiology, two case studies are presented below.

Tuberculosis Transmission in Enclosed Spaces – A Homeless Shelter and a Factory

The dynamics of localized TB transmission within enclosed facilities such as homeless shelters or factories is little understood. Traditional Medical Geography, involving disease diffusion mapping precludes detailed analysis of the dynamics of TB transmission in enclosed spaces. For example, the spatial patterns of individual movement, pathogen characteristics, airflow and other specifics of the facility that trigger transmission are not easily modeled in a GIS.

The case studies cover tuberculosis transmission in a factory and a homeless shelter. Results of initial analysis suggest that proximity of workspace to infected person is a major determinant of infection. After showing the shortcomings of traditional medical geography and disease mapping for modeling dynamics of disease transmission, preliminary results of a simulation model using advanced computational tools, are presented. The new tool of computational epidemiology allows the spatial distribution of risk to be defined not in terms of large regions but in micro-space, literally feet and inches. The potential of such computational tools for disease transmission in enclosed spaces is demonstrated.

The number of tuberculosis cases in the United States is at its lowest point in history, with 15,075 cases reported in 2002 and a TB case rate of 5.2 per 100,000 [17]. Consequently recent research suggests that molecular based studies focusing on dynamics of TB transmission in specific locations, such as homeless shelters, and social settings such as bars [15, 18, 19] is a much-needed final push to TB control. For example, the homeless and those living in marginal housing and overcrowded areas [22] constitute reservoirs of TB infection. Recent research conducted in Los Angeles and Houston suggest that locations at which the homeless congregate are hot spots of tuberculosis transmission, and measures that reduce tuberculosis transmission should be based on locations rather than on personal contacts [23, 24]. Yet, little research exists on the dynamics of localized TB transmission within a homeless shelter or other enclosed facility.

While much emphasis has been placed on homeless shelters, little attention has been paid to other enclosed facilities such as factories, warehouses and classrooms where long-term exposure usually in close contact situations that may facilitate transmission of pathogens, is usually the norm. For example, tuberculosis transmission is a recognized risk to patients and workers in health-care facilities (CDC 1994). Factories and warehouses, where people usually work in close proximity for long periods, may also be areas of concern.

Methodology

Data for these case studies were based on data collected prospectively on all persons newly diagnosed with culture positive tuberculosis at the Tarrant County Health Department (TCHD) between January 1, 1993 and December 31, 2000. Each eligible patient was prospectively enrolled and participated in a structured interview as part of their routine initial medical evaluation. As part of an on-going Center for Disease Control and Prevention (CDC) study of the molecular epidemiology of tuberculosis, all positive isolates obtained from persons residing in Tarrant County are sent to the Texas Department of Health (TDH) for DNA fingerprinting. All patients are interviewed at the time of the initial evaluation, using a data collection instrument designed to obtain demographic information and medical history. The results of the DNA fingerprinting were incorporated into the database using patient identification numbers. Epidemiological factors included in this study were age, country of birth, date of entry, race/ethnicity, onset of symptoms, date of diagnosis and physical address. Any patient who did not have both PCR-based spoligotyping and RFLP-based IS6110 analysis performed on their corresponding MTB isolate, and/or did not live within Tarrant County at the time of collection were excluded from the geographical analysis.

M. tuberculosis culture isolation, identification, and drug susceptibility was conducted at the Texas Department of Health Bureau of Laboratories. Clinical isolate IS6110-based RFLP and PCR-based spoligotyping methods were utilized to identify patients infected with the same *M. tuberculosis* strain using published methods (van Embden JD, et al., 1993; Kamerbeek, et al., 1997). Since the discriminatory power of the IS6110 probe is poor for strain differentiation among specimens with five or fewer of the insertion elements, additional genotyping using the PCR-based spoligotyping was utilized (Kamerbeek, et al., 1997). We consider isolates representing a cluster when two or more patients had identical number of band copies, IS6110-RFLP, and spoligotyping patterns.

The first case study describes the dynamics of tuberculosis transmission within a homeless shelter with 800 beds providing both long and short-term occupancy for homeless people in Tarrant County, Texas. We seek to understand how location within a homeless shelter influences risk of tuberculosis infection. The data set comprises screening records for each case including age, race, date tested, status of tuberculosis, location in the facility, length of time spent in the facility, and other variables. Within the Shelter the 800 beds can be assigned to major areas – Men's Mats, Men's Beds, Men Over 50, Female Mats and Females Over 50 Beds. Each of these areas varied in bed density, floor space and occupants (Figure 1). The Mats area, (both male and female), is occupied by transients with no regular source of food, shelter, or shower. The Beds and Over 50 areas (male and female) are less dense overall, with more permanent residents. Results of initial analysis suggest that TB risk is not uniformly distributed but depends on the location of the sleeping bed and duration and frequency of stay at the night shelter. For example, 12 of the 17 active cases (63.2%) had been visiting the shelter for more than 5 years.

Table 1. Who Sleeps Where and TB

Category	Total People	Active TB
Men's Mats	1220	1.0%
Men's Beds	51	3.9%
Men's Over 50	87	3.4%
Female Mats	265	0.0%
Female Over 50	63	0.0

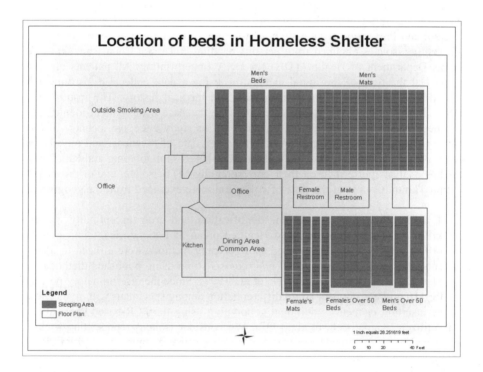

Fig. 1.

We need to examine certain dynamics of the Homeless Shelter that promotes or inhibit TB transmission such as the air circulation system. For example, while the men's and women's areas had different airflow systems, it appeared that air flow in the women's section was more effective than in the men's section. Is this a factor in TB transmission? The movement patterns of residents also need to be addressed. How much time do they spend in common areas such as the dining area, the smoking area, the TV area and rest rooms? Another factor to consider is the lighting in different parts of the Homeless Shelter. Does the heat put off by the lighting affect dispersion of the bacilli?

Addressing all of these is clearly beyond the capacity of any GIS or simple disease mapping. HPC is required to simulate the movement pattern of residents, TB bacilli, lighting, the air circulation system and other variables.

Case Study 2 – Factory TB Outbreak

The second case study covers TB outbreak in a factory that produces airplane bridges. Out of a total of 64 workers, 32 were ultimately infected with the same strain of TB presumably from one Index case (Table 2).

Table 2. Workspace and Tuberculosis Risk

TB Test Result	Assembly	Maintenance	Office	Painting	Welding
Positive	8	0	2	10	12
Negative	18	2	2	2	2
Total	26	2	4	12	14

In the factory, Figure 2, in addition to basic screening records as collected for the homeless shelter, other available data include measures of duration and proximity to infected person such as hours per week in the factory, hours per week in the same workspace, hours per week within 3 feet of infected person, and usual work area. Results of initial analysis suggest that proximity of workspace to infected person was a major determinant of infection. In fact almost 100% of those who worked directly in the same space with one infected person were infected with the same strain of TB.

Hours spent each week in the factory was not a statistically significant determinant of TB risk. Rather, hours spent in the same work space and hours spent within 3 feet of Index case were the significant determinants of risk. In short active TB risk in the factory depends not so much on time spent in the factory but on time spent where in the factory. Simple mapping of TB occurrence in the factory does not go far enough. We need to simulate actual transmission considering factors such as the dynamic movements of individuals in the factory, shared common areas and amount of time spent there, the air circulation system, and related variables. Clearly more sophisticated tools are required to handle multiple variables in a dynamic system.

This rich data set provides the opportunity to implement a model to calibrate the dynamics of TB transmission in enclosed facilities using computational epidemiology.

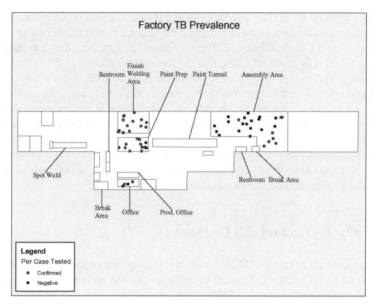

Fig. 2.

Conclusion

This study examined tuberculosis transmission in a homeless shelter and a factory with ongoing TB transmission. To understand the dynamics and determinants of transmission in enclosed spaces, traditional medical geographic approaches such as GIS are not suitable for modeling dynamics of disease transmission. Computational epidemiology allows the spatial distribution of risk to be defined not in terms of large regions but in micro-space, literally feet and inches. The potential of such computational tools for simulating and explaining disease transmission in enclosed spaces is high.

References

Acevedo-Garcia D. 2001. Zip-code level risk factors for tuberculosis: neighborhood environment and residential segregation in New Jersey, 1985 – 1992. *American Journal of Public Health*; 91(5): 735 – 741.

Barnes PF, El-Hajj H, Preseton-Martin S, et al. 1996. Transmission of tuberculosis among the urban homeless. *Journal of American Medical Association* 275:305 – 307.

Centers for Disease Control and Prevention 1994. Guidelines for Preventing the Transmission of Mycobacterium tuberculosis in Health-Care Facilities, 1994. *MMWR*; October 28, 1994 / 43(RR13);1-13200.

Centers for Disease Control and Prevention. 2003. *Reported Tuberculosis in the United States, 2002*. Atlanta, GA: CDC.

Cromley, E.K. 2003. GIS and Disease. *Annual Review of Public Health*. 24:7-24.

de Lepper, M.J.C., H.J. Scholten, and R.M. Stern (eds). 1995. *The Added Value of Geographical Information Systems in Public and Environmental Health*. Boston: Kluwer Academic Publishers.

de Savigny, D., and P. Wijeyaratne. 1995. *GIS for Health and the Environment*. Ottawa: International Development Research Center.

Diwan, V. K and A Thorson. 1999. Sex, Gender and Tuberculosis. *Lancet* 3/20/99, Vol. 353 Issue 9157, 1000-1001.

Gatrell, A. 2002. *Geographies of Health: An Introduction*. Oxford, Blackwell.

Gatrell, A., and M. Senior. 1999. Health and Health Care Applications. In: *Geographical Information Systems: Management Issues and* Applications - Volume 2, ed. P.A. Longley, M.F. Goodchild, D.J. Maguire, and D.W. Rhind, 925-938. New York: John Wiley & Sons, Inc.

Goldman, D.A., and J.D. Brender. 2000. Are Stanardized Mortality Ratios Valid for Public Health Data Analysis. *Statistics in Medicine* 19:1081-1088.

Hathcock, A.L., Greenberg, R.A., and A.W. Dakan, 1982. An Analysis of Lung Cancer on a Microgeographical Level. *Social Science in Medicine* 16:1235-1238.

James, W.L., R.E. Cossman, J.S. Cossman, C. Campbell, and T. Blanchard. 2004. A Brief Visual Primer for the Mapping of Mortality Trend Data. *International Journal of Health Geographics* 3:7.

Klovdahl AS, Graviss EA, Yaganehdoost A, et al. 2001. Networks and tuberculosis: an undetected community outbreak involving public places. *Soc Sci Med*; 52(5):681-94.

Leonhardt KK, Gentile F, Gilbert BP, Aiken M. 1994. A cluster of tuberculosis among crack house contacts in San Mateo County, California. *Am J Public Health*; 84(11): 1834 – 1836.

Melnick, A.L. 2002. *Introduction to Geographic Information Systems in Public Health*. Gaithersburg, Maryland: Aspen Publications.

Melnick, A.L. 2002. *Introduction to Geographic Information Systems in Public Health*. Gaithersburg, Maryland: Aspen Publications.

Pickle L.W. 2002. Spatial Analysis of Disease. In: *Biostatistical Applications in Cancer Research*. ed. C. Beam, 113-150. Boston: Klewer Academic Publishers.

Pickle, L.W., M. Mungiole, G.K. Jones, and A.A. White. 1996. *Atlas of United States Mortality*. U.S. Department of Health and Human Services, Public Health Service, Centers for Disease Control, National Center for Health Statistics.

Pickle, L.W., M. Mungiole, G.K. Jones, and A.A. White. 1996. *Atlas of United States Mortality*. U.S. Department of Health and Human Services, Public Health Service, Centers for Disease Control, National Center for Health Statistics.

Pickle, L.W., M. Mungiole, G.K. Jones, and A.A. White. 1999. Exploring Spatial Patterns of Mortality: The New *Atlas of United States Mortality*. *Statistics in Medicine* 18:3211-3220.

Ricketts, T.C. 2003. Geographic Information Systems and Public Health. *Annual Review of Public Health* 24:1-6.

Ricketts, T.C. 2003. Geographic Information Systems and Public Health. *Annual Review of Public Health* 24:1-6.

Rushton, G. 2003a. Epidemiology and Biostatistics: Public Health, GIS, and Spatial Analytic Tools. *Annual Review of Public Health* 24:43-56.

Rushton, G. 2003b. Public Health, GIS, and Spatial Analytical Tools. *Annual Review of Public Health* 24:43-56.

Scholten, H.J., and M.J.C. de Lepper. 1990. The Benefits of the Application of Geographical Information Systems in Public and Environmental Health. *World Health Statistics Quarterly* 44:160-171.

Yaganehdoost A, Graviss EA, Ross MW, et al. (1999). Complex transmission dynamics of clonally related virulent Mycobacterium tuberculosis associated with barhopping by predominantly human immunodeficiency virus-positive gay men. *Journal of Infectious Diseases* 180(4):1245-51.

An Infectious Disease Outbreak Simulator Based on the Cellular Automata Paradigm

Sangeeta Venkatachalam and Armin R. Mikler⋆

Department of Computer Science, University of North Texas
Denton, TX 76207, USA
{venkatac,mikler}@cs.unt.edu

Abstract. In this paper, we propose the use of Cellular Automata paradigm to simulate an infectious disease outbreak. The simulator facilitates
the study of dynamics of epidemics of different infectious diseases, and
has been applied to study the effects of spread vaccination and ring vaccination strategies. Fundamentally the simulator loosely simulates SIR
(Susceptible Infected Removed) and SEIR (Susceptible Exposed Infected
Removed). The Geo-spatial model with global interaction and our approach of global stochastic cellular automata are also discussed. The
global stochastic cellular automata takes into account the demography,
culture of a region. The simulator can be used to study the dynamics of
disease epidemics over large geographic regions. We analyze the effects
of distances and interaction on the spread of various diseases.

1   Introduction

Nowadays, the problem of emergent diseases and re-emergent diseases like influenza and SARS, have caused increased attention towards public health in general and epidemiology specifically. With the ever-increasing population and ability to travel longer distances in short time, the spread of communicable diseases
in a society has been accelerated [16,17]. Growing diversity of the population,
and globalization are leading towards increasing interaction among individuals.
Constant exposure to public health threats is raising people's concern and necessitates pro-active action towards preventing disease outbreaks. Further, greater
emphasis on infections and epidemics is rooted in the imminent threat arising
from bioterrorism. As a result, Public Health professionals have been focusing on
identifying the factors in the social, physical and epidemiological environment
which aid to faster spread of diseases.

As the significance of Public Health is being recognized, the role of epidemiologists has become more prominent. Epidemiology deals with the study of cause,
spread, and control of diseases. The goal of epidemiologists is to implement mechanisms for surveillance, monitoring, prevention and control of different diseases.
To accomplish the above mentioned, epidemiologists need to deal with large data

⋆ This research is in part supported by National Science Foundation award: NSF-
0350200

T. Böhme et al. (Eds.): IICS 2004, LNCS 3473, pp. 198–211, 2006.

sets of disease outbreaks. These data sets are often spatially and/or temporally distributed. It is in fact ironic that, for epidemiologists to study the dynamics of different diseases, it is vital for an outbreak to occur. Epidemiologists have been studying and analyzing the data sets using primarily statistical tools. In the vast variety of infectious diseases, expertise is needed in terms of epidemiologists for every disease. Statistical tools, prove to be inadequate and fragmentary, when focusing on large spatial domains. These tools have been deemed limited, particularly in view of an emerging global computational infrastructure that facilitates high performance computing. Hence, it is imperative to develop new tools that take advantage of today's computational power, and help epidemiologists to analyze and understand the spatial spread of diseases. The computational tools also enhance the quality of information, accelerate the generation of answers to specific questions and facilitate in prediction. Such tools will take on an important role in surveillance, monitoring, prevention and control of different diseases.

1.1   Cellular Automata

In the domain of computational tools, the Cellular Automata paradigm has been in use for several decades [14]. Nevertheless, in the field of modeling epidemics, this paradigm has rarely been utilized to its full potential [1,10,14,8]. A cellular automata as defined by Lyman Hurd is a discrete dynamical system, where space, time, and the states of the system are distinct [15]. CA has been exemplified as an array of similar processing units called cells. The cells arranged in a regular manner constitute a regular spatial lattice. Figure 1 shows a regular lattice of cells. The fundamental property of each cell is a state, where the states of cells change based on a update rule, either local or global. The update rule is applied synchronously throughout the lattice and the state transitions of the cells are based on few of the close by cells, known as the neighborhood. For a two-dimensional lattice the most common neighborhoods defined are von Neumann and Moore neighborhood as shown in figure 1 [15]. In the von Neumann neighborhood, the state of cell C_i,j depends on the states of the four neighborhood cells namely $C_{i+1,j}$, $C_{i-1,j}$, $C_{i,j+1}$, $C_{i,j-1}$. In the Moore neighborhood, the state of cell $C_{i,j}$ depends on the states of the eight neighborhood cells namely $C_{i+1,j}$, $C_{i-1,j}$, $C_{i,j+1}$, $C_{i,j-1}$, $C_{i+1,j+1}$, $C_{i-1,j-1}$, $C_{i-1,j+1}$, $C_{i+1,j-1}$.

As mentioned before, the CA's evolution is based on a global update rule applied uniformly to all the cells. The signature of this rule can be thought of as a state transition from time *t-1* to *t*. As shown in the figure 2 the state of the center cell changes to a state, which is in majority among the cells in the neighborhood. The update rule determines the deterministic or stochastic behavior of a CA. Stochastic behavior is seen by probabilistic update rules in non-deterministic state transitions.

Our efforts to design and implement a Cellular Automata based simulator has been necessitated by the need to study the dynamic of spread of a vast number of infectious diseases. Towards this goal, this paper proposes the use of CA paradigm to simulate an infectious disease outbreak. Specifically, this paper focuses on the design and evaluation of EPI-SIM, a global disease outbreak sim-

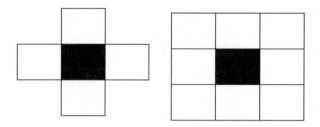

Fig. 1. von Neumann and Moore Neighborhood

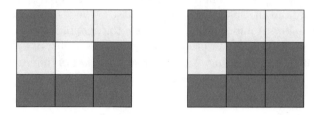

Fig. 2. Cellular Automata Update from time step *t-1* to *t*

ulator. The following section summarizes some of the research effort in modeling disease epidemic and highlights principle approaches. The design of EPI-SIM is discussed in Section 3. Section 4 presents the experimental analysis and results of the simulator. Section 5 discusses the Geo-Spatial model and the approach towards the global model to account for different demographics. Section 6 concludes the paper with a summary and direction for future work in the area of modeling infectious diseases outbreaks.

2   Related Work

Most of the work in modeling infectious disease epidemics is mathematically inspired and based on differential equations and SIR/SEIR model [3]. Differential equation, SIR modeling rely on the assumption of constant population and neglect the spatial effects [5,6]. They often fail to consider individual contact/interaction process and assume populations are homogeneously mixed and do not include variable susceptibility. Considerable research has been conducted in SIR(Susceptible, Infectious, Recovered) modeling of infectious diseases using a set of differential equations. Both partial and ordinary differential equation models are so deterministic in nature that they neglect the stochastic or probabilistic behavior [8]. Nevertheless, these approaches/models have been shown to be effective in regions of small population [8]. Other approaches for modeling disease epidemics have been using mean field type approximations [12]. Even though the MFT models are similar to the differential equations, they add a probabilistic nature by adding different probabilities for the mixing among individuals. Although, according to Boccara [5] mean field approximations tend to

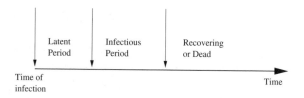

Fig. 3. Infection Time-line

neglect spatial dependencies and correlations and assume that the probability of the state of cell being susceptible or infective is proportional to the density of the corresponding population. This approach relies on the quantitative measures to predict local interaction. Boccara and Cheong [5] study the SIS model of spread of infectious disease in a population of moving individuals, thereby introducing non-uniform population density. In every update the cells take up a state of being either susceptible or infectious and randomly choose a cell location to move to.

Ahmed *et al* [2] model variations in population density by allowing cyclic host movement. Other approaches in modeling variable susceptibility of the population, have been done by inducing immunity in the population. Ahmed *et al* [1] introduce incubation and latency time, and suggest that the parameters have an accelerating impact on the spread of a disease epidemic. Nevertheless, the underlying assumption is spontaneous infection of individuals. Boccara and Cheong [6] concentrate on SIR epidemic models and take into consideration the fluctuation in the population by births and deaths, exhibiting a cyclic behavior with primary emphasis on moving individuals. Di Stefano *et al* [8] have developed a lattice gas cellular automata model to analyze the spread of epidemics of infectious diseases. The model is based on individuals, where individuals can change their state independent of others and can move from one cell to other. However, this approach does not consider the infection time-line of latency, incubation period, and recovery which have been shown to be important to model a disease epidemic.

3   EPI-SIM Disease Outbreak Simulator

In our model the basic unit of cellular automata is a cell, which may represent an individual or a small sub-population. For each cell we use the Moore (8) neighborhood definition. Each cell can be characterized with its own probability for risk of exposure, probability of contracting the disease and state. Unlike the SIR model, every cell comes in contact with the cells in its defined neighborhood. The time-line for infection that we consider is shown in figure 3. However, the moore neighborhood is restricted in modeling population demographics and travel patterns. The limitation is eliminated in the next version of the simulator with a global neighborhood which will be proposed in future publications. The following sections discuss the definitions, features and rules of the model and simulator.

3.1   Definitions

In order to understand the functioning of the simulator, we define definite number of states a can exists in, and define the infectious time-line. The following section describes the different states and definitions considered in the model.

States of a Cell

State 'S' for Susceptible is defined as the state where, the cell is capable of contracting a disease from its neighbors. In the infectious state, 'I' the cell is capable of passing on the infection to its neighbors. In the recovery state, 'R' the cell is neither capable of passing on the infection, nor is capable of contracting the infection.

Parameters for the Simulator

Infectivity ψ, at any given time is defined as the probability of an susceptible individual to become infectious, if it has an infectious cell as a neighbor. Latency λ, is defined as the time period between, the cell becoming infected and it becoming infectious. Infectious period θ , is the period of time, when the infected cell is capable of spreading the disease to other cells. Recovery period ρ is defined as the time period, the cell takes to recover, wherein it is neither capable of passing on the infection, nor is capable of catching the infection.

3.2   Rules for Spread of Disease

The following rules are applied to the CA for simulating the spread of the disease. The rules describe the state transitions of individual cells.

1. A cell's state changes from susceptible S to Latent L when it comes in contact with an infected cell in its defined neighborhood. The cell acquires the disease from the infected neighbor based on the probability of given by the parameter of infectivity ψ. The cell remains in the latent state for the number of time steps (updates) as defined by the parameter latency λ.

2. The state of the cell changes from latent L to infectious I after being in state L for the given λ. In this model we assume for simplicity, that every cell exposed to the pathogen, will become infectious. In the state I, the cells are capable of passing on the infection to neighborhood cells. For example if for a disease $\mathcal{D}$, λ= 2 units, then after two time steps the cell will enter the infectious state I.

3. After a time period, defined by the infectious period θ, the state of the cell changes from infectious I to recovered or removed R. Once the cells enter the state R, the cell is no more capable of passing on the infection.

4. From the state R, the cell's state changes back to either susceptible S or it remain in state R, signifying complete immunity. The 'healing mode' turned on determines the transition from state R to state S and vice versa.

3.3 Features

While modeling a disease epidemic, few parameters that are considered important are neighborhood radius, contact between individuals, infection probability (variable susceptibility), immunity, latency, infectious period and recovery period. The simulator is highly parameterized to let the user change and modify the above parameters. The neighborhood of every cell can be changed from a 8 neighborhood to 4 neighborhood depending on the region being simulated and the contacts among the individuals of the region. As mentioned, the infection probability represented as infectivity ψ is a significant parameter for the spread of a disease. In the case of our model, ψ is based on the virulence of the disease and contact rate among individuals. For some diseases individuals attain lifetime immunity, after being infected, while for disease like common cold, individuals attain temporary immunity. Thus, to take this fact into consideration, the simulator has a feature of healing mode. With the healing mode enabled the simulation is executed in a mode that forces cells to turn into susceptible after the recovery state and with healing turned off, the cell attains complete lifetime immunity.

As mentioned above, the infection time-line is also an important factor in modeling a disease epidemic. Thus the time periods of latency λ, infectious θ, and recovery ρ are all expressed as time units, for example, latency of two days, can be represented as $\lambda=2$ units. The simulator allows the user step through the simulation at each time step, or execute it continuously. We will see in the next section, how changing these parameters, can change the dynamics of spread of diseases.

4   Experiments and Results

An epidemic is a severe outbreak of an infectious disease which spreads rapidly to many people. For example, the occurrence of Influenza in a region is considered as an epidemic. When a disease spreads to larger geographic regions or throughout the world it is known as pandemic.

Moving along the same direction an endemic is defined as a disease that is always present in certain group of the population. Using our model we show both an epidemic and endemic. An epidemic is characterized by an exponential growth of the infected individuals in a population. In the case of an endemic the number of infected individuals fluctuates around a mean, there is no exponential growth.

Experiments were conducted on a 140 by 140 grid cellular automata with different values of ψ, λ and θ. The results in this section represent the mean over multiple random experiments and different random graphs of the same type. The analysis of results in this section have been conducted with reference to the above definitions.

4.1 Analysis of Variation in Infectivity ψ

As mentioned earlier, ψ is an important factor in the analysis of spread of a disease. Figure 4(a) and 4(b) show the results of executing the simulation of a

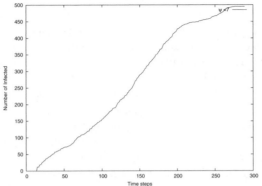

(a) The growth of number of infected individuals per time step is represented for $\psi = 7$.

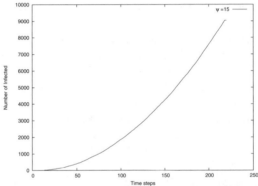

(b) The growth of number of infected individuals per time step is represented for $\psi = 15$.

Fig. 4. Variation in spread for different ψ's

disease $\mathcal{D}$ with ψ of 7 and 15 respectively. Figure 4(a) depicts that the number of infected reached around 500 in 300 time steps, whereas in figure 4(b) with ψ of 15 the number of infected reached around 10000 in 300 updates. Thus, this depicts that the growth is rapid with ψ of 15 as compared to ψ of 7. Figure 5(a), shows the comparison of the different values ψ's, which are 7,10,12,15. The curves represent the growth rate. The curve is much steeper for ψ of 15 as compared to others. The experiment was conducted with the $\lambda = 2$ units, $\theta = 3$ units and $\rho = 2$ units. Healing option was turned off. This shows the sensitivity of the parameter ψ.

4.2   Effects of Vaccination

Vaccination has contributed significantly towards the eradication and reduction of effect of many infectious diseases [7]. The following experiments were con-

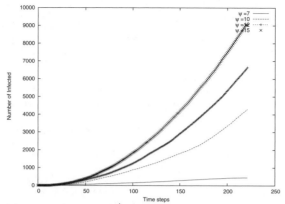

(a) Comparison of ψ's of 7,10,12,15 is shown. The
curve with ψ represents faster growth of infected individuals than ψ of 7,10,12

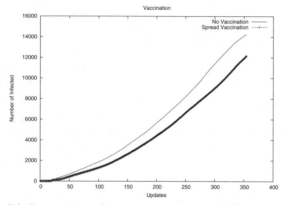

(b) Comparison of Random Vaccination (5% of population was vaccinated) and no Vaccination

Fig. 5. Comparison of ψ's and Comparison of Random Vaccination and no Vaccination

ducted on the simulator by vaccinating about 5% of the population at random
and infecting few cells. Figure 5(b), shows the growth of infected individuals
in a vaccinated and non vaccinated population. Figure 5(b) depicts that the
growth of infected individuals in a population with only 5% of the population
vaccinated, is considerably less as compared to the growth in a non-vaccinated
population.

We study the effects of spatial distribution of population, by vaccinating a
part of the population using the random vaccination and ring vaccination. Every
time a new vaccine is discovered, the question arises as to how should the vaccine
be distributed to minimize the spread of a disease and maximize the effect of
vaccination. Thus, in this experiment we compare the random vaccination, which

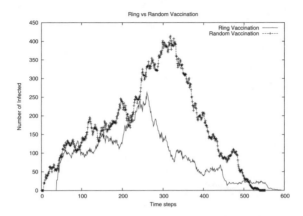

Fig. 6. Comparison of Random and Ring Vaccination with N doses of vaccination available for both strategies

is also known as uniform strategy [9], and ring vaccination. The doses of vaccine available at our disposal is often limited, thus for the purpose of experiment we consider N doses of vaccine to be available to vaccinate the population, where N is about 5% of the population. In random vaccination, the N vaccines, are randomly distributed to individuals in a population, independent of the other. In the ring vaccination, individuals are vaccinated in a ring surrounding an area. The thickness and circumference of the ring depends on N. As Figure 6 shows, using random vaccination many more individuals are infected as compared to the ring vaccination. This experiment validates the result shown by Fukś and Lawniczak in [9].

4.3 Conclusion from Experiments

The previous model described poses a limitation of neighborhood. The model considers a neighborhood of 8 cells, because of which after a time period the number of susceptibles reduce and saturate the neighborhood . In such a situation the variance of infectivity parameter plays no role and has the same effect on the spread of the disease. Also, the need to simulate a disease, where an infective can spread the disease to twelve other individuals in one time step, will not be possible to simulate. Another important issue to note is the movement of people, migration, or travel is not considered. Some models, we saw in the previous section deal with movement of individuals from one cell to another in the defined neighborhood, where again the neighborhood is restricted. The saturation of neighborhood occurs due to overlapping of neighborhood, when more than one cell is infected in a neighborhood. Cells in a neighborhood may get infected more than once in one time unit.

5   Geo-spatial Model

The Geo-spatial model is designed for simulating global outbreak of a disease in a environment with global interaction. Even for this model the basic unit of CA

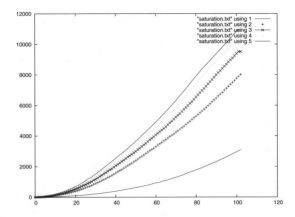

Fig. 7. Represents saturation of neighborhood ψ

is a cell, which represents an individual. The neighborhood as defined for this model is global, where in a region of n cells every cell has n-1 neighbors.

For the functioning of this model, the definitions for the states of cell, parameters for simulation are same as the ones for SIR model discussed earlier. This model has an additional parameter of contact rate and the definition is as follows.

Contact rate parameter defines the number of contacts made by an individual per time unit. Instead of having the same contact rate parameter for every cell in the lattice, for simulation purposes this parameter has a Poisson distribution over the cells. The simulation of spread of disease is discussed further.

1. In a time step a cell chooses k cells at random from the pool of n-1 neighbors, where k is the contact rate defined for that cell. Thus the cell has now established contacts with k cells.
2. Once a contact has been established between cell 'a' and cell 'b', depending on the virulence of the disease defined by the infectivity parameter, cell 'a' can pass the infection to cell 'b' if cell 'b' is in a susceptible state S. If cell 'a' is not infected currently and cell 'b' is infected then cell 'a' can acquire the infection from 'b'. Thus the infection can pass on in both directions.

5.1   Experiments on Geo-spatial Model

The Geo-spatial model is different from the SIR type model in terms of the neighborhood. The neighborhood saturation problem posed by SIR type model is overcome by this model. However, this model is restricted in modeling population demographics and travel patterns. The choice of cells for contact, is random and is not based on distance from the cell or any other parameter.

To study the effects of **position of index case** on spread of a disease, the simulation was run with different initial positions. After a certain time unit it is seen that locations of new infected cases are not very different for the two

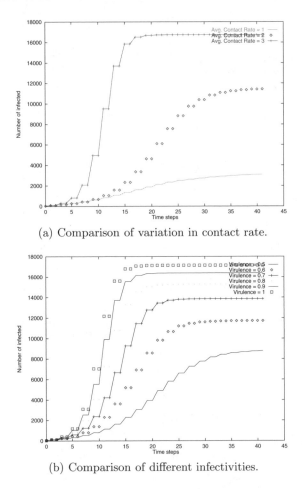

(a) Comparison of variation in contact rate.

(b) Comparison of different infectivities.

Fig. 8. Analysis of contact rate and infectivity

simulations. This shows that the position of index case does not matter. In the SIR type model the same experiment was done and the locations of new infected cases were different for different positions of index cases. The new cases were closer to the index case. In the Geo-spatial model because of global neighborhood and global interaction the positioning of index case does not matter.

To analyse the **contact rate** the experiment was done with three different contact rates for cells. The result shows that as average contact rate increases, the number of infected individuals also grows. For this model the contact rate is directly proportional to number of infected individuals. It is important to note that the contacts made by cells are random. Figure 8(a) shows the comparison.

As seen before in the other model, as **infectivity parameter** ψ increases the number of infected individuals increases. The average contact rate was fixed for this experiment. Figure 8(b) shows the comparison.

5.2   Accounting for Different Demographics

The models described above may be used for simulating diseases over small regions with local interaction and global interaction respectively. As mentioned before, these models do not take into account the demographics of the region and may not be accurate for simulating disease spread over large geographic regions because of the neighborhood constriction posed by them. Thus the global stochastic cellular automata with demographics will facilitate to understand the effects of different demographics, the population density, socio-economics of a region and culture. It can also be used effectively for investigating different vaccination strategies and understanding the effects of travel.

5.3   Global Outbreak Simulator

In the following section we discuss the design of a global outbreak simulator with a global interaction and demography. Even for this model the basic unit of CA is a cell, which represents an individual or a small sub-population. The neighborhood as defined for this model is global, where in a region of n cells every cell has n-1 neighbors.

The **neighborhood** for a global SCA is defined using a fuzzy set neighborhood. The definition of Fuzzy set neighborhood is as follows.

The set $F \subset S$ where S is a set of all the cells
$$F: \{\langle s,p\rangle | s \in S, 0 \leq p \leq 1\}$$
$\langle s,1 \rangle$: Total/Complete membership
$\langle s,0 \rangle$: No membership

The variable p maintains the state of infection, 1 if infected else 0.

5.4   Characteristics of a Cell

State of infection δ is defined as any number between 0 and 1, indicating the level of infection present in the cell. 0 indicates not infected, 1 indicates fully infected.

Interaction Coefficient i for a particular cell is defined as the interaction between that cell and every other cell in the lattice space. It is calculated as the reciprocal of the euclidean distance between the cells. Euclidean distance as derived from the GIS gravity model.

$$i_{C_{i,j},C_{k,l}} = \frac{1}{\sqrt{\langle i-k\rangle^2+\langle j-l\rangle^2}}$$

Global interaction coefficient Γ of cell Ci,j is the summation of all the individual (n-1) interaction coefficients of the cell. Every cell has one global interaction coefficient and n-1 interaction coefficients.

The **infection factor I** is calculated as a fraction of the interaction coefficient to the global interaction coefficient Γ, for every cell to cell interaction. It is also based on the virulence of the disease and the state of infection of the infecting agent.

$$I_{C_{i,j}} = \sum\nolimits_{\forall C_{k,l}\neq C_{i,j}} \frac{i_{C_{i,j},C_{k,l}}}{\Gamma_{C_{i,j}}\times\delta_{C_{k,l}}\times\psi}$$

5.5   Simulation Based on Population

The global interaction coefficient and the interaction coefficients are calculated based on the distance. As the distance in between the cells reduce, the interaction coefficients increase which indicates more chances of interaction between them.

$$\Gamma_{C_{i,j}} = \sum_{\forall C_{k,l} \neq C_{i,j}} \frac{1}{\sqrt{(i-k)^2 + (j-l)^2}}$$

5.6   Simulation Based on Population and Distance

The global interaction coefficient and the interaction coefficents are calculated based on the distance and population. The distance between the cells and the populations of the cells are considered. For better understanding, the cells are considered to be small regions having certain populations. The product of the populations of the two cells, acts as a factor for the interaction coefficients. The population factor is directly proportional to the interaction coefficient and the distance between them is inversely proportional to the interaction coefficient.Thus two cells with high populations are assumed to interact more than two cells with low populations, when the distance between them is same.

$$\Gamma_{C_{i,j}} = \sum_{\forall C_{k,l} \neq C_{i,j}} \frac{1}{\sqrt{(i-k)^2 + (j-l)^2}} \times P_{C_{i,j}} \times P_{C_{i,j}}$$

6   Conclusion and Future Work

This paper describes a disease outbreak simulator using the cellular automata paradigm. The results show the variation in the spread of the disease for different parameters of infectivity ψ. The simulator has also facilitated the study of different vaccination strategies. Geo-spatial model helps us in simulating disease spread in an environment with global interaction including travel and migration. In the same direction the global model can be used to simulate disease spread over large geographic regions. It deals with global interaction and the demographics of the region. While still working on the development of computational tools to facilitate surveillance, monitoring, prevention and control of dynamics of different diseases, the current simulators prove as valuable tools to study the dynamics of different diseases. Global stochastic versions of the CA are currently being developed.

References

1. Ahmed E., Agiza H.N. On Modeling epidemics. Including latency, incubation and variable susceptibility*Physica A 253 (1998)*, pp. 347-352
2. Ahmed E., Elgazzar A.S. On some applications of cellular automata*Physica A 296 (2002)*, pp.529-538
3. Bagni, R., Berchi, R., and Cariello, P. A comparison of simulation models applied to epidemics. *Journal of Artificial Societies and Social Simulation 5 (2002)*,3

4. Barfoot, T. D. and D'Eleuterio, G. M. T. Multiagent Coordination by Stochastic Cellular Automata *Presented at the International Joint Conference on Artificial Intelligence (2001)*

5. Boccara N. Cheong K. Critical behavior of a probabilistic automata network SIS model for the spread of an infectious disease in a population of moving individuals.*Journal of Physics A :Mathematical and General 26:5 (1993)*, pp. 3707-3717

6. Boccara N. Cheong K., Oram M. A probabilistic automata network epidemic model with births and deaths exhibiting cyclic behavior.*Journal of Physics A :Mathematical and General 27 (1994)*, pp. 1585-1597

7. Del Giudice G., Vaccine. *21 Suppl 2:S83-8. (2003)*

8. Stefano, B. D., Fukś, H., and Lawniczak, A. T. Object-oriented implementation of CA/LGCA modelling applied to the spread of epidemics.*In 2000 Canadian Conference on electrical and Computer Engineering 1*, IEEE, pp. 26-31.

9. Henryk Fukś and Anna T. Lawniczak. Individual-based lattice model for spatial spread of epidemics *Discrete Dynamics in Nature and Society 6 (2001)*, pp. 191-200

10. Hokky Situngkir, Epidemiology through Cellular Automata Case of Study: Avian Influenza Indonesia *Working Paper WPF2004,* Bandung Fe Institute.

11. James C. Thomas and David J. Weber. Epidemiologic Methods for the Study of Infectious Diseases. Oxford Press (2001)

12. Kleczkowski, A., and Grenfell, B. T. Mean-field-type equations for spread of epidemics: The 'small world' model. *Physica A 274, 1-2 (1999)*,pp. 355-360.

13. Ricardo Mansilla, Jose L.Gutierrez. Deterministic site exchange cellular automata models for the spread of diseases in human settlements.*Bulletin of Mathematical Biology*

14. Shih Ching Fu and George Milne. Epidemic Modelling Using Cellular Automata. *To appear in Australian Conference on Artificial Life 2003*

15. Wolfram, S. Statistical Mechanics of Cellular Automata. *Reviews of Modern Physics 55* pp. 601-644.

16. Yaganehdoost A, Graviss EA, Ross MW, et al. Complex transmission dynamics of clonally related virulent Mycobacterium tuberculosis associated with barhopping by predominantly human immunodeficiency virus-positive gay men. *Journal of Infect Diseases. 180(4) (1999)* pp.1245-51.

17. Youngblut, C. Educational uses of virtual reality technology. *Technical Report IDA Document D-2128 (1998)* , Institute for Defense Analyses, Alexandria, VA

Agent-Based Simulation Tools
in Computational Epidemiology

Padmavathi Patlolla, Vandana Gunupudi, Armin R. Mikler, and Roy T. Jacob

Department of Computer Science and Engineering
University of North Texas, USA 76203

Abstract. An agent-based approach is evaluated for its applicability as
a new modeling technology in the emerging area of Computational Epidemiology, a research domain that attempts to synergistically unite the
fields of Computer Science and Epidemiology. A primary concern of epidemiologists is investigating the spread of infectious diseases. Computer
Scientists can provide powerful tools for epidemiologists to study such
diseases. The existing simulation approaches available to epidemiologists
are fast becoming obsolete, with data being stored in newer formats
like GIS formats. There is an urgent need for developing computationally powerful, user-friendly tools that can be used by epidemiologists to
study the dynamics of disease spread. We present a survey of the state-
of-the-art in agent-based modeling and discuss the unique features of
our chosen technique. Our agent-based approach effectively models the
dynamics of the spread of infectious diseases in spatially-delineated environments by using agents to model the interaction between people and
pathogens. We present preliminary results of modeling an actual tuberculosis disease outbreak in a local shelter. This model is an important
step in the development of user-friendly tools for epidemiologists.

1 Introduction

Computational epidemiology is a developing research domain that attempts to
unite the disparate fields of computer science and epidemiology. Epidemiologists
are primarily concerned with investigating disease outbreaks and risk assessment
in spatially delineated environments, investigating vaccination strategies to control the spread. Thorough understanding of the dynamics of disease transmission
is key to predicting the spread of a disease and controlling it. Epidemiologists
employ various statistical methods to analyze the data relating to a disease, but
there are no specific tools that they can use to study a disease, its spread, the
spread of the infective agent and other factors. With the emergence of new infectious diseases like Lyme disease, Hepatitis-C, West Nile Virus, and HIV, the
need to develop tools that epidemiologists need to study these diseases becomes
apparent. As more strains of diseases like tuberculosis and pneumonia become
resistant to antibiotics, it becomes imperative to track the progression/mutation
of these strains. The method of field trials, currently available to epidemiologists,
is either prohibitively expensive or unethical. Applying mathematical models and

T. Böhme et al. (Eds.): IICS 2004, LNCS 3473, pp. 212–223, 2006.

using computers to process the copious amounts of data related to a particular disease outbreak can aid in understanding the dynamics of the disease spread to a certain extent. But, even today, in spite of the availability of computational resources to process the huge data involved, epidemiologists face tough challenges in trying to understand the results obtained by applying the mathematical models and computer programs. Epidemiologists are not trained to understand the intricacies of mathematical theories or the subtleties of computer programs. This is where computer scientists can step in, by harnessing the power of powerful computing resources now available and developing user-friendly tools that epidemiologists can use.

Epidemiologists are often faced with the challenge of dealing with data that are sparse, widely distributed, and incomplete (often due to confidentiality and other constraints). This may result in conflicting information that confound or disguise the evidence, leading to wrong conclusions. Today, the role of epidemiologists has become even more pronounced as the significance of Public Health has been recognized. To meet the increasing demands, the field of Epidemiology is in need of specific computational tools that would enable the professionals to respond promptly and accurately to control and contain disease outbreaks. Increased globalization, highly mobile populations, and possible exposure to infectious diseases pose new public health threats. It is vital to develop new tools that take advantage of today's communication and computing infrastructures. Computational models for the simulation of global disease dynamics are required to facilitate adequate what-if analyses. This necessitates adapting fundamental Computer Science concepts to the specific problems in Epidemiology.

One of the primary challenges that Computational Epidemiologists face today is trying to understand the spread of a disease globally. The results obtained from the processing of the available data are difficult to analyze because of the sheer size of the population involved. In such scenarios, providing visualization tools would allow the scientists to process available data and draw relevant conclusions. For example, consider the critical issue of limiting the spread of an infectious disease in a particular area (city or town, for example). The data immediately available to epidemiologists may include information about the extent of disease spread, the areas the epidemic has spread to and the number of vaccine doses available for immunization. If the number of doses is limited, a decision must be made about vaccination strategies, *i.e.* what is the optimal way to vaccinate in order to effectively limit the spread of the disease. The goal is to provide epidemiologists simulation tools that will allow them to analyze the effect of various immunization strategies to derive an optimal strategy for immunization with the available resources. For example, they may arrive at the conclusion that ring vaccination, i.e. vaccinating in the area of 1 mile radius around the infected area, will contain the spread of the disease.

In 2003, an outbreak of SARS in a province of China spread quickly to geographically-remote parts of the world like Toronto. When such a disease outbreak occurs, epidemiologists must study the outbreak to predict its spread. At this time, there are no general-purpose computational tools available to epidemi-

ologists to model disease outbreaks. Outbreaks like SARS in 2003 illustrate the
need for developing tools that epidemiologists can use to model an outbreak
quickly and predict its spread successfully. These include mathematical or computational modeling tools to effectively monitor the spread of a disease, track
mutations of different strains, and implement effective vaccination strategies,
and investigate the spread of diseases.

Computational Epidemiology addresses the broader aspects of epidemiology,
primarily disease tracking, analysis and surveillance. An example of the synergistic collaboration of computing power and biology is the genome research project,
which involved mapping the human genome. Similarly, we can use high performance computing and data visualization techniques to develop tools to simulate
disease outbreaks and aid in the investigative process allowing them to respond
promptly and effectively contain the spread of diseases. The availability of data
from geographic information systems (GIS), new visualization techniques (like
virtual reality) and high-performance computing paradigms, such as cluster and
grid computing, will greatly contribute to the development of tools that facilitate
the work of today's epidemiologists.

2   Outbreak Models

Mathematical models are important tools that can be combined with analytical
tools to model disease outbreaks, study mutations of viruses, help in developing
effective immunization and vaccination strategies. When combined with other
analytical methods, they can become powerful tools for epidemiologists. Mathematical models can predict future outbreaks, present risk analysis, compare
alternatives and methods, and even help prepare effective response strategies for
bioterrorism attacks. In order to provide epidemiologists with user-friendly tool,
a synergy is required between computer scientists and epidemiologists to help
in the utilization of currently available tools and development of new ones. It is
imperative that both computer scientists and epidemiologists cooperate in order
to develop effective tools.

Dynamical modeling and statistical methods have been used in epidemiology for many years, but their role is changing now due to increasing size of the
associated data. There has been little effort until now to harness the power of
computational resources and apply them to existing approaches. Other modeling
paradigms, such as agent-based modeling and stochastic cellular automata, can
now be applied to epidemiology since we can use available data sets in the form
of GIS data and large computer databases. The SARS outbreak was a global
outbreak, whereby the disease that originated in a remote part of China spread
rapidly to other parts of the world like Toronto. Global outbreaks of diseases are
dependent on a number of factors like demography, geography and culture of a
region, socioeconomic factors, and travel patterns. Local disease outbreaks, on
the other hand, are outbreaks of diseases in spatially delineated areas like factories, homeless shelters. The spread of the disease is thus dependent on airflow
rates, heating and cooling, the architectural properties of the delineated space,
and social and spatial interactions.

3   Computing Paradigms

Different computational paradigms have been used to model the behavior of biological phenomena like disease outbreaks. Depending on the nature of the outbreak, different paradigms are required. For example, the same computing paradigm cannot be used to model both global and local outbreaks. Stochastic Cellular Automata is a novel paradigm that can successfully model global disease outbreaks, taking into account the factors responsible for the outbreak. Modeling global outbreaks is a particularly challenging task for which stochastic cellular automata are a useful modeling tool. Each region consists of cells, where each cell is influenced by its neighbors. The state of each cell is dependent on the state of its neighbors. This paradigm is useful for modeling vaccination strategies such as ring vanninations. It can also be used to model other vaccination strategies.

Whether it is global or local, modeling a disease outbreak is particularly challenging. The sheer complexity of the problem overwhelms traditional analytical tools. A particularly promising paradigm for modeling local outbreaks is that of agent-based modeling, which involves assigning an agent to each object in the environment that we want to model. We can exploit the features of agent-based modeling to address problems that can be intractable using traditional models. We discuss agent-based modeling in the following section.

3.1   Agent-Based Modeling

Agent-based models are simple but allow modeling of complex phenomena. An agent can be defined simply as an entity that acts on behalf of others, while displaying some form of autonomous behavior in choosing its actions. Using this simple definition of an agent, we can build very complex systems. By assigning agents to the entities in a system, we can run controlled experiments that allow us to change some parameters of the system while keeping the others constant. In this manner, an entire history of the system can be developed. Agent-based modeling is particularly useful for modeling local disease outbreaks and can be combined with other techniques and, by harnessing computational resources, used to effectively simulate local disease outbreaks.

The functionality in an agent-based system is implemented through the interaction of agents. Assigning agents to different interacting entities in the outbreak will allow is to model the spatial and social interactions in spatially delineated environments. The infected people as well as the infectious bacilli or viruses can be agents and purposeful movement can be incorporated to simulate the disease in a realistic manner. Purposeful movement implies that the agents can move of their own volition, simulating the movement of the objects (people and bacilli) in the actual disease.

Incorporating purposeful movement is not a simple task. We need first to investigate the type of environment and the nature of the entities we want to model, study their desires and model them as a function of some parameters. When the desire function reaches a threshold, agents tend to change their behavior, such as move in a different direction or perform a certain action. For example, if we are trying to model humans with desires to smoke and to drink, we associate with each an agent, with variables representing their present level of desire to smoke or drink. When its desire level hits a threshold, an agent will perform an action, such as moving toward the smoking or toward the drinking fountain.

Figure 1 shows the desire levels as a function of time and threshold values.

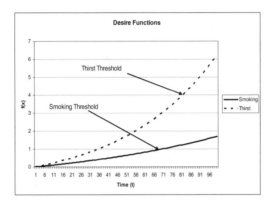

Fig. 1. Desire Function

Now when the desire level reaches the threshold, the agent, which is in the area A in Figure 1 tries to move towards the area D, here it can quench its thirst. In order to move toward the destination D from the source A, we can design a Source/Destination routing table which will help the agent move in the right direction and reach the destination with least effort.

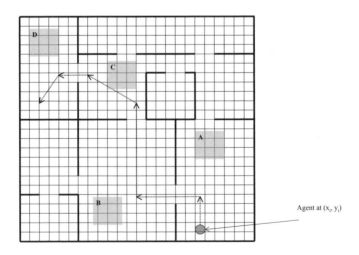

Fig. 2. Grid Environment

S/D	A	B	C	D	...
A	-	B	C	B	...
B	A	-	C	C	...
C	A	B	-	D	...
D	C	C	C	-	...
...	...	...	...	...	...

Fig. 3. Source/Destination Routing Table

3.2 State-of-the-Art in Agent-Based Modeling

Agent-based modeling has been used in the biological domain extensively, and various modeling tools are available. The following section presents a brief overview of the current state-of-the-art in agent-based modeling. This section outlines some of the agent-based computational tools that are currently available.

Swarm. Developed at the Santa Fe institute, Swarm [13] provides a set of libraries that can be used to model complex systems. As the name suggests, the basic component of agent organization is a "swarm", a collection of agents with a schedule of events over the collection. The swarm represents the entire model, i.e, the agents as well as the evolution of these agents over a time period. Swarm is a very powerful and flexible agent platform. However, it is very domain-specific in that extensive knowledge of the Java programming language is required. Consequently, this tool cannot be used directly by many epidemiologists.

Ascape [14], which is modeled on Swarm, is a platform that allows users to develop complex models. It has been used to develop the well-known Sugarscape simulation. Easier to learn and use than Swarm and providing many user-friendly tools. it is also implemented using Java. Some knowledge of the language is required to be able to use it effectively.

RePast [15] is a framework for creating agent-based simulations. Developed by the University of Chicago's Social Science Research Group, it requires knowledge of Java. It has built-in GIS, Excel import/export facility, and support to produce charts and graphs and allows objects to be moved by the mouse. It aims to model the agents using recursive social constructions and to replay the simulations with altered assumptions.

StarLogo [12] is a multi-agent simulation tool developed at the MIT Media laboratory. It is specifically aimed toward providing support to build decentralised multi-agent simulations. Starlogo is an extension of the programming language Logo, which allows us to define the movement of an agent called turtle on the computer screen by giving it commands. Starlogo extends this idea and provides support to create and control thousands of turtles in parallel, allowing them to move around a world defined by the user. Starlogo provides support to program thousands of patches that make up the turtles world. This allows a purposeful movement for the turtles in which they can sense their surroundings and move by choice. Starlogo is very easy to learn and provides a graphical user interface that allows epidemiologists with no prior programming experience to use it easily. It provides support for plotting graphs, allows the user to define slide bars, buttons and monitors allowing the user to control the simulation, monitoring the various parameters of the simulation and observing how they change with time.

3.3 What's New

Even though agent-based modeling tools useful to epidemiologists exist today, the unique features of epidemiology require the development of new tools. Data from various sources and in different formats need to be input into these models, highlighting the need for developing tools to convert existing data into uniform formats. Also, data are most commonly available in GIS format, but agent-based tools are not able to directly read data from these sources. Therefore, either existing tools need to be modified to read GIS data or new tools must be designed that read the data in GIS format and output the simulation results.

4 TB Outbreak in a Homeless Shelter

Tuberculosis (TB), an extremely infectious disease, is of particular concern when people interact in spatially-delineated environments like factories and homeless shelters. It was a leading cause of death in the 19th century. It spreads through the air, with the bacilli having a settling rate of 3 feet/hour. The tuberculosis bacilli reside in the lungs, so the immune system responds quickly to the infection. Most infected individuals never develop TB, *i.e.* they never become infectious. Most exposed individuals remain "latent-for-life," but around 10 percent of those exposed become infectious. The reasons that TB persists in the United States are co-infection with HIV/AIDS, lack of public knowledge about transmission and treatment, and immigration, which accounts for a large number of new cases. We propose to model the dynamics of an outbreak that occurred in 2000 to model the spread of infection from patient zero to other infected individuals. Using agent-based modeling, we can simulate the outbreak and study the transmission patterns unique to this setting. We model the layout of the homeless shelter and the interacting entities. The bacilli and the individuals are modeled as agents. Each individual is given a color indicating its level of infection.

4.1 Data Collection

Data was collected through interviews during targeted surveillance screenings of homeless people who use the shelter. The facility opens daily at 4 p.m. and people line-up outside the shelter, waiting to enter it. These individuals are tested at least once a week, with non-regular people being tested more often than the people who sleep at the shelter regularly. The data has been sanitized in compliance with HIPAA regulations, whereby all identifying information has been removed. This data has been provided to us by local health authorities in GIS format and is incorporated into the agent-based model. For the homeless shelter, the data used in the model includes the following information in each case:

- Date tested (relative to t_0)
- Status of tuberculosis
- Location in the facility
- Length of time spent in the facility

4.2 Agent-Based Simulation of the Outbreak

We have modeled this disease outbreak using StarLogo, an agent-based modeling tool that uses "turtles" and "patches" to model the interaction in the environment. Figure 4 shows a screen shot from the simulator giving the layout of the homeless shelter.

The shelter contains mats and beds, with the mats shown in light-grey and the beds shown in dark-grey (see Figure 4). The occupants of the beds are regular inhabitants of the homeless shelter who pay a nominal rent in return for being guaranteed a bed. The people who sleep on mats are usually short-term occupants who sleep in the shelter sporadically. There are separate sleeping areas for men and women, with different sleeping areas for people over 50. The simulation shows the placement of the beds and mats in the different sleeping areas. The upper left-side section shows the beds occupied by men that sleep at the shelter regularly. The lower left-side shows the placement of the mats occupied by men who sporadically sleep at the shelter. The upper right corner shows the beds used by the men that are over fifty years of age. Finally, the lower right area shows the women's sleeping area that has both beds and mats.

The model shows that the beds are spaced further apart from each other than the mats, which illustrates the difference in the infection rate in these areas. The small compartments that are between the men's and the women's area are the restrooms and the lower area without mats and beds is the smoking area. People ocassionally wake up during the night to smoke, congregating in that

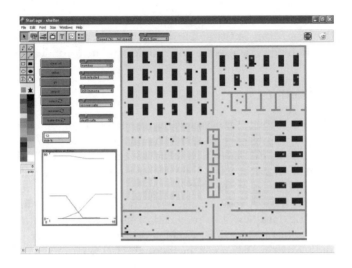

Fig. 4. StarLogo Screen Shot

area. Incidentally, people enter the shelter through the smoking area. The figure shows the queues near the smoking area from which people enter the shelter.

We use different colors (not shown in Figure 4) to represent people in various stages of infection and resistance to tuberculosis. For example, green dots are used to denote healthy people, people who are immune (already immunized) are represented using black, and red is used to represent the infected people. The people, represented as agents, move about randomly in the homeless shelter. Whenever they approach a bed or mat, they may choose to sleep on it for a random amount of time. The amount of time an agent rests on a bed or a mat can be varied in order to simulate the different behaviors of the people. For example, there is more interaction among people during the daytime hours than in the nighttime hours. Accordingly, the agents linger on the beds or mats for a longer time when we want to simulate the nighttime behavior. In our model, the days and nights continue in a cycle until we stop the simulation.

We also simulate the behavior of smokers by allowing the agents to randomly move about the smoking area. The risk of infection among smokers is different from that of non-smokers due to the complexities of the transmission of the tuberculosis infection. Since smoke lingers in the air for a while, the bacilli may survive in the smoke-filled air for a longer time than in recirculated air, so we use different settling rates for the tuberculosis bacilli in recirculated air than for smoke-filled air. In a future paper, we plan to take on the difficult task of modeling the air-flow in the homeless shelter, in order to predict the spread of the infection.

The model shows the spread of infection from the infected people to the healthy people who are not immune. Whenever a healthy person encounters an infected person, he may get infected with probability p. Infected people can take medication, recovering to become immune to future infections. The infected people can also die in which case they disappear from the population. The functional parameters of the simulation can be controlled using the slider bars shown in Figure 4. In this model we have one slider to indicate the total number of people in the homeless shelter before we start to run the simulation, the number of initially infected people, number of initially immune people, the death rate and the recovery rate. The model allows us to drag on the sliders, increasing and decreasing the functional parameters to engage in a what-if analysis and arrive at useful conclusions about the transmission of infection among the population.

The movement of the people, the spread of infection among individuals, and the rate with which they recover or die, can be examined visually from the model. At any time, the precise number of people that fall into the infected, recovered (immune), healthy, and dead classes can be seen from the graph plot at the lower left side of the screen shot. Also at any time, the percentage of infected (sick) people is displayed in a small monitor box.

The simulation can be controlled using control buttons that can be switched on or off during the simulation. We have one button each to control the spread of infection, process of recovery, and process of death. We can at any time switch these off or on as needed to analyze the effect of a factor on the spread of infection.

The infection can spread through direct contact between agents while they are moving around in the homeless shelter or by exposure to bacilli that are in the air. The simulation can model these aspects to show that the smoking areas and the restrooms are the areas with high risk of TB infection. The model can be extended to include the other architectural details of the shelter such as the elevation. Ventilation which was better on the women's side than the men's side, may prove to be the reason why the men's side shows high risk of infection.

4.3   Analysis

Primary results show that we are able to model the outbreak in a spatially delineated environment successfully by incorporating "purposeful movement" in the agent entities. This simulation can be extended to incorporate other parameters such as the effect of smoking in the spread of this infection.

The dynamics of the spread were studied using the graphical output generated by the simulation and the behavior of the spread is exactly that explained by the classical SIR model. Also, the threshold levels of the SIR model could be related and observed by using the graphical outputs. There were certain points where the infection rapidly spread, and other points where it slowed. These were related to the threshold levels calculated using the SIR model. Also, we could see that few areas in the shelter had high risks of TB infection. This was due to the differences in air flow, the distance of separation between the beds, and the proximity to the smoking area and restrooms where people usually gather.

5   Conclusion

We have presented a survey of the state-of-the-art in modeling tools for computational epidemiology. We looked at different computational paradigms and how they can be used to model disease outbreaks. We proposed simulating the outbreak of TB in a local homeless shelter and presented preliminary results.

In order for effective tools to be developed for epidemiologists by computer scientists, a synergistic union of the disparate fields as well as existing computational paradigms is required. Every year millions of dollars are invested by US in research towards finding ways to improve public health and lower the risk of epidemics and disease spread. Recently, attention has also shifted towards bio-terrorist attacks. In such cases, it becomes imperative to understand the social network and its behavior in order to understand the spread of the disease. Once sufficient knowledge about the social groups of the network is established, multi-agent simulations help in modeling and analyzing the risk of disease spread through socially connected groups. In order to do so, we first have to understand the characteristics of the social group, the disease, and the environmental factors that affect the spread of the disease.

The tools discussed above can successfully model social behavior, the interactions, the air flow, the air suspensions, the atmospheric conditions favorable or unfavorable for spread of any disease, the characteristics of the infection spreading agents and their behavior and responses to different prevailing conditions. This helps in analyzing the risk of propagation, the spread of propagation, and the medium of propagation, and helps in mitigating the risk of such spreads or, in some cases, totally eradicating the disease through immunization strategies or other measures. Being able to do so would take the epidemiologists a step further in the way of analyzing disease outbreaks and the spread of epidemics. The results of the simulations and the associated graphs can help to improve understanding of the dynamics of transmission and to take better steps towards the prevention and control of disease spread.

References

1. Gimblett, H. Randy, "Integrating Geographic Information Systems and Agent-based Modeling Techniques", Santa Fe Institute, Oxford University Press, 2002.
2. Carley K. M., & Schreiber, C., "Information Technology and Knowledge Distribution in C3I Teams", 2002 Command and Control Research and Technology Symposium, Monterey, CA, 2002.
3. Buckeridge, DL, Graham, J, O'Connor, MJ, Choy,MK, Tu, SW, Musen, MA., "Knowledge-Based Bioterrorism Surveillance", American Medical Informatics Association Symposium, SanAntonio, TX, November 9-13, 2002.
4. Barrat, Rod, "Atmospheric dispersion modeling: an introduction to practical applications", Earthscan,2001.
5. Carley, K. M. and Hill, V., "Structural Change and Learning Within Organizations", in A. Lomi and E. R. Larsen (eds), *Dynamics of Organizations: Computational Modeling and Organization Theories*. Menlo Park, CA: MIT Press/AAAI, 2001.
6. Lawson, Andrew B., *Statistical Methods in Spatial Epidemiology*, John Wiley & Sons, 2001.
7. Meselson, Matthew, "Note Regarding Source Strength", *ASA Newsletter*, article 01-6a (www.asanltr.com).

8. Carley, K.M., & Gasser, L., "Computational organization theory", in G.Weiss (ed.), *Multiagent Systems: A Modern Approach to Distributed Artificial Intelligence*, MIT Press, 1999.
9. Turner, D. Bruce, "Workbook of Atmospheric Dispersion Estimates: An Introduction to Dispersion Modelling", Lewis Publishers, 1994.
10. Carley, K.M., "A theory of group stability", *American Sociological Review 56(3)*, pp. 331-354, 1991.
11. Miller RA, Pople HE, Myers JD, "Interist-I, An Experimental Computer-based Diagnostic Consultant for General Internal Medicine", N Engl J Med 307, pp. 468-76, 1982.
12. Documentation available from: http://education.mit.edu/starlogo/, Last Accessed: May 3, 2004.
13. Documentation available from: http://swarm.org, Last Accessed: May 3, 2004.
14. Documentation available from: http://www.brook.edu/es/dynamics/models/ascape/, Last Accessed: May 3, 2004.
15. Documentation available from: http://repast.sourceforge.net, Last Accessed: May 3, 2004.

ITSUMO: An Intelligent Transportation System for Urban Mobility

Bruno Castro da Silva, Ana L.C. Bazzan*, Gustavo K. Andriotti,
Filipe Lopes, and Denise de Oliveira

Instituto de Informática, UFRGS, C.P. 15064, 91501-970, Porto Alegre, RS, Brazil

Abstract. It is well-known that big cities suffer from traffic congestion and all consequences that come with it. This is an especial problem in cities in developing countries where the public transportation system is not reliable and where the fleet of vehicles tend to be old thus increasing air pollution. There is no turnkey solution for this problem, but several improvements have been suggested in the field of urban and traffic management, provided an information system is built which can provide information to both the traffic experts and the user of the system. Such an information system has to incorporate features of an ITS and an ATIS. An underline assumption is that there is a simulation model to provide certain kinds of information in forecast. This paper discusses the model and implementation of such an information system which is based on a microscopic model of simulation and on cellular automata and is implemented using agent technologies and with a bottom-up philosophy in mind. We give here an overview of the project, the details of the modules (data, simulation, driver and information/visualization), as well as discuss an application of the simulation tool.

1   Introduction

The increasing urban mobility poses challenges to traffic engineers, urban planning experts, and researchers involved with optimization and information technology. One way – certainly not the only one, but one to be used in conjunction with others – to cope with this problem is to approach it from the information point of view. Our assumption is that urban mobility both produces information and increases the demand for it, a loop which has been the motivation for previous works [1,2].

One way to deal with this information loop is to collect data, produce a forecast and broadcast it to the traffic system users. It is well-known that the *same* information when provided to *all* users can be harmful. This is certainly a point but will not be directly tackled in this paper, although the simulation infrastructure provided here can deal with such situations and in fact we have already been doing case studies [3]. In order to produce the information to be broadcasted, a fast simulation model is necessary. We use the Nagel–Schreckenberg approach [4] which is a microscopic model for traffic simulation originally based on cellular–automata (CA), as detailed in Section 2.

The motivation for the development of the simulation module is twofold. First the fact that although several similar tools exist, they are built normally with the objective to tackle isolated problems. Currently traffic engineers only have a collection of isolated

---

* Corresponding author

T. Böhme et al. (Eds.): IICS 2004, LNCS 3473, pp. 224–235, 2006.

tools to i) track and log flow and density of vehicles (induced loop detectors, cameras, etc.); ii) perform off-line simulations (e.g. to evaluate the impact of building a shopping mall); iii) adjust timing of traffic lights. None of these tools is really suitable for forecast. The new generation of traffic simulators are usually too slow for the faster-than-real-time simulations which are needed for traffic forecast, or are too expensive for budgets of cities in developing countries.

Second, both commercial and academic tools are black-box systems in the sense that generally one has no access to the source code. This is no big problem to users like traffic engineers working in control centers of municipal traffic authorities with a reasonable budget. But that poses a problem for i) anyone working in research; ii) anyone who wants minimal changes in output reports or, more important, to those who want to finetune the simulation model; iii) those aiming at integrating the simulator to other tools.

Therefore, driven by the incentives given by Brazilian funding agencies regarding free software, the project SISCOT (Integrated System for Simulation, Control and Optimization) was developed [2]. The aim of this project was to build a traffic simulator based on free software and on a CA model, to be used freely for academic and operational purposes.

We are now developing an extension of the SISCOT project, called ITSUMO – Intelligent Transportation System for Urban Mobility[1]. One of the aims of the project is to create an information system for urban mobility capable of integrating different functionalities, such as a simple traffic control (mostly based on control of traffic lights), traffic management and real-time information providing via internet and/or mobile phone. The idea is to distribute the system under free-software license.

The development of the project involves people with different backgrounds: physicists (microscopic traffic simulation model), computer scientists (modeling the driver and integration of it to the anticipatory traffic forecast tool), and traffic engineers (as users and evaluators of the approach). Once this infrastructure is ready, it can be used both for academic purposes (e.g. testing new approaches for synchronization of traffic lights, simulating drivers decision-making, etc.) or for operational purposes.

To address these objectives, a novel feature added to the basic simulation model is the possibility to easily define other modules such as drivers as intelligent agents, in contrast to the current models that are pure reactive and ignore the mental state (informational and motivational) from the drivers.

The kernel of the simulator is ready and was programmed using the object-oriented paradigm in order to facilitate the portability and increase the quality of documentation. The idea is that anyone can aggregate further code when necessary. Also a database and a visualization module are at final development stages, as well as the basic information module which is closely tied to the visualization, in case of information via internet.

To illustrate the benefits of our approach, consider this fact which has been taken from the daily newspaper "Folha de São Paulo" (online edition of April 21, 2005): "São Paulo (city) reaches traffic jam record: 178 Km. of jam were recorded at 7 p.m.". In Feb. of 2002, that amount was 130 kilometers. Since then, such level of traffic jam was reported many times due to the lack of timely information to users of the traffic system (public transportation, trucks and vehicle drivers).

---

[1] http://www.inf.ufrgs.br/~mas/traffic

The benefits for users is clear: once a forecast is provided or at least some information is given to them, they are able to better plan their trips. This has an impact on travel times, fuel consumption and acceptance of public transportation.

The remaining of this text is organized as follows: the next section details the microscopic simulation model. Section 3 presents the overview of the project and the main modules: data model, simulation kernel, infrastructure / module to model drivers decision-making, visualization and information to the users. Section 4 presents and discusses the use of ITSUMO project in a a traffic simulation of a region of the city of Porto Alegre, Brazil. The last section concludes and outlines the future research directions.

2 Microscopic Simulation: Nagel–Schreckenberg Model and Extensions

Basically, there are two approaches to model traffic movement, namely the macroscopic and the microscopic. The former is mainly concerned with the movement of platoons of vehicles, focusing on the aggregate level. At this level, the system as a whole behaves as if all traffic agents (drivers) make decisions in a deterministic and rational way. It considers only averaged vehicle densities but not individual traffic participants. On the other hand, in the microscopic model of simulation, one may go to the individual level. Each road can be described as detailed as desired, given the computational restrictions, thus permitting a more realistic modeling of drivers' behavior. In the microscopic approach both travel and/or route choices may be considered, which is a key issue in simulating traffic since those choices are becoming increasingly more complex. Also, individual traffic lights can be modelled according to several approaches, from classical off-line coordination to recently proposed ones (negotiation, communication-free, via game theory, reinforcement learning, swarm intelligence, etc).

2.1 Nagel–Schreckenberg Model

In this project, in order to achieve the necessary simplicity and performance, we use the Nagel–Schreckenberg model [4] which is a microscopic model for traffic simulation originally based on cellular–automata (CA).

In short, each road is divided in cells with a fixed length. This allows the representation of a road as an array where vehicles occupy discrete positions. Each vehicle travels with a speed based on the number of cells it currently may advance without hitting another vehicle. The vehicle behavior is expressed by rules that represent a special form of car–following behavior. This simple, yet valid microscopic traffic model, can be implemented in such an efficient way that is good enough for real-time simulation and control of traffic.

Given that every vehicle has a nonnegative integer speed (v, limited to $vmax$), the following four rules are verified simultaneously for all vehicles in a CA way:

1. Movement: each vehicle advances v cells at each time step;
2. Acceleration: each vehicle's speed is increased by one unit, up to $vmax$ (the maximum speed) or the gap (the number of empty cells in front of a vehicle);
3. Interaction: if the vehicle ahead is too close, v is decreased by one unit;

4. Randomization: vehicles decelerate with probability p in order to simulate the non-deterministic dynamics of vehicle movement, which occurs mainly because of the different driving behaviors.

These CA rules imply that certain conditions must be met. First, the simulation must be discrete both in time and space. Second, all network cells must be updated simultaneously. This condition implies that the vehicles' movement must occur in two steps: a) all drivers must take their decisions of movement and b) all vehicles' status must be updated by taking into account the driver decision and the restrictions and limitations of the vehicle and the scenario being simulated.

Although these rules might seem too simplistic, investigations reported in the literature showed that the cellular automaton model is capable of reproducing macroscopic traffic flow features including realistic lane changing behavior (for an overview see [5]). Later on, this basic model was extended to deal with enhanced scenarios [6,7,8]. In the urban traffic scenario, there was the need to add more elements such as traffic lights and more complex intersections.

The first concept of the Nagel–Schreckenberg model was a very simple CA that only intend to mimic a single-lane circular circuit on a highway. Improvements have been made on that basic model to make it possible to simulate other scenarios. There are two major extensions to the model to make it suitable for more complex simulations:

– Multi-lane extension: several different extensions had been made to achieve this characteristic, such as [5] and [9]. These improvements allow to perform realistic simulations with more than one lane, since vehicles can change lanes. Therefore it is possible for the vehicles to perform a take-over maneuver and avoid slowing down by changing to a faster lane.
– Density inversion: This characteristic observed in real traffic is important to make simulations more realistic. Density inversion is a phenomenon that occurs when the flow of vehicles reaches a certain threshold. Then the lane on the left side gets a higher density than the lane on the right side. This empirical phenomenon is reproduced to some extensions of the original model (see [9] and [10]).

2.2   The Traffic Network Representation

As for the network representation, each road is described as a composition of nodes and edges representing intersections and roads, respectively. Each edge is composed by a set of connected sections. A section represents a portion of the road that is delimited by two nodes. Each section is formed by a set of lanesets, which represent groups of lanes with the same orientation. The lowest-level structure in the network representation is the lane itself. Lanes are subdivided into cells of fixed length, which can be either empty or occupied by a vehicle. The cell size is chosen so to represent the average space a vehicle occupies in a traffic jam, but this value can be adjusted. It is important to do this adjustment so that each time step in the simulation corresponds to the desired time frame, that is, the simulator must be adjusted in order to use discrete values that faithfully represent real-life measurements.

As said before, a node is an important component of a road. It represents the connection between two sections and is an abstraction of a real-life crossing. A node may contain four different objects: sources, sinks, sensors and traffic lights[2]. Sources and sinks are objects used to adjust the simulation parameters to known values of traffic flow (e.g. collected by loop induced detectors). This way, the traffic manager or the user responsable for the simulation may configure a node in a way that vehicles are inserted into the network according to fixed rules. Currently, nodes equipped with a Source object can generate vehicles according to a constant flow, a constant probability, a variable probability or a variable flow. The Sink object is just the opposite of the Source. It is responsible for removing vehicles of the simulation. Note that dead-end streets must obligatorily be linked to a Sink object. Currently the simulator can automatically handle this kind of requirement preventing the user from facing the tedious task of adapting the real-life traffic network to the simulator standards.

Moreover, the simulator supports two other objects: Sensors and Traffic Lights. The purpose of a Sensor object is to collect all sorts of information about the scenario being simulated, such as the lane occupation rate, the average vehicle speed in a street, in/out flow of vehicles in a specific laneset, etc. Traffic Lights control a set of signal plans which reflects the movement constraints of the real traffic network.

3   Description of the System

3.1   Overview of the Project

The ITSUMO project uses data from several sources, which can be both off-line information (maintained by different providers), and on-line information (e.g. traffic flow). The network topology data, for instance, is provided by traffic authorities. Currently, given that there is a lack of on-line data, which is not collected in the city of Porto Alegre so far, we work basically with off-line data. However, the system is designed to use real-time information.

Most of the information is stored in a database, described in the next section. There is also a module for definition of drivers decision-making, which is optional. If the user does not define particular classes of drivers, then the simulation is performed using the standard driver model described in Section 2. In any case, the simulator kernel retrieves the necessary information from the database, performs the computation of the vehicles' movement, updates the network state and stores this in flat files. If special drivers are defined, then the simulator also loads such models in a way described in Section 3.4.

A visualization module retrieves data originated from the microscopic simulation and exhibits a graphical representation of the traffic simulation. The ITSUMO system is thus composed by four distinct modules: the data module, the simulation kernel, the driver definition module, and the visualization module. These modules are further detailed next.

3.2   Data Module

This module manages the traffic information data that serves as the basis to the microscopic simulation. This information is stored in a relational database, which means that the data is represented in the form of tables. Queries to these tables are made by means of the SQL language.

---

[2] Sources and Sinks are inspired in the proposals discussed in [7,8,11].

The data module uses the PostgreSQL relational database system[3]. Since performance is a key issue in real-time simulation, a database with simple interface and quick response is required. PostgresSQL is a free implementation of SQL/92 standard with a fair time response to the database queries. Another important issue is the possibility to work with spatial data in order to make use of geographically referenced data. This capability is provided by PostGIS, an extention of PostgreSQL to support spatial data and geographic objects. Note that the topological data existing in the database is not yet geographically referenced, although we plan to use these capabilities in the future. Actually, spatial positions are implemented by means of a series of attributes on each node, such as its spatial cartesian coordinates. Besides that, the database makes use of several foreign-key constrains in order to guarantee the consistence of the spatial relationship between objects.

The database structure reflects the way the simulation occurs. Thus, the data module is in charge of providing the necessary means to specify several topology details and network constrains. The database entities and the attributes they model are described below:

- **General Settings:** topology name, traffic system orientation (right-handed, left-handed), cell size, real-life correspondence of each iteration, frequency of sensor measurements, starting hour of the simulation and *default* deceleration probability
- **Network:** network name and its settings
- **Node:** cartesian coordinates of the node and the associated network
- **Street:** street name and the associated network
- **Section:** section name, whether it is preferential, delimiting nodes and the associated street
- **Laneset:** length, associated section
- **Lane:** maximum speed, width, associated laneset
- **Laneset Probability:** set of probabilities of moving a vehicle to a specific laneset upon passing through a node and the associated lane where these probabilities are valid
- **Turning Probability:** set of allowed vehicle movements according to its current lane
- **Traffic Light:** set of signal plans, associated with a node
- **Signal Plan:** set of lane-to-laneset allowed movements in a specific order, cycle time and offset
- **Sink:** probability of removal of a vehicle and the associated node
- **Source:** source behavior (insertion of vehicles according to fixed values per iteration, insertion of vehicles according to constant/variable probabilities, etc), laneset where the vehicles should be inserted and the node which contains this Source.

The above entities also describe the relationship between the several traffic network components. For instance, each lane is associated with exactly one laneset, and each section is composed by exactly two nodes. The data module was designed in a way to ease the task of specifying the traffic network topology.

---

[3] Actually all technologies used in this project are free software, such as PHP, Apache Web Server, Java, JVM and Debian servers.

3.3 Simulation Module

This module was developed using C++/PostgreSQL platform and is responsible for simulating the traffic flow in a given traffic network. The simulation kernel was implemented over the ideas of a previous version of the simulator [2]. The simulator implemented in [2] imposed serious restrictions to the feature-adding process, making it hard to add new functionalities and delaying the process of implementing the necessary extensions.

The current version of the simulator solves an issue inherent to the basic microscopic model described in Section 2, namely the difficulty to represent urban scenarios. Thus, the simulation tool we developed supports different kinds of elements, such as lanes, lanesets, streets, sections, vehicles, sources and sinks (of vehicles), sensors and detectors, traffic lights, etc. Some special functions are still under development, which will be briefly explained in Section 5.

The simulation occurs in discrete steps and is implemented as a series of updates in the drivers' decisions of movement, followed by simultaneous updates in the vehicles' positions in the network and finally updates in the status of objects such as nodes, sources, sinks and traffic lights. Each update in a node or traffic light may modify its current behavior depending on its internal state and on the current traffic flow. Sources and sinks are also activated whenever a vehicle passes over a crossing. This is the moment in the simulation when vehicles might be inserted or removed from the network. Note that special drivers (such as floating cars) are not removed from the simulation. Also, they do follow specific routes, in opposition to standard drivers which move through the network in a non-deterministic way. The last action to be performed in each iteration is to fire the sensors and detectors, updating their internal status and eventually displaying partial simulation results.

The simulation results can be formatted according to the user needs. The most usual formats are the "cell map" and the "laneset occupation map". The former is a representation of a set of cells associated with each lane in the network. This set of cells indicates which portions of the lane are occupied by which vehicle, providing the most detailed output possible. On the other hand, the "laneset occupation map" is a high-level output which specifies the rate of occupation (density) for each laneset in the network. This output is generally more useful since it hides the individual status of the vehicles and focus on the overall stochastic behavior of the simulation.

3.4 Driver Model

Modeling a driver can be approached in different ways, depending on the purpose of the simulation. In most cases, the objective is to simulate the collective or macroscopic behavior. However, this behavior emerges out of individual ones. Simple algorithms, like the Nagel–Schreckenberg model, can be used to describe vehicles movement without loosing significant simulation fidelity with reality.

A driver model can be splitted into two different components: decision about movement and planning. These two parts together can guide a vehicle in the network. The movement decision is responsible for a vehicle's short-time movement. On the other hand, the planning decision is related to a more sophisticated decision-making, e.g. which direction to turn and what to do in case a jam exists.

The movement decision-making is in charge of local optimization, i. e., to decide whether it is better to take-over the headway vehicle, to change lane and to avoid collisions with other vehicles. More complex than the former, the planning decision-making component is in charge of deciding which path to follow from one point to other in the traffic network. To make such decisions it is necessary to observe the traffic forecast (if available), the path restrictions, etc. Moreover, it is necessary to implement some kind of learning skills in the driver module so that it improves future decisions. Most of the optimization performed intends to reduce the amount of time to travel from an origin to a destination. The planning component can use several heuristics and methods to perform those tasks.

3.5   Visualization Module

This is the module that allows the graphical visualization of the simulation results. The visualization can be either in a macroscopic or microscopic level. At a macroscopic level, the visualization considers only data which reflect the overall behavior of the network, abstracting details and providing an useful tool to capture the big picture of what is happening in a specific scenario. It is useful to provide this kind of information via the internet, as it has been the case in [12].

On the other hand, the microscopic level visualization provides an interface through which one can see, both in 2D and 3D manner, individual vehicles movement. In order to obtain a more realistic and detailed visualization, this module is being developed using the OpenGL graphic library, enabling features such as walk-through navigation and detail-focused interfaces. An example of the visualization is depicted in Figure 1.

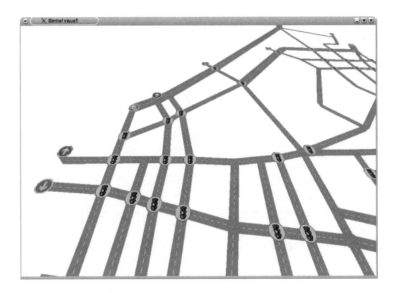

Fig. 1. Example of the visualization module interface

The visualization of data at microscopic level is the kernel of the information system for the traffic engineer and/or the urban planning experts. At this level, the whole system can be used to perform simulations in order to check what happens if a shopping mall is built in a specific place, or a new arterial is added to the network (as it was the case recently in Porto Alegre), or traffic lights are synchronized in a given way. In the next section we discuss a scenario from Porto Alegre in which the ITSUMO system was used: a simulation of an arterial with different rates of vehicles insertion in given nodes of the network.

4   Experiment: A Scenario from Porto Alegre

The ITSUMO system is capable of simulating traffic flow considering several simulation parameters. These parameters, such as the probability of inserting new vehicles in a given street and the deceleration probability reflect the overall behavior of the network being simulated as well as the drivers' behavior.

The probability of inserting vehicles in the simulation reflects the inflow of vehicles in a given location. The deceleration probability, on the other hand, represents the tendency of drivers to slow down occasionally, which is a known cause for quick and sporadic traffic jams.

The ITSUMO system was applied in a scenario which models an important part of an arterial street located in Porto Alegre. This street, called Independencia, is composed by several sections and traffic lights. There are six points of insertion of vehicles (sources): five of them are located in the transversals and insert vehicles with a constant rate of 0.1 per iteration. The insertion probability of the other source, located in the beginning of the Independencia street, will be one of the varying parameters of the simulation. Note that since we measure the vehicle density only in the Independencia street itself, we chose to keep the insertion probability in transversal streets as small as possible in order to minimize their influence on the main traffic.

The scenario also contains four traffic lights, as shown in figure 2, each one operating with two phases. The first phase gives green time to the flow in the main street (75% of the cycle time); the other phase gives green time to the flow in streets that cross the Independencia avenue (25% of the cycle). The traffic lights are not synchronized in any way. All vehicles leave the network in the last node of Independencia, depicted as the rightmost node in Figure 2.

The goal of this test scenario is to show that this type of simulation can be done with the ITSUMO system, and how the results can be used in order to re-plan and optimize the already existing traffic infrastructure.

In order to depict the effect of two important simulation parameters, namely the deceleration probability and the inflow of vehicles in the Independencia street, we present a table containing the average vehicle density in the street according to the variation of these parameters.

Table 1 shows how the traffic flow varies according to the parameters. Note that an increase in the probability of deceleration leads to a proportional increase in the street density, since the average speed decreases and the effect of a deceleration is cumulative in the street. In a similar manner, an increase in the probability of insertion of vehicles leads to a proportional increase in the density, since there are more vehicles using a

Simulating Independencia Av. and transversals

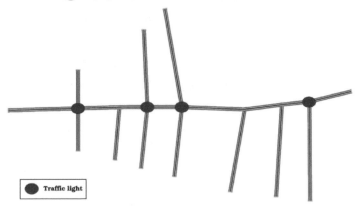

Fig. 2. 3D visualization of the Independencia avenue

Table 1. Density on Main Street after 20000 time steps

	Deceleration probability			
Main Source Probability	0.1	0.3	0.5	0.75
0.1	0.10	0.10	0.11	0.12
0.25	0.13	0.14	0.15	0.21
0.5	0.19	0.21	0.25	0.46
0.75	0.27	0.29	0.36	0.51
1.0	0.34	0.39	0.45	0.52

limited street area. Moreover, the density values depicted in Table 1 depend on the relation between the street length and the duration of the traffic light phase. This relation is important due to the fact that longer traffic light phases tend to create cycles of density with great amplitudes. This effect, which causes the density of vehicles in the street to vary between zero and something close to the maximum possible value (1), can be seen in Figure 3.

In order to optimize network parameters such as the traffic light cycle time and the phase time, one can estimate parameters like sources probabilities according to data generated by induced loop detectors, cameras, etc. These data is thus used to calibrate the simulation parameters and allows the usage of the ITSUMO system to control and optimize the existing traffic infrastructure.

5   Conclusion and Outlook

The ITSUMO system is capable of dealing with several aspects of the simulation of a traffic scenario, such as the driver behavior, traffic lights coordination, traffic jam prediction, among others. The driver module makes the simulation more realistic since it allows the modeling and use of several and arbitrary drivers behavior simultaneously.

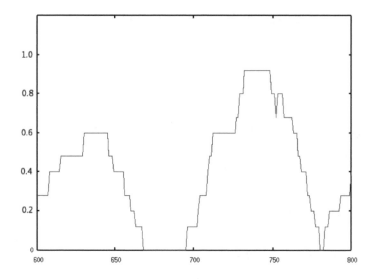

Fig. 3. Variation of density over time

Currently, the ITSUMO system provides an useful tool to simulate and predict traffic conditions, as well as to support urban planning tasks. The system itself is independent of driver model and supports the adjustment of several parameters that can be used to reflect the characteristics of the traffic network. The use of the ITSUMO simulation module facilitates the implementation of concrete actions that can lead to a better traffic flow control, reducing the average commuting time thus promoting a better life quality in cities with complex urbanization.

We plan to extend ITSUMO to consider other kinds of information such as those related to weather forecast. Our future goal is to focus on the development of ITSUMO as an information system for urban mobility, making it capable of integrating functionalities that will vary from simple traffic control to information providing via internet and/or mobile phone.

Acknowledgments

Filipe Lopes was supported by CNPq (project SincMobil). CNPq also partially supports Ana L. C. Bazzan. Denise de Oliveira's master scholarship was funded by CAPES.

References

1. Bazzan, A.L.C., Wahle, J., Klügl, F.: Agents in traffic modelling – from reactive to social behaviour. In: Advances in Artificial Intelligence. Number 1701 in LNAI, Berlin/Heidelberg, Springer (1999) Also appeared as Proc. of the U.K. Special Interest Group on Multi-Agent Systems (UKMAS), Bristol, UK.

2. Andriotti, G.K., Bazzan, A.L.C.: An object-oriented microscopic traffic simulator. In: Proceedings of the XXVIII Latin-American Conference on Informatics (CLEI 2002), Montevideo, Uruguay (2002)
3. Klügl, F., Bazzan, A.L.C.: Route decision behaviour in a commuting scenario. Journal of Artificial Societies and Social Simulation **7** (2004) http://jasss.soc.surrey.ac.uk/7/1/1.html.
4. Nagel, K., Schreckenberg, M.: A cellular automaton model for freeway traffic. J. Phys. I France **2** (1992) 2221
5. Nagel, K., Wolf, D.E., Wagner, P., Simon, P.: Two-lane traffic rules for cellular automata: A systematic approach. Phys. Rev. E **58** (1998) 1425
6. Esser, J., Schreckenberg, M.: Microscopic simulation of urban traffic based on cellular automata. International Journal of Modern Physics C **8** (1997) 1025
7. Esser, J., Neubert, L., Wahle, J., Schreckenberg, M.: Microscopic online simulation of urban traffic. In Ceder, A., ed.: Proc. of the 14th ITS, Pergamon (1999) 535–554
8. Rickert, M., Nagel, K., Schreckenberg, M., Latour, A.: Two lane traffic simulation on cellular automata. Physica A **231** (1996) 534
9. Wagner, T., Garvey, A., Lesser, V.R.: Complex goal criteria and its application in design-to-criteria scheduling. In: Fourteenth National Conference on Artificial Intelligence. (1997)
10. Knospe, W., Santen, L., Schadschneider, A., Schreckenberg, M.: A realistic two-lane traffic model for highway traffic. J. Phys. A (2003) 3369–3388
11. Nagel, K., Esser, J., Rickert, M.: Large–scale traffic simulations for transport planning. Ann. Rev. Of Comp. Phys. (2000) 151–202
12. Hafstein, S.F., Chrobok, R., Pottmeier, A., Schreckenberg, M., Mazur, F.C.: A high-resolution cellular automata traffic simulation model with application in a freeway traffic information system. Comp-aided Civil Eng **19** (2004) 338–338

Automatic Bottleneck Detection Based on Traffic Hysteresis Phenomena: An Application to Paris Highway Network

Oscar Sánchez[1] and Omar Mekkaoui[2]

[1] Facultad de Ingeniería Universidad Autónoma del Estado de México
Cerro de Coatepec s/n, Ciudad Universitaria, 50130, Toluca, Estado de México, Mexico
osanchez@uaemex.mx
[2] THEMA-Université de Cergy-Pontoise, 33, Bd du Port, 95000, Cergy, France
Omar.mekkaoui@eco.u-cergy.fr

Abstract. This paper refers to the problematic that the phenomenon of traffic hysteresis induces from a macroscopic overview. Firstly, the document presents a topological analysis of traffic hysteresis in two levels of variation: density and flow. The referred analysis takes into account temporal and spatial components of the phenomena and is based on empirical data obtained from a freeway bottleneck configuration. Secondly, a mathematical model supported on the basic traffic equation is formalized in order to describe the phenomenon of hysteresis. The econometric adjustment of the model follows this stage with a discussion about the possible extensions of this model. Finally, the proposed model is applied to the A-14 highway and presented later on. Thereafter, some implications of the hysteresis phenomenon are discussed on the basis of economical planning and evaluation of transport systems.

1 Introduction

Several mathematical models and techniques have been proposed with the purpose of formalizing the relation between different macroscopic variables of traffic, such as speed, flow and concentration. This formalization related to the empirical studies and the inclusion of external factors that impact traffic stream has lead us into a paradigm renewal about the relation that those variables maintain over the years (e.g. see [1]).

The restating of paradigms merges from different circumstances that have an impact on the relationship vehicle-infrastructure-driver. (a) The technological advance that implies infrastructure improvements as well as vehicle performance inducing less wheel friction, and enhancing high speed stream. (b) The adaptability nature of drivers that guide them to take more risks, particularly, in the reduction of vehicle-to-vehicle safety margin. The process of constant renewal is important due to the fact that most of the planning, socioeconomic, and infrastructure management studies lie on such paradigms. Following this renewal process, this document not only revises the previous overview about hysteresis, but also includes spatial and temporal factors. The first ones are related to the configuration of the infrastructure while the second ones relate to the variation of the demand. Is precisely bottleneck infrastructure that induces queue formation as well as the traffic phenomenon known as traffic hysteresis (see [2]). The proposed approach is empirical and consists generally, in analyzing such phenomenon by using macroscopic traffic data and the relations of their basic

T. Böhme et al. (Eds.): IICS 2004, LNCS 3473, pp. 236–251, 2006.

equation. A theoretical treatment of hysteresis based on a microscopic approach can be revised in [3] or [4].

Diagram flow-concentration is particularly used in model building that embodies different stages of hysteresis. The development of such models is supported firstly, in the analysis of the flow-time (q-t) diagram characteristics as well as the speed-time (u-t), flow-speed (q-u) and flow-concentration (q-k) diagrams applied to an urban bottleneck road configuration in the Parisian A-14 Highway. Secondly, the model is based on the characterization of hysteresis phenomenon stages through the flow-speed and flow-concentration diagrams. These two model components, retaken on section 2, were described in [5] and are essential to characterize the four phases of hysteresis (section 3) in which the assumption is, a linear behavior tendency in each of them by simplicity. On the knowledge of these considerations, the analytical solution to the model is simple. However, its complexity lies on the identification of break points tendencies between two consecutive phases. In order to solve this difficulty two econometric techniques are proposed. The first one is a hypothesis trial based on Chow's test that allows the identification of tendency rupture (section 4). The second one is a structural econometric model often applied in time series estimation. Due to the fact that the amount of processing information required to adjust the model is elevated, an algorithm, for the first approach, is proposed (section 5) to find break points of each hysteresis stage. This last tool is considerable to identify or surveying conflictive road sections (black points) in dense congested or highly demanded networks. This conflictive section identification allows to detail studies to reduce or eliminate external effects of congestion heading the transport system to a more efficient performance level.

2 Traffic Hysteresis

In this section an empirical and inductive procedure is followed in order to introduce the hysteresis concept. Pursuing this goal, in first place, the theory of traffic stream based on a macroscopic approach for describing different traffic regimes is pointed out. In second place, and based on empirical data, the temporal variation of macroscopic traffic variables, such as flow and speed, presented in a bottleneck configuration structure are analyzed. Finally, the theoretical and empirical elements are put together to prove hysteresis phenomenon presence in diagrams q-u and u-k.

2.1 Relating Macroscopic Variables, Traffic Regimes and Hysteresis

The macroscopic relation of traffic was first introduced by Wardrop in 1952 [6] and after reformulated by Gerlough and Huber in 1975 [7]. The relation could be valid when variables of traffic are treated as a continuous or discrete variable (see respectively [8] and [9]). In the discrete variable case:

$$q_i = \overline{u}_i \overline{k}_i. \tag{1}$$

In which q represents vehicular flow measured in the i point of a transversal section. Variables $\overline{u}_i$ and $\overline{k}_i$ represent, average speed and concentration respectively (see [10] or [11]). Several studies have tried to determine the relation between two out

of the three variables of this equation. Empirical studies (e.g. [9]) show that the diagram flow-speed indicates four regimes to measure traffic congestion (see [8]), which
are shown in diagrams *q-u* and *k-q* on figure 1.

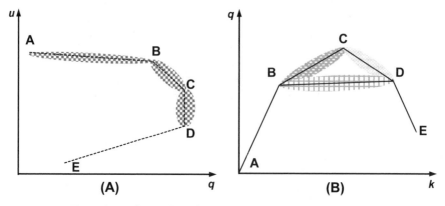

Fig. 1. Saturation regimes for flow-speed (a) and flow-stream (b)

2.1.1 Uncongested Regime

This regime known also as not congested [9], is formed by two stages: (a) *free flow*. It
occurs when demand is relatively low. The number of vehicles in the infrastructure is
reduced and motorists drive at a desired speed; (b) *Car following*: during this stage,
infrastructure endures a crescent vehicular volume without reaching its full capacity.
Drivers are restricted by front vehicles and cannot drive at the desired speed. During
first stage (segment A-B on figure 1a), average speed varies around top speed limits.
This tendency prolongs for an important interval of stream. During the second stage
(segment B-C on figure 1a), speed begins to decrease and the transition regime is
reached. slope line in *q-u* and *k-q* diagrams identifies uncongested regime.

2.1.2 Transition Regime

It is also known as discharged queue stages. At this stage infrastructure receives
maximum traffic and discharges it according to its capacity. When this level is
reached, an additional incorporation of vehicles leads into the formation of queues
(peak hour). Once the demand begins to diminish (after peak hours), infrastructure
begins to discharge queues (segment C-D on figure 1.a). The phenomenon of hysteresis takes place in this regime. This phenomena means that the trajectory followed by
the traffic variables (i.e. *q-u* or *q-k* relationship) during the loading phase of the infrastructure is not the same as in the unloading one. Diagram *k-q* on figure 1.b shows
this phenomena. In the limits of car-following regime (point C on figure 1.b) a tendency rupture between the represented segments B-C and C-D appears. Indeed, while
the B-C segments reflects that flow and concentration level increase, the C-D segment
shows an increasing on the concentration (induced by an increasing demand) along
with a diminishing on flow levels. In the limit of D a new tendency rupture appears.
This is due to the absence of more traffic (the hyper saturated regime will be reached
if more traffic arrives to the infrastructure). The infrastructure begins to unload in a
different trajectory this time. The last situation is indicated in figure 1b by segment D-C

(whenever there is more traffic, the supersaturated system will be shown). Theoretically and empirically ([5] and [12] respectively) it had been shown that traffic hysteresis is not only motivated by the increasing or decreasing of demand. But also because of the recurrent congestion in peak hours (i.e. that induced by vehicle interaction) as well as the not recurrent one (e.g. blocking, accidents, bad weather, temporary reduction of infrastructure capacity).

2.1.3 Hypercongested Regime

In this regime, flow and speed decrease, but concentration continues to grow. This tendency prevails until all vehicles remain immobile during a certain time interval (segment D-E figure 1a). At his moment, average speed is null, concentration is the highest and the flow null. This system is completely unstable; it is also called "within a queue" and should be treated carefully in planning studies (see discussion on this topic in [5]).

2.2 From Empirical Studies to Hysteresis Morphology

The goals in this case study are multiple. (a) Validate and select the obtained data on the field about recurrent and not recurrent congestion. (b) Analyze the repercussion of demand variation over the basic equation relations through a dynamic perspective (adding time variable to the whole analysis). (c) Study each and all different stages of the blocking phenomenon (i.e. beginning, propagation and disappearing), the formation and propagation of waiting lines in relation to time (demand variation), and space (corridor configuration).

2.2.1 The Case Study

The case study corresponds to a section of the urban highway A-14 tunnel located in the La Défense sector (Northwest Paris). Such two lane section is 1.4 kilometers long (segment 1-5 in figure 2) and channels traffic which runs towards either Porte de Paris-La Défense or to the Boulevard (Boulevard Périphérique) coming from the Norwest suburbs. Two ramps inside the tunnel allow vehicles in and out towards Paris and Puteaux respectively. At the tunnel exit (section 5 in figure 2) a pair of kilometers ahead, a traffic light system regulates the entering of traffic towards Paris. This road section is equipped with five loops that automatically register (measurement section) traffic flow and speed (transversal section 1-5 in figure 2) every five minutes. The analyzed information takes into consideration include 5-days from 6 to 23 hours of registering during the months of January and March 1998.

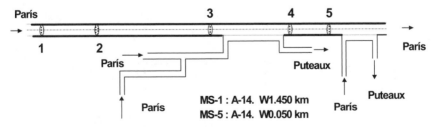

Fig. 2. Location and configuration of observation points (MS) in A-14 French Highway (La Défense sector)

2.2.2 Impact of the Temporal and Spatial Factors
over Flow-Speed Relationship

The configuration of the studied section shows, a priori, that traffic conditions in the Measurements Sections (MS) are not equal. Therefore, the resultant macroscopic relations will reflect different traffic phenomenon (see [9]). In section 3-5, for example there is shown vehicles transference, and the stream continuity previous to section 3 is disturbed. Similarly happens in section 5. Indeed when we observe flow and speed variation along the day at MS-5, we will notice recursive reduction of the average speed during peak hours (from 8:00 a.m. to 9:12 a.m. in the morning and from 19:00 to 20:12 in the afternoon (see figure 3). Moreover, a slight diminishing on stream can also be seen (the variation tending to decrease is more important in the morning than in the afternoon). If macroscopic traffic stream theory states that in a hypercongested regime flow decreases with speed: why does the flow remain constant when speed decreases? Not recurrent congestion and vehicle interaction are the cause of speed reduction. As mentioned before, at the latest part of section 3 (section 3-5) there is a stream transfer zone due to ramps. Anytime the traffic is higher, the transference is more intense: downward vehicles in section 5 stay blocked longer time intervals and their average speed reduces. After passing the transfer section, vehicles running into Paris could be stopped: the regulation system imposed by the red light on the traffic lights. This kind of delay is more likely to appear in peak hours due to the fact that the quantity of vehicles waiting for the green light increases; thereafter, a queue is formed and propagated downward section 5-3 inducing new blocking zone. In order to verify this hypothesis, a look on average speed and flow variation should

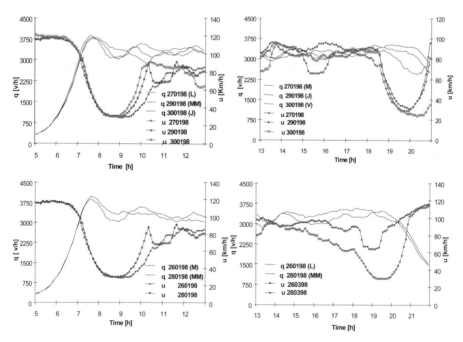

Fig. 3. Stream variation and average speed along the day (PO 5, 2 lanes)

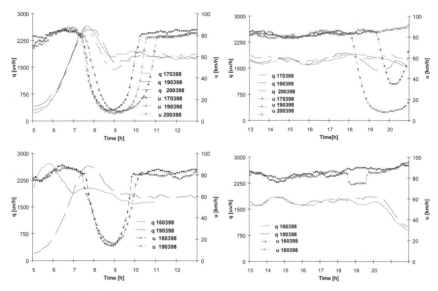

Fig. 4. Speed-flow diagrams and traffic hysteresis (PO 1, 2 lanes)

be taken to a section beforeMS-5. In the MS-1, for example, we have on the one hand, at the beginning of the day, the flow is not high (2500 v/h, see figure 4). However, the same speed reduction phenomena appear even in infrastructures of constant capacity (2 lanes road as in section 5). Consequently, one may conclude that vehicle interaction hardly contributes to speed reduction. On the other hand, the beginning of speed reduction in section 1 and 5 is out of step (about 30′ minutes in the morning). This out of step time corresponds to the queue propagation time generated by access infrastructures (ramps), which work as bottleneck; as well as by the traffic lights.

It is also noticeable that the reduction in average speed has, above all, an exogenous and not recurrent nature due to the fact that it is not presented neither systematically nor in frequency (i.e. no speed variation on March16, 17 and 18 in the afternoon) or in magnitude (i.e. speed variation on March 17, 19 and 20 in the afternoon). Let us see how this situation is reflected in the case of the basic diagram.

2.3 Basic Diagrams and Hysteresis

Few studies have analyzed in a detailed way the implication of traffic hysteresis in terms of stream conditions. In [12], all macroscopic traffic relations in the previously mentioned A-14 section Highway are analyzed (see section 1.2). Figure 5, extracted from the herein analysis, shows the way in which traffic conditions evolve along the morning in MS-5. Diagram flow-speed values display a great dispersion in the transition regime. Between 7:00-7:54 the flow decreases same as speed. Between 8:00-8:54 flow tends to decrease but speed starts increasing. This effect is reflected in the basic diagram k-q due to the loop alike trajectory described by the data. All this leading us to the phenomenon of traffic hysteresis: concentration values (obtained through equation 1) during the loading phase of the infrastructure (the flow between 7:00-7.54 h)

do not correspond to the ones from the unloading phase (the flow between 10:00 -
12:54). The variation on traffic concentration is explained by the formation of queues
as well as by demand variation (number of cars arriving to highway). Let us have in
mind that transfer zone and traffic light systems eliminate continuum flow causing
queues at peak hours. When peak hour start (after 7:00), a few vehicles are delayed
(low concentration 40-60upc/km). As time goes by demand increases to its top limit,
the number of blocked vehicles grows and the lines grow too (between 7:00 -7:30)
Demand starts diminishing as well as blocked vehicles in the line (unload phase between 9:00-12:54). At this moment concentration levels are the lowest respect to
loading phase. Once queue formation in MS-5 has been displayed, what effect pro-
vokes its propagation? Figure 6, a very illustrative view of macroscopic relations in
section 1 brings some answers to this question. Firstly, we confirm that loading and
unloading phases of transition regime are more evident, which at the time indicates
that queue from section 1 is more important. Vehicles remain blocked for a longer
time interval; therefore their average speed is much more reduced. Secondly, notice
that the quantity of vehicles passing trough section 2 is inferior to those passing
through section 5. Basic diagram also reflects the dichotomy of the transition regime
so hysteresis is much more marked. Indeed, the propagation of waiting lines has a
notable influence on hysteresis appearing, which at the time marks the so mentioned
dichotomy. Bottleneck starts queue formation, that is a fact, but it is also a fact that
those lines are propagated downward inducing vehicles to be blocked during a longer
time period, therefrom their average speed is much more reduced. As a consequence
of such phenomenon, vehicle stream in downward sections would be inferior to the
stream in next to bottleneck sections.

The previous analysis states that intrinsic factors on the phenomenon of congestion
have an impact on hysteresis intensity. However, there are external factors that lead
into its formation such as: adverse weather conditions, not recurrent congestion presence (infrastructure maintaining or accidents), infrastructure configuration, road signs,
traffic regulation devices, infrastructure location, etc. The evaluation of these factors
influence on hysteresis goes beyond the scope of this analysis and will be matter of
new studies. As for now, we will only limit this document to propose a model to characterize the different phases of the already described phenomenon.

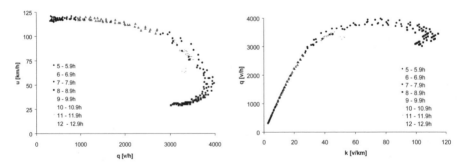

Fig. 5. Traffic hysteresis in q-u and k-q relations in MS 5 of study studied section

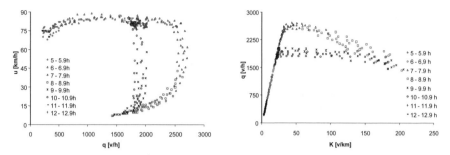

Fig. 6. Traffic hysteresis in q-u and k-q diagrams in MS1

3   The Proposed Models

The proposed model does not correspond directly to the macroscopic relations shown in section 2 due to the fact that congestion process is considered to be formed both by the uncongested regime and the transition regime. (cf. Section2) Actually, supersaturated or hyper-congested regime [13] represents in anyway a second level of hysteresis, which may be linked to not recurrent congestion presence (accidents, maintaining or infrastructure building) and that will be matter of future investigations. So far, the present model limits itself to the study of recurrent congestion effects parting from the flow-concentration relation. The following paragraphs make a description about the way in which the already mentioned traffic regimes (see section 2.1) have been characterized.

3.1   Modeling Traffic Regimes

Consider the basic diagram shown in figure 7. In this diagram hysteresis has been represented by two regimes: uncongested regime(*segment O-F-S*) and transition regime(segment *S-H-F*), as well as the tendency break points *F, S* and *H*.

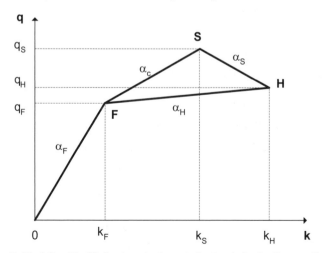

Fig. 7. Modeling Traffic hysteresis characterization in basic diagram (k-q)

3.1.1 Uncongested Regime

As indicated in section 2.1, the flowing regime takes two phases: steady stream or free flow and strained stream or car following. Steady stream corresponds to segment *O-F* and can be characterized by slope line α_F. During that phase there is a proportional increment in both concentration and stream that ends up in *F* point associated to stream q_F and concentration k_F. Such point means a frontier (break point) that marks the tendency rupture that starts the new strained stream stage (segment *F-S*). In this stage, there still is a proportional stream and concentration increasing though in a slower ratio (in relation to steady stream), which is defined by the slope α_C. In a strained stream condition, infrastructure continues receiving traffic until it reaches its capacity limit (critical point S defined by q_S and k_S). This occurs when a new tendency rupture takes place and the free flow regime becomes transition regime.

3.1.2 Transition Regime

Starting from *S* point, infrastructure capacity is exceeded and the quantity of vehicles running continues to grow (saturation phase). Queue is considerable now and starts propagating themselves downwards. At this moment, total of vehicles running out of the analyzed section diminish. However, concentration continues growing with a slope α_S. Concentration reaches its limit (*H* point, defined by k_H *and* q_H) marking the beginning of the phase nominated as hysteresis in which traffic diminishes (indicated by the decreasing of concentration), as well as flow a α_S ratio. Provided additional cars do not enter to the section, infrastructure will continue unloading until reaching its critical point *F* representing the frontier between steady and strained stream. Due to the intensity of hysteresis phenomenon observed in diagram *q-k* on the empirical studies, it had been considered that the transition process among regimes might be estimated by using a straight line. Nevertheless even though intensity is more important, the described principles would be valid as long as not lineal curves are employed.

3.2 Identifying Break Points

In the proposed model, the identification of initial/terminal points of each hysteresis phase is characterized by a regular increasing of flow and concentration. In first stage, the congestion first stage is represented by a regular increment of these variables until the arrival of their limits, point in which a difference in growing tendencies between steady and strained stream phases (*F* point in figure 7) can be distinguished. Afterwards, in the saturation phase, concentration may continue increasing, but infrastructure is not able to unload the quantity of vehicles that run into it anymore. Subsequently, queue formed and flow decreases (section *S-H*, figure 7). Finally, in the hysteresis phase, when demand levels decrease, the intensity of vehicles running into is lower in relation to the preceding phase. The vehicles remaining blocked in waiting lines start abandoning infrastructure, action that reduces both stream and concentration, but at more inferior rates than in the preceding stage. This way, the characterization of the described model could be outlined by identifying the infrastructure's initial points of the demand state: loading and unloading vehicles.

3.2.1 Traffic Stream Loading State

It is characterized by positive variation in concentration between two consecutive intervals of time t, and is conformed by the steady stream and strained stream phases of the non-congested regime as well as by the saturation phase of the transition regime. Taking into account the linear hypothesis which links break points with the geometrical relation from figure 1, it is possible to determine in an analytical way the slope variables and resultant stream for each of those phases. Table 1 summarizes the result from that operation. It is important to mention that in free flow regime, regime u_F represents the maximum circulation speed observed.

3.2.2 Traffic Stream Unloading State

The characteristic of this state is the negative variation of the concentration along two consecutive instants. The hysteresis phase within the transition regime and the steady stream within the flowing regime form it. As in the previous state, results are shown in table 2 and were obtained by considering geometrical relations in figure 7.

Table 1. Analytical values of the loading stream state

Phase	Condition	Validity	Slope	Flow
Uncongested (F)	$\dfrac{\Delta q(+)}{\Delta k(+)} > 0$	$0 \le k_j \le k_F$	$\alpha_F = \dfrac{q_F}{k_T}$	$q_j = u_F k_j$
Transition (T)	$\dfrac{\Delta q(+)}{\Delta k(+)} > 0$	$k_F < k_j \le k_S$	$\alpha_T = \dfrac{q_S - q_F}{k_S - k_T}$	$q_j = q_T + \alpha_F(k_j - k_T)$
Congested (S)	$\dfrac{\Delta q(-)}{\Delta k(+)} < 0$	$k_S < k_j \le k_H$	$\alpha_S = \dfrac{q_S - q_H}{k_S - k_H}$	$q_j = q_H + \alpha_S(k_H - k_j)$

Table 2. Analytical values of the unloading stream state

Phase	Condition	Validity	Slope	Flow
Hysteresis(H)	$\dfrac{\Delta q(+)}{\Delta k(-)} < 0$	$k_T < k_j \le k_H$	$\alpha_S = \dfrac{q_T - q_H}{k_T - k_H}$	$q_j = Min\{q_T, q_H\} + \alpha_H Min\{k_T + k_H\} - k_j$
Uncongested (F)	$\dfrac{\Delta q(-)}{\Delta k(-)} > 0$	$k_S \le k_j \le k_T$	$\alpha_F = \dfrac{q_T}{k_T}$	$q_j = u_F k_j$

4 Model Econometrics

Two models that could be implemented to adjust the proposed hysteresis model have been developed.

4.1 Identifying Breaks Points Based on Chow's Test

In the previous section some expressions to calculate each of the proposed model parameters have been derived, but by using empirical data it is necessary to verify that indeed every break point is presented so that the model strength is guaranteed. In this sense Chow's contrast (see [14] or [15]), applied to a hypothesis test procedure, allows the determination of the behavior homogeneity for the observed group T respect to the two sub samples T_1 y T_2 where $T = T_1 + T_2$. For linear cases, formally:

- Hypothesis
  Null Hypothesis

$$H_o: \qquad y = Xb + u, \tag{2}$$

  Alternative Hypothesis

$$H_A: \qquad \begin{aligned} y_1 &= X_1 b_1 + u_1, \\ y_2 &= X_2 b_2 + u_2, \end{aligned} \tag{3}$$

- Decision Rule

$$H_o \text{ rejected if } f > f_\alpha^*,$$
$$f_\alpha^* : \Pr\{F_{(k, T-2k)} > f_\alpha^*\} = \alpha \tag{4}$$

Where f_α^* represents the critical reliance value α according to Fisher Law, while f equals Chow's contrast (see. Equation 4):

$$f = \frac{\dfrac{SCR_c - (SRC_1 + SRC_2)}{k}}{\dfrac{(SRC_1 + SRC_2)}{T - 2k}}. \tag{5}$$

In the equation 5, SRC_1 y SRC_2 respectively represent, the error sum of squares from the separate regressions to group 1 and 2, $- SCR_c$ represent the error sum of squares from the pooled regression, k variable represents the estimated parameters and T_1 and T_2 are the number of observations in the two groups

4.2   A Structural Econometric Model

In order to estimate the four regimes of traffic flow over a given day, a structural econometric model is used. This kind of model often applied in times series estimation. In the case of one traffic flow regime, the relation between average speed, $u(q)$, and average flow, q, can be formulate as:

$$u(q) = aq + b \tag{6}$$

Where a and b represent parameters to estimate. As shown in the theoretical part, the parameters a and b correspond respectively to the traffic density and to an additive constant.

Consider U a column vector which represents average speed data observed over the day. The exogenous data are represented with de matrix X and which include also the flow observed over the same day. As shown in the theoretical part, each value of average flow q is associated to a value of average speed u. Parameters to estimate are grouped in a vector column denoted B.

The simple linear model given above can be written in a matrix form as:

$$U = XB' + E \Leftrightarrow \begin{bmatrix} u_1 \\ \vdots \\ u_n \end{bmatrix} = \begin{bmatrix} q_1 & 1 \\ \vdots & \vdots \\ q_n & 1 \end{bmatrix} \begin{bmatrix} a \\ b \end{bmatrix} + \begin{bmatrix} e_1 \\ \vdots \\ e_n \end{bmatrix} \tag{7}$$

The vector column E represents the unobserved estimation errors.

In order to show the matrix form for the structural model, we consider an example with two regimes:

$$u(q) = a_1 q + b_1$$
$$u(q) = a_2 q + b_2$$

(8)

Parameters a_1 and b_1 describe the relation between flow and speed in the first regime and parameters a_2 and b_2 describe the same relation for the second regime.

To estimate these regimes, we consider that we have a set of observed data composed of n speed-flow couple. The first p couples describe the observed first regime and $2<p<n<2$. In this case the relation (6) became:

$$U = XB' + E \Leftrightarrow \begin{bmatrix} u_1 \\ \vdots \\ u_p \\ u_{p+1} \\ \vdots \\ u_n \end{bmatrix} = \begin{bmatrix} q_1 & 1 & 0 & 0 \\ \vdots & \vdots & \vdots & \vdots \\ q_p & 1 & 0 & 0 \\ 0 & 0 & q_{p+1} & 1 \\ \vdots & \vdots & \vdots & \vdots \\ 0 & 0 & q_n & 1 \end{bmatrix} \begin{bmatrix} a_1 & a_2 \\ b_1 & b_2 \end{bmatrix} + \begin{bmatrix} e_1 \\ \vdots \\ e_p \\ e_{p+1} \\ \vdots \\ e_n \end{bmatrix}$$

(9)

The problem of this model is to define to optimal regime sub-sets. The approach used for that is based on a grid over variation of speed and flow as describe in the theoretical part.

In this model, we describe the variation of speed and flow over each four regimes and between two successive regimes (Figure 8). The first regime represents the free-flow regime. This case starts when the flow is null and the speed is higher. Over this regime, when flow start to increase, speed increase but it is still less sensible to the flow's variations. When speed became sensible to the flow's variations, the transition regime start. The grid to define the end of the free-flow regime is made around of the value of the couple of speed and flow which represents the end of this regime and observed data that describes this first regime are grouped.

The second regime, named transition regime, is characterized by a sensible variation of both speed and flow in other words, speed continue to decrease and flow continue to increase. When the flow starts to decrease but speed continue to decrease the end of the second regime is reach and the third regime start.

The third regime, named congested regime, is characterized the decrease of both speed and flow. This situation persists over the third regime until the speed starts to increase in order to return to free-flow regime or transition regime.

The fourth regime named hysteresis regime and last one is characterized by an increasing variation of speed and a decreasing variation of flow.

5   Application and Model Estimation

5.1   Test Chow Example

The empirical data on stream, speed and concentration obtained from the broadcasting station in the previously described and studied zone (cf. section 2) at MS-5 point (PK

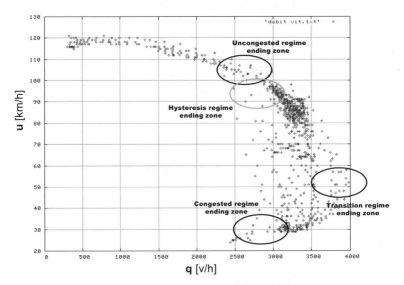

Fig. 8. Provided ending zone regimes

A14+0500 in direction to Paris) were used to apply hypothesis test described above. The variable values correspond to the 6-minutes aggregated data from 6:00- 13h on 21/01/98. The results are summarized in table 3 in which Chow test was apply to flow-concentration relationship in order to identify consecutive phases of the proposed model (see section 2, table 1,2): Free Flow (F) vs. transition (T), transition (T) vs. Saturation (S) and saturation (S) vs. hysteresis (H). These phases were noted down in tables $F+T$, $T+S$ and $S+H$, respectively.

There were a total of 60 observations analyzed. In the table 2 and 3, the number of data take into account in each phase tested is indicated by the n. It may be observed that while in the three comparisons, null hypothesis is rejected, so that sample does not present homogeneity so tendency rupture points between the two compared phases do exist; Chow's contrast values (f) are less marked between steady stream and strained stream, as well as much higher for the other contexts. This stating agrees with the macroscopic variable diagrams described in section 2.

Table 3. Results of Chow test example

Restricted	Not restrict.	n	$f > f_\alpha^*$	Restricted	Not restrict.	N	$f > f_\alpha^*$
F+T	F	21	440.34>19.5	S+H	S	15	12735>19.5
	T	5			F	40	
T+S	T	5	5630>19.5				
	S	15					

5.2 Structural Model Example

The data used in estimation represent flow and speed variations over the five days of the week (from Monday to Friday). These data are represented in figure 8. However, no reasonable estimation can be produced specially for the hysteresis regime. Two solutions can be used. The first one consists in considering only data that describe a typical day. The second solution consists in using average speed and flow value. For each time of the day, we calculate an average speed and flow over the five days. In this paper, we apply the second one. Results of this manipulation are illustrated in the figure 9 and table 4.

In table 4, the values in brackets represent the standard variation. All parameters are significant at 5% except for the value of *a* in the first regime. The adjusted R-square is equal to 0.98. The sign of each parameter is in the correct sense. Representation of the fitted models is represented in the Figure 9.

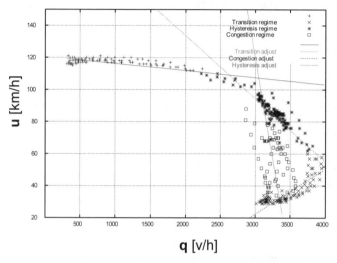

Fig. 9. Linear estimation by the structural econometric model proposed

The table 5 shows the value of the speed-flow couple. They are calculated by intersection between each two successive regimes. As long as speed is less than 19,15 *km/h*, the free-flow regime persist and the increase of the flow does not influence the speed. When flow is close 2624 *veh/h*, the second regime begins and speed starts to decrease. The congested regime starts when flow reach 4072,61 *veh/km* and speed decreases quickly and in the same time flow also decreases. The hysteresis regime is reached when flow is equal to 3346,30 *veh/km* and speed equal to 32,03 *veh/km*. In this case and in order to return to transition regime or free-flow regime, flow continues to decrease but speed starts to increase. The last column in the table 5 represents the density in each breaking point between two successive regimes. These values are calculated using the fundamental low. For example, the transition regime begins when the density is around 24 veh/km.

6   Final Comments

Three important contributions have been pointed out, firstly, an alternative to characterize traffic hysteresis phenomenon in an effective way through macroscopic data.

That characterization is based on the empirical analysis of the macroscopic traffic variables where a bottleneck urban road section and continuum is presented. Secondly, two econometric techniques have been proposed in order to identify the break points of each traffic regime, which at the time demonstrates the proposed model real efficacy. Finally, with the purpose of solving frontier points finding problematic, an algorithm for locating them through tendency rupture points has been developed; moreover, model adjustments can be done. This tool is necessary to analyze dense road networks containing a number of traffic broadcasting stations. As an example, in the case of Paris urban highway net, there are about 500 permanent stations registering traffic variables every 6 minutes. Despite this advance, improvements on process rapidity in real time usage should be worked on. Project which may be left out in future works.

Table 4. Estimation results for structural econometrics model

Regime	Model parameters	
	A	b
Uncongested	-0.00437	120.62
	(0.0022)	(2.8808)
Transition	-0.03926	212.19
	(0.0078)	(25.819)
Congested	0.02792	-61.41
	(0.0072)	(25.205)
Hysteresis	-0.25302	878.70
	(0.0395)	(128.43)

Table 5. Breaking point regimes for structural econometric model

PHASES	Flow [veh/h]	Speed [km/h]	Density [veh/km]
Uncongested – transition	2624.55	109.15	24.04
Transition – congested	4072.61	52.31	77.85
Congested – hysteresis	3346.30	32.03	104.47

Implications about integrating this phenomenon in the planning of infrastructure are important. Any applications concern instant travel time predictions as well for socio-economical evaluation. For instance, for the studied section MS-5 point (section 2.1), the proposed approach allows travel time prediction with a relative average error margin of -3%. On the contrary, a traditional approach, based in a delayed function (i.e. [16]), BPR travel time function adjusted to minimize quadratic errors among empirical values and function forecasting values by the function, show a relative average error margin of 40%.

Another field of potential application of the model is referred to planning dynamic models (i.e. [17]), in which users decisions (time, schedule, departure times) are strongly affected by travel times in a certain instant of time. The integration of hysteresis phenomenon implications to that type of processes will be matter of new studies.

Acknowledgements

This research was funded by the Mexican National Research Council (CONACYT) and the University Autonomous of Mexico State (UAEM) through the projects 41078 and 1597/2002 respectively. Same way, we would like to thank The Regional Direction of Parisian Infrastructure (DREIF) for gladly providing us data and the required information about the case study.

References

1. Hall, F. Traffic stream characteristics. In TRB-NRC (Ed) Traffic Flow Theory : A State of Art Report. Monograph. TRB-NRC, Washington DC. (1997)
2. Treiterer and Myers J. A.: The hysteresis phenomenon in traffic flow. Proceedings of the 6th International Symposium of Transportation and Traffic Theory, Sydney. 13-38. Bucley, D. J. (editor). (1974)
3. Zhang, H. M. : A Mathematical theory of traffic hysteresis. TR B 33, 1-23. (1999)
4. Chowdhury, D., Santen, L. and Schadschneider A.:Statistical physics of vehicular traffic and some related systems. Physics Report Vol. 329, 199-329 (2000)
5. Sánchez, O and de Palma A. "Relación fundamental, congestión en un cuello de botella y histeresis: análisis y evidencias en la autopista parisina A-14" In Lindau, Ortùzar et Strambi (eds) Ingeniería de tráfico y transportes: avances para una era de cambio. 145-158. ANPET. Gramado. (2000)
6. Wardrop, J. G. : Some Theoretical Aspects of Road Traffic Research. Proceedings of the Institution of Civil Engineers 2(1), 352-362. (1952)
7. Gerlough, D. L. and Huber M. J.: Traffic Flow Theory: a Monograph. Special Report, TRB, Washington (1975)
8. Newell, G. F.: Applications of Queuing Theory. Chapman and Hall, London (1982)
9. Hall, F., V. F. Hurdle and Banks J.H.: Synthesis of recent work in the nature of speed-flow and flow-occupance (or density) relationship on freeways. Transportation Research Record 1365, 12-18. (1992)
10. Daganzo, C.: Fundamental of Transportation and Traffic Operations. Pergamon, New York. (1994)
11. Leutzbach, W. :Introduction to the Theory of Traffic Flow. Springer-Verlag, Berlin. (1998)
12. Sánchez, O. Planification d'infrastructures de transport routier : théorie et applications selon une approche de simulation discrétisée. Septentrion, Lille (2000)
13. Small, K.: Urban Transportation economics. Harwood Routledge, Taylor and Francis. (2001)
14. Chow: Test of equality between sets of coefficients in two linear regressions. Econometrica, Vol. 28, 591-605 (1960)
15. Guajarati, D.: Essencial of econometrics- Mc Graw Hill, New York (1999)
16. Spiess, F.: Conical Volume-Delay Fonctions. Transportation Science. 153-158. (1990)
17. de Palma, A., F. Marchal and Nesterov. Y. : METROPOLIS : A Modular System for Dynamic Traffic Simulation. Transportation Research Record 1607. 178-184. (1997)

Are Static and Dynamic Planning Approaches Complementary? A Case Study for Travel Demand Management Measures

Oscar Sánchez[1] and André de Palma[2]

[1] Facultad de Ingeniería Universidad Autónoma del Estado de México
Cerro de Coatepec s/n. Ciudad Universitaria, 50130. Toluca, Estado de México, Mexico
osanchez@uaemex.mx
[2] THEMA-Université de Cergy-Pontoise, 33, Bd du Port. 95000. Cergy, France
Andre.depalma@eco.u-cergy.fr

Abstract. We determine the relevance of the displacement management measures in an urban road network. The main contribution, limitations and the balance among the static and dynamic planning approach are evaluated. In order to compare results from these approaches, four criteria to evaluate effects induced by simple and combined travel demand measures are established: configuration of the road network, efficiency rates, additivity of effects and multicriteria analysis. These criteria are quantified in two prototype networks which allow choosing between a series of flexible measures these ones which improved current circulation conditions. The obtained conclusion contribute to the decision making process because the managing authorities of urban transportation could know the effects induced by these measures, their spatial distribution and advantages or disadvantages from each modelling approach.

1 Introduction

Traditionally, urban transportation systems' analysis is based on a static modelling point of view. This approach admits all journeys and infrastructure service level as constants, during a determined time interval (usually an hour or a peak period), taking into account that this hypothesis, methods, algorithms (e.g. [1] or [2]) and commercial software (emme 2, TransCad, Estraus, Davisum, etc.) have been developed to find a network's equilibrium state (e.g. [3]). Based on this approach, alternative solutions to the urban transport essential problem are proposed: given a limited capacity transport network (supply) and some population's mobility characteristics (demand) to find the journeys' optimum assignations where transportation costs would be the most efficient (minimum) supposing that the assignment is implicitly linked to infrastructure's performance level.

Based on urban centres' developing stage and financial resources availability, the solutions to urban congestion were oriented to increase infrastructure capacity. Simulation tools, based on static approach, were sufficient in this way for transport network's planning (network design, infrastructure's capacity etc.) mostly because travel pattern and travellers' behaviour were more or less constant. Correspondence between model's hypothesis and simulated reality were consequently coherent. Actually, this paradigm has lost robustness due to societal changes [4], congestion levels induced in mobility decisions and more flexible and unstable day after day travel patterns. The fact is that the static approach is not enough to deal with this reality [5].

T. Böhme et al. (Eds.): IICS 2004, LNCS 3473, pp. 252–265, 2006.
© Springer-Verlag Berlin Heidelberg 2006

Nowadays, relentless growing in motorized mobility, perverse or negative effects (Myrdall circle) induced by an increment in infrastructure's capacity policy (see for example [6]), the over-offering automotive industry, the limited financial resources for new infrastructures, and high urban population density, have turned the possibility to continue with the same not feasible treatment of transport problems.

An alternative treatment is viable, in which management of demand must be included: the travel demand management (TDM). In the 90 a series of transport policies based in this new paradigm emerged [7]. Nevertheless, even such planning approach's theory was founded in the 70 [8]; few operational tools lived up to be feasible. The evaluation of such policies couldn't be more coherent. As a matter of fact, congestion phenomenon is characterized by its variability: firstly, traffic conditions are not the same throughout the day, neither days of the week or months of the year. This is due to infrastructure performance variation with demand's level (non-linear relation). Secondly, user's behaviour is not fixed, too. Travellers change mobility decisions (e.g. selection of start time to travel, itinerary, transportation modes, etc.). to adapt to current traffic conditions. Considering these components in the phenomenon treatment have caused an alternative approach called dynamic ([8], [9]), it is theoretically appropriate to analyse the effects of TDM [10].

Although the mentioned approaches are different (philosophy, modelling approach, algorithms, etc.), they are used to help transportation planning decision, but which one is more pertinent? And under which circumstances? Under which parameters are they reliable? These are only some of the questions that transport authorities can set. The objective of this article is to give answer elements in this way. That is the reason to analyse the implications of defining a journey's policy based on static and dynamic simulation approaches. Such analysis has been oriented into four directions: network's configuration, spatial distribution effects, additional flexible measures and alternatives' selection.

Following the traditional transport planning procedure (e.g. [11]), firstly, supply and demand characteristics for two prototype networks are introduced (sections 2 and 3, respectively); then, supply and demand equilibrium criteria is described for each one of the approaches mentioned (section 4); afterwards, stages oriented towards TDM's flexible measures are described (section 5); and finally, obtained results are analysed (section 6) and final comments are presented.

2 Modelling Supply

To show the representation of a generic transport system, two prototype networks of transport were modelled, they have been called reticular and circular configurations. The components of each network are as usual: centroids, arcs, nodes, and links, while centroids were located in the geometrical centre of each area, limited by streets (blocks). Nodes were located in each intersection of the network and were considered as self-regulated which means that no penalisation coefficients were used for turns. The road sections between two intersections were characterised by arcs and their physical properties such as: maximum permitted speed, number and capacity of lanes. Performance of such arcs was represented by means of BPR delay functions (e.g. [12]). Prototype networks' characteristics are detailed below.

2.1 Zones

To have comparison elements among the networks, simulation approaches and data comprehension, two spatial addition levels were set. The first is formed by each one of the 100 zones resulting from the criterion previously mentioned. The second, very much more added, sums the last 100 zones in six macro zones and its names depend on their orientation: Central Business District (CBD) A and B on the city centre, northeast, southeast, southwest and northwest (see fig. 1).

2.2 Radial Network

This configuration represents European and some Latin American cities. The network was constructed from two basic perpendicular axes North-South and East – West which drive the vehicle flow to city centre and also to three concentric peripheral rings, which drive the flow to secondary roads. The basic structure of this network is formed by concentric rings, separated by 500-metres each. These rings are linked with road segments, which do not follow a geometric pattern, for their aim is to provide a number of nodes similar to the reticular network. Thus, for a five-kilometre diameter outer ring, the radial network has: 120 nodes, 852 arcs in an over 342-kilometres length. Note that radial net is smaller in dimension than the reticular one. This situation is due to the configuration. In fact, arcs' average length compares this last thing: 0.4-km. of radial net against 0.42-km. of reticular net. This particularity will have implications comparing efficiency in journeys that we will show it in section 6.

2.3 Reticular Network

This prototype network represents American cities' drawing and is illustrated in figure 1B. Analogically to radial network, it is made up by two axes that divide the city. These axes do not cross the city centre (CBD) but feed two avenues that drive around the first and second city squares. The aim of these two avenues is to distribute the vehicular flow into the secondary roads. Secondary two-way roads, every 500 metres with north-south and east-west direction, complement the former basic structure. A node represents every intersection. Under this configuration and considering a network extension of 25 km^2, 121 nodes and 824 arcs were obtained in a 354 kilometres net's length.

3   Modelling Demand

Travels' spatial distribution was made considering the existence of an attractive geometrical centre (historical centre or CBD). Attraction and / or emission of travels were fading as the edge was reached. The travel's pattern previously described represents cities typically centralised, in which diversity, quality and quantity of goods and services are more concentrated in downtown area while the periphery is used as residential area.

(A) **(B)**

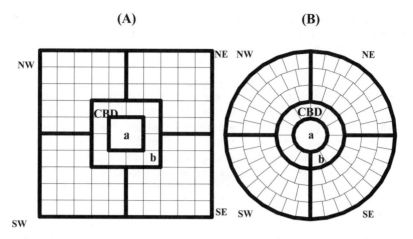

Fig. 1. The macro zones and the prototype networks: (A) Circular Network, (B) Grid network

3.1 Users

A homogeneous population was assumed with respect to its socio-economic characteristics and all the evaluations were done in travel time terms to use them as a comparative measure. Consequently, in the static model approach (see section 4.1), it was not necessary to define a value of time (VOT). Even though, due to dynamic model's considerations (see section 4.1) it was necessary to define the following parameters: VOT $\alpha = 1$USD / hour; the unit cost parameter for late arrival $\gamma = 2.5$ USD / hour; the unit cost parameter for early arrival $\beta = 0.8$ USD / hour; and the flexible arrival period (not penalised arrival time) $\Delta = 10$ minutes. All these parameters are medium values of normal distribution (see details in [13]). Additionally, a uniform distribution of desired arrivals was considered. Unitary cost parameters was described considering wages and time in absolute terms to emergent countries and in relative terms to obtain relations empirically (e.g. [14], [15], [16]). These values were lightly modified to reach an important users' concentration in the rush hour. We only consider work-home travels due to their regularity and importance, measured by the sum of journeys.

3.2 Trip Generation and Distribution Models

To obtain a centralised travel's spatial distribution, an enclosed exponential distribution model was used:

$$V_{i,j} = A_j P_j * \exp\left(-\frac{tt_{i,j}}{\mu_k}\right) \quad if \quad tt_{i,j} > tt_p \atop V_{i,j} = 0 \qquad\qquad if \quad tt_{i,j} \le tt_p . \tag{1}$$

In this equation $tt_{i,j}$, represents the travel time from i zone to j zone in minutes; tt_p shows the maximum travel time on foot expressed in minutes, that people are willing to spend by going to destination in minutes; V_{ij} are the travels made from i zone to j zone (travels /peak hour). Finally μ_k is a model's parameter in minutes. Equation 1 lets us know the travel's distribution to each zone whenever user's travel time is greater than bearable time on foot by the inhabitants of the selected zone (normally 5 minutes). To value the accessibility as well as zone attraction, services, equipment, facilities and commercial centres were considered to represent the city centralism. Finally, μ parameter was adjusted to the travel's frequency to be minimum compared to the user's total travel time, as if it was equal to the travel time from CBD to an outer point of the network. In this way two different coefficients were used to represent both behaviour of outer inhabitants and drivers from centre to suburbs. The reason for this separation is justified because central inhabitants have few reasons? To moving to get high quality services and goods, and suburbs inhabitants are used to move into downtown to get high quality services and goods.

3.3 Results

The previous model's adjustment sets the possibility of knowing the total amount of travels within a peak hour. In this way, an origin-destination matrix was obtained. The matrix consisting of 8,700 elements represents 151,819 trips. Table 1 shows spatial distribution in the five macro zones described before. Generated travels from/to network's centre (CBD) were divided in two parts, being the closest CBDa and a ring CBDb. From Table 1, it can be verified that more than 40% of the total amount of travels have CBD as destination, while internal travels to CBD represent about 9% of the total; and generated travels from CBD reach a 16%. Travels among macro zones, excluding CBD reach only 42% of the total.

Table 1. O/D matrix agregated by macro zones

Mzone	CBD-a	CBD-b	NE	SE	SW	NW	Total
CBD-a	0	2252	2812	2508	1259	2246	**11077**
CBD-b	3165	7636	3221	4966	3313	4946	**27248**
NE	3576	6433	9750	5006	102	4014	**28882**
SE	10030	9951	4996	9401	4548	439	**39366**
SW	5032	6622	102	4545	9649	4087	**30035**
NW	3827	4136	542	204	3068	3435	**15211**
Total	**25630**	**37031**	**21423**	**26630**	**21940**	**19166**	**151819**

4 Supply and Demand Equilibrium

The essential difference among the dynamic and static simulation approach is located in the hypothesis of users' behaviour which determines the transportation system equilibrium. In the static model the individual characteristics of mobility are fixed in the period of analysis (origin-destination or o/d matrix, departure time and traffic conditions). In the dynamic model, the user faces every moment an alternatives set: make travel or not, departure time choice, transportation mode choice, itinerary choice, etc. In this way, the modelling demand in our static approach is define as aggregated and uses almost exclusively physical notions while the dynamic one is individual or disaggregated and it is based on micro-economical notions of the user's behaviour.

4.1 The Static Approach Equilibrium

The equilibrium principle of this approach is based mainly on the traffic macroscopic theory (e.g. [2], [17], [18]) and on the fundamental relationship (e.g. [19] reformulated in [20]), in which the travel time is bounded by the speed-flow relation by means of a delay function. This function measures the performance of each road section according to their saturation level. It is the base on which the users, or a group of users, choose their itinerary (sequence in the use of links), in an interactive way and according to search criterion. The stationary state or equilibrium supply-demand is reached when *"the journey times in all used routes are equal or less than those which would be experienced by a single vehicle on any unused route"* (Wardrop's first principle or optimum individual [19]), or *"when the travel times are the minimum for the all the users"* (Wardrop's second principle or optimum social). There is a series of variants for the two types of equilibrium mentioned, as well as diverse algorithms that permit to reach them. For more details see for example [2] or [3].

4.2 The Dynamic Approach Equilibrium

The dynamic approach, proposed initially by Vickrey [8], is based on the model of individual election of departure time: the users choose among avoiding the congestion setting off before or after its usual time or to reach its destination at the desired time but with a more extended time of journey (time of the journey elapsed in longer time of journey). In this way, for any displacement, the individuals support a generalized cost C that depends on: the departure time (td), the effective travel time (tt), the desired arrival time (t^*) and a flexible arrival period (Δ) which supposes a null cost, due to a not penalty, for the user (cf. equation 2). Under these premises, we have three cases related to the arrival time (ta): early arrival ($ta < t^*$), late arrival ($ta > t^*$) and arrival on time ($ta = t^*$). Generalized cost function is given by:

$$
\begin{aligned}
C(td) &= \alpha tt(td) + \beta\left\{\left(t^* - \frac{\Delta}{2}\right) - [td + tt(td)]\right\} & si \quad ta < t^* \\
C(td) &= \alpha tt(td) + \gamma\left\{[td + tt(td)] - \left(t^* + \frac{\Delta}{2}\right)\right\} & si \quad ta > t^* \\
C(td) &= \alpha tt(td) & si \quad ta = t^*
\end{aligned}
\tag{2}
$$

In the previous equations, (α) is the value of the time, (β) is the unit cost parameter for early arrival, (γ) is the unit cost parameter for late arrival. From both theoretical (see [8]) and empirical (see [21] or de [22]) points of view, the costs due to the early or late arrivals (schedule delay cost) can result on half of the general cost of the journey. In this way, the static focus does not permit to determine an important part of the total travel cost (see also Table 3). Underestimation of this cost is important since this variable is determining in the analysis of the modal distribution or in the calculation of the benefits induced by TDM. The model previously described represents the heart of the dynamic focus and its complement for the consideration of the adaptive aspect of the users. The last one is characterized by a learning process that leads the system into a stationary state (see [13]). In a transportation system, conformed by N heterogeneous users with its preferences of election and with its VOT (journey, early and late arrival), there will be a distribution in the schedules of arrival that, combined to the duration of each one of the trips, implies that travelers use the network at the same time causing congestion and that the users will incur in an excessive transportation costs (due to incomplete information about traffic conditions). Nevertheless, as the time goes by, such costs will tend to be reduced and the user will adapt its habits of displacement (alternatives of election). Finally, the system tends to be stabilized once the users minimize its generalized costs of transportation: At the equilibrium, no driver can modify her/his departure time in order to strictly decrease the travel cost (Wardrop's first principle applied to dynamic approach). It's important to mention that the election models for departure time, way of transportation, itinerary are discrete choice model (e.g. [23]) correspond to the simulation of stochastic processes for which the stationary state of the system is achieved after an important number of interactions (see [16]).

5 Scenerii Design

According to the centralized structure of the trips' spatial distribution (see figure 1), it is expected that the greatest problems of congestion are in the central macro-zone called CBD. From the purpose to improve the circulation in this zone, TDM measures are used to describe a variety of auxiliary actions to reduce or to modify the intensity of displacement [7]. TDM concept has got success since the 70's. It's due to the mobility increment and its advantage is that the employed measures do not generally require an increase in the capacity of the infrastructure. Globally, the demand in the systems of transportation surpasses the diagnosed limits in the statements of its services and the public authorities responsible for this management, are not willing or do not have the financial requirements to improve, to adapt, or to build the required infrastructure. The policies based on TDM are an answer to the problems originated by the increase of urban congestion, since these intend to diminish it through the application of flexible measures that do not require large investments.

The management of demand in transportation involves different measures, among the following: internalize congestion costs, electronic toll, shared trips, access interdiction to CBD, rearrangement of circulation ways, etc. In this paper, we take into account only the two last measures mentioned above. The main objectives of these measures, in the medium term, are [24]:

To modify the travellers' behaviour: the most common objective is to reduce the number of trips, as well as to change the users' attitude in order to use another transportation mode or a different schedule to reduce the traffic concentration periods to get a better demand distribution throughout the day.

To diminish environmental damages: the construction and transportation services operation is always going to cause environmental impact such as air pollution at local (ozone, CO, suspended particles, etc.) and global level (weather changes, consequences caused by ozone), noise and water contamination.

To diminish the dependence of the car: the easy access to a specific place implies a commercial and housing development. Because of it, the measures of management of demand intend to reduce this damage based on urban design that diminish the dependence toward the individual use of vehicles, and besides, they help the cyclists and pedestrian circulation.

To increase the security of the trip: if the number of trips is reduced, possibly the number of accidents, collisions, damage to vehicles, fatalities, injuries and emergency calls can be reduced too.

In the next subsection, we describe the analysed measures based in TDM. It is important to mention that different TDM measures were added on the base case in order to evaluate additive effects.

5.1 The Base Case

It represents the "current traffic conditions" in the network corresponding to the supply and demand characteristics described before (see section 2 and 3). From the purpose to establish a comparative framework among both networks prototype and among the measures implemented, the system's performance was analyzed "without congestion" (SC) that comes to represent the minimum travel time for the origin-destination matrix described synthetically in table 1. In a way, to fixed demand, any TDM policies implemented will not be able to obtain better levels of performance with this situation (see tables 3, 4 and 5).

5.2 Scenery 1

The main measure of this Scenery consists in providing a pedestrian zone in the first square/ring of the city centre. This zone is close to the car circulation. As mentioned before (section 2), the structure of the networks and the travel demand induced high levels of traffic in the CBD (see section 6). To compensate the loss of capacity that implies the prohibition mentioned, we proceeded to eliminate the public parking in the streets around the mentioned first square/ ring. This measure allows gaining an additional lane to car circulation. We considered that other actions were implemented to increase circulation speed too. These actions mean an increase of 5km/h the speed.

5.3 Scenery 2

In this case, we include supplementary (additional) measures for the Scenery 1. They vary according to the kind of network. In the reticular network, the street ways for the first square of the city were changed in a one-way clockwise circulation while the public street parking in the second square was restricted to gain an additional lane. Thus, same improvements were carried out to increase the circulation speed in 5km/h. In the circular network they only improved the conditions of circulation in the second peripheral ring enlarging its capacity in a lane and the circulation speed in 5km/h. These measures come from a series of simulations using software based on the static approach EMME2 [25]. The results showed by this software indicate that the average travel time through was lowered in comparison to the current situation (base case) in both networks.

5.4 Scenery 3

In this Scenery, our research focused towards circulation way changes that contributed to alternative itineraries to the users who travel towards the center of the city. In the reticular network and based on the modifications of Scenery 2, two unidirectional parallel group lanes were implemented. The first one runs in North-South and south-north direction and the second one runs in East-West and West-East direction. Each one of the unidirectional parallel group lanes doubled its capacity according to the number of lanes due to the fact that the parking restriction was not established. For the circular network, the first peripheral ring was considered as unidirectional. Hence, three lanes were obtained ready to circulation.

5.5 Scenery 4

Additional measures were included in this case to improve the circulation conditions of Scenery 3. In the reticular network the unidirectional parallel group lanes lengths were reduced being limited to the second square of the city. In the circular network, changes of direction in the road sections, that feed the periphery of the first square, were made. Four sections were modified to become one-way with the consequent duplicity of the circulation lanes.

6 Results

Due to the fact that the results obtained by both simulation approaches are comparable in terms of travel time only, this criterion was used for the first level of analysis. The results obtained for the benefits spatial distribution for sceneries considered are commented in a brief way (for a detailed description see [26]). The second level of analysis is exclusive of the dynamic focus and refers to the measures of effectiveness (MOEs). These measures are used to analyse transportation system's performance.

6.1 Spatial Distribution of Benefits (Static Model)

Although the measures of management implemented contribute, in general terms, to decrease the travel time, it is necessary to determine in what zones the population obtains the circulation improvements. We introduce two levels of analysis to evaluate effects induced by measures in sceneries considered from static approach point of view. The first one concerns the spatial distribution of effects (how benefits for each zone are different). The second one is related with the magnitude of effects (how many the total travel time is reduced). A summary of comparative analysis is described in the next lines:

In the reticular network the users of the external zones obtain the greatest benefits in travel time reduction terms, while for those who arrive or leave the CBD, the travel time increases. The results are valid for all the analyzed sceneries.

There is an almost homogeneous benefits distribution in the circular network about the reduction/increase of the travel time, even for the scenery that contributes the most to the reduction of travel time (Scenery 2). The highest benefits are for the users that enter/leave the city center (CBD).

In a non-congestion situation, the travel time is, in general terms, upper in the reticular network. Only in the relations NE-SE and NE-CBD this situation is reverted.

The justification of the mentioned results and the detailed analysis of other distribution conditions are described in [26].

6.2 Measures of Effectiveness

In dynamic approach, the simulations were carried out using the METROPOLIS software [10] which produces aggregated MOE's from aggregation of individual data. Due to the extension of this work, all the results related to the costs (schedule delay cost and individual travel costs) will be omitted. However, the next variables will be used: the average travel time, the total average travel cost, the congestion level, the average vehicles-kilometer, and the average number of links used by motorist.

6.3 Comparing Approaches

The table 2 provides information of the travel time for each prototype and to each modeling approach. Taking into account the total travel time as the criterion for election of the measures to implement, it is known that:

The modelling approach does not end up to the same conclusions. In the static approach we need to improve total travel time with extra flexible measures whereas in the dynamic approach the additional measures only give marginal improvements (reticular network) and can even increase the travel time (circular network).

The relation among the induced improvements, in terms of travel time, in the reticular and circular networks is independent of the simulation approach when the actions on the network are equivalent. This conclusion is verified by the relation: average travel time in the reticular network against that in the circular network represented in the column "RET/CIRC" of table 2, since for scenery SC, BC, 1 and 2 have values of around 1.06. Sceneries 3 and 4 differ completely from each one of the networks (see section 5). That is why the measures implemented are not equivalent.

Table 2. Results by simulation approach based on total average travel time comparison

Scen.	STATIC APPROACH			DYNAMIC APPROACH			STAT/DYN	
	Circr	Grid	G/C	Circ	Grid	G/C	Circ	Grid
NC	5.06	5.35	1.06	5.00	5.28	1.06	1.03	1.03
BC	8.13	8.56	1.05	**6.35**	6.87	1.08	*1.28*	1.25
1	8.50	8.90	1.05	6.72	7.02	1.05	1.27	*1.27*
2	**8.04**	**8.51**	1.06	6.40	**6.86**	1.07	1.26	1.24
3	9.04	10.21	**1.13**	8.80	8.28	**0.94**	1.03	1.23
4	9.40	10.18	1.08	6.98	7.71	1.10	1.35	1.32

6.4 Additivity of Effects

In terms of travel time, the implemented measures do not always induce positive effects; the aforesaid effects vary according to the modelling approach that is being used. Table 2 shows that, for scenery 2 and according to the static approach, the additional measures improve the conditions of circulation with regard to the "current situation" and to the situation where traffic circulation in the CBD was prohibited. Therefore, the positive effects are added. It is not established in sceneries 3 and 4, whose measures worsen the conditions obtained in scenery 1. In the dynamic approach, the additional measures do not contribute to neither beneficial nor additional effects.

For the dynamic approach, the MOE's are not always directed on the additivity of effects. In the table 3, it can be observed that, except for a cell, the MOE's values are over the "current situation" (base case), this shows that any taken measure will come to worsen the circulation conditions. On the other hand, the minimum values of the indicators for each network do not always belong to specific scenery. This justifies the need to employ a ranking alysis to make hierarchical the TDM measures.

Table 3. MOE's for dynamic approach where results were normalized to "current situation" values

	GRID				RET			
Scen.	Time [min]	Cost [$]	Congest [%]	Veh-km	Time [min]	Cost [$]	Congest [%]	Veh-km
1	1.02	1.09	1.18	1.00	1.06	1.03	1.22	0.99
2	**1.00**	**1.07**	1.23	**0.98**	**1.01**	**1.00**	1.13	**0.98**
3	1.20	1.25	1.50	1.19	1.39	1.24	2.58	1.10
4	1.12	1.18	**1.12**	1.17	1.10	1.06	**1.05**	1.09

6.5 Scenery Ranking

There is some information about the multicriteria analysis in tables 4 and 5 applied to the circular and reticular networks respectively. In order to obtain the final note of sceneries considered, the value of a specific MOE was normalized in respect of their average value in the analysed scenery. Subsequently normalized value was affected by a K factor. Finally, these values were added up, so that the minimum value belongs to the best alternative. The mentioned tables permit to verify that none of the sceneries obtains a better rang than the present situation. Only scenery 2 presents the closest testing to the present situation, for both the reticular and the circular networks. It could be said that the two simulation approach match in indicating that scenery 2 is the one with the most "benefits".

Table 4. Ranking scenarii for the grid network (dynamic approach)

GRID Scen.	Time [min]	Cost [$]	Congest [%]	Veh-km	Narcs	Ranking
K	5	4	3	2	1	
Average	7.00	2.58	20.7	0.41	5.99	15.0
NC	5.28	2.31	0.0	0.36	5.38	10.0
BC	6.87	2.36	20.6	0.39	5.76	14.4
1	7.02	2.57	24.3	0.39	5.79	15.4
2	6.86	2.52	25.3	0.38	5.67	15.3
3	8.28	2.94	30.9	0.46	6.73	18.4
4	7.71	2.77	23.06	0.46	6.62	16.5

Table 5. Ranking scenarii for the circular network (dynamic approach)

GRID Scen.	Time [min]	Cost [$]	Congest [%]	Veh-km	Narcs	Ranking
K	5	4	3	2	1	
Average	7.00	2.58	20.7	0.41	5.99	15.0
NC	5.28	2.31	0.0	0.36	5.38	10.0
BC	6.87	2.36	20.6	0.39	5.76	14.4
1	7.02	2.57	24.3	0.39	5.79	15.4
2	6.86	2.52	25.3	0.38	5.67	15.3
3	8.28	2.94	30.9	0.46	6.73	18.4
4	7.71	2.77	23.06	0.46	6.62	16.5

7 Final Comments

The results obtained allow showing that, to spatial distribution of continuous trips, the effects induced by the TDM depend so much on: the network configuration, the evaluation criterion chosen and the simulation approach used. In the static model case, it is clear that the access interdiction of motorists to the city center have to be compensated by other measures. In the dynamic model case, the preceding idea is not verified in reference to the type of measures proposed. Nevertheless, the effects of other flexible measures, such as fixing a toll on fuel or the implementation of flexible arrival schedules, are topics to explore. There are some other non-analyzed alternatives:

The spatial distribution patterns of trips. In our analysis, we considered a fixed volume and trip spatial distribution. Nevertheless, it is necessary to evaluate whether the described conclusions are still valid for other levels of demand (consequently different infrastructure's saturation levels) and another kind of spatial distributions.

Spatial distribution of effects. The comparative analysis of the induced effects by sceneries analysed was based on the addition of the total travel time. However, the distribution of these effects in each zone and the definition of criteria that allows gathering together this kind of considerations, have not been analyzed in testing benefits as an alternative.

Evaluation of effects on a multimodal system. The O/D matrix considered corresponds only to the trips in private cars. In a more realistic case, we need include alternative transportation modes. This would modify aforementioned conclusions. Thus, it is recommended to include, in further analysis, multimodal transportation networks.

Situation for each individual. Differing from the static one, the dynamic focus allows knowing, individually or in a separated way, a wide variety of performance rates that inform about the measurements used and that affect all kind of users. Therefore, an analysis of this kind, would allow defining measurements according to the needs of all people.

All the aforementioned represents a fascinating field of investigation which will be explored in future works.

Acknowledgements

This work was carried out according to the project 35692U (CONACyT-UAEM). We acknowledge O. Mekkaoui (THEMA-TTR). F. Marchal (IEEE), Ricardo Valdés and Roberto Galicia (UAEM), who provided us with technical support and helped in the creation of diagrams.

References

1. Beckman, R. J., McGuire, C. B. y Winsten, C. B. *Studies in the economics of Transportation.* Yale University Press. New Haven (1956*)*
2. Sheffi, Y.: Urban Transportation Network. Prentice-Hall, Englewood. (1985)
3. Miller, H. J.: Towards Consistent Travel Demand Estimation in Transportation Planning : A Guide to Theory and Practice on Equilibrium Travel Demand Modelling. TMIP Report. (1997)
4. Giuliano, G.: Urban travel patterns in B. Hoyle and R. Knowles, *eds.* Modern Transport Geography, 2nd edition. Chichester, GB: John Wiley & Sons. (1998)
5. Goldman, T (editor): Transportation models in the police-making process: uses, misuses and lessons for the future. Proceedings from a symposium of the problems of transportation analysis and modeling in the world of politics. UCB, Berkeley. (1998)
6. Button, K.: Transportation economics. Elgar, Published, London (1996)
7. Button, K. and Hensher, A.: Handbook of Transport Systems and Traffic Control. Vol. 3, Pergamon. Oxford (2001)
8. Vickrey, W.S.: Congestion Theory and Transport Investment. American Economic Review (articles and communications). Vol 59. 251-261. (1969)
9. Ran, B. and D. Boyce E. : Dynamic Urban Transportation Network Models: Theory and Applications for IVHS. Springer-Verlag, Heidelberg (1994)
10. de Palma, A., F. Marchal and Nesterov. Y. : METROPOLIS : A Modular System for Dynamic Traffic Simulation. Transportation Research Record 1607. (1997) 178-184.
11. Ortúzar, J. de D. and Willumsen L. G. : Modelling Transport: Third edition. Wiley, Chichester. (2002)
12. Spiess, F.: Conical Volume-Delay Functions. Transportation Science. (1990).153-158.
13. de Palma, A. and Marchal, F. Real Cases applications of the fully dynamic METRÓPOLIS tool-box: an advocacy for large-scale mesoscopic transportation systems. Networks and spatial economics, Vol 2. (2002) 2: 347-369.
14. Small, K.: Urban Transportation Economics. Harwoord, Chur. (1992)
15. de Palma, A. and Rochat D. : Congestion Urbaine et Comportament des Usagers: analyse de la composante horaire. Revue d'Economie Urbaine et Regionale. Vol 3. (1998) 467-488.
16. THEMA-TTR QUATUOR : Outils dynamiques de simulation pour la gestion des déplacements dans la région parisienne. PREDIT 00MT66 Report. Université de Cergy-Pontoise. (2001)
17. Leutzbach, W.: Introduction to the theory of traffic flow. Springer-Verlag. Berlin (1988)
18. Daganzo, C.: Fundamentals of transportation and traffic operations. Oxford, Pergamon. (1997)
19. Wardrop, J. G.: Some Theoretical Aspects of Road Traffic Research. Proceedings of the Institution of Civil Engineers. Vol 2(1), 352-362. (1952)
20. Gerlough, D. L. and M. J. Huber Traffic Flow Theory : a Monograph. TRB Special Report, Washington. (1975)
21. de Palma, A. and Marchal F. : From W; Vickrey to Large-scale dynamic traffic models. European Transport Conference, Loughborough University, U. K. (1998)

22. de Palma and Fontan, C. Departura time choice: estimation resylts and simulation to Paris Area. Proceedings 10th ICTBR : 39 (2003)
23. Ben-Akiva, M. and Lerman S.: Discrete Choice Analysis: Theory and Applications to Travel Demand. The MIT Press, Cambridge (1985)
24. Victoria Transport Policy Institute: Online TDM encyclopedia, http://www.vtpi.org. Victoria, BC: Victoria Transport Policy Institute. (2000)
25. INRO: EMME/2 User's Manual Software. INRO, Montreal. (1998)
26. Sánchez, O.: Análisis paramétrico basado en los enfoques de modelización estático y dinámico: estudio comparativo. UAEM-CIITRA. Working paper 5/2002. (2002)

On-Request Urban Transport
Parallel Optimization

Arnaud Renard, Michaël Krajecki, and Alain Bui

Université de Reims Champagne Ardenne, CreSTIC
Département Mathématiques et Informatique, Moulin de la Housse
BP 1039, F-51687 Reims Cedex 2, France
{arnaud.renard,michael.krajecki,alain.bui}@univ-reims.fr

Abstract. Transport problems are generally rather complex. The number of temporal, material, social and economic constraints makes it difficult to solved it both in theory (the problem is NP-complet) and in practice.
This paper presents a pick-up and delivery transportation problem with time window and heterogeneous fleet of vehicles. Its objective is to provide an efficient schedule for drivers and the best service for users with the lower cost. This paper will explain the methodology used to compute and optimise the driver schedule. The goal is to assign more than eight hundreds fares to about forty drivers using thirty vehicles.
Constraints programming approach makes it possible to treat instantaneously the local insertion of one journey in an optimised way. This local insertion was simply solved by an engine of constraints resolution in 1996 [MS88]. In addition, this method allows also the local insertion of several transports which was used to implement a total optimization of the schedule as a multitude of local displacements of few transports.
This method becomes too slow when it moves more and more transport to improve quality of the solution. In this paper, a parallel solution, based on PVM, is introduced and some interesting results are provided. It is now possible to manage the collaboration of independent optimization engines working with different parameters. Experimentally, this robust solution is most of the time able to provide the best known sequential result.

Keywords: On-request transport, collaboration engine, Parallelization, optimization, constraint programming, vehicle routing, pick-up and delivery, time windows, heterogeneous fleet, cartography, PVM.

1 Introduction

Transport and mobility by road or by train play an important part in modern life. That is why the social integration of people with reduced mobility cannot be efficient without a complete mobility in the city. The G.I.H.P. is a non-profit organisation which manages the public service of transport inside a district for people with reduced mobility.

T. Böhme et al. (Eds.): IICS 2004, LNCS 3473, pp. 266–275, 2006.

Everyday, this association has to treat requests of users by phone. Each request has to be rejected or approved in real time, while the user is holding on the line. Users can change their transport up to the day before the transport in the afternoon. The first functionality is to treat requests on a real time basis.

The aim of this study is to planning routes for buses and establishing daily working schedule for drivers.

It is not so simple to treat such a transport considering each compatibility between users and vehicles with or without special equipment, between users and drivers who can or not carry the user in staircases. The resolution of a single insertion was resolved in 1996 [ACDK96] using a representation by constraints of the problem and thanks to a constraints resolution engine called NCL [Zho98a]. This method of resolution will be described in the first part of this paper.

The second part of the problem consists in optimizing a whole schedule to treat more transports if some of them have been rejected by the system but accepted by the operator and to use fewer drivers. The implementation of the optimization was made to be close to the insertion method and use the insertion itself. This method seems to be efficient and produce good results for years. In fact, this method makes local optimization using displacements and exchanges of transport between drivers. Such an optimization can be finished after six hours so it is possible to launch the processes only during the night and not before the edition of the mission sheets for drivers at 6pm.

The idea to speed-up the optimization processes by exploiting low-used computers came few years ago. In this paper, the parallel method using PVM will be introduced and the experimental results will be discussed.

The paper is organised as follows: in the next section, the vehicule routing problem is described. Some backgrounds are given and the main characteristics of the specific routing problem studied in this paper are discussed. Next, the principles of the sequential optimization are exhibited. Section 4 is dedicated to the parallel optimization: the mechanism of collaboration between the agents and the different heuristics used are presented. We, then, comment the results obtained by the experimental analysis which show that the parallel solution is interesting. Finally, the paper ends up by some concluding remarks and future works.

2   Vehicle Routing Resolution

2.1   Backgrounds

A vehicle routing problem occurs when several vehicles can be used to tread an amount of requests at different places. Vehicles can be cars, planes, trucks, or a man. The request can be rather complex. To resolve the problem, you need to affect a vehicle to each request, respecting capacity, time, cost and some other constraints. It is quite natural to try to resolve such problems using constraint programming which allow to describe the problem easily [Ros00][BPK01]. Each variable has a finite domain, each constrain involves variables, and the resolution method is well known [BC94][Pro93].

Other types of methods to resolve vehicle routing problem are constructive. Those methods, are part of meta-heuristics [Hol75][OL96] and are more and more used to resolve optimization problems. Ant Colony system [DG97b] is one of them. A lot of agents are building a solution for the problem and the best can share its solution with the others to influence them. After several generations and with special controls, the optimised solution is found [DPST03].

To reduce the execution time, parallel implementation of meta-heuristics has been proposed and proved efficient in pratice [BHPT98][CMRR01].

2.2   Description of the Problem

The G.I.H.P. is a non-profit organisation which manages public transport inside an urban district for people with reduced mobility. The project to build an optimization tool takes place in the middle of the nineties while the amount of transport was growing up and was tricky to be treated manually. At the beginning, the goal was to insert one transport in an existing schedule. Each insertion is made by minimising its cost in an optimal way without modifying the current planning. To answer instantaneously the user who telephones to reserve a transport, the operation of insertion must be very fast. In order to insert a transport correctly, a certain number of parameters and constraints must be respected; the system must also consider a whole day to manage legal duration of work for drivers.

Drivers and Vehicles. There are two types of resources to manage; the drivers and the vehicles.

Maximum working time and duration for drivers are set to respect the social legislation and agreement. A driver can work in one, two or three parts during the day. Between each part, the driver has a break at a specified address. Each driver can have a special cost for the first transport of the part and next a cost for every hour of work. That is useful to give a kind of priority to each driver but to use expansive drivers not only for one ride. Drivers must also respect the transport legislation and the system automatically manages total driving time for each of them.

A vehicle is available for the whole day or can be unavailable for a while to have it serviced or repaired. Some of them must be used more than others. Each vehicle has several configurations which describe the number of seats, number of places for wheelchair or folding chair. The modification from a configuration to one other can sometimes need consequent handling in the depot. There is also a compatibility relation between vehicles and drivers due to different driving licences or big vehicles.

Geographical Data and Requests. The geographical data is an important point for the vehicle routing resolution. It consists in a black box that gives us the outdistance between two addresses (which is not very important element in the cost evaluation) and the journey time between them at the specified time of the specified day. This geographical engine can really evaluate journey duration differently whether if it takes place either during night or midday. The evaluation is made using data from cartography and some speed matrix which has different values during the day.

Requests have a lot of properties. Each request has a pick-up and a deposit address, a pick-up and a deposit time window, the duration of those operations, a vehicle compatibility list (some users require special equipment) and a driver compatibility list (some users need to be helped by one or two strapping drivers). A request explains how many seats or wheelchairs it needs. Other information precise if the user can stay alone in the vehicle, if the driver has to leave the vehicle for his pick-up, for his deposit. The user can also be transported directly or with a special duration in place of the time calculated by the default function depending of the direct trip duration. A request can also represent a group of basic requests. This complex definition will be detailed later.

Pick-up and deposit times are defined in a very flexible way. They are, in fact, time windows of about twenty minutes. This theoretical time window is the reference given to the user. The inference engine can use this period of time to group users together and to optimize the global schedule. An other constraint imposes to drop wheelchair users in a reversed order than their pick-up. Each day, more than 800 fares are assigned to about forty drivers using thirty vehicles.

3   Actual Optimization Process

In this section, the solution used in practice by the G.I.H.P. is introduced. The constraint programming approach is used both for the local and the global optimization.

3.1   Model of the Insertion Problem

Constraint programming contains two points, the constraint model and the search strategy. As explained in [DKZ98a], only a good model can make an efficient search strategy. Driver scheduling and vehicle despatching are seen as two independent problems. Each compatibility, each cost and each dependence is represented as a constraint. The inference engine contained in the scheduling engine is NCL.

NCL combines Boolean logic, integer constraints and set reasoning over finite domains. Concerning its syntax, NCL fully adopts mathematical notations and provides literate-style solutions. Compared to some other modelling languages, one of NCL's features is: Though NCL handles several data types such as Boolean, integer, set, index, array, tuple and reference, there is no need to separate data from a problem model. Concerning constraint handling capability, logical and meta controls such as quantification, search strategy, logical switch, multi-criteria optimization, and meta expression are introduced in a natural and flexible fashion [Zho98b] [Zho98a].

NCL is available at *http://www.loria.fr/~zhou/ziran.html*

Our optimization engine uses the natural constraint propagation engine to resolve the problem. It instantiates first the different constraints for drivers and vehicles, adds the constraints for each already scheduled journeys and finally adds the constraints for the new journey. The constraint propagation engine is launched to find a good solution which satisfies all the constraints. If one solution is found, the system tries to find a better solution. The cost of the global schedule is a self modifiable constraint; the search strategy tries to find a solution with a lower cost than the current one. If a new solution is found, it becomes the current solution and its cost, the new current cost.

3.2   Global Optimization Using Insertion Abilities

The main capability of the scheduling engine is to add several transports in a schedule. This ability is also used for the optimization of an existing schedule. Regularly or during the night, the optimization occurs. One round of optimization is a large set of micro-optimizations. A micro-optimization proceeds in unscheduling few transports (three to five) and adding them together into the schedule with the standard insertion method. By this way, we hope we could find a better place for each of them. In the worst case, those transports will find their initial place. When all the journeys of the day are treated, if the new schedule has lower cost than the previous one, an other optimization round can be executed. According to the parameters, a whole optimization can take from two to fifteen rounds, and from five minutes to five hours. The value of the parameters has a huge influence on the quality of the solution and on the execution time.

The first parameter, called *size*, is the number of transport which will be rescheduled together. The more this parameter is important, the more the research tree will be big; what makes increase the execution time considerably. When the inserted request is composed of a group of journeys, the exploration mechanism becomes very long. The number of possible affections between drivers, vehicle and rides is exponential. This is the main limitation of the optimization method. This parameter is usually set to 1,2,3 or 4 to avoid too consuming time optimizations.

The second parameter is the *step* between two micro-optimization selections. This parameter must be set between one and *size*. This parameter means that

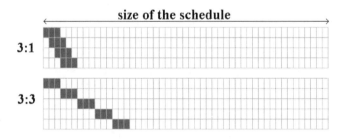

Fig. 1. Size and Step of micro-optimization

two consecutive micro-optimizations will have (*size-step*) common rides. Figure 1 illustrates two modes of selection, the first uses a micro-optimization with 3 transports and a step of 1. The other uses a micro-optimization with 3 transports and a step of 3. A combination of *step* and *size* is enough to create an optimization parameter. This method was first implemented because it was easy to set and gives good results; the quality is very dependent of the parameters used.

During our experimentations of the sequential method, a large set of values for the parameters was tested using ten typical example days. Given that the best solution was never generated with the same set of values for the parameters. This is the reason why the best result is memorized as a reference. Two sets of values are also studied as real optimization parameters since they are used in real condition (in the company). The first one is called *express optimization* and the second one is *thorough optimization*, see table 1. The express optimization has a very small *size*. The thorough optimization has a bigger *size* and a small *step*. Initially, journey were treated using a chronological order because it was the best method to have the chance to select close requests which are potentially group able, mixable or exchangeable.

4   A Collaborative Method to Parallelise the Sequential Optimization

The main defect of the initial optimization method is that we must try a lot of parameters to get a good result and it takes a long time. The principle of the parallel resolution is to make collaborated several optimization engines which use each one a different strategy. We are now able to try several strategies on the same time.

The global optimization is parallelised using the message passing paradigm: one agent which is running on one computer can share information and data with other agents on other or same computer directly with sending the data by message to the addressing agent. This parallel tool can work either on windows, linux, unix or big shared-memory multi-processors computers simultaneously. To manage the exchanges between the agents, PVM has been considered [GBD⁺94]. A client/server scheme is used to make the collaboration between the agents effective: in particular, the manager is in charge of the management of the best known solution.

In concrete terms, as the reader can see it on Figure 2, several agents can load or share their current solutions to the manager which deals the solutions and the strategies. An agent can load dynamically a new strategy (step=3) or can share its computed solution with the manager (solution_cost=22). The manager can decide if the new solution given by the agent is better or not than the current solution. It can also decide to ask one agent its solution or to give it the new current best solution. When the manager detects stagnation of the solution cost and when no other strategy can be used, it decides that the parallel optimization is finished.

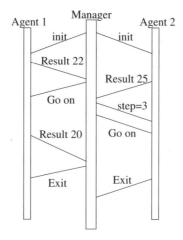

Fig. 2. The collaborative method with two agents

4.1 The Different Heuristics

Different parallel heuristics have been tested. All of them are time-oriented, it means that journeys to be re-scheduled together are chosen thanks to their theoretical begin time. In this paper, heuristics are based on the four parameters: size, step, the first journey selected to begin the optimization and the time orientation. Three interesting heuristics are summarized in the following.

1. **Three agents are beginning to select journeys at various moment of the day.** Agents are using the same *step* and *size* parameters. The first is beginning to select the first journey of the day, the second is beginning at one third of the day and the last agent is beginning at two third of the day.

   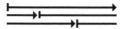

2. **Four agents are working either with chronological way or in the other way.** Agents are using the same *step* and *size* parameters. The first is beginning to select the first journey of the day; the second is beginning at half of the day. They are both selecting the rides chronologically. The third and the fourth agents are selecting fares in the other way and beginning at the end or at the middle of the day.

   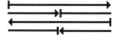

3. **Different step and size values.** Three agents are using *size* parameter of 3, 4 and 5. *Step* value is either equal to one or the value of the *size*.

4.2   Experimental Analysis

We will compare 10 parallel strategies to the sequetial reference results in term of speed-up and efficiency. For more stability in the results, the experimentations were conducted several times on a parallel computer[1].

The table below shows average values for ten experimentations. For each experimentation, the parallel heuristic and the parameters used is detailed. Each experimentation's result is compared to the *express* and the *thorough* methods which are used everyday in the company, and to the *best known* parameters, which we introduce in section 3.2. The value represent the efficiency of the parallel version compared to the 3 sequential versions. And important element is the speed-up between the best known solution and the parallel execution.

Table 1. Experimental results

Try	Heuristic	*Size:Step*	Efficiency of the parallel version compared to (%)			speed-up
			best	express	thorough	
1	1	3 :3	91,83	101,30	99,57	3,03
2	1	3 :1	93,09	103,00	101,10	2,24
3	1	4 :4	96,09	106,98	104,29	1,70
4	1	4 :1	95,42	106,01	103,42	2,05
5	2	3 :3	97,99	108,62	106,35	2,20
6	2	3 :1	94,30	104,44	102,25	1,39
7	2	4 :4	97,53	108,68	105,91	1,53
8	2	5 :5	98,31	109,12	106,61	0,92
9	2	5 :1	103,31	115,02	112,13	0,28
10	3	3 :3 ;5 :5	102,83	116,73	111,72	0,80

The reader can clearly see that parallel optimization gives good results which are very closed to the best known solution almost always better than the solutions given by the express and thorough methods. In the same time, time profit is significant.

For example, the most interesting strategy (number 5) uses the second heuristic with a *size* of 3 and a *step* of 3. Its results are very closed to the best known results (97,99%) and the time profit is very good (220,70%).

5   Conclusion and Future Works

The aim was to resolve the schedule construction for forty drivers. Each day, eight hundreds on-request journeys are added to the schedule. Originally, the scheduler engine was able to make local insertions of a ride in an existing schedule. The insertion was optimized without modifying existing schedule while managing

---

[1] The parallel computer of the University of Reims Champagne-Ardenne is a Sunfire 6800 (SMP 24 x UltraSparc III @900MHz, 24 Go of memory).

every parameter. A first optimization method is used since 2001 to improve the quality of the schedule but the quality of the solution depend on the parameters that are used.

Thanks to the parallel optimization, the scheduler staff does not need to try three or four basic optimizations with different values of the parameters to obtain a good solution. With this parallel method, the result is very close to the best result they could hope and the compute time is light. Robustness is the main benefit of this method which is running since summer 2004. An other key advantage of the parallel solution is the time execution which allows the staff to use it not only during the night, but also during the day.

The next part of the study will be the implementation of a constructive method like Ant Colonies Systems [Hol75][DG97a] to make the optimization more efficient and melt it with other meta-heuristics [OL96].

Acknowledgment

We want to give a special acknowledgment to Eric Domenjoud [DKZ98b] [DKZ98c] who is working on the problem as a consultant now and has been a researcher for years.

References

ACDK96.   Farid Ajili, Carlos Castro, Eric Domenjoud, and Claude Kirchner. Rapport de fin de pré-étude du problème d'affectation des courses pour le GIHP-Champagne. Rapport de fin de contrat, November 1996.

BC94.   Christian Bessiere and Marie-Odile Cordier. Arc-consistency and arc-consitency again. In Manfred Meyer, editor, *Proceedings ECAI'94 Workshop on Constraint Processing*, Amsterdam, 1994.

BHPT98.   V. Bachelet, Z. Hafidi, P. Preux, and E.-G. Talbi. Vers la coopération des métaheuristiques. *Calculateurs parallèles, réseaux et systèmes répartis*, 9(2), 1998. in french.

BPK01.   Philippe Baptiste, Claude Le Pape, and Wim Nuijten Kluwer. constraint-based scheduling: applying constraint programming to scheduling problems. *International Series in Operations Research and Management Sciences*, 39, 2001.

CMRR01.   Van-Dat Cung, Simone L. Martins, Celso C. Robeiro, and Catherine Roucairol. Strategies for the parallel implementation of metaheuristics. *Essays and Surveys in Metaheuristics (C.C. Ribeiro and P. Hansen, editors), Kluwer, 2001*, 2001.

DG97a.   Marco Dorigo and Luca Maria Gambardella. Ant colonies for the traveling salesman problem. *BioSystems*, 1997.

DG97b.   Marco Dorigo and Luca Maria Gambardella. Ant colony system: A cooperative learning approach to the traveling salesman problem. *IEEE Transactions on Evolutionary Computation*, 1(1):53–66, April 1997.

DKZ98a.   Eric Domenjoud, Claude Kirchner, and Jianyang Zhou. Generating Feasible Schedules for a Pick-Up and Delivery Problem. In Michael J. Maher and Jean-Francois Puget, editors, *Proceedings of CP-98*, volume 1520 of *LNCS*, page 467. Springer, 1998. (Poster).

DKZ98b.   Eric Domenjoud, Claude Kirchner, and Jianyang Zhou. *Le manuel de ROUTER*. LORIA, October 1998.

DKZ98c.   Eric Domenjoud, Claude Kirchner, and Jianyang Zhou. The ROUTER transport scheduling system. Technical report, LORIA, October 1998.

DPST03.   Johann Dréo, Alain Pétrowski, Patrick Siarry, and Eric Taillard. *Métaheuristiques pour l'optimisation difficile*. Eyrolles, 2003. French book.

GBD⁺94.   A. Geist, A. Beguelin, J. Dongarra, W. Jiang, R. Manchek, and V. Sunderam. Pvm 3 user's guide and reference manual. Technical report, Oak Ridge National Laboratory, September 1994.

Hol75.   J.H. Holland. Adaptation in natural and artificial systems. *Ann Arbor, Michigan, The University of Michigan Press*, 1975.

MS88.   Kim Marriott and Peter J. Stuckey. *Programming with constraints: an introduction*. Mit Press, 1988.

OL96.   I. Osman and G. Laporte. Metaheuristics in combinatorial optimization, 1996.

Pro93.   P. Prosser. Hybrid algorithms for the constraint satisfaction problem. *Computational Intelligence*, 9:268–299, 1993.

Ros00.   Francesca Rossi. Constraint logic programming, 2000.

Zho98a.   Jianyang Zhou. A Unified Framework for Solving Boolean, Integer and Set Constraints. In *Third International Conference on Systems Science and Systems Engineering, Beijing (China)*, pages 205–210, Beijing, China, August 1998. Scientific and Technical Documents Publishing House.

Zho98b.   Jianyang Zhou. *The Manual of NCL - Version 1.2*. Loria, Campus Scientifique - BP 239, 54506, Vandoeuvre-les-Nancy, France, 1998.

A General Multi-agent Modelling Framework for the Transit Assignment Problem – *A Learning-Based Approach*

Mohammed Wahba[1] and Amer Shalaby[2]

[1] Ph.D. student in Transportation Engineering, Department of Civil Engineering,
University of Toronto, 35 St. George Street, Toronto, Ontario, Canada M5S 1A4
Tel: (416) 978-5049
medhat@cantab.net
[2] Assistant Professor, Department of Civil Engineering, University of Toronto,
35 St. George Street, Toronto, Ontario, Canada M5S 1A4
Tel: (416) 978-5907
amer@ecf.utoronto.ca

Abstract. This paper presents the conceptual development of an innovative modelling framework for the transit assignment problem, structured in a multi-agent way and inspired by a learning-based approach. The proposed framework is based on representing passengers and both their learning and decision-making activities explicitly. The underlying hypothesis is that individual passengers are expected to adjust their behaviour (i.e. trip choices) according to their knowledge and experience with the transit system performance, and this decision-making process is based on a "mental model" of the transit network conditions. The proposed framework, with different specifications, is capable of representing current practices. The framework, once implemented, can be beneficial in many respects. When connected with urban transportation models – such as ILUTE – the effect of different land use policies, which change passenger demand, on the transit system performance can be evaluated and assessed.

1 Introduction

The problem of predicting passenger loads and levels of services on a given transit network that consists of a set of fixed lines is known as the Transit Assignment Problem (TAP), which is an important topic of public transport system analysis. Transit assignment models are widely used as an important planning tool at the strategic and operational levels. They are, therefore, a critical component of multimodal network models of urban transportation systems. Important decisions concerning investment in public transport infrastructure or services are normally supported by evaluation methodologies based on transit assignment models.

Assignment procedures, in general, form the core of any comprehensive transportation model. By modeling passengers' travel behaviour on their journey from origins to destinations, such procedures distribute a given travel demand on a network and attempt to model the interaction between the travel demand and the network supply. Not only does this help determine traffic volumes in roads and transit lines, but it also reflects the service quality of the transport network. The main differences between the various transit assignment models are the hypotheses made, either explicitly or implicitly, on the user's behaviour when faced with route choice decisions. As such, any transit assignment model includes, at its core, a path choice model that describes the

T. Böhme et al. (Eds.): IICS 2004, LNCS 3473, pp. 276–295, 2006.
© Springer-Verlag Berlin Heidelberg 2006

behaviour of transit riders with regards to their choices of transit stops and routes to travel between trip origins and destinations.

Currently, mircosimulations, which allow one to model dynamically individual objects, make it possible to couple the behavioural demand generation models with plausible traffic dynamics allowing for logically consistent feedback. This paper presents the conceptual development of an innovative modeling framework for the transit assignment problem, structured in a multi-agent way and inspired by a learning-based approach. In the framework, it is recognized that individual passengers decide on their travel choices (e.g. departure time, origin/destination transit stops, route choice) for a transit trip on consecutive days; this decision-making process is based on the passenger's experience of the transit system performance.

2   The Transit Assignment Problem

Assignment procedures, in general, attempt to predict traveler flows and levels of services on a given transport network. Although much attention has been given to auto-traffic assignment models, it is well addressed in the literature that the transit assignment process is more complicated than auto-traffic assignment [1, 2]. This complexity is due to:

- Parallel lines, with the same or different frequencies are common features of public transport networks. In addition, how to assign weights to out-of-vehicle time versus in-vehicle time is not a straightforward task.
- While car drivers may depart at any time and free to choose a route which appears convenient to them, transit riders are strongly restricted by the line network and the timetable.
- Transfers and waiting times are significant factors for the transit assignment process. Some passengers may prefer routes with minimum number of transfers, while others minimize their in-vehicle travel time.
- In addition to that transit passengers may need to transfer, they are also faced with connection problems, which encompass temporal constraints such as departure and arrival times at all chosen stops.
- Different sub-modes and the transit mode-chain add more complexity. Not only may different sub-modes have different levels of services, but they may also be perceived differently among passengers.
- Choices in public transport networks are often dependent, as the choice of the next line at a terminal depends on the preceding choice.
- The public transport network structure is very complicated, and the assumption that each passenger is aware of all feasible routes may not be feasible.

Therefore, it has always been a practice to develop special assignment procedures for the transit assignment problem rather than applying variations of traffic assignment algorithms.

2.1   The Current State-of-Art

In the early stages of development, only heuristic algorithms were proposed to solve the TAP, where many of them represent simple modifications of road network assignment procedures; e.g. the all-or-nothing assignment. Prior to the early 1980s, several authors had dealt with the TAP, either as a separate problem or as a subproblem of more complex models. Some important examples of procedures and algorithms proposed to solve the TAP are by Dial [3], Le Clercq [4], Chriqui [5], Chapleau [6], Andreasson [7], and Rapp et al. [8]. Scheele [9], Mandle [10], and Hasselstrom [11], on the other hand, considered the TAP in the context of transit network design models, while Florian [12] and Florian and Spiess [13] dealt with multimodal network equilibrium. One serious limitation of the aforementioned procedures, however, was neglecting congestion effects over the transit system. Last and Leak [14] was the only exception. Nonetheless, their procedure is only appropriate for very special radial networks, which renders the algorithm practically inapplicable to real-world applications [15].

The first mathematical formulation for the TAP was proposed by Spiess [16] and Spiess and Florian [17]. Based on the assumption that passengers minimize "generalized travel times", they proposed a linear programming model and a solution algorithm for the TAP. They assume that passengers face 'strategies' rather than simple paths to make their origin-destination trips over a transit network. De Cea [18] and De Cea and Fernandez [19], later, formulated another linear programming model of the transit assignment, based on the concepts of "common lines" and "transit routes", inspired by early contributions of Le Clercq [4] and Chriqui [5]. Both mathematical models assume flow independent travel and waiting times, and hence do not consider congestion effects.

The next development phase of TAP procedures considered the congestion effects, which is known as the Transit Equilibrium Assignment Problem (TEAP). Many models have been developed to consider this phenomenon, such as De Cea and Fernandez [20]. These models define *passenger-flow-dependent* generalized cost functions and transit riders behave according to Wardrop's first principle [21]. Recognizing the potential differences between passengers' preferences, different stochastic user equilibrium transit assignment models have been proposed, such as Nielsen [1] and Lam et al. [22]. Recently, and accounting for the dynamics and the complex structure of the transit network, dynamic transit assignment models have been developed (such as [23] and [24]); most notably the schedule-based transit assignment model [25].

Although some improvements were made to incorporate congestion effects on passenger waiting time and behaviour, there still are some major limitations that question the applicability of the existing models.

2.2 Limitations of Existing Models

Most of the previously developed models have, either explicitly or implicitly, bounding assumptions that sometimes limit their applicability and/or question the results to be realistic. For instance, some of these assumptions are necessary to speed up the solution algorithm to a reasonable running time, such as the assumption that waiting times at boarding stops or at transfer stops depend only on the headway of the following transit line [2]. While it speeds up computation, it fails to consider the coordination of the timetables, an important feature of the transit network.

Some assume that vehicles always operate on schedule [23, 24], a critical assumption that is always not applicable to congested transit (and transport) networks. Most of the models assume that all passengers are subject to the same weights in their decision-making process on route choice. This sometimes is interpreted that all passengers can access the same or have full information about the system (e.g. through user traveler information system). This is not usually true, as passengers might still choose different routes for the same OD pair according to their different preferences and perceptions of waiting times, walking times, in-vehicle times and transfer penalty.

Some assumptions may be violated by the dynamic nature of the transit-transport network. For instance, it is often assumed that taking over between transit vehicles is not allowed [23]. A typical situation where slow lines depart just before fast lines reveals a possible violation. The unlimited capacity assumption has unrealistic consequences: some lines might be loaded with passengers much beyond the actual capacity while other lines serving the same OD pair are greatly underutilized [22]. Rather than assuming that transit vehicles have unlimited capacity, it has been assumed that all transit vehicles have a fixed capacity [24]. Again, a typical real-sized transit network may operate different vehicle capacities.

The transit assignment process has many choice dimensions, such as departure time choice, origin/destination stop choices, transfer stop(s) choices and route choice. Normally, only one or two dimensions have been considered in previous modeling efforts, e.g. only route choice is considered in Poon et al. [24].

The strategy-based approach [17] is usually criticized for the bias towards over-assigning riders to lines with high combined frequency of transit services and under-assigning riders to those with low combined frequency of services. In addition, with the introduction of Intelligent Transportation Systems (ITS) and Advanced Public Transport Systems (APTS) that provide pre-trip/en-route information, certain segments of the network and many transit riders may not comply with the behavioural assumptions of the model. Moreover, low frequency transit lines may not be assigned as a travel option at all. This procedure does not explicitly calculate transfer times but rather assumes that they depend on the headway. In other words, the coordination of the timetable is not considered.

The schedule-based approach [25], which uses a "diachronic" graph to represent the transit network, also has some drawbacks. The diachronic graph does not represent congestion effects on travel times, unless the graph's structure itself depends on the flow pattern, which will add more complexity. This is important to mention, as the supply variations (i.e. transit system performance) need to be modeled appropriately. The complexity of the assignment process increases more than linearly with the transit line frequencies, because this implies the growth of graph's dimensions. When schedule-based procedures use a shortest path algorithm, they unfortunately have two more weaknesses [2]:

- They may require long computing time. To determine all connections with a shortest path algorithm, it is necessary to perform a search for each possible departure time at the origin stop within the examined time interval. Since acceptable computing time may only be achieved through a significant reduction in departure times, this approach will usually fail to find all connections.
- They may not find all relevant connections. In some networks, even a connection which departs earlier and arrives later than an alternative connection may be attractive for some passengers; e.g. if it is cheaper or requires fewer transfers.

In order to address some of the above limitations, we propose in the next section a general *multi-agent learning-based* modeling framework for the transit assignment problem, using methods from Artificial Intelligence (AI), microsimulation and Geographical Information Systems (GIS).

3 A General Multi-agent Framework

The need for a new modeling framework for the transit assignment problem is increasing. While current models try to capture congestion effects, they do not explicitly deal with:

- The effect of travel time uncertainty on departure time choice. In other words, current transit assignment models do not consider the change in departure time as a response to congestion.
- Formal models of knowledge and cognition. It is important to analyze how departure time and other trip choices take place in daily decision-making, which makes up the transit congestion settings. Without explicitly representing how new experiences are integrated in a passenger's cognitive model, it would be hard to predict passenger's reactions.

Transit assignment is a process of interactions between individual passengers and transit services. These interactions are in both directions: the execution of route choices leads to congestion, yet the expectation of congestion influences choices; and such interactions cannot be overlooked. In reality, this logical deadlock is typically approached through a *feedback mechanism,* usually represented by a learning process [26]. While the task of any transit assignment procedure is to find 'acceptable' routes for each passenger, defining 'acceptable' often leads to the assumption that passengers employ user equilibrium (UE) principles. Nonetheless, the UE formulation presents the mathematical construct of such an assumption, not necessarily the solution to the original transit assignment problem. A different methodology to approach the original problem is using *learning algorithms*, in which passengers search for better routes based on some kind of historic information. It is arguable that learning algorithms do not guarantee a UE solution. One can, however, assume that learning algorithms converge to a fixed point (if every thing is deterministic) or go towards a steady-state density (for stochastic systems if they are Markovian) [26].

In the proposed framework, the underlying assumption is that individual passengers decide about their choices (departure time, origin/destination stops, transfer/connection stops) for a trip on consecutive days and this decision process is based on a "mental model[1]" of the transit network conditions. For a given day d, each passenger has a perception of the transit network conditions as stored in his mental model. This perception is built up over time through experience with the transit system. For day d, a set of choices are made by each individual passenger (e.g. departure time choice and route choice), with the aim to realize a Desired Arrival Time (DAT) at the destination.

Each passenger has an *action space* – a joint set of feasible network paths and departure times for a transit trip. The passenger's action space will possibly be devel-

---

[1] Similar to the concept provided in Ettema et al. [27], for the dynamic traffic assignment problem

oped based on transit stops near trip origin and destination, maximum acceptable number of transfers and timetable information. The outcome of individuals' choices constructs a stochastic process that has to be simulated using a microsimulation model. The specification of the stochastic process largely depends on the interaction between different individuals as well as the transit network performance. The microsimulation model then returns new experience information (e.g. in-vehicle travel time and waiting time) for each individual, which is used to update the mental model for the next day ($d +1$) decision process.

The multi-agent framework structure is presented in Figure (1). The framework shows six agents that can be classified into two categories: *Active Agents* including a GIS-Agent, a Passenger-Agent and a Microsimulation-Agent; and *Assistant Agents* including a Feeder-Agent, a Loader-Agent and a Feedback-Agent. Active agents usually support the decision making process. For example, the GIS-agent decides on the catchment area (i.e. available/accessible transit stops) for a Passenger-agent. Assistant agents facilitate the interaction between active agents. For instance, the loader-agent dynamically establishes connections between passenger-agents and the microsimulation-agent.

The microsimulation-agent is essential to the framework, as services in a transit network are time-dependent. Although there may be pre-defined schedule, transit service performance differs by the time of day and the day of week. Therefore, the optimal path from an origin to a destination also varies by the time of day and among days. In order for passenger-agents to experience these variations, a microsimulation representation of the transit network is important. Representing passengers as agents is critical to account for the differences not only in passengers' preferences but also passengers' learning and adaptation mechanisms. Due to the complicated topology of the transit network, the GIS-agent appears necessary. Complicated structure, such as one stop serving multiple lines and asymmetry in minimal-time paths between the same OD pair, is easily handled using powerful capabilities currently available within GIS packages. Individuals are linked to the transit network simulator to create a simulation system in which both individual decision-making process and system performance (and interactions between both) are adequately represented.

The learning-based approach works as follows. For a given day, the feeder-agent is responsible for handling the input process. The inputs to the framework can be through user interface in the form of an OD trip matrix for the transit mode, or the framework can be integrated with a larger trip-based (or emerging activity-based) urban transportation model that provides the OD transit mode matrix. For each passenger-agent, the GIS-agent communicates to the feeder-agent the catchment area (available/accessible transit stops) and expected access/egress walking times to/from origin/destination transit stops. The outcome of this interaction is a set of possible combinations of departure time and route choices for each passenger-agent – i.e. *action space*. Each passenger-agent has a *planner* component that is responsible for selecting only one combination that reflects that passenger-agent's preferences and is based on the mental model of previous experiences. This results in a stochastic process of different choices for individual passengers; therefore the loader-agent's task is to communicate dynamically passenger-agents' choices to the microsimulation-agent. Then, the microsimulation-agent handles the dynamics of the transportation network according to the passengers' choices and provides experienced measurements for

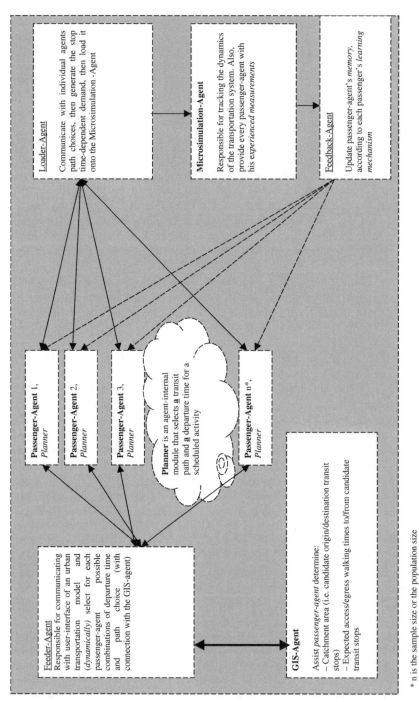

Fig. 1. A General Multi-Agent Transit Assignment Model

individual passengers. Afterwards, the feedback-agent is responsible for updating each passenger-agent's *memory*, according to every passenger's learning mechanism. The whole process repeats for many days.

In principle, this stochastic process should be simulated over multiple runs in sequence, each representing a day, and the decision-making process of an individual passenger should be traced over time. While this sounds simple in principle, it is difficult to implement. Another challenge is that useful results are attainable only with a deep understanding of the learning mechanism. On the one hand, assuming UE conditions has the advantage of describing the state of the system, without really caring how the computational system arrives at it. On the other hand, it is increasingly recognized that socio-economic (e.g. transportation) systems do not necessarily operate at a user equilibrium point [26, 28].

Compared with the stochastic user equilibrium approach, the passenger-agent approach seems to be more robust. In the stochastic UE approach, there is some *external* module that calculates the utility of all options for each passenger and then makes a random weighted draw between these options (e.g. discrete choice theory). When not all options have been previously tried out, the *external* module needs to make assumptions about the option's performance. This might lead to inconsistencies [26]. Agents collect information about their environment as they interact with it, and use it to develop anticipatory models of the environment. The decision process arises from an adaptive learning process driven by the agent's desire to maximize some payoff through its actions over time. The proposed approach is well suited to test and evaluate a broad range of policies that consider, for example, situations with pre-trip and/or en-route information being available to users. For instance, en-route choices occur at stops and are relative to the decision to board a particular run or to wait for another run of the attractive set. The choice of boarding stops is considered to be made before starting the trip, since it is not influenced by unknown events. The agent-based representation allows for different passenger types to be accommodated, for example frequent users (who travel frequently and know routes and scheduled timetables, as well as real system functionality based on previous experience, *fully-informed users*) and occasional users (who sometimes use transit services, so they only know some line routes, the most important routes and their scheduled timetable, but no information about the real system functionality, *ill-informed users*).

In the proposed framework, it is assumed that trip generation and mode choice are constant, and that learning and adaptation takes place only with respect to the transit assignment choice dimensions (departure time choice, origin/destination stops choices, route choice). Therefore, passenger-agents should well represent the population not only in preferences such as DAT and value of travel and waiting times, but also in cognitive parameters such as speed of learning and learning strategies.

It is recognized that the proposed framework may be challenging to implement. However, there is always an unavoidable trade-off between simplicity and elegance on the one hand, and accuracy on the other. Where real life applications are important, as in transportation systems, the accuracy is much more important if the contributions of the research are judged with regard to their relevance to real-world systems [28].

4 The Passenger-Agent

The proposed framework is based on representing passengers and both their learning and decision-making activities *explicitly*. The underlying hypothesis is that individual passengers are expected to adjust their behaviour (i.e. trip choices) according to their experience with the system and the information provided to them. Individual passengers base their daily travel decisions on the accumulated experience gathered from repetitively traveling through the transit network on consecutive days and the information they receive on the day of the trip through, for instance, traveler information systems. It is important to note that all transit passengers may have full knowledge about the transit system (through ITS, APTS), but they might still use different routes for the same OD pair according to their preferences.

Building on this, it is concluded that without explicit *proper* representation of how new experiences are integrated in a passenger's cognitive system, it would be hard to predict passenger's reaction to the experience with the transit system. Therefore, individual behaviour should be modeled as a cyclic process of repetitively making decisions and updating the perception, according to a learning process. Every passenger has a *memory*, where he stores previous experiences, and it reflects the passenger's perception (i.e. knowledge) about the transit network conditions. At the end of day d, the passenger's memory is *updated* with the new experience; the updating process is governed by a *learning mechanism*. The updated passenger's memory, coupled with his decision-making component, is the base for trip decisions at day $d+1$. The decision-making component directs trip decisions to reflect the passenger's preferences (e.g. more preference towards less number of transfers).

It is well established in psychology sciences that alternatives are generated after heuristic search in a solution space, evaluated according to designated criteria, then selected and implemented [28]. The practice has always been to use the random utility choice theory, from the microeconomic field. There are, however, two critical issues about using random utility theory:

- The definition of utility is not clear; which leads to this circular situation: A person chooses an alternative X over Y because s/he prefers it; X is preferred over Y because the person chooses it [29]. Apart from curve fitting to hypothetical variables that lack theoretical foundation and may have logical meanings, the utility definition is still vague.
- By specifying some variables that are believed to affect choices, it is usually assumed that persons have the information about these variables or have the ability to correctly predict their values. In a situation of incomplete information (or even misinformed person), the previous assumption should be relaxed.

In the agent-based framework, there is an underlying assumption that each passenger decides on his travel choices rather than an external utility function that decides for all passengers. The benefit is believed to be twofold. First, while it may yield the same results when sensitivity coefficients attached to the different components of the generalized cost function are randomly generated from a known density function, it gives the flexibility to represent different population characteristics that may not follow a certain distribution. The current practice is to use the error term in the utility function to account for the differences between individuals; this requires some assumptions which are usually not satisfied in the transit assignment problem (e.g. the independence of alternative choices). Second, the assumption, that all individuals are optimizers and they want to maximize their utility, may not hold for the whole population. Optimizers as well as acceptors (and others) behaviour should be represented. Moreover, representing different types of passengers, such as frequent users who have full knowledge about the system and occasional users who have little or no information about the system, is now possible.

The passenger-agent representation means that passengers are treated as agents, who have a memory of previously tried strategies and their respective performance. In general, they choose the strategy with an 'acceptable' performance according to designated criteria, but from time to time they re-try one of the other strategies just to check if its performance is still unchanged. For example, other individual choices to not travel on a specific route may turn this route 'acceptable' for another passenger. Meanwhile, new strategies may be generated and added to the memory.

4.1 The Learning Process

It should be mentioned that the generalized cost of the transit trip is what the passenger learning and adaptation is about. Trip generation and mode choice are assumed to be constant. The generalized transit trip cost usually consists of four components (a) in-vehicle time (b) waiting time (c) penalty of transfer (d) access/egress walking time. The in-vehicle time represents the time spent during the whole trip in a transit run (or sequence of runs). The waiting time consists of three sub-components: waiting time at the origin stop, waiting time at the transfer stop(s), and hidden waiting time where passengers arrive too early/late (i.e. schedule delay) at the destination [1]. The transfer penalty may consist of a fixed cost for making a transfer and a variable cost for the number of transfers. The access/egress walking times depend on the choice of the origin/destination stops, and accordingly will affect the route choice (and the transfer choice as well).

By weighting the trip generalized cost function components, it is permissible for an *acceptable* path to be slower than others in real time provided that it is more attractive in other aspects, such as less number of transfers. With optimizer behaviour, passengers are assumed to travel on a path with a minimum generalized cost; while with satisfying behaviour, passengers are assumed to select the first path that satisfies certain criteria. A certain path with specific values for the four generalized cost components may be perceived differently by different passengers due to different preferences.

The proposed approach assumes that passenger-agents have the ability to make predictions about the transportation network conditions, which have been gained through past experience. Passengers interpret each new experience in the context of previous knowledge to assess whether behaviour should be adjusted. The day-to-day evolution of attributes that make up the generalized cost function, hence, can be explicitly considered through a learning process. It is also assumed that passengers base their perception on the events stored in memory. Individuals will not store information for all possible conditions, but only distinguish between conditions of states that are significantly different in terms of outcome of the event. In other words, passengers classify their experience to differentiate between travel conditions for which expectations of generalized cost function is relatively comparable. In this context, different learning mechanisms can be implemented and tested.

The learning process is concerned with the complete specification of the generalized cost function components, according to which passengers consider their choices on day *d*. This requires explicit treatment of how experience and information about those components on previous days influence the choice on the current day. The proposed approach assumes that learning occurs both with the evolution of within-day and the evolution of day-to-day. The generalized cost function has some fixed components that do not change from day-to-day or within-day, such as the number of transfers for a certain path; no learning is required for these components. Some components change due to within-day dynamics; these attributes are direct functions of service features, such as waiting time and comfort levels. Passenger-agents learn how to estimate these components, or, in the case of available ITS and ATIS, this information is supplied by the system. Other components, which passenger-agents should learn about, include in-vehicle time and transfer time – the learning process involves the estimation of such components. It is important to mention that the existence of ITS or ATIS will not replace the learning process, since information supplied by the system does not totally *overwrite* passengers' memory. Passengers consider new information in the context of past experience; they base their perception on the events stored in memory. Hickman and Wilson [30] developed a framework to evaluate path choices in public transit systems where passengers receive information in real time regarding projected in-vehicle travel times. They reached the conclusion, based on a case study corridor at the Massachusetts Bay Transportation Authority (MBTA), that real time information yields only very modest improvements in passenger service measures (e.g. origin-destination travel times). This reflects that passengers rely more on their *expectations*.

4.2 The Planning Process

Individual passengers are decision makers, who choose a departure time, an origin stop, a destination stop and a route between a given origin and a destination each day. As rational individuals, their aim is to maximize their perceived outcome of their trip by minimizing the generalized cost in relation to some DAT (e.g. work start time). The decision process is based on a cognitive system (i.e. mental model) of the generalized cost of the transit trip, which is updated each day, after the outcome of the trip decision is known. The passengers' knowledge of the transit network will have an effect on the decision making process; simply, unknown routes will not be tried. In this context, different levels of knowledge can be represented, such as frequent users and occasional users. Even when full information is assumed for all passengers, different passengers' preferences will result in different evaluations for the 'acceptable' path for each passenger.

The proposed path choice model considers the home departure time choice, the stop choice and the run (or sequence of runs) choice. The home departure time and stop choices are assumed to be *at-home* choices (i.e. pre-trip), in which passenger-agents consider available information obtained from previous days and the information available from the system (if applicable). The cost associated with a stop includes stop-specific components, such as presence of shops, and components that represent the average cost associated with all runs available at this stop (i.e. *effectiveness of a stop*). Once a passenger-agent arrives at a stop, a specific run choice is considered an adaptive choice, in which, besides previous information, the passenger considers situations that occur during the trip, for example waiting time. The existence of information, through

ITS and APTS, will influence the passenger-agent adaptive choice behaviour at stops. It is important to mention that, because of the dynamic representation of the transportation network (i.e. a microsimulation model), the adaptive choice is relative not only to the transit line, as in static models, but also to the specific run of each line. In other words, the proposed approach considers the path choice as time-dependent.

The mental model reflects the outcome of the new trip as well as the outcome of previous trips, all stored in memory. Each passenger has a memory, in which relevant aspects of previous trips are stored, but not all are retrievable. This may be because some experiences are too old or not considered as representative. Using the mental model and accessing resources in the memory, each passenger plans his transit trip decisions each day; i.e. a departure time, an origin stop, a destination stop and a route. There could be an assumption that there is no en-route replanning, so that passengers are committed to their plans for the whole trip duration; or they can have adaptive choice behaviour throughout the trip; for example, a passenger may have a *master plan*, and in case of difficulties pursuing it s/he switches to a *backup plan*. Where ITS and APTS exist, en-route re-planning can take place.

The UE assumption considers that no passenger believes that he can improve his perceived trip utility with unilaterally action. This, in fact, means conducting a search process for all available paths and selecting the best one. Where a path has not been tried before, a utility value is to be assigned to that path, and it does not necessarily have to be consistent with the actual performance. The decision-making activity has a mechanism of selecting remembered plans that are stored in the memory. For each plan, there is a generalized cost value, which measures the plan performance. This also can be called the *score* of the plan, so that agents can compare scores of different plans stored in memory and choose based on the performance. The generalized function can include other performance criteria, which can be agent-specific in some cases to reflect different preferences between passengers. Other selecting mechanisms can be easily implemented. For example, a *stress-based*[2] mechanism which reflects the reluctance of passengers to change their *preferred* routes (i.e. routes that have been used more frequently), even they are no longer the optimal ones, can be easily implemented. In this way, one can test different policies that address the stress-threshold of passengers in order to promote different service characteristics or introducing new services (e.g. BRT systems). Also note that transit riders do not usually change their choices frequently, even after a bad experience. Each individual, therefore, may have an exploration period, during which the passenger does not change his transit option.

The main idea is that it is never the case that passengers choosing among alternatives are informed about probabilities of the outcomes. They normally support their own expectations about the outcomes in evaluating different alternatives, based on their previous experience. The existence of information about the expected performance of the transit system (e.g. ITS, APTS) will affect the passenger choices. This information, when provided to the passenger, can be interpreted as a *recent* experience, added to the memory, and then combined with *previous* experiences for the usage in the decision-making process. Planning requires that passengers can anticipate the consequences of their choices, presumably by developing an internal model of the environment through experience.

---

[2] The idea of stress-based mechanism is illustrated in Salvini [32]

5 The Microsimulation-Agent

The microsimulation component is important for modeling transit system networks, in which both line service frequency and OD trip demand are time varying. The transit network is highly dynamic because service characteristics change constantly during the day and among days. Moreover, schedule coordination is essential for path finding within the transit network, and the optimal path is very sensitive to the time of the trip. Transit networks need to be treated dynamically, as active traversals and transfer nodes of the network are dynamic [31]. To capture the dynamics of the transit system, a time-dependent self-updated representation is needed, i.e. a microsimulation model.

In previously developed approaches, all transfers between lines are described by timetables. Accordingly, different routes will be optimal based on given criteria during the day, thus different assignment models can be used (usually called deterministic time-dependent models). Current assignment models do not consider properly the interaction between transit vehicles and other general traffic sharing the same road, although transit vehicles are usually delayed by other general traffic. In principle, to describe these delays, auto and transit assignment models should interact at the link-level. The argument that these delays are usually reflected by the timetables does not hold for long-term forecasting, where it might be easier to model delays instead of specifying in-vehicle time manually for each planned scenario [1].

A typical dynamic problem with network graph representation instead of a microsimulation model is illustrated by this simple situation. When a passenger leaves a transit vehicle and arrives at a boarding link for a transfer, the network loading process for this passenger has to be suspended at this moment in time until the movements of all other passengers have been simulated at least up to this moment, in order to calculate, for example, the correct dwell time at the current boarding link [24]. Such situation is likely to occur in any transit network. The difficulties in dealing with such dynamics in a network graph representation raise the need for microsimulation models as a potential candidate that it is structured to take care of this kind of dynamics.

Other dynamics of the transit system include congestion effects and asymmetric interactions between individual passengers. For a congested transit network with bottlenecks, only a portion of passengers may get the first arriving vehicle at some stations/stops. The residual passengers will be served by the next coming vehicles or transfer to alternative routes. Hence, the passenger overload delay at a station/stop should be determined endogenously to the system. This can be done according to the equilibrium characteristics of the congested transit network, such as in Lam et al. [22]; this, however, is based on the equilibrium conditions that may not apply. The asymmetric interactions can be of two kinds [24]:

- The costs of users in successive time periods influence each other: the cost of arriving passengers at stops is influenced by earlier passengers boarding the transit vehicle, but not the reverse way.
- The cost of boarding passengers is influenced by the number of passengers occupying the transit vehicle, but not the reverse way.

In addition to the aforementioned dynamics of the transit network, the current practice of using *nominal frequencies* to determine the set of attractive lines for a given pair of nodes is no longer correct. Nominal frequencies should be replaced by *effective frequencies*, which depend on the flows over the transit network. This means that attractive transit links cannot be defined in advance. In other words, the trip assignment process and defining attractive sets cannot be separated.

The transit network is dynamic in nature, as available services of the network keep changing through time. In order to account for all the transit network dynamics, the microsimulation-agent is introduced. Simulation, in general, is an appropriate tool when analytical methods have little predictive power. Not only do microsimulation models describe the behaviour of individual decision makers, but they also capture the interaction between the system level and the individual level, due for instance to limitations of system capacity. Interactions between individuals and with the system level affect the assignment process; for example, the trip duration is influenced by the occurrence of congestion that is determined by interaction between transit supply and decisions of other individuals to use the transit network at particular times on particular routes. The microsimulation-agent is expected to handle the transit network dynamics and asymmetric costs involved in the transit assignment process. Microsimulation models have recently been considered as an essential component in urban transportation planning models, such as ILUTE [33].

6 The GIS-Agent

The purpose of the GIS-agent is to store the geocoded data of transit trips (origin and destination of each trip), to define for each transit trip access/egress walking times between any trip origin/destination and a particular transit stop. It is also used to define the catchment area for individual passengers, in order to determine the available/accessible transit stops for each passenger-agent. The GIS-agent is essential to define for each passenger-agent the initial set of possible/eligible transit paths, where temporal and/or spatial constraints may apply (e.g. catchment area of 300 meters).

Not only does the access walking time to an origin transit stop affect the route choice, but also the egress walking time and/or accessibility from the destination transit stop. While it has always been overlooked, the stop choice is very critical to the transit assignment process and may affect considerably the loads on all routes; changing a stop most probably results in changing the route (and hence the transfer connection).

It is acknowledged that the topology of the transit network is very complex. In the transit network, one stop may serve multiple transit routes and many routes may be run on the same street. In addition, the minimal-time path in the transit network is not symmetric in terms of origin and destination pairs [34]. Recently, some transit applications have included a GIS model as an essential component to treat the complex nature of the transit network, with different public transport modes, lines and transfer points [31]. The GIS-agent is important to test and evaluate land-use policies, especially when spatial analysis is required.

7 Assistant-Agents

There are three assistant-agents: the feeder-agent, the loader-agent and the feedback-agent. The purpose of the assistant-agents is to build modularity into the framework and separate the major three active-agents via 'bridges'. These bridges enable all the combinations of different technologies and/or architectures of the active-agents implementations. Besides, each assistant-agent has another task for the transit assignment process.

The feeder-agent is responsible for communicating either with users or other large-scale land-use and transportation models for the input process. The feeder-agent holds information about passenger's initial (or preferred) departure time and other constraints that may restrict departure time changes (these constraints can be agent-specific). In addition, the feeder-agent is the bridge between the GIS-agent and each passenger-agent to supply each passenger with a list of feasible plans for the transit trip. These plans are generated based on the available/accessible transit stops to that passenger supplied by the GIS and the preferred departure time obtained by the feeder-agent. This list can be supplied once, that contains all possible plans for a given trip origin-destination, or can be dynamically updated every time the departure time is changed.

The chosen plans by different individual passengers are output to the microsimulation-agent; this connection is made using the loader-agent. The loader-agent keeps track of each stop time-dependent demand and dynamically loads and establishes connections between passenger-agents and the microsimulation model. When the simulation is finished, its output is processed by the feedback-agent. The feedback-agent is responsible for collecting information about each passenger's trip cost components (i.e. waiting times, in-vehicle times, transfer times[3]). It is also in charge of updating each passenger's memory with the new experience according to every passenger's learning mechanism; this can be governed, for example by Reinforcement Learning principles [35].

8 Connectivity with Activity-Based Urban Transportation Models

The evolution of travel demand modeling is now leading to the new activity-based models, as the core of the next generation of transportation forecasting models. This evolution has been driven by the need for greater sensitivity to policies that affect more than just the broad characteristics of urban form, and target the mechanisms that produce human travel behaviour.

Transit assignment is a key component of activity-based land-use and transportation models. Activity-based microsimulation models require transit assignment models to be sensitive to dynamic variations in travel demand, and have the ability to provide feedback on average transit travel times in a way that is consistent with traffic congestion and service interruptions. Both requirements are included in the proposed multi-agent learning-based approach, by its very nature.

The proposed framework structure is formulated in a way that is compatible with the recently developed activity-based models for urban transportation systems. The agent-based concept implemented here facilitates direct connectivity with agent-based activity-based urban transportation models, such as ILUTE [33]. Within ILUTE, each person is represented as a distinct entity that makes detailed travel plans in both time and space. With specific manipulation of the feeder-agent, passenger-agents can represent the same individuals modeled in the activity-based models that happen to choose transit as the primary mode of travel (and even borrow the same characteristics to maintain consistency, such as waiting time preference) – see Figure (2). Besides, the introduction of the GIS-based component allows for appropriate handling of spatial land-use issues that are difficult to be addressed by a transportation microsimulation model alone.

[3] Access/egress walking times are assumed to be fixed and pre-determined by the GIS-agent

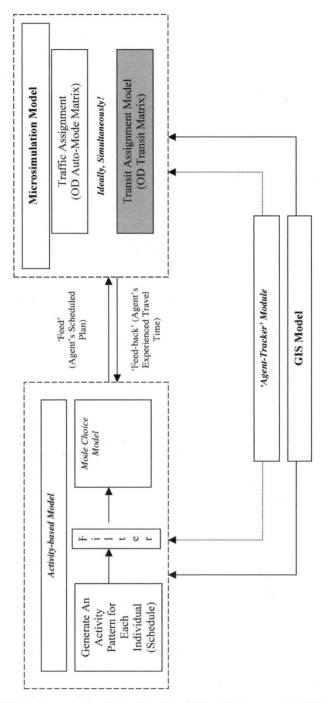

Fig. 2. Connectivity with Activity-Based Urban Transportation Model

By connecting with emerging activity-based microsimulation urban transportation models, the multi-agent learning-based approach becomes suitable for operational planning of transit services as well as for long-range strategic planning. It has usually been conceived that highly detailed, dynamic transit assignment models are not adequate for strategic planning as they require precise input data for detailed network planning, which are not generally available for long future scenarios; or that precise forecasts are not necessary for strategic planning. ILUTE, for example as a microsimulation model for long-range transportation planning, is likely to be capable of providing inputs for long-range scenarios at a fairly accurate level of detail.

9 Comments and Future Research

The proposed *multi-agent learning-based* transit assignment approach could accommodate all the different views of the transit assignment problem, as well as tries to resolve many of the limitations of existing approaches. The framework, inspired by a learning-based approach, is able to represent different behavioural hypotheses, such as user equilibrium as well as others. It has been shown that learning and adaptation methodology is a powerful tool in modeling the dynamics in responses over time. The transportation system, in particular the transit system, is complicated, and given the systems' path dependencies and the time-varying factors, system equilibrium is often not achieved. This represents a great challenge to equilibrium-based models. Therefore, in the absence of explicit equilibrium conditions, a future state of the transportation system can only be estimated by explicitly tracing the evolutionary path of the system over time, beginning with current knowledge conditions [36]. The multi-agent-based representation increases the possibility of emergent behaviour to be predicted, which is not *hardwired* into the model.

As already indicated, the proposed multi-agent framework, with different specifications, is capable of representing current practices. For example, a simple network graph representation may replace the microsimulation model and acts as the microsimulation-agent. While this is not desirable for the previously mentioned reasons, this is still possible because of the modular approach.

The proposed approach can simultaneously predict how passengers will choose their routes and estimate the total passenger travel cost in a congested network, as well as run loads on different transit routes. It results in a dynamic network manipulation (through the microsimulation model), time-dependent trip choices, and a dynamic network loading procedure. The framework, once fully implemented, can be beneficial in many respects. It can be used to model long-term planning activities (e.g. the introduction of BRT services), as well as short-term (temporary) planning activities (e.g. construction site scenario). It can be used to simulate the performance of an existing transit system operating on pre-announced schedules under variable passenger demand conditions, or to evaluate the effects of changes in schedules, routes or passenger demand on the system performance. In cases of congested transit networks, it can be used to test different alternative methods of relieving congestion. New services and modifications to existing service characteristics can be evaluated and assessed under different passenger behavioural patterns. The model can also be used to evaluate the impact of different situations on the transit assignment process, even if they are not directly related to the transit service. It reflects the impacts of non-related transit activities on the transit service conditions, and consequently passenger travel behaviour – e.g. construction site (temporary) impact on the transit assignment process. When connected with urban transportation models – such as ILUTE – the effect of different land use policies, which change passenger demand, on the transit system performance can be evaluated and assessed.

The proposed framework emphasises the importance of representing the supply side and the demand side simultaneously. The change of the transit service affects passenger's travel behaviour, yet passenger's travel behaviour affects the transit service. When connected to trip-based (or activity-based) models, the model can be used to test the impact of the implementation of measures, such as new BRT systems, on mode choice. The multi-agent approach provides the most consistent way of combining traffic and transit in a simultaneous modeling framework; therefore it is able to represent the impact of roadway congestion on transit service and *vice versa*. This approach *explicitly* accounts for different preferences and characteristics of the transit population. By adding more factors to the transit option generalized cost function, one can model behavioural situations where, for example, passengers may walk a further distance to get a seat on the bus or may choose transit options with higher travel times to avoid overcrowding. These factors can be general such as comfort level or transit route reliability, or agent-specific such as preferences for stops with shopping malls.

The proposed approach acknowledges the importance of maintaining explicit representation of information available to passengers, so that it allows for explicit modeling and evaluations of operational impacts of investing in new technologies for traveler information systems (e.g. ITS and APTS). It is also possible to analyze and evaluate different planning polices at the operational level, such as Transit Signal Priority (TSP) and control operation strategies that address reliability issues (e.g. holding policy), as well as at the strategic level, such as the introduction of a new BRT line or schedule changes.

An operational prototype of the proposed modelling framework has been developed and tested. The purpose of this prototype is to demonstrate the feasibility and applicability of the new framework. A hypothetical transit network has been developed in the Paramics™ microsimulation platform. A population of transit riders has been synthesized and the multi-agent learning-based algorithm has been coded. Reinforcement Learning principles are used to represent passenger's adaptation and learning process – for more details, refer to Wahba and Shalaby [37]. The implementation of the prototype raised many issues that need to be addressed in future research, refer to Wahba [38] for a detailed discussion. The prototype is intended to reflect the proposed structure with all connections, but possibly with simple implementation of subcomponents. In the near future, a full implementation, possibly using medium-size real transit system, will be conducted.

References

1. Nielsen, O.A. (2000). "A stochastic transit assignment model considering differences in passengers utility functions", *Transportation Research Part B, 34:377-402*
2. Friedrich, M., I. Hofsaess and S. Wekeck (2001). "Timetable-based transit assignment using branch and bound techniques", *Journal of Transportation Research Record 1752:100-107*

3. Dial, R. B. (1967). "Transit pathfinder algorithm", *Highway Research Record, 205:67-85*
4. Le Clercq, F. (1972). "A public transport assignment method", *Traffic Engineering and Control, 14(2):91-96*
5. Chriqui, C. (1974). "Reseaux de transport en commun: Les problemes de cheminement et d'acces", *Center of Transporation Research: University of Montrea. Publication No. 11.*
6. Chapleau, R. (1974). "Reseaux de transport en commun: Structure informatique et affecta-tionn", *Center of Transporation Research: University of Montrea. Publication No. 13*
7. Andreasson, I. (1976). "A method for the analysis of transit networks", in: M. Ruebens, ed., *2nd European Congress on Operations Research. Amsterdam: North-Holland*
8. Rapp, M.G., P. Mattenberger, S. Piguet and A. Robert-Grandpierre (1976). "Interactive graphics systems for transit route optimization", *Journal of Transportation Research Record, 559:73-88*
9. Scheele, C.E. (1977). "A mathematical programming algorithm for optimal bus frequencies", *Institute of Technology, University of Linkoping*
10. Mandle, C. (1980). "Evaluation and optimization of urban public transportation networks", *European Journal of Operational Research, 5:396-404*
11. Hasselstrom, D. (1981). "Public transportation planning: A mathematical programming approach", *PhD thesis, University of Goteburg*
12. Florian, M. (1977). "A traffic equilibrium model of travel by car and public transit modes", *Transportation Science, 11(2):166-179*
13. Florian, M. and H. Spiess (1983). "On binary mode choice/assignment models", *Transportation Science, 17(1):32-47*
14. Last, A. and S.E. Leak (1976). "Transept: A bus model", *Traffic Engineering and Control, 17(1):14-20*
15. De Cea, J. and E. Fernandez (2002). "Transit Assignment Models", Chapter 30 in: *Handbook of Transport Modeling* (ed. David A. Hensher and Kenneth J. Button): *Pergamon*
16. Spiess, H. (1983). "On optimal route choice strategies in transit networks", *Center of Transport Research, University of Montreal, Publication No. 286*
17. Spiess, H. and M. Florian (1989). "Optimal strategies: A new assignment model for transit networks", *Transportation Research B, 23(2):83-102*
18. De Cea, J. (1986). "Rutas y estrategias optimas en modelos de asignacion a redes de transporte publico", presented at: *IV Congreso Panamericano de ingenieria de transito y transporte, Santiago*
19. De Cea, J. and E. Fernandez (1989). "Transit assignment to minimal routes: An efficient new algorithm" *Traffic Engineering and Control, 30 (10):491-494*
20. De Cea, J. and E. Fernandez (1993). "Transit assignment for congested public transport systems: An equilibrium model" *Transportation Science, 27:133-147*
21. Wardrop, J.G. (1952). "Some theoretical aspects of road traffic research", *Proceedings of the Institution of Civil Engineering, Part II:325-378*
22. Lam, W.H.K., Z.Y. Gao, K.S. Chan and H. Yang (1999). "A stochastic user equilibrium assignment model for congested transit networks", *Transportation Research Part B, 33:351-368*
23. Tong, C.O. and S.C. Wong (1999). "A stochastic transit assignment model using a dynamic schedule-based network", *Transportation Research Part B, 33:107-121*
24. Poon, M.H., S.C. Wong and C.O. Tong (2004). "A dynamic schedule-based model for congested transit networks", *Transportation Research Part B, 38:343-368*
25. Nuzzolo, A., F. Russo and U. Crisalli (2003). "Transit Network Modelling: The schedule-based approach.", *Collana Trasnporit, FrancoAngeli s.r.l., Milano, Italy*
26. Raney, B and K. Nagel (2003). "Truly agent-based strategy selection for transportation simulations", *Transportation Research Board Annual Meeting, Washington, D.C., Paper 03-4258*

27. Garling, T. (1998). "Behavioural assumptions overlooked in travel-choice modelling", chapter 1 in: *Travel Behaviour Research: Updating the State of Play* (ed. Juan de Dios Ortuzar, David Hensher and Sergio Jara-Diaz): *Pergamon*

28. Ettema, D., G. Tamminga, H. Timmermans and T. Arentze (2003). "A Micro-Simulation Model System of Departure Time and Route Choice under Travel Time Uncertainty", *10th International Conference on Travel Behaviour Research, Lucerne, August.*

29. McNully, T.M. (1990). "Economic theory and human behaviour", *The Journal of Value Inquiry, 24:325-333*

30. Hickman, M. D. and N. H. M. Wilson (1995). "Passenger Travel Time and Path Choice: Implications of Real-Time Transit Information." *Transportation Research 3(4): 211-226*

31. Huang, R. and Z.R. Peng (2001b). "An object-oriented GIS data model for transit trip planning systems", *Transportation Research Board, the 81st Annual Meeting, Paper 02-3753, November*

32. Salvini, P. (2003). "Design and development of the ILUTE operational prototype: a comprehensive microsimulation model of urban systems", *Ph.D. Thesis, Graduate Department of Civil Engineering, University of Toronto, Toronto*

33. Salvini, P. and E.J. Miller (2003). "ILUTE: An operational prototype of a comprehensive microsimulation model of urban systems", *paper presented at the 10th International Conference on Travel Behaviour Research, Lucerne, August*

34. Huang, R. and Z.R. Peng (2001a). "An integrated of network data model and routing algorithms for online transit trip planning", ", *Transportation Research Board, the 80th Annual Meeting, Washington, D.C., Paper 01-2963*

35. Sutton, R.S. and A.G. Barto (1998). "Reinforcement Learning: An Introduction", *Cambridge, Massachussetts: MIT Press.*

36. Miller, E. (2003). "Microsimulation." Chapter 12 in: *Transportation System Planning: Methods and Applications* (ed. Konstadinos G. Goulias). *CRC Press*

37. Wahba, M. and A. Shalaby (forthcoming). "A Multi-Agent Learning-Based Approach to the Transit Assignment Problem: A Prototype." *accepted for presentation at the 84th TRB Annual Meeting, January 9-13, 2005: Washington, D.C. and for publication in the Journal of Transportation Research Record*

38. Wahba, M. (2004). "A New Modelling Framework for the Transit Assignment Problem: A Multi-Agent Learning-Based Approach." *M.A.Sc. Thesis (unpublished), Graduate Department of Civil Engineering, University of Toronto, Toronto.*

OLSIM: Inter-urban Traffic Information

Daniel Weber, Roland Chrobok, Sigurdur Hafstein, Florian Mazur,
Andreas Pottmeier, and Michael Schreckenberg

University Duisburg-Essen
Lotharstr. 1, 47048 Duisburg, Germany
{weber,chrobok,hafstein,mazur,pottmeier,
schreckenberg}@traffic.uni-duisburg.de
http://www.traffic.uni-duisburg.de

Abstract. Nowadays detailed and reliable information about current
and future traffic states is a crucial requirement not only for each modern
traffic control centre, but also for driver accessible traffic information
applications. In this work the novel traffic information system OLSIM
is presented that is based on three components. The first is a highly
realistic traffic flow model with which all vehicles in a large scale network
are simulated. The second component consists of efficient data processing
and forecast algorithms that form heuristics from a large database that is
fed every minute by traffic data of 4,000 inductive loop detectors across
the road network. The third is a graphical user interface which can be
accessed at www.autobahn.nrw.de. More than 200,000 users each day
indicate the importance of such a system.

1 Introduction

The vehicular traffic has risen in a dramatic manner, particularly in densely
populated regions. Whereas at first the autobahns could handle the traffic demand easily, nowadays, the existing autobahn network has reached its capacity
limit. This is in particular true for the German state of North Rhine-Westphalia
with its large urban areas in the Rhine-Ruhr region (Dortmund, Essen, Duisburg, Düsseldorf) and around Cologne. The daily occurring traffic jams cause
significant economic and ecological damage, and an enlargemant of the existing network is usually not possible. The prognosis for the future paints an even
worse picture as the demand will increase further. New information systems and
traffic management concepts are thus truly needed. Therefore, we established
the advanced traffic information system OLSIM (**OnL**ine Traffic **SIM**ulation)
which gives the internet user the opportunity to get information about the current traffic state, a 30, and a 60 minute prognosis of the autobahn traffic in
North Rhine-Westphalia. Our approach to generate the traffic state in the whole
autobahn network is to use locally measured traffic data, as the input into an
advanced cellular automaton traffic simulator. These measured data, which are
delivered minute by minute, are mainly provided by about 4,000 loop detectors
and include especially the number of vehicles and trucks passed, the average

T. Böhme et al. (Eds.): IICS 2004, LNCS 3473, pp. 296–306, 2006.
© Springer-Verlag Berlin Heidelberg 2006

speed of the passenger cars and trucks, and the occupancy, i.e., the sum of the times a vehicle covers the loop detector. The simulator does not only deliver information about the traffic states in regions not covered by measurement, but also gives reasonable estimates for other valuable quantities like travel times for routes, a quantity that is not directly accessible from the measurements of the detectors. As a further improvement we combine the current traffic data and heuristics of aggregated and classified traffic data to forecast the future traffic state. In the first step we gave a short-term forecast for 30 minutes, which was extended in the next step by a 60 minute prognosis. This information is completed by the temporal and spatial road work and road closures. All these valuable traffic information is integrated in a Java applet that can be accessed by every internet user at `www.autobahn.nrw.de`.

2   Outline of the Traffic Information System OLSIM

The intention in developing the traffic information system OLSIM is to offer the opportunity to inform the road user fast and efficient about the current and the predictive traffic state. Therefore, the information mentioned above has to be collected and prepared in a manner that is useful for the user. The general setup of the traffic information system OLSIM is depicted in Fig. 1.

First of all the different kinds of data have to be collected. Especially, the traffic data are stored in a database. These are sent from 4,000 loop detectors to the central OLSIM server every minute. The same holds for the data of the control states of about 1,800 variable message signs (VMS) that are located across the network. Furthermore, the data of road works are sent from the traffic centrals to OLSIM. The messages of short term construction areas are sent daily, those of permanent construction areas every two weeks. The data include the location and the duration of the construction area and an estimate whether the construction area will cause a congestion or not.

Another data source are the so called RDS/TMC-messages. These messages are information provided by the traffic warning service and include all kind of warnings concerning the current traffic like traffic jams, accidents, road closures, and reroutings. These data are sent to the OLSIM server immediately when they are generated.

To generate a valid picture of the traffic state many kinds of data fusion techniques are needed. First, the actual traffic data are integrated into the microscopic traffic simulator. Using it, every vehicle that is measured at any time at one of the 4,000 loop detectors is directly fed into the simulation and virtually moves on. In this way the point information of the loop detectors is merged into a network wide traffic state. Such simulations are running for the current traffic state, for the 30 minute, and for the 60 minute forecast. In contrast to the online simulation, the forecasts are based on a combination of the actual traffic data and heuristics that are frequently generated and stored in a second database.

These heuristic traffic patterns are aggregated data which are classified in different days (work days, holidays, etc.) and secondary data like road constructions, variable message signs, and special events.

The second level of data fusion is done in the java applet at the website
www.autobahn.nrw.de. Traffic state, construction areas, and road closures are
integrated in one graphical user interface. Here each section is colored according
to its calculated traffic state. Moreover, the construction areas and the road
closures are marked in the map at their location. Their temporal parameters are
shown in the status bar. The user can easily choose between the current traffic
situation, the 30, and the 60 minute prognosis.

The microscopic traffic simulation, on which the core of the information system
tem is based, is focused on in the next section.

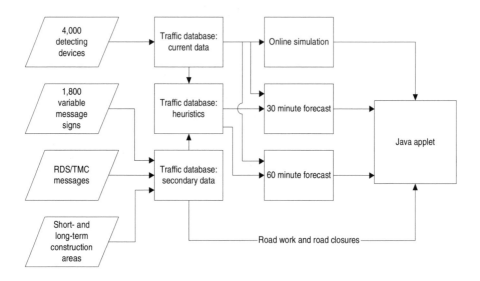

Fig. 1. The architecture of the traffic information system OLSIM

3   Simulation Model

The kernel of the online simulation is an advanced and highly realistic traffic
simulation model. Because the data is fed into the simulator and processed by it
every minute it has to be at least real-time. Due to their design cellular automata
models are very efficient in large-scale network simulations [1]. The first cellular
automaton model for traffic flow, that was able to reproduce some characteristics
of real traffic, like jam formation, was suggested by Nagel and Schreckenberg in
1992 [2]. Their model has been continuously refined in the last 10 years. The
model we implemented in our simulator uses smaller cells in comparison with
the original Nagel-Schreckenberg model, a slow-to-start rule, anticipation, and
brake lights. With these extensions the cellular automaton traffic model is able
to reproduce all empirically observed traffic states. Further, we use two classes
of different vehicles, passenger cars and trucks, where the trucks have a lower
maximum velocity and different lane changing rules.

Smaller cells allow a more realistic acceleration and more speed bins. Currently an elementary cell size of 1.5 m is used, in contrast to the 7.5 m in the original Nagel-Schreckenberg model. This corresponds to speed bins of 5.4 km/h and an acceleration of 1.5 m/s² $(0 - 100$ km/h in 19 s) which is of the same order as the "comfortable" acceleration of about 1 m/s². A vehicle occupies $2 - 5$ consecutive cells. By using velocity dependent randomization [3], realized through the introduction of "slow-to-start rules", meta stable traffic flows can be reproduced in the simulation, a phenomenon observed in empirical studies of real traffic data [4]. The inclusion of anticipation and brake lights [5] in the modeling leads to a more realistic driving, i.e., the cars no longer determine their velocity solely in dependency of the distance to the next car in front, but also take regard to its speed and whether it is reducing its speed or not.

There is only one global parameter in the Nagel-Schreckenberg model, the probability constant (or dawdling parameter) p, and every vehicle, say vehicle n, is completely determined by two parameters: its position $x_n(t)$ and its velocity $v_n(t) \in \{0, 1, ..., v_{max}\}$ at time t. When the vehicle n decides in the time-step $t \mapsto t + 1$ how fast it should drive, it does this by considering the distance $d_{n,m}(t)$, i.e., the number of empty cells, to the next vehicle m in front. The modifications mentioned above of the Nagel-Schreckenberg model imply that we have to add few new parameters to the model. When the simulation algorithm decides whether a vehicle n should brake or not, it does not only consider the distance to the next vehicle m in front, but estimates how far the vehicle m will move during this time-step (anticipation). Note, that the moves are done in parallel, so the model remains free of collision. This leads to the effective gap

$$d_{n,m}^{\text{eff}}(t) := d_{n,m}(t) + \max(v_m^{\text{min}}(t) - d_S, 0)$$

seen by vehicle n at time t. In this formula d_S is a safety distance and

$$v_m^{\text{min}}(t) := \min(d_{m,l}(t), v_m(t)) - 1,$$

is a lower bound of how far the vehicle m will move during this time-step. $d_{m,l}(t)$ is the number of free cells between car m and car l in front of it. Brake lights are further components of the anticipated driving. They allow drivers to react to disturbances in front of them earlier by adjusting their speed. The variable $b_n(t) = $ on if car n has its brake lights on and $b_n(t) = $ off if they are off.

Several empirical observations suggest that drivers react in a temporal- rather than a spatial-horizon [7,8]. For this reason the velocity-dependent temporal interaction horizon

$$t_n^S(t) := \min(v_n(t), h)$$

is introduced to the model. The constant h determines the temporal range of interaction with the brake light $b_m(t)$ of the car m ahead. Car n does only react to $b_m(t)$ if the time to reach the back of car m, assuming constant velocity $(v_n = const.)$ and car m standing still, is less than $t_n^S(t)$, i.e.,

$$t_{n,m}^h(t) := \frac{d_{n,m}(t)}{v_n(t)} < t_n^S(t) .$$

The estimations for h vary from 6 s [7], 8 s [8], 9 s [9] to 11 s [10]. Another estimation can be obtained from the analysis of the perception sight distance. In [11] velocity-dependent perception sight distances are presented that, for velocities up to 128 km/h, are larger than 9 s. Therefore h is set to 6 s as a lower bound for the time headway [12].

The third modification of the Nagel-Schreckenberg model implemented in the simulator is a velocity dependent randomization, which means that the probability constant p is replaced with a probability function dependent on the velocity of the vehicle. Further, the probability is also a function of the brake light of the next vehicle in front. In every time-step for every vehicle n with vehicle m next in front, the probability that the vehicle n brakes is

$$p_n = p(v_n(t), b_m(t)) := \begin{cases} p_b, & \text{if } b_m(t) = \text{on and } t_{n,m}^h(t) < t_n^S(t), \\ p_0, & \text{if } v_n(t) = 0, \\ p_d, & \text{default} . \end{cases}$$

The parameter p_0 tunes the upstream velocity of a wide moving jam and p_d controls the strength of the fluctuations.

With this parameter set the model is calibrated to the empirical data. The best agreement can be achieved for $d_s = 7$ cells, $h = 6$, $p_b = 0.96$, $p_0 = 0.5$, and $p_d = 0.1$. For a detailed analysis of the parameter set see [12]. To sum up, to move the vehicles forward in the network the algorithm executes the following steps in parallel for all vehicles n:
Move forward (drive):

- Step 0: Initialization:
  For car n find the next car m in front.
  Set $p_n := p(v_n(t), b_m(t))$ and $b_n(t+1) := $ off.

- Step 1: Acceleration:

$$v_n(t + \frac{1}{3}) := \begin{cases} v_n(t), & \text{if } b_n(t) = \text{on or } (b_m(t) = \text{on and } t_n^h(t) < t_n^S(t)), \\ \min(v_n(t) + 1, v_{\max}), & \text{default.} \end{cases}$$

- Step 2: Braking:

$$v_n(t + \frac{2}{3}) := \min(v_n(t + \frac{1}{3}), d_{n,m}^{\text{eff}}(t)).$$

  Turn brake light on if appropriate:

$$\text{if } v_n(t + \frac{2}{3}) < v_n(t), \text{ then } b_n(t+1) := \text{on.}$$

- Step 3: Randomization with probability p_n:

$$v_n(t+1) := \begin{cases} \max(v_n(t + \frac{2}{3}) - 1, 0), & \text{with prob. } p_n, \\ v_n(t + \frac{2}{3}), & \text{default.} \end{cases}$$

Turn brake light on if appropriate:

$$\text{if } p_n = p_b \text{ and } v_n(t+1) < v_n(t+\tfrac{2}{3}),$$
$$\text{then } b_n(t+1) := \text{on.}$$

- Step 4: Move (drive):

$$x_n(t+1) := x_n(t) + v_n(t+1).$$

Free lane changes are needed so that vehicles can overtake slower driving passenger cars and trucks. When designing rules for the free lane changes, one should take care of that overtaking vehicles do not disturb the traffic on the lane they use to overtake to much, and one has to take account of German laws, which prohibit overtaking a vehicle to the left. Further, it is advantageous to prohibit trucks to drive on the leftmost lane in the simulation, because a truck overtaking another truck forces all vehicles on the left lane to reduce their velocity and produces a deadlock that may not resolve for a long time.

One more variable is needed for the free lane changes, $l_n \in \{\text{left}, \text{right}, \text{straight}\}$ notes if the vehicle n should change the lane during the actual time-step or not. This variable is not needed if the lane changes are executed sequentially, but we prefer a parallel update of the lane changes for all vehicles and that renders this variable necessary. For the left free lane changes the simulator executes the following steps parallel for all vehicles n:
Overtake on the lane to the left:

- Step 0: Initialization:
  For car n find the next car m in front on the same lane, next car s in front on the lane left to car n, and the next car r behind car s. Set $l_n := \text{straight}$.

- Step 1: Check lane change:

$$\text{if } b_n(t) = \text{off and } d_{n,m}(t) < v_n(t)$$
$$\text{and } d_{n,s}^{\text{eff}}(t) \geq v_n(t) \text{ and } d_{r,n}(t) \geq v_r(t),$$
$$\text{then set } l_n := \text{left.}$$

- Step 2: Do lane change:

$$\text{if } l_n = \text{left, then let car } n \text{ change lane to the left.}$$

The definition of the gaps $d_{n,s}^{\text{eff}}(t)$ and $d_{r,n}(t)$ in the lane-change-blocks is an obvious extensions of the above definition; one simply inserts a copy of the car n on its left or right side. These overtake rules used by the simulator can verbally be summed up as follows: first, a vehicle checks if it is hindered by the predecessor on its own lane. Then it has to take into account the gap to the successor and to the predecessor on the lane to the left. If the gaps allow a safe change the vehicle moves to the left lane. For the right free lane changes the simulator executes the following steps parallel for all vehicles n:
Return to a lane on the right:

- Step 0: Initialization:
  For car n find the next car m in front on the same lane, the next car s in front on the lane right to car n, and the next car r behind car s. Set $l_n :=$ straight.

- Step 1: Check lane change:

  if $b_n(t) =$ off and $t^h_{n,s}(t) > 3$ and $(t^h_{n,m}(t) > 6$
  or $v_n(t) > d_{n,m}(t))$ and $d_{r,n}(t) > v_r(t)$,
  then set $l_n :=$ right.

- Step 2: Change lane:

  if $l_n =$ right, then let car n change lane to the right.

Thus, a vehicle always returns to the right lane if there is no disadvantage in regard to its velocity and if it does not hinder any other vehicle by doing so. It should be noted, that it is not possible to first check for all lane changes to the left and to the right and then perform them all in parallel without doing collision detection and resolution. This would be necessary because there are autobahns with three lanes and more. To overcome this difficulty, the lane changes to the left, i.e., overtake, are given a higher priority than the lane changes to the right. For a systematic approach to multi-lane traffic, i.e., lane-changing rules, see, for example, [13]. For a detailed discussion of the different models see, e.g., [6] and the references therein.

4   Implementation of the Topology

An important point in the design of a simulator is the representation of the road network. Therefore, the network is divided into links. The main links connect the junctions and highway intersections representing the carriageway. Each junction and intersection consist of another link, like on/off-ramps or right/left-turn lanes. The attributes of each link are the length, the number of lanes, a possible speed limit, and the connecting links. In case of more than one connecting link, like at off-ramps or highway intersections, there is also a turning probability for each direction. The turning probability is calculated by taking into account the measured traffic data. All these spatial and functional data was collected to build a digital image of the topology of the whole network.

Another crucial information concerns the positions of the installed loop detectors. They also have to be included in the digital map of the network. The positions in the simulation are called checkpoints, and at these checkpoints the simulation is adapted to the measured traffic flow of the loop detectors. Table 1 shows some design parameters of the network. North Rhine-Westphalia is approximately one fifth of whole of Germany with respect to many numbers, e.g., number of cars, inhabitants, length of the autobahn network, et cetera.

Table 1. Design parameters of the North Rhine-Westphalian autobahn network

Area	34,000 km^2
Inhabitants	18,000,000
On- and off-ramps	862
Intersections	72
Online loop detectors	4,000
Offline loop detectors	200
Number of links	3,698
Overall length	2,250 km

5   Traffic Data and Forecast

The simulation describes the dynamics in a network but lacks information about the boundaries. Especially for forecasts, reasonable data has to be incorporated. Many approaches to predict traffic states have been investigated in the past, such as Box Jenkins techniques [14], heuristics [15,16], neural networks [17,18], Kalman filtering [19], and nonparametric regression [20], as well as several comparisons [21] and combinations [22]. The result of the forecast methods strongly depend on the prognosis horizon. For short-term forecasts the current traffic data is of an enormous importance and many complex forecast methods are outperformed by simple models like the single smoothing average or the moving average model. For longer horizons the experience from the past in form of heuristics creates better results.

Because of this fact different forecast methods for the 30 and the 60 min traffic predictions are used. After an intensive statistical analysis of different kinds of traffic data [23], a 14-day classification is chosen considering the different day to day traffic. The average flow and velocity data $x_{\text{hist}}(t_{\text{p}})$ of the last 20 days of each class is averaged and used as a pattern for long-term forecasts. As the short-term forecast method the smoothing averaged values of the last recent minutes $x_{\text{c}}(t_0)$ are used.

Finally, for the prognosis horizons $\Delta\tau = 30$ min and $\Delta\tau = 60$ min the predicted traffic value $x_{\text{pred}}(t_{\text{p}})$ at the time t_{p} is the sum of the average $x_{\text{hist}}(t_{\text{p}})$ of the sample class and the difference of $x_{\text{c}}(t_0)$ and $x_{\text{hist}}(t_{\text{p}})$ weighted with k:

$$x_{\text{pred}}(t_{\text{p}}) = x_{\text{hist}}(t_{\text{p}}) + k \cdot \Delta x(t_0),$$

with

$$\Delta x(t_0) = x_{\text{c}}(t_0) - x_{\text{hist}}(t_0),$$

$$k = \begin{cases} \eta \left(1 - \frac{\Delta\tau}{\Delta\tau_{\max}}\right), & \text{if } 0 < \Delta\tau \leq \Delta\tau_{\max} \\ 0, & \text{if } \Delta\tau > \Delta\tau_{\max} \end{cases}$$

$$\Delta\tau = t_{\text{p}} - t_0.$$

t_0 is the point in time when the forecast is made. Obviously, for $\Delta\tau > \Delta\tau_{\max}$ the heuristics is used as forecast. The factor η is a coefficient determining the relevance of the current and historical data respectively. Reasonable is $0 < \eta < 1$; for $\eta = 0$ only the heuristics are used, for $\eta = 1$ the prognosis uses the current value.

6   Implementation of Traffic Data

To incorporate the real world measurements from the loop detectors into the simulation vehicle-moving, inserting, and removing algorithms have to be applied. This is done at the so-called checkpoints, which are located at those places in the network where a complete cross-section is available, i.e., all lanes are covered by a loop detector. Every time, when checkpoint-data is provided, the simulator uses the measured values to adjust the traffic state in the simulation. The first step is to try to move vehicles behind the checkpoint in front of it and vice versa. If this is not enough to adjust the traffic state, vehicles are inserted or removed. This should be preferred to pure insert/removal strategies, because these can completely fail due to positive feedback if a non-existing traffic jam is produced by the simulation. In this case the simulation measures a low flow in comparison with the real data, so vehicles are added periodically to the ever growing traffic jam leading to a total breakdown.

7   Web-Based Information

The design of the simulator was financially supported by the Ministry of Transport, Energy and Spatial Planning of North Rhine-Westphalia, the reason being, that it wanted a novel web-based traffic information system for the public. This information system is provided by a Java applet at `www.autobahn.nrw.de` (see Fig. 2). The Java applet draws a map of North Rhine-Westphalia, where the autobahns are colored according to the level of service of the simulated traffic state, from light green for free flow, over dark green and yellow for dense and very dense synchronized flow, to red for a traffic jam. Additionally, after numerous requests, we integrated a color-blind mode, where dark green is replaced by dark grey and yellow by blue. Further, construction areas are drawn at the appropriate positions on the map and their estimated influence on the traffic is shown through red construction signs for a high risk of a traffic jam and green construction signs for a low risk. Road closures, which have a deep impact not only on the specific track the closure happens, but also on the traffic in a wide part of the network, are shown as well. To make orientation easier the number and name of each junction is also written in the status bar when the mouse moves over the pictogram of the junction. All this valuable information assists the road user to choose the best route and the best starting time for his trip.

The rising accesses to OLSIM and the nearly throughout positive feedback shows that this information system is accepted by many people and used regularly. The daily requests increased from about 20,000 on work days at the beginning in September 2002 up to 200,000 regular accesses after the implementations of the 30 minute forecast in March 2003 and the 60 minute forecast in December 2003.

Up to now, we have restricted OLSIM on the autobahn network. The next step will be to incorporate the national streets (*Bundesstrassen*) as well as some of the heavily used urban streets.

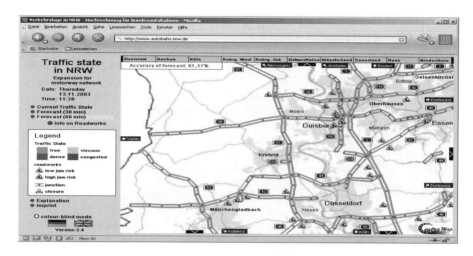

Fig. 2. Screen shot of the visualization of the 60 minute traffic forecast of North Rhine-Westphalia (here one can see the area around Duisburg). For further information about this application and to see the current and future traffic state see: http://www.autobahn.nrw.de

8   Summary

In this paper we present a new advanced traffic information system OLSIM which gives the internet user the opportunity to get the information about the current traffic state and a 30 and 60 minute prognosis of the autobahn network of North Rhine-Westphalia. The system rests upon a microscopic traffic simulator which uses an advanced cellular automaton model of traffic flow and adjusts the traffic state in accordance with measurements of the real traffic flow provided by 4,000 loop detectors installed locally on the autobahn. The cellular automaton model, the abstraction of the network, the guidance of the vehicles, and the data integration strategies to periodically adjust the traffic flow in the simulation in accordance with the measured flow on the autobahn were discussed, as well as some details on the efficient implementation of the dynamics and the presentation of the simulated traffic state to the public. A graphical user interface implemented by a Java applet can be accessed by every internet user. In a simple to navigate window the user can choose between the current traffic state, the 30, and the 60 minute prognosis. Additional information like road works can be chosen with a simple click.

References

1. J. Wahle, R. Chrobok, A. Pottmeier, and M. Schreckenberg.: A Microscopic Simulator for Freeway Traffic. Network and Spatial Economics **2** pp. 371–386, (2002).
2. K. Nagel and M. Schreckenberg.: A cellular automaton model for freeway traffic. J. Physique I **2**, pp. 2221–2229, (1992).

3. R. Barlovic, L. Santen, A. Schadschneider, and M. Schreckenberg.: Metastable states in cellular automata for traffic flow. Eur. Phys. J. B **5**, pp. 793–800, (1998).
4. D. Helbing.: Empirical traffic data and their implications for traffic modelling. Phys. Rev. E **55**, pp. R25–R28, (1996).
5. S.F. Hafstein, R. Chrobok, A. Pottmeier, J. Wahle, and M. Schreckenberg.: Cellular Automaton Modeling of the Autobahn Traffic in North Rhine-Westphalia. In: I. Troch and F. Breitenecker (Eds.), Proc. of the 4th MATHMOD, Vienna, Austria, pp. 1322–1331, (2003).
6. D. Helbing, H.J. Herrmann, M. Schreckenberg, and D.E. Wolf (Eds.).: Traffic and Granular Flow '99, Springer, Heidelberg, (2000).
7. H.P. George.: Measurement and Evaluation of Traffic Congestion. Bureau of Highway Traffic, Yale University, pp. 43–68, (1961).
8. A. Miller.: A queuing model for road traffic flow. J. of the Royal Stat. Soc. B1, 23, University Tech. Rep. PB 246, Columbus, USA, pp. 69–75, (1961).
9. Highway Capacity Manual. HRB Spec. Rep. 87. U.S. Department of Commerce, Bureau of Public Road, Washington, D.C., (1965).
10. L.C. Edie and R.S. Foot.: Traffic flow in tunnels. Proc. HRB **37**, pp. 334–344, (1958).
11. R.C. Pfefer.: New safety and service guides for sight distances. Transportation Engineering Journal of American Society of Civil Engineers **102**, pp. 683–697, (1976).
12. W. Knospe.: Synchronized traffic: Microscopic modeling and empirical observations. Ph.D. Thesis, University Duisburg-Essen, Germany, (2002).
13. K. Nagel, D.E. Wolf, P. Wagner, and P. Simon.: Two-lane traffic rules for cellular automata: A systematic approach. Phys. Rev. E **58**, pp. 1425–1437, (1998).
14. S.A. Ahmed.: Stochastic Processes in Freeway Traffic. Transp. Res. Record **19–21**, pp. 306–310, (1983).
15. D. Wild.: Short-term forecasting based on a transformation and classification of traffic volume time series. Int. J. of Forecasting **13**, pp. 63–72, (1997).
16. S. van Iseghem and M. Danech-Pajouh.: Forecasting Traffic One or Two Days in Advance - An Intermodal Approach. Recherche Transports Securite **65**, pp. 79–97, (1999).
17. M.S. Dougherty and M.R. Cobbett.: Short-term inter-urban traffic forecasts using neural networks. Int. J. of Forecasting **13**, pp. 21–31, (1997).
18. H. Dia.: An object-oriented Neural Network Approach to Short-Term traffic forecasting. Euro. J. Op. Res. **131**, pp. 253–261, (2001).
19. J. Whittaker, S. Garside, and K. Lindveld.: Tracking and Predicting a Network Traffic Process. Int. J. of Forecasting **13**, pp. 51–61, (1997).
20. A.S. Nair, J.-C. Liu, L. Rilett, and S. Gupta.: Non-Linear Analysis of Traffic Flow. In: B. Stone, P. Conroy, and A. Broggi (Eds.), Proc. of the 4th International IEEE Conference on Intelligent Transportation Systems, Oakland, USA, pp. 683–687, (2001).
21. H.R. Kirby, S.M. Watson, and M.S. Dougherty.: Should we use neural networks or statistical models for short-term mororway traffic forecasting? Int. J. of Forecasting **13**, pp. 43–50, (1997).
22. M. Danech-Pajouh and M. Aron.: ATHENA: a method for short-term inter-urban motorway traffic forecasting. Recherche Transports Sécurité - English issue **6**, pp. 11–16, (1991).
23. R. Chrobok, O. Kaumann, J. Wahle, and M. Schreckenberg.: Different methods of traffic forecast based on real data. Euro. J. Op. Res. **155**, pp. 558–568, (2004).

Author Index